Samantha Battams (Photo by Tania Gaylor)

Dr Samantha Battams is an Australian author specialising in non-fiction historical books. Her books combine meticulous research with compelling narrative to explore the social and historical forces shaping individuals and communities. With a PhD in Public Health and a Bachelor of Arts (Social Science, Honours in Sociology) she brings depth to the art of historical storytelling. Her earlier works include true crime histories *The Secret Art of Poisoning: The True Crimes of Martha Needle* and *The Rhynie Poisoning Case: The True Crimes of Alexander Newland Lee*, which examined some of the most sensational criminal cases in Victorian and South Australia history, and the societies in which they occurred. She also wrote, with Les Parsons, *The Red Devil: the Story of South Australian Pioneer Aviator Captain Harry Butler* (Wakefield Press), a biography of a community hero in the wake of WWI. Her latest book, *Paving the Way,* turns to family history, tracing pioneer ancestors from England, Ireland, Prussia and Bavaria to the colonies of South Australia and New Zealand between 1837 and 1859. Beginning with a search for her biological grandparents, the story unfolds across six generations and explores migration, social change, the lives of pioneering women, and the complex legacy of colonisation. When not researching history, she is an avid painter.

Paving the Way

Pioneer Ancestors from England, Ireland, Prussia and Bavaria to South Australia and New Zealand

Samantha Battams

First published by Samantha Battams in 2026
This edition (v.1.2) published in 2026 by Samantha Battams

https://twitter.com/BattamsSamantha
https://www.samanthabattams.com

Paving the Way:
Pioneer Ancestors from England, Ireland, Prussia and Bavaria to South Australia and
New Zealand
POD: 978-0-6483728-9-9
EBOOK: 978-0-6483728-7-5

Cover design by Rose Miller
Front cover Photo: Edith Miller with baby Leonard, 1890
(S. Battams)

Contents

Dedication

This book is dedicated to the ancestors and to my great nieces and nephews who are the 8th generation of our family in South Australia. May they continue with the courage of the pioneering ancestors!
Also to my younger self, who started on this journey with very little information about the family to go on, especially on my father's side.

First Nations Acknowledgement

I acknowledge the Aboriginal peoples as the First Nations peoples of South Australia and the Māori people as the First Nations peoples of Aotearoa New Zealand. I acknowledge Aboriginal and Torres Strait Islanders as traditional owners and custodians of Country, and recognise their continuing connection to the land, sea, waterways, culture and heritage and sovereignty was never ceded. I pay my respects to their Elders past, present and emerging. I acknowledge the traditional owners of all the places mentioned in this history, including the Kaurna, Ramindjeri, Ngarrindjeri, Ngadjuri, Nukunu, Adnyamathanha, Wirangu, Mirning, Kokatha, Meru (Yirawirung - Erawirung) peoples. I also wish to acknowledge the Māori people as tangata whenua and Treaty of Waitangi partners in Aotearoa New Zealand.

Cultural Sensitivity Warning and Disclaimer

The content is based upon document and image research, personal accounts and stories passed down. This book contains some topics that readers may find distressing, including sorry business, adoption, forced relinquishment, missions that have been linked to the stolen generation, stillbirth, suicide, substance misuse, interpersonal violence, colonisation, warfare, murder, racism, death (including in custody), challenging life experiences, sexual assault, post-traumatic stress disorder, and animal cruelty. Descriptions in newspaper articles represent views at the time, and do not represent the views of the author. Some wording in historic newspaper accounts has been changed [as indicated by brackets].

Whilst every effort has been made to handle these topics with care and sensitivity, some readers may find certain sections distressing. If you are affected by the content of this book, please consult a qualified professional or seek support from a trusted helpline in your region.

Aboriginal and Torres Strait Islander peoples should be aware that this book contains names of deceased Aboriginal and Torres Strait Islander peoples.

Every effort has been made to ensure accuracy. If you notice something that does not seem right, I would be grateful if you could inform me so I can review it. This is a work in progress and may change as new information comes to light.

There were a number of old photos of family members identified through Ancestry or other sources that I have not been able to use in this family history, as I have not been able to obtain permission in time for publication (or people who could give permission are not contactable). These photos may appear in future editions of the book.

We all grow up with the weight of history on us. Our ancestors dwell in the attics of our brains as they do in the spiralling chains of knowledge hidden in every cell of our bodies.

The frontier will nevertheless survive in the attitudes a few of us inherited from it. One of those attitudes – to me a beatitude – is the conviction that the past matters, that history weighs on us and refuses to be forgotten by us, and that the worst poverty women – or men – can suffer is to be bereft of their past.

Abbott, S. (1998) Womenfolks: Growing Up Down South. University of Arkansas Press

Introduction

It started as an Adoption Story

"What is your ancestry?" Until 1997, my siblings and I were unable to come up with any definite answers to questions regarding our biological grandparents on our father's side, due to his adoption. The main questions I was initially trying to answer through family history research were: Who were our paternal grandparents? What were their cultural backgrounds? And, why was our father given up for adoption?

Dad only found out he was adopted when he was 30 years old and required his birth certificate to apply for a government job with the Municipal Tramways Trust. His adoptive father told him the secret as he handed over the document. Our father never wanted to find out who his birth parents were and said that his adoptive parents were the only ones he had ever known, and had been good parents. He may never have been able to find out who his biological parents were at the time anyway, for legal or other reasons. I was to later discover that his birth was a secret in his biological mother's family.

My interest in researching Dad's family was also spurred on by the fact that Dad died when I was just six years old, and both his birth and adoptive parents died before I was born. My maternal grandfather was long gone, whilst my maternal grandmother passed away when I was 3 months old. This situation is partly explained by being born to older parents, who came from what I thought was an entirely working class background (where life expectancy is lower) - although undertaking this family history challenged some of those conceptions.

Initially my family history relied upon a sometimes unreliable narrator who had snippets of information - my mother. Mum had once seen Dad's birth certificate, and said that Dad's mother was 'Irene Fahy,' and that grandpa had told her he'd 'brought up a poor little rich kid,' and that the Fahy's owned hotels. It is a name linked to the hotel industry in South Australia and Victoria. I was to discover that I could trace his line back to a famous name linked to the wine industry in South Australia (Gramp).

The search for Dad's biological family turned into wider research on both parents' ancestry, along with that of my stepfather's family, and their early arrival in the Colony of South Australia. The research was conducted, and resulting book has been written, on and off across 30 years.[1] I acknowledge the work done by previous family historians on my mother's side: *The Rumbelows of Encounter Bay (2005)* (by Peter Rumbelow et al.), and *The Miller Family* (2005) (by the late Margaret Miller), which I have drawn from there.

Pioneers of South Australia

In this book I trace my direct line from England, Ireland and Germany (the states of Bavaria and Prussia) to their arrival in South Australia or Aotearoa New Zealand. The stories of these families are closely connected to the complex early colonial history of South Australia and have been contextualised as much as possible.

All of the South Australian ancestors were European pioneers to the Colony, arriving between the 1830s and 1850s. Those who arrived in the first 10 years (1836-1846) include: Johann **Gramp** (1837) (per the *Solway*) and his wife Johanne **Nitschke** (1838) (*Zebra*), Johann Gottfried **Schulz** and wife Johanne Eleonore nee **Rau** (1838) (*Prince George*), and the **Boormann** (1840) (*Skjold*) family. These Prussians and one ring-in Bavarian (Gramp) arrived before all of my English and Irish ancestors, and yet they remained outsiders in the new Colony for some time. The German community in South Australia was again ostracised during the World Wars, even though many individuals of German descent (like Australian Commander John Monash) became allied soldiers.

My English ancestors to first arrive in the Colony included Henry **Lomman** and Martha nee Strong (1840) (*John*), William **Heading** and Ann nee Brooks (1840) (*Joseph Rowan*), and William **Glassenbury** and Esther nee Mansfield (1840) (*Fairlie*).

Families included in this book include my father's biological ancestors (**Fahy**, **Schulz** and **Gramp**), along with his adoptive family (**White** family), my mother's ancestors (**Lomman, Rumbelow, Heslop** and **Miller** families), and my stepfather's family (**Battams**). I also include some history on the women who married into these families including the **Holman**, **Heading, Glassenbury** and **Boorman** families.

Some of these families were European pioneers of regions in South Australia, including **Kangaroo Island** (Gramp), **Barossa Valley** (Gramp/Schulz), **Minnipa** (White), **Kapunda** (Fahy) and **Moorak** (Fahy), **Encounter Bay** (Rumbelow), **Paradise** and **Athelstone** (Lomman) **Campbelltown** (Heading), **Norwood** and **Payneham** (Battams) and **Moorook** (Battams) in South Australia.

This book is also the story of the **Heslop**, **Thompson**, **Parsons** and **Miller** families who migrated from the United Kingdom and were pioneers in **Lyttelton, Christchurch and Timaru**, Aotearoa New Zealand, before the **Miller/Abbott** families moved to Victoria, Australia.

Most of the English ancestors were Wesleyan Congregationalists and Methodists (later the Uniting Church), whilst the Irish were Catholics and the Bavarians / Prussians were Lutherans (the latter fleeing religious persecution) from Kavel's group (later the Immanuel Synod). In Aotearoa New Zealand, the **Heslop** family were Presbyterians who had Scottish origins.

The White, Fahy and Schulz families were working-class families who came out as Labourers, the English **White** family via assisted government passage, whilst the Irish **Fahy** family were miners sponsored by Scotsman

Edward Stirling. The **Schulz** family, farmers, were sponsored by George Fife Angas from the South Australia company, along with Pastor Kavel's group.

Due to DNA testing, we have been able to bust some myths along the way, including that we have Māori heritage. However, another DNA surprise turned up in 2025, which will be revealed in this book.

I have also taken the opportunity to reflect upon my travels (at the end of some chapters) where I have returned to countries and places that my forebears came from.

Interactions with Aboriginal communities

Stories about my pioneer ancestors and other early pioneer settlers are also part of a larger story of colonisation, displacement and dispossession for Aboriginal communities with intergenerational impacts, which cannot be ignored. Within this book I have tried to include reports of any interactions between my ancestors and Aboriginal (or Māori) peoples and communities where I have found these.

There were some records of encounters with local Aboriginal peoples, for example the Kaurna people of the Adelaide plains, Ramindjeri (part of the broader Ngarrindjeri peoples) of Encounter Bay/Ramong, and Ngadjuri. One relative's report (in a contemporary newspaper) of Kaurna people at Paradise was recently used in contemporary Aboriginal cultural awareness training for the City of Campbelltown.[2] The Gramp and Schulz family were significantly involved in Lutheran Aboriginal Missions that may have involved Wirangu, Mirning, Kokatha, and Pitjantjatjara people, among other Aboriginal communities in South Australia. There is also a tragic story of a death of an Aboriginal man in custody of police constables in 1849 near Wirrabara.

My motivation for including stories of these interactions between my family and First Nations peoples (as a non-Aboriginal author) comes from a sense of responsibility to ensure that the truth is being documented and to confront the truth, despite its brutality. The previous family histories in my family that I have read have made little mention of interactions between my pioneer ancestors and the Aboriginal peoples or Māori communities and the legacy of colonisation, apart from the reference to Caroline Cakebread's (nee Rumbelow) encounter with an individual Aboriginal man who came to her property.[3] The same is also true of other historical accounts in the public domain – for example, *The Orlando Way: A Celebration of 150 Years 1837-1987*[4] which has a preface by His Excellency Sir Donald Dunstan (KBE, CB), Governor of South Australia, makes no reference to the central role that the Gramp family had in the Lutheran Aboriginal Missions. I was therefore surprised to find that Gustav Gramp (son of Johann Gramp) was head of the Lutheran Synod (the Immanual Synod) which oversaw the operation of many such missions in South Australia and the Northern Territory.

More information has also now become readily available regarding contemporary accounts on Trove (albeit told from European perspectives), however I have also made an effort to seek out information. I think it is important to acknowledge and confront our past to avoid 'whitewashing' history, as part of an attempt to understand the impacts of colonisation and to make ongoing progressive steps towards reconciliation in the future.

Women in the family

From what I originally knew about my family history when I was growing up, I thought that the women in the past largely accepted their lot in life; that they stayed with dubious men, endured violence and unfaithfulness, didn't separate or divorce, hid children born out of wedlock, largely stayed at home rather than pursued careers or travelled, kept in line with social mores, put up and shut up. A common refrain of my mother who was born in 1930 was *'What will people think?'*

I was surprised to find through my research some women ancestors who did not put up with abusive or alcoholic spouses, did not stay with philandering husbands, were single (or separated) and economically productive even wealthy, and enjoyed the privilege of travel. I had not heard about some of these women as they were on my father's biological side, but many were on my mother's side. *Why were their stories not passed down?*

On mum's side, great-great grandmother **Elizabeth Abbott** (nee Heslop, later Miller) was a bigamist (leaving her first spouse), lived in three continents and travelled frequently, said she was 8 years younger than her true age, and at her death was the Manager of a Warehouse in Melbourne. She survived her charlatan second husband, Albert James Abbott, whose scandals were frequently and tiresomely reported in the Melbourne newspapers. I felt that I was nudged along to write Elizabeth Abbott's story, through a series of coincidences. I would meet someone with her maiden name, Heslop. At another time, when I was walking along the wild, wind-swept beach at Semaphore during winter with only a handful of people on it, someone came up to me and said 'is this yours?' – it was a lost credit card, with the name Shirley Abbott on it! I googled and found that Shirley Abbott (1934-2019) was the name of an American writer, editor, feminist, family historian and memoirist who spoke French, had lived in France and who wrote for a public health magazine for 25 years (I speak French, lived in a francophone country, have written non-fiction historical books and been a public health researcher and academic!). She was from Portland, Oregon, where my great-great grandmother Elizabeth Abbott's brother Mowbray Heslop once lived! I was propelled along by discovering Shirley Abbott and have included some quotes from her book *Womenfolks* at the start of this book.

On mum's side, great-great-great grandmother **Martha Lomman** nee Strong was strong by name and nature. Her husband Henry was tried for murder in the Supreme Court for attempting to shoot their son and he was then interned in the Adelaide and then Parkside Lunatic Asylums. Martha managed the farm with the support of her sons, at least two of whom signed the Women's Suffrage Petition in Adelaide, probably spurred on by the plight of their mother.

Also on mum's side, great great Auntie **Alice Rumbelow** (Jeliff/Bolger), was responsible for hawking the Rumbelow catch, along with raising both her own and her late sister Mahalia's children. On Dad's biological side, another great-great Auntie **Alice Fahy** (who never married) owned her own store in Adelaide's West End (250 Wright Street, Adelaide) near the Prince Albert Hotel, and was mentioned in the social pages for her attendance at mayoral events and tours of south-east South Australia and New South Wales.

On the Rumbelow side, **Mahalia Philps** was a prominent Lady Mayoress of Adelaide, who is in the Rumbelow family history book. I was reminded of her when my sister Raelene sent a link to her story in the City of Adelaide's Women in History project – HerStory Project on Adelaidia.[5] Mahalia was active during the Second World War as the President of the local Red Cross, and it was said that she was 'deeply interested in the then called 'Home for the Incurables' – the Julia Farr Centre. However, post WWII there was intense focus in the newspapers on what she was wearing at the many charity events for causes she championed!

On Dad's biological side, great-great grandmother **Anna Schulz**, daughter of famous winemaker Johann Gramp, left her violent alcoholic spouse who was barred from being served alcohol in the Barossa Valley, managed a large farm at Hallet's Valley with her son and died a wealthy woman. In the research for this book, a scandalous rumour was uncovered about the fate of her spouse. Her daughter Helena Fahy nee Schulz was a 'black sheep' who married an Irish catholic miner, travelled to Western Australia and lived with him for a few years before marrying, and later catered at large functions which he organised in the South East of South Australia.

Perhaps one of the most extraordinary women was Miss **Mary Jane (May) Battams**. She was blind from the age of 9, but travelled remote parts of Australia with missionary Annie Lock by pony and buggy, translated hundreds of books and educational resources into Braille, memorised Scripture and hymns, wrote poetry, played musical instruments, made her own clothes, was the first blind woman in Australia to weave, and was an inventor making a number of innovations for blind people which were used across Australia, England, America and Egypt.

If only my mother only knew about some of the family stories I have uncovered! I hope you enjoy reading this family history, it has been a time-consuming labour of love developed over a considerable period of time and has hopefully fulfilled some curiosity.

Pedigree Charts

GENERATIONS IN AUSTRALIA

First Generation	Second Generation	Third Generation	Fourth Generation	Fifth Generation	Sixth Ge
Father's Paternal Ancestry (adoptive)					
Stephen **WHITE** & Hannah Luxford (arrived **1849** on the "Marion" born Sussex, UK)	Stephen Jnr **White** Sarah James	David Edward **White** Linda Cox	Stephen William **White** Margaret Ethel **Holman** (mother was nee Vierk, also a German background)	Stephen Raymond **White** (born Jack Fahy) Valma Jean Miller	Lynette Margret Cheryl Raelene Samantha
Father's Maternal Ancestry (biological)					
Patrick Fahy (Clare, Ireland) James O'Leary (Kilkenny, Ireland	Edmund/Edward **Fahy** Margaret O'Leary (Fahy arrived **1857** via "Lady Ann" born Ireland)	Michael Patrick **Fahy** Helena Marie Schulz	Iris Marie **Fahy** (married Henry John 'Jack' McDermott) Father of 'Jack Fahy' Unknown		
Johann Gottfried **SCHULZ** &Johanna Eleonore Rau (arrived **1838** "Prince George" From Brandenburg, Prussia)	Friedrich Wilhelm **Schulz** & Anna Dorathea Gramp (Rowland Flat)				
Johann **Gramp** Johanne Eleonore Nitschke [Johann Gramp, arrived **1837** on the "Solway" from Eichig (Aichig), Kulmbach, Bavaria					
Nitschke family arrived on the "Zebra" in **1838** from Lochow, Zullichau, Brandenberg, Prussia]					
Mother's Paternal Ancestry			*(Maternal Grandparents)*		
Miller (unknown) (possibly Scotland) (biological ancestor: **Hazlehurst** from Christchurch NZ)	Charles **Miller** Elizabeth Heslop	George Heslop **Miller** Edith Thompson	Leonard Albert **Miller** Stella Lillian **Rumbelow**	Valma Jean **Miller**	
George **Heslop** Jane Kitchener [HESLOP family arrived from Durham, UK to NZ **1859** via the "Zealanda") "Lincoln"]		[THOMPSON family arrived NZ **1867** from Yorkshire, UK via the			
Mother's Maternal Ancestry					
Malin **RUMBELOW** 1st Alice Pitches Arrived **1854** on the "Pestonjee Bemanjee" born Suffolk, UK	Malin **Rumbelow** 2nd Mary Glassenbury	Godfrey **Rumbelow** Ada Louisa **Heading**			
William **Glassenbury** Esther Mansfield (later McDonald) Arrived **1840** on the "Fairlie" from Gloucestershire, England, UK					
William **Heading** Ann Brooks Arrived **1854** on the "Joseph Rowan' From Cambridgeshire, England	John **Heading** Martha Ann Lomman				
Henry **Lomman** Martha Strong Arrived **1840** on the "John" from Pitminster, Somerset, England (Lomman roots in Devon)					

Stepfather's Ancestry

George **Battams** Sarah Wesley Arrived **1847** on the "Phoebe" settled at Marden, SA from Buckinghamshire, UK	William Alfred **Battams** Caroline Neale	William Alfred **Battams** Hannah Gilbey (went to Moorook, Riverland)	Leonard George **Battams** Meta Otillie **Bormann**	Leonard Frank **Battams** Valma Jean Miller
Johann Gottfried **Bormann** arrived on the "Skjold" **1841** from Posen, Prussia	Wilhelm Ernst **Bormann** (settled at Milendilla, Riverland)	Johann Frederick **Bormann** Lydia Otillie Heffner (or Heppner)		

Left: Stephen William White and Margaret Ethel (nee Holman) (adoptive parents) with Ethel (nee White) and Jim Graham 18th November 1919

Above: Michael Patrick Fahy, Helena (Lena) (nee Schulz), Dorothy Fahy (Boulder-Kalgoorlie 1905)

Above: Iris McDermott (nee Fahy) with Henry James 'Jack' McDermott circa 1945

Above: Stephen Raymond (Ray) White (formerly Jack Fahy) & **Valma (nee Miller)** 30th October 1950, Port Adelaide

Paternal Ancestry

Part 1: Paternal (Adoptive) Ancestry

1849: White Family: Working-Class, Oddfellows, Churchgoers, Shepherds and Soldiers

Chapter 1: First Three Generations of the White Family

Introduction

The White family was my father's adoptive family. Dad was born John/Jack Fahy and renamed Stephen Raymond White, continuing a long tradition of Stephens in his adoptive family, including the ancestor who first arrived in the Colony. They were a working-class family who started as unskilled Agricultural Labourers and Shepherds in Sussex, England (near the coastal region of Brighton). Upon arrival in South Australia, they moved from North Adelaide to the Northern Flinders and back to the city, where they had strong connections to the coastal regions Glanville, Semaphore and Port Adelaide. They became skilled tradespeople and after the First World War landowners at Minnipa on the Eyre Peninsula, where my grandfather was a soldier settler, before returning to the Port Adelaide region.

1st Generation to arrive in Australia

The first of the White family to arrive in Adelaide was **Stephen White**, his wife Hannah, and three children: Stephen, John and Edward.[6] The family travelled on the ship *Marion* which left London 27th October 1848 via Plymouth, and arrived at Port Adelaide nearly four months later on the 10th February 1849.[7]

Stephen White was the son of Samuel White, a Shepherd, and Lucy Muggridge.[8] He was christened on the 21st September 1817 in Rodmell, Sussex. Rodmell is a small village which is part of the District of Lewes in East Sussex, 10 kilometres from Brighton and the southeast coast of England. More recently, Rodmell was the residence of Virginia Woolf for several years and where she wrote many of her novels. Her home at Sussex (the 17thC Monk's House) was frequently visited by members of the Bloomsbury group of writers, activists and artists, and is now a National Trust building and tourist attraction.[9]

The Lewes area was a prominent site for the Romans. In West Sussex is the Fishbourne Roman Palace (AD75-80), which was the largest roman residence north of the alps.[10] I thought I could see some influence of the romans in the White family centuries later, with my grandfather and his siblings having olive tanned skin and brown eyes.

When the Roman government fell in the 5th century, the Anglo-Saxons held the Kingdom of Sussex (the name deriving from 'South Saxons') until the Norman conquest. After the Battle of Hastings, an 11th century castle was built by William de Warenne, William the Conqueror's lieutenant, now known as Lewes Castle.[11]

Stephen White was 23 years old when he married Hannah Luxford. She was six years older and pregnant when they married on the 27th May 1840 at the Church at All Saints for the Parish of St John's, Lewes, Sussex.[12] Her father was Edward Luxford, Gardener and her mother was Mary. Hannah was baptised on the 23rd September 1810 at Lewes St John the Baptist sub Castro. Like many who came to South Australia, Stephen and Hannah White were Wesleyan Methodists (a Protestant-Baptist religion).

Before they left England, the couple lived in several places. In 1841, they were at Scabes Castle Cottage, with their local Parish being St Peters, Brighthelmstone (now Brighton). Scabes Castle Cottage was part of Scabes Castle Farm Estate, which included a farm with a large house, lodge and cottage. Stephen was a Shepherd like his father, and he and Hannah (24 and 30 years respectively) lived with their 3 month old son, Stephen. Also living in the same cottage were the Trigwell family with their three children (where the head of the family was also an Agricultural Labourer) and unrelated people, all likely to be servants working on the farm estate.[13]

In 1843, Stephen and Hannah White christened their second son John George at which time their abode is listed as All Saints, Lewes. In the following year, their child Henry was baptised at St John the Baptist sub Castro when they are living in St Mary's Lane, Lewes but sadly dies three days later and is buried at the same place he was christened.[14] Another two years later, in 1846, their child Edward is baptised when they are living in Denton, South East of Lewes and part of the St Leonard Parish, near the Port of Newhaven. They were on their way to Portsmouth to embark upon their journey.

When the family emigrated to South Australia, it was at the height of the British empire and industrialisation in England. They were a part of the UK assisted passage scheme to South Australia, which was in need of farm Labourers.[15] Whilst the shipping record lists Stephen as being 30 and Hannah 37, the couple were actually 31 and 38 when they arrived in the colony. The upper age limit for government assisted passage to Australia for men was 30 years, which could explain the 'age adjustments.'

Ship **Marion**, 904 tons, Captain McKerlie, from London 27th October 1848 and Plymouth 1848, arrived at Port Adelaide, South Australia 10th February 1849. Passengers: R. McLash Esq surgeon-superintendent and Mrs Alwyn in the cabin and the following emigrants in the steerage. 4th ship from England to S.A. with government passengers for 1849. *South Australian Register* Wednesday 14th February 1849

Stephen and Hannah White first settled in in Tynte Street, North Adelaide, which would have been very different from what it is today.[16] They struggled both financially and through the deaths of their children as daughter Mary Hannah Sarah died aged 6 months in 1852, whilst the following year 10 year old son John George died.[17]

Stephen White was a military volunteer in Company 2, North Adelaide in 1855.[18] However, paid employment was unstable. The family was in arrears for the rates of the Adelaide Corporation (Council)[19] as well as the mortgage. On the 17th August 1858 a newspaper alerted of the sale of their property:

> *By order of the mortgagee Wicksteed, Botting, Townsend & Co are instructed to sell by auction, at their Mart, on Tuesday 7 at 12 o'clock. All that piece and parcel of land being portion of town acre*

no 835, having a frontage of 24 ½ feet to Tynte Street by 210 feet in depth. Together with the house and erections therein situate, as now in the possession of Mr Stephen White. For particulars and conditions of sale, apply to the Auctioneers; or to Messers Bagot & Labatt, solicitors to the mortgagee, Clark's buildings, Hindley Street.

The Advertiser[20]

Perhaps the family maintained the home or rented the home back, as they were still living at Tynte Street in 1868. The White family were members of the Odd Fellows Lodge (Ancient Independent Order of Odd Fellows, IOOF), an assortment of those in lesser and poorer trades, and so may have got lodge assistance to support their family. Lodge or Benefit Societies have been likened to other fraternal groups such as Freemasons societies, and historically many working-class people were organised in these, which provided a kind of insurance in the event of sickness and other events.[21] Lodge membership was important at a time when there was no public welfare.

Stephen White[22] was employed by the Adelaide Corporation for the month of March 1869, specifically by the City Inspector, to shoot unregistered dogs around the city, with the horrible practice of skinning the dogs required as proof to the City Inspector in order to be paid. At the time the *Dog Act* stated that *'any dog not being in the custody of any person, and not having a collar round its neck with the name of its owner and registered number upon it, could be destroyed.'*[23]

White was charged by Police Inspector Bee for shooting one white French poodle on 9th April 1969 in Symon's place,[24] between Gilbert and Halifax Street, Adelaide, and faced Presiding Magistrate Mr Beddome at court on 27th April for this terrible work.[25] In the meantime, on 24th April 1869, there was a letter written to the editor of *South Australian Chronicle* by a man living on Barton Terrace, North Adelaide (where I once lived) complaining of Stephen White who was shooting dogs *'almost on a daily basis'* around the city, and asking *'on whose authority?'* he was doing this.[26]

During the court case, it was described how a child had just walked around the corner when a gun went off, said to be fired in her direction. Stephen White was charged with wantonly shooting and had to pay 10s and costs, £2 7s in total. At the same court hearing he faced an accusation of animal cruelty in relation to scalping one poor creature before it had died, for the reward from the Legislature. Another citizen had anonymously reported this 'brutal conduct' to the newspaper.[27] The Magistrate determined that the dog had been tortured but that this act had not been done intentionally and fined White £1 12s. The City Inspector stated that he had employed White for this work and recommended a refund of the fine. His Worship did not grant the City Inspector's request and said he thought it unacceptable to discharge firearms in the city.

Being the owner of an adored dog, it was hard to read about White's employment and the treatment of dogs. Despite his horrible work, White was a popular member of the community (or the IOOF Lodge) and community members unsuccessfully lobbied the Public Works committee to refund the fine. Unsurprisingly, the case and the publicity surrounding it resulted in a large increase in the registration of dogs. The Adelaide Corporation continued to employ Stephen White in other roles, as in 1868-69, he was employed as a Ganger, or a foreman of a gang of Labourers.

Glanville, Port Adelaide, and Semaphore

In the late 1870s, Stephen and Hannah moved with their family to LeFevre's Peninsula, which was named after Sir John George Shaw Lefevre, South Australian Commissioner and lawyer who enthusiastically advocated for the Colony and was employed in the Colonial Office.[28] The White family soon established a strong link to the region, and one member of the family ended up with Lefevre as their middle name!

Stephen White became a Smelter at the Junction Smelting Works, which treated sulfide ore (for nickel, copper, and cobalt) and carbonate ore from various mining operations in the state.[29]

Hannah died aged 68 in 1878,[30] and was buried in the Walkerville Wesleyan Cemetery, where a number of well-known South Australians are at rest, including Sir John Cleland and suffragist Mary Lee.

Stephen would live another 17 years and spent his last years at Glanville. He was one of the 157 Glanville ratepayers petitioning Governor Robinson in 1880, opposing establishment of the Semaphore municipality – then the 'beach ward' of Glanville. At the time, citizens actively participated in democracy through the *Government Gazette,* and prayers were referenced in relation to political announcements by both the Governor and petitioners.

> *Your petitioners, while not objecting to a corporation acceptable to the ratepayers and based in equity would respectfully urge that no grounds whatever exist for the granting of the proposed municipality so limited and so unfair to the other portion of the district.*
>
> *Your petitioners therefore humbly pray that your Excellency will be pleased not to grant the prayer of the aforesaid memorial.*
>
> *And your petitioners will ever pray, &c.*
>
> *The South Australian Government Gazette, 18th October 1883*

The ratepayers opposed the establishment of Semaphore for reasons including that it had already had its full proportion of tax income expended on streets and roads; that public officers' salaries in small districts are greater in proportion to those in large districts and there would be less money to spend on public works; as building streets and roads would impact upon the streets and roads of Le Fevre's Peninsula and Glanville; that the proposed boundaries of Semaphore were limited and expenses would be considerable and lead to less funding available for public works.[31] It appears that they were most concerned about missing out on funding for the Glanville District. The protest was unsuccessful, and the Corporate Town of Semaphore was established three months later, on 17th January 1884.

When Stephen was later hospitalised in 1886 he still worked as a Labourer, but was living at Reedbeds.[32] In 1895 when Stephen is 78 he was admitted to hospital due to pericarditis (and was living at Exeter at the time). He died the following day, 25th June 1895.[33] His death was not reported in the newspaper, and he was buried at Cheltenham Cemetery rather than Walkerville where his wife was at rest.

2ndGeneration in Australia

Stephen and Hannah's son **Stephen Junior White** (19 years) (born January 1841-died 1st Oct 1868) married **Sarah Ann James** (18 years) on the 1st August 1861 at the Wesleyan Chapel, Norwood, SA.[34] Sarah was born in 1843 in England, to William and Margaret James.

Photo: Wesley Church and School, Norwood, c1900. The small church on the right was the marriage place of Stephen Junior White and Sarah James in 1861. State Library of South Australia B 17555

Stephen jnr and Sarah lived in North Adelaide, Mount Serle, Prospect and Glenelg.[35] They had the following children:

George William White (born 18th Apr 1862, North Adelaide[36])
<u>**David Edward White**</u> (born 8th Oct, 1864, Mt Serle, d. 1949)[37]
Mary Hanna Sarah White (born 23rd Aug 1866, Prospect Village,[38] d. 24th Aug 1886, Port Adelaide, SA, aged 20 years – married William Jacobs).[39]
Stephen White (3rd) (born 21st February 1869, North Adelaide, SA, died 1870)[40]

Mount Serle – Owieandana Station

Stephen White worked as a shepherd in Owieandana near Mt Serle[41] (Arta-wararlpanha) in the Northern Flinders Ranges, which at that time was a brave move due to the tension between Europeans and Aboriginal people in the north (Adnyamathanha people). There were a number of reports of conflict between local Aboriginal people and settlers in the preceding years, with Europeans taking over land (and food and water sources) and local Aboriginal people allegedly stealing or attacking cattle and sheep for food (or destroying them in protest), particularly in times of drought when food was scarce.[42]

In 1860, some cattle were killed on Samuel Stuckey's station at Umberatana[43] to the north of Mount Serle (north of the Gammon Ranges) and in 1864, Stuckey confronted an Aboriginal Chief, Pompey, about robbing an outstation on the Umberatana property[44], and then pursued, shot and killed him when he ran off. Stuckey was tried for manslaughter.[45] Around April the following year, it was alleged that a Shepherd (John Walter Jerrold)[46] working for John Jacob north east of Mt Serle at Paralana station (which was sold and renamed Wooltana Station)[47] near Mount Fitton[48] was murdered by local Aboriginal people in retaliation.

In April 1865 another police station was established in the area, which was the most northerly police station in South Australia – but the police could not respond to the 1865 murder investigation as there were no fit horses, and due to the drought, the station was abandoned in October of the same year.[49]

In 1866 Stepehen White was living care of J. Campbell, Owieandana northeast of Mount Serle[50] – where there is still a homestead. John Campbell was one of four Scottish brothers who settled in the Mount Remarkable district in 1845.[51] Campbell was foreman of the local jury on the Stuckey case, and in a letter to the editor of a South Australian newspaper he discussed the Coroner's inquest held at Umberatana station in February 1864, with him being head,[52] and complained that the local case was going to be retried in Adelaide.[53]

A later report describes a journalist meeting an Aboriginal man, 'Big Bobbie' at Owieandana station in 1873, when it was managed by 'old John Campbell' who describes the wonder and fear of his people observing Eyre's party when the Europeans first arrived in the region.[54]

Mt Serle was the European name given by explorer Eyre on his 1840 trip to Northern Australia. By the 1860s, Mt Serle was a farming station where the pastoral lease was initially acquired by Walter and Thomas McFarlane in 1856, along with Owieandana, but the brothers left in 1859 and it was purchased by Abraham Scott in 1860.[55] It was part of a number of Northern land parcels owned by A. Scott, R. B. James[56] and J. F. Haywood. Abraham's younger brother Henry Scott[57] (who had taken over his brother's wool brokering business in 1866) advertised the Mt Serle station (with 10,000 to 15,000 sheep) for sale in June 1868.

> *Five leases, having a total area of 352 square miles, were also stocked at Mount Serle, the next post office being Yudanamutana." ... when, on account of a difference of opinion, Messrs. Scott, James and Haywood parted company in 1869, Canowie was carrying 63,000 sheep, and the run fetched £61,000.*[58]

John Jacob also was an early pastoralist in the region, first farming at Beetaloo in the southern Flinders Ranges and Outalpa (to the north east, near Bimbowrie), before settling in the far north at Paralana (now Wooltana Station), where John and his brother William owned the lease from 1856 to 1860.[59] Due to drought conditions in 1863, the brothers left the region and pastoral pursuits, with William Jacob focusing on Moorooroo (Jacob's Creek, Barossa Valley) and John Jacob commencing as an agent at Mintaro.

In the 1970s the land was managed by its traditional owners, the Adnyamathanha people through the Yadlhiauda Aboriginal Corporation and in 2009 following native title claims by Adnyamathanha people, land rights were reclaimed as Adnyamathanha Traditional Lands and managed by the Adnyamathanha Traditional Lands Association (Aboriginal Corporation).

Sarah White gave birth to my great-grandfather David White at Mount Serle station in 1864. But by 1866, the White family was back living in Prospect Village, the home of the James family (in-laws), where their daughter Mary was born.

Stephen then turned to fishing, and in June 1868 there is a report that he had a bag of oysters stolen from the Glenelg jetty.[60] When Stephen (2nd) died at North Adelaide in 1868 aged only 27 years of Albuminuria, at North Adelaide[61] he was then listed as a Fisherman with his usual residence at Glenelg.[62] Albuminuria is a condition where albumin, a kind of protein is present in the urine and can be a sign of kidney disease. His death notice read:

> *3rd October 1868*
> *White – On the 1st October, at his father's residence. Tynte Street, North Adelaide, Stephen White, late of Glenelg, aged 27. He sleeps in Jesus.*[63]

The undertaker for Stephen junior was Phillip Le Cornu. The lodge posted the following notice about his burial:

> *Ancient Independent Order of Oddfellows*
> *Loyal Cumberland Lodge No 8*
> *The members of the Lodge and Order are requested to MEET at the Lodge-room, Wellington Inn, Wellington square, North Adelaide on Sunday next, at half past 2 o'clock p.m. to FOLLOW the REMAINS of our late Brother STEPHEN WHITE from his late residence, Tynte street, to the Walkerville Cemetery. By order of the N.G., WM REYNOLDS, Secretary.*[64]

Stephen junior left behind three children and a five month pregnant wife Sarah who would be a 26 year old single parent with four children in 1869. The baby that was born posthumously on the 21st February 1869, at North Adelaide was also named Stephen, and tragically died of intestinal problems only a year after his birth, on 6th February 1870. Stephen junior's parents had lost three of their four children. Only Edward White remained – he married (Susana Elizabeth Barden) and had a large family of nine children.

There are no records indicating that the White children were boarded out or in the Destitute Asylum, so it appears they were assisted by their family. However, the Oddfellow's Lodge had a widow and orphan's fund, which Sarah likely benefited from. The James family (or at least mother) also likely moved to Port Adelaide with the White family, as Margaret James died at Port Adelaide in 1894.

Within a year Sarah White remarried (on the 11th July 1871) to George Graham[65] who was a Carter of Portland Estate. The marriage took place at the Primitive Methodist Parsonage, Wellington Square, North Adelaide[66], the residence of Reverend William Colley, Primitive Methodist Minister. He had been a missionary throughout Australasia,[67] and regularly gave public lecturers, including on the fear of 'The Russia War.'[68] Reverend Colley was to die only two months after Sarah's wedding.[69]

Sarah had four more children to George Graham, including Margaret (on 3rd December 1871) at Bowden, John William (5th April 1873) at North

Adelaide, William Hugh (14th October 1875) at Cannon Street, Port Adelaide and May (17th September 1878) at Port Adelaide. In 1892 the family were living at Solomontown (near Port Pirie) when their daughter Margaret (spouse John Brealey) died. George Graham died and Sarah married for a third time, to Soloman Harris at Solomontown, on the 9th February 1904. The marriage registration states that the bride's age was 59 (the same age as the groom), however she was actually 61 years.[70] Sarah died on the 3rd February 1916, aged 73, at Port Pirie.

3rd Generation in Australia

David Edward White was born 8th October 1864 at Mt Serle to Stephen Junior White and Sarah James, when his father was a Shepherd.[71] His birth was registered by his grandmother, Margaret James of Prospect Village, on the 28th October 1864, leaving her 'X' in recording the birth, indicating she was illiterate. David White was fatherless just before his fourth birthday.

On the 2nd July 1881, David (aged 18 years) married **Linda Cox**[72] (aged 19 years) at the Baptist Church, Flinders Street, Adelaide.[73] Linda (or Linder as recorded on the birth registration) was born 11th Jan 1863 at Port Adelaide, to William Cox and Mary Ann Ellis[74] and christened 15th Feb 1863. Linda had siblings William (born 6th Sept 1864), Rebecca (born 1st Nov 1872),[75] Frederick (born 1870) and Charlotte (born 1874 - died 1917). Their mother died in 1884, when Linda was 21 years of age.

William and Mary Ann Cox from Queenstown had separated and petitioned for divorce on the 16 Jan 1861,[76] however there were no reports of this divorce being granted, and the five children of the couple were all born after this date. This petition may have been related to alcoholism, as William Cox was arrested a number of times for drunkenness, foul language and assault (in Adelaide and Port Adelaide). A William Cox died in 1893 (of alcoholism) and there was a coronial inquest into his death.[77]

David and Linda White and family lived at Glanville Blocks, Adelaide, Victoria and at Minnipa on the West Coast of South Australia. Like many people from South Australia, due to a financial depression in the late 1880s and early 1890s the family moved to Victoria, and three of their 10 children were born there.[78] There were 23 years between their oldest and youngest children, and one of their children (Walter) died at a young age. Their children were as follows:

Mary Ann White b 20th Feb 1882 Port Adelaide[79] (married Michael Maguire, went to Western Australia)

Stephen William White (4th) b 18th Nov 1883 Glanville[80]

Mabel Eveline White b 6th Mar 1886 Port Adelaide[81]

Ethel Maud White b 1890 Essendon Victoria[82]

David White b 1892 Victoria[83]

Linda White b 1894 Northcote, Victoria[84] (married Robert Siviour)

Sarah ("Sadie") Elizabeth Victoria White b 1888 Ascot Vale, Victoria[85] (married Albian William Whiting)[86]

David Edward White (junior) b 16 Oct 1899[87] Glanville Blocks

Frederick John White b 11th Jan 1902[88] Williamstown, Semaphore

Clarence ("Clarry") White b 13th July 1905, Glanville Blocks[89]

Walter White b 13th July 1905, Glanville Blocks[90]

Stevedores and Waterside Workers

Prior to and after WWI, David White was a waterside worker – a stevedore. This could be precarious work - in 1905 an article reports of David having a serious work accident:

> *On Monday morning David White, a stevedore resident at Glanville, Blocks, met with an accident while engaged in the coaling of the steamer Bombala at Port Adelaide. He slipped off the overhead tramway, and fell between the coal lighter and the hull of the steamer — about 20 ft. He was conveyed to a surgery for medical attention.*

Evening Journal, 7 November 1904

> *It was found that he was suffering from a bad concussion of the brain, while his side was considerably bruised. No bones appeared to have been broken, and after his injuries had been dressed by a medical man he was conveyed to his home.*

The Register, 8 Nov 1904

Much later, David's namesake David Edward White junior, who was a motor driver (in 1939) and boiler attendant (in 1945), also had a serious workplace accident where he was pinned by a two and a half ton box in an engineering shop at Port Adelaide.[91]

Building the Glanville Methodist Church

In 1906, David White was involved in jointly owning a piece of land (under the Trustee Act 1893) where a Methodist church would be built at Carlisle Street, Glanville (which is now a private home) – this was jointly owned by his cousins Joseph Stephen White and Frank Ernest White of Exeter (his Uncle Edward's children) and other church members from Alberton, Port Adelaide, Exeter and Glanville.[92]

GLANVILLE METHODIST MISSION

Photo: Glanville Methodist Mission, Carlisle Street, *Australian Christian Commonwealth*, 24 Dec 1937, Trove

Minnipa

David and Linda moved to Minnipa on the Eyre Peninsula around 1921, with their son Stephen White (who had soldier settlement land there), their other adult children, and foster son Bill Surman. The West Coast of South Australia was where many soldier settlers were granted land under the *Soldier Settlement Act* following World War I.

Below: Linda Cox, far right, with her daughter Linda Siviour nee White and son-in-law Robert Siviour on a country road, possibly near Minnipa, circa 1920s, Christine Tovey, Ancestry

In 1927 Minnipa featured prominently in the news, as someone by the name of James Curran died from strychnine poisoning in the government camp for the South Australian Railways, and Detectives Slade and Goldsworthy were sent to investigate.[93] A Swedish Labourer, Carl Bystedt, who had an argument with the cook on the camp the night before, was put on trial for murder, but the Crown decided not to proceed with the case due to a lack of evidence.[94]

After Minnipa, the White family moved back to Port Adelaide, and their residences included Glanville, Robert Street, Sandwell (Birkenhead),[95] Church Place West, Port Adelaide,[96] and later (in 1939) King Street, Alberton, a house which is still standing.

At the age of 80 years, David White went to the Royal Adelaide Hospital for over 4 months (125 days), and was discharged to 9 College Street, Portland, his son Stephen's home.[97] However it was his wife Linda White who predeceased him, dying on the 18th July 1935, aged 62 years of age, whilst David White died in 1949, aged 85 years.

Photo: David and Linda White in older age (prior to July 1935), Christine Tovey, Ancestry

Chapter 2: Grandfather Corporal White and the 6th Field Artillery Brigade of WW1, the 'Fair Dinkums'

4th Generation in Australia

Stephen William White was born 18th Nov 1883, Glanville, Port Adelaide, to David Edward White and Linda Cox, [98] a third generation 'Colonial.' A Carpenter, Blacksmith and Wheelwright by trade, he was the first member of his family to travel back to Europe since his great grandparents arrived in the colony of South Australia sixty-six years earlier.

At that time, it was common for carpenters to work underwater and be experienced divers, required to work on jetties and bridges. In 1913, Stephen White was working on a jetty extension at Wallaroo when there was a double fatality, and he reported to an inquest on the death of Frederick James Stephensen and John Putris.[99] The deaths were caused by a leak in the oxygen pump of the diving apparatus.

At 31 years old, White joined the first Australian Infantry Force (A.I.F.) on the 13th July 1915 that was to serve in Egypt, France and Belgium in World War 1. Upon enlistment at Keswick, he states he is 30 (one year and one month younger than he actually is) and a 'Bridge Carpenter'. The enrolment officer's description: dark complexion, brown eyes, dark hair, 5ft 9in and 148lb, tattoo both forearms, single. He would later become a 'Fitter' (or engineer) in the army.

His mother was listed as Mrs Linda White of Church Place West, Port Adelaide, formerly of Robert Street, Sandwell via Port Adelaide[100]. Like the majority of those who enlisted, he was single at the time. Stephen White was first listed as a 'Wheeler', (24/7/1916) and then is promoted to Bombardier (04/08/1917). In early Sept 1917 he spent some time on leave in the UK, in Dec 1917 he is promoted to temp Corporal, then in Feb 1918 to Corporal, and shortly after that he is hospitalised for good before he returns home.

Stephen William White is the fourth Stephen in his family lineage in Australia, his great grandfather Stephen White who arrived in Australia from England died when he was 12 years, his grandfather Stephen Junior White died before he was born, and he also had an Uncle Stephen White only 14 years his senior. He appeared to be close to his large family of siblings, particularly Ethel White and her husband Jim Graham, and his 'brother' Alec/Alex who was brought up as a brother to Stephen, but was really a nephew and the illegitimate and secret son of his older sister Sadie.

According to my mum Val Battams, Grandfather Stephen White (4th) would apparently tell stories about his forebears such as that his grandfather hailed from South Africa, and owned part of what was referred to as 'No Man's Land' in Port Adelaide (a name commonly used in WW1 to refer to territory between opposing trenches). These stories perhaps referred to William Cox, his mother's father, however this has not been verified.

It was the handwriting of Linda[101] on the enlistment form for her son Stephen to join the call to arms for WW1 where 65% of soldiers would become casualties[102]. Propaganda posters around this time were targeting mothers of potential soldiers. An Australian recruitment poster for World War 1 reads '*Whose son are you?*'.[103] Under this slogan, pictured at left, is a man with waistcoat and hat with his fancily dressed mother's arms wrapped around his neck, declaring *'I didn't raise my son to be a soldier'*. A second big-bosomed mother on the right, with plainer clothing, is more distantly spaced from her soldier son, shaking his hand whilst patting him on the back and replying to the first mother *'I did'*. Between the divide of these clearly distinguished women are the words '*Enlist today*'. The advertisement appeared to be tapping into and reinforcing values of independence and courage.

Image: 'Whose son are you?' Propaganda poster, WW1[104]

The only previous clues about 'Old Grandpa White' included remnants such as a gold necklace charm he had engraved with his initials, a ruby and garnet and gold ring that had been passed down to his son (and then grandson), and a silver letter opener with an eagle engraved as the handle which he had obtained in France during World War 1. There were also his war service medals (the 1914/1915 cross, British War Medal and Victory Medal), the Honor Roll of the 18th Battery 6th Field Artillery Brigade[105], the suede covered trench series 'Digger Smith' book by C.J. Dennis and the 1967 Returned Sailors Soldiers and Airmen's Imperial League (Australia) badge. There was a grandfather clock and an impressive miniature wooden model of St Peter's cathedral in North Adelaide (the original built during his lifetime – he built two such churches) that he had intricately carved, and some old hand-held shears.

There were also black and white photographs such as the one showing a handsome young soldier looking very dignified and proud in his uniform in 1915, and a somewhat aged man in his wedding photo of only four years later. There is also the photograph taken at Glanville in the 1940s with his wife and younger brother, and his young nephew where he has a wry smile. His personal King James Bible is still intact within which he penciled the dates of his mother's and his wife's deaths inside the front cover, in addition to curious scribbling that looked like a secret code. Apart from material possessions there was also ever-changing oral history. Most of the clues were from an intense three-year period of war that would have a profound effect.

The spirit of adventure and curiosity about Europe, as well as the propaganda of war could be well understood but there may well have been material reasons for grandfather's enlistment because as a Carpenter, the building industry had been affected by shipping supplies causing many to be unemployed[106]. This is apparently why his occupation was listed as a 'Bridge Carpenter' on the application form.

July 1915 was the peak time for enlistment in the war in Australia, with three times as many enlistments as in the previous month, spurred by the news of the Gallipoli landing,[107] the June announcement that there had been 10,000 Australian casualties, and the June call from Britain of 'every available man wanted'.[108] This group who enlisted after the casualty figures were announced were known as the 'fair dinkums' as they knew their chances of survival.[109]

A copy of the story of the 18th Battery, 6th Field Artillery Brigade, First Australian Imperial Force[110] was to provide some details of his war experiences. This account by fellow Carpenter and later 'Driver' Dyer describes the battery first training as the 34th Battery at Artillery Base Camp at Mitcham. They later transferred to Glen Osmond for further training where it became the 18th Battery led by Major Dean (later Colonel) and then left Adelaide on the 18th October 1915 to join and form the 6th Field Artillery Brigade in Essendon North, Victoria. A larger group comprising Victorians and Tasmanians then formed the 6th brigade, including the 16th, 17th and 18th Batteries which left Australia via Port Melbourne. The 18th Battery 6th Field Artillery Brigade was declared to be the 'first and only complete Field Artillery Battery to go on active service from South Australia'.[111]

Photo: Stephen William White, 1915 Source: S. Battams

3

Description of *Stephen William White* on Enlistment.

Age *30* years *7* months Height *5* feet *9* inches Weight *148* lbs. Chest Measurement *35 37½* inches Complexion *Dark* Eyes *Brown* Hair *Dark T.G* Religious Denomination *Methodist*	Distinctive Marks. *Vac R4/6 L4/9* *Vacc L4 Inf* *Tattoo both Forearms*

CERTIFICATE OF MEDICAL EXAMINATION.

I have examined the above-named person, and find that he does not present any of the following conditions, viz.:—

Scrofula; phthisis; syphilis; impaired constitution; defective intelligence; defects of vision, voice, or hearing; hernia; hæmorrhoids; varicose veins, beyond a limited extent; marked varicocele with unusually pendent testicle; inveterate cutaneous disease; chronic ulcers; traces of corporal punishment, or evidence of having been marked with the letters D. or B.C.; contracted or deformed chest; abnormal curvature of spine; or any other disease or physical defect calculated to unfit him for the duties of a soldier.

He can see the required distance with either eye; his heart and lungs are healthy; he has the free use of his joints and limbs; and he declares he is not subject to fits of any description.

I consider him fit for active service.

Date *9 · 7 · 15*

Place

[signature] CAPTAIN A.A.M.C.

Signature of Examining Medical Officer.

CERTIFICATE OF COMMANDING OFFICER.

I Certify that this Attestation of the above-named person is correct, and that the required forms have been complied with. I accordingly approve, and appoint him to *M Group Base Inf Depot* ~~BATTERY, 6th F.A.B.~~

Date *13 July 1915* *[signature] Lieut*

Place *Mitcham* Commanding

for Major, Camp Commandant.

Photo: Description of S.W.White from war registration form Source: National Archives of Australia, WWI collection, record 1850441

The Battery left Australia via the cargo passenger liner *Persic* on the 22nd November 1915, arriving on the 18th December at Pt Suez. It spent some months near Cairo and Tel-El-Kabir, fighting on the Sinai Peninsula, Egypt. Gunner Melville of the 18th Battery who arrived in Egypt earlier repeatedly tells of the 'hard day's work' here and sometimes illicit pleasures ….

> *August 23rd (Monday)*
> *Did hard days work and managed to steal a tin of sardines, 2 tins of treacle, 2 loaves bread and a tin of sardines from Quartermasters store. This might keep us going for a day or two. By the way it is not called stealing here. The goods stick to your hands*[112].

PRG 280/1/27/48

Photo: Australian Troops in Egypt negotiating a price for the hire of donkeys near the pyramids at Giza, c1915, State Library of South Australia [PRG 280/1/27/48]

According to Dyer the 18th Battery left Alexandria for France in March 1916. They first arrived in the port town of Marseilles, in southern France. They then crossed France via a 58 hour train journey from Marseilles to Le Havre in the upper Western region of France, and eventually on to the

Somme and the Great Western Front. The 6th Field Artillery Brigade supported the Second Australian Division on the Somme.

The initial six week battle of the Somme began on 1st July 1916 where the 1st ANZAC corps suffered severe wounds and 23,000 casualties.[113] In September 1916, the 18th Battery relieved the 1st ANZAC corps at Menin Gate, Ypres (now Ieper), Belgium[114], where they spent the next 17 days and were to eventually spend the winter in terrible conditions and much of the following year. Gunner Colin Twist from the 18th Battery describes these days…

> *3.9.16 Took Thiepval & Mouquet Farm. Had to retire midday from Thiepval with heavy casualties. Fighting all night. Saw two of our planes descend near our lines. One engine trouble and one wounded pilot. 6 wounds from Fokker.*
>
> *4.9.16 Guns came out of action at 4pm. Fritz started shelling us at 7pm. One horse wounded. Raining cats and dogs...mud up to ankles. Harnessed up and moved out. Fritz still shelling. Moved about 1 mile and stayed there till morning Absolutely the worst night I have ever experienced. Wet through and foot deep I walked about all night. I think rum saved our lives.*[115]

After a break from the Somme, the 18th Battery marched back to the to the region…

> *28th to 31 Oct What happened between these dates I don't rightly remember. What with forced marches, nothing to eat and no sleep. Mud up to our thighs. It was an absolute nightmare.*
>
> *1.11.116 Arrived firing line Longueval*[116] *– Again in the Somme battle. Shot one of our horses – broke his leg in the mud. Shell just missed our dugout and killed 3 men.*
>
> *2.11.16 Shelling all around. Oh! What a hole – a hell hole. Saw a 'Tank'.*[117]

The Honor Roll from this Battery records that Bombardier Stephen White was wounded on the 15th November, 1916 at the Somme. Private Colin Twist wrote in his diary[118] of the event…

> *[Top of page] (Gunner Pearce reported missing)*
>
> *15.11.16 Fritz strafed our trenches like hell. Bdr White wounded with bomb dropped from Taube[119]. Shell dropped 10 yards away whilst I was asleep and wounded one horse which had to be shot.*[120]

Private Melville from the 18th Battery also wrote in his diary of these events…

> *Nov 14th Big stunt in morning. Our lads took some trenches on right. Pearce killed at wagon lines. Recently came in from D.A.C[121]. Fritz strafed pits in evening and killed one wounded one in 16th. Did all night stunt. Barrage.Nov 16th*
>
> *Bomb White wounded at ammunition dump. Fierce weather. Plenty doing. All night barrage.*[122]

Grandpa White would later tell the story of this wounding with the detail of the horse being shot. The heaviest battles the battery faced would be around a year later….

> *Known as the Menin Road Battle it was the most strenuous, drawn out, and dangerous the Battery had been in. Seven members of the Battery were killed and twenty-two wounded)...Menin Road was known as the first step, and Polygon Wood, the second...the Battle for Polygon Wood on the September 26th [1917] was an epic of courage and bravery for all Australian troops engaged...German guns searched and swept the area and only one gun was left in action. Casualties were heavy...The Battery was relieved after twenty-three days in action on the 3rd October and moved back to rest area La Motte near Hazebrouck.* (Dyer, 1965, p 21)

This marked the wounding of fellow soldier Private Melville and his return to England, with significant wounds being called 'blighty's' as they could bring soldiers back to England which was known as 'Blighty'[123] …

Photo: Somme, Winter 1916, Source: AWM E0092

> *Monday Sept 24th*
>
> *Started a stunt at 5.30am and Fritz retaliated. Result I get a blighty in the back and Sal Gordon in the head. Lark[124] shelters in a trench where I had crawled and thought my last hour had come. After the strafe was over was carried on stretcher to 2nd Dressing Port. From there was taken to Dressing Stn on Menin Road. Had to wait a long time for ambulance. Wound pained a bit. Had a rough ride to Dressing Stn outside Menin Gate where wound was dressed. Then got another bus on to the Canadian CCS[125]. Had a long painful wait there. Underwent operation at 9pm and came to, freed up about 10 with nice little souvenir in my leg. Waited until morning for train.[126]*

On the 26th September 1917 Corporal Carr from Port Adelaide, Gunner Hensen (or Henson) from Glanville, Gunner Bodholdt from Rosewater, and

Bombardier Paterson from the UK, all in the 18th Battery, were killed in action at Menin Rd, Ypres, and all buried at the Hooge Crater Cemetery, Zillebeke, Belgium.[127] Bombardier Gray was acknowledged for his efforts on the same day in packing ammunition under heavy fire at Hooge via a meritorious service medal. The death of Corporal Carr was reported as follows:

> *Corporal L. W. Carr, third son of Mr. and Mrs. G. E. Carr, of Leadenhall Street, was killed in action on September 26. He enlisted in August 1915, and left for Melbourne in November. After seeing active service in Egypt, he proceeded to France, and among other engagements he was in the battles of the Somme, Ypres, Hill 60, Pozieres, and Mouquet Farm. For 9 months prior to enlisting, Corporal Carr was doing duty at Fort Largs with the Garrion Artillery. He was educated at the Port Adelaide Public school, and was in the employ of Messrs. W. Thomas and Co. He was of a bright disposition, and highly respected. He was only 22 years old. An elder brother, Private G. E. Carr, is on service in France [with the 43rd Battalion].*

Port Adelaide News, 9th November 1917

Gunner Alfred Hensen enlisted one month after Stephen White and:

> *left Melbourne on the 28th November 1915 with the 6th Army Field Artillery Brigade. Previous to enlisting he served five years in the navy. He was born at Bucknall road, Glanville, and was educated at Lefevre Peninsula School. He left a widow and two little girls.*

The Advertiser, 30th October 1917

Gunner A. L. Bodholdt's death was reported on the 355th Casualty List for South Australia,[128] and through a Family Notice. He was also listed in the legal notices section by the Public Trustee which indicated he was formerly a Seaman.

BODHOLDT – Killed in action in France, on September 26, Gunner Arthur L. Bodholdt, 18th Battery, F. A. B., youngest dearly beloved son of A. and I. Bodholdt, Rosewater.

The Express and Telegraph, 20th November 1917

This incident of these men dying possibly related to a story told by Stephen White where he had just left a trench and it was subsequently blown up with three of his mates in it… according to family legend, his hair went white overnight.[129] However, according to his pay records, around this time Stephen White spent some time in the 16th Battery, Australian Field Artillery (from 4th August 1917 to 12th Nov 1917).[130] As Stephen married a woman whose fiancé had been killed in the war, I wondered if this she was either the fiancé of someone he knew, such as Corporal Carr or Gunner Bodholdt.

The 26th September 1917 had marked the commencement of the Battle for Polygon Wood and occurred in the middle of 23 continuous days of fighting action for the Battery that was not relieved until the 3rd October 1917.[131] A total of 14 men from the 18th Battery died in the 3rd Battle of Ypres.[132] Before the relief from this battle, on the 1st October 1917 Stephen White was wounded in action[133] and evacuated on the 7th October 1917. Apart from the bloodshed, weather conditions were atrocious around this time, with mud and rain considered to be worse than at Flers on the Somme.[134] Menin Gate led to 'Hell Fire Corner' where:

there is a small stone by the roadside stating that this is where the German Army were stopped in their advance. The Menin Gate memorial [see photo in Conclusion], built into the ramparts of Ypres, has on the East side a figure of the British Lion with the words "they shall not pass"...this memorial carries the names of over 6000 Australians killed in these battles with no know grave.

(Dyer 1965: 23)

Photo: 'Australian wounded on the Menin Road, near Birr Cross Road, on September 20th, 1917 (Frank Hurley, National Library of Australia)

On the 1st October 1917 Stephen White was injured at Menin Road a month after his leave (according to Honor Roll) and this was recorded on the 2nd October 1917.[135] He was next wounded on the 21st October 1917. The 18th Battery resumed action on the 18th October 1917[136] near Zillebeke, and Stephen was next wounded a few days later on the 21st October 1917. On the same day a letter is dated to Mrs Linda White from the Australian Military Force (Base Records Office, Victoria Barracks) which informs her that her son Wheeler S.W. White is wounded, with no further information.[137] On the 29th October 1917 she responds to this information with a letter:

> *Dear Sir*
>
> *I have just received your notification informing me that Wheeler S.W White no 8427 6th Army Brigade is reported wounded.*
>
> *I would be glad if you could give me any information as to the nature of his wounds and when he was wounded. For which I will be very thankful to you.*
>
> *Thanking you in anticipation.*

I am yours Faithfully,

Mrs L White

Church Street West

Port Adelaide

South Australia

On the 1st November 1917, Mrs Linda White receives a reply from the Base Records Office saying that there is no further information, that her son's condition was 'not serious' and therefore it could be assumed he is making satisfactory progress.

Bombardier White was sent back to the trenches on the 17th November 1917, however fellow soldiers Twist and Melville by this stage were both in England due to injuries. That Christmas was spent by the 18th Battery in a camp between Bailleul and Armentieres in France, being a white Christmas where snow commenced early on Christmas day.[138] The troops enjoyed turkey followed by pudding and a parcel for each soldier and thanks to the 'Australian Comfort Fund' it was deemed the best Christmas ever by these troops, according to Dyer.[139] The Battery was to receive special parcels prepared by the 18th Battery Club, formed from the wives, mothers and sisters of troops in Adelaide.[140]

On the 20th February 1917 a set of gun pits had been built ready for occupation at short notice, but just prior to this many men lost their voice by accumulating gas affected timber in order to build the pits.[141] Stephen White also may have been affected as he went to the field hospital by ambulance around the 20th February 1918 with 'Bronch Catarrh' (Bronchitis) and on the 28th February 1918 also declared to have 'Trench Fever' and sent to the 2nd Australian General Hospital in Boulogne. He embarked for England on the 4th March 1918 via the ship 'Pieter de Connick' and was admitted to East Suffolk & Ipswich General Military Hospital, Colchester on the 4th March and then sent to the 3rd Auxiliary Hospital in Dartford, Kent on the 21st March 1918.[142]

On the 10th and 17th April 1918, Linda White receives a note stating that her son Stephen has been admitted to the General Military Hospital in Colchester, a good 6 months after he is hospitalised. On the 10th April 1918, she receives another letter stating that he has been admitted to a hospital in England. She responds to the letter regarding her son's hospitalisation …

> *Dear Sir*
> *I today received notification of my son Bmdr S.W. White's illness of trench fever and as he is in a lodge or Benefit Society could I get a Drs certificate to treatment to the lodge, as I cannot get his sick pay without one, also a certificate for the time he was wounded last October, as according to the lodge rules a certificate on and off the funds must be privated to the lodge, and if you could supply me with same I will be very thankful to you,*
> *Thanking you in anticipation*
> *I am yours Faithfully*
> *Mrs L White*
>
> (NAA record 1850441)

Many families at this time were receiving financial support from their son's regular payments from part of their war service income, with minimum and maximum specifications suggested by the army going to men with wives and children. According to his pay records, Stephen White was regularly paying his mother in 1916 and 1917.[143] The lodge provided some form of health insurance during times of illness or injury.

Stephen White went to hospital around the 20th February 1918, in Boulogne, France, with Trench Fever. This was likely to be the 2nd Australian General Hospital at Wimereux, near Boulogne, where the famous Matron Ethel Gray worked (she was the only member of the Australian Army Nursing Service to be awarded the Medaille de la Reconnaissance Francaise).

Stephen White embarked for England on the 4th March 1918 via the ship 'Pieter de Connick' and was admitted to East Suffolk & Ipswich General Military Hospital, Colchester.[144] He was then transferred to the 3rd Australian Auxiliary Hospital at Dartford on the 21st March 1918. On the 27th April 1918 he appeared on the 392nd Casualty List in the Adelaide newspapers.[145]

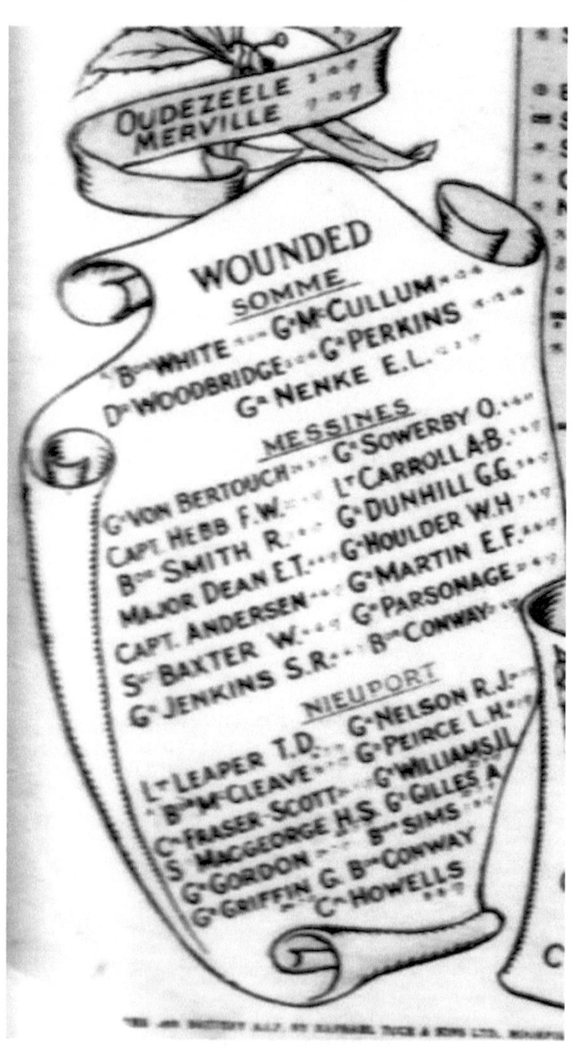

OUDEZEELE
MERVILLE

WOUNDED

SOMME

BDR WHITE — GR McCULLUM
DR WOODBRIDGE — GR PERKINS
GR NENKE E.L.

MESSINES

GR VON BERTOUCH — GR SOWERBY O.
CAPT HEBB F.W. — LT CARROLL A.B.
BDR SMITH R. — GR DUNHILL G.G.
MAJOR DEAN E.T. — GR HOULDER W.H.
CAPT. ANDERSEN — GR MARTIN E.F.
SR BAXTER W. — GR PARSONAGE
GR JENKINS S.R. — BDR CONWAY

NIEUPORT

LT LEAPER T.D. — GR NELSON R.J.
BDR McCLEAVE — GR PEIRCE L.H.
CR FRASER SCOTT — GR WILLIAMS J.L.
S MACGEORGE H.S. — GR GILLES A.
GR GORDON — BDR SIMS
GR GRIFFIN G. — BDR CONWAY
CR HOWELLS

Image above: Extract from Honor Roll Second Year's Record Indicating wounding of Bombardier White on the Somme. He was listed on the 392nd Casualty List in The Chronicle (27th April 1918).

Above: British soldiers marching past the ruined Cloth Hall, Ypres, Belgium, 25 October 1917. Source: Australian War Memorial

On the 2nd May 1918 Grandpa White was discharged to No 2 C.D (Australian Command Depot) and the following day he was marched in from the 3rd Australian Auxiliary Hospital at Dartford, Kent. But just a month later, on the 6th June he had another casualty. On the 12th June, Corporal Stephen White was received from the I.B. 500 R. (Infantry Brigade) and sent back to Australia via the ship 'Barambah' departing from Liverpool, and on 16th June 1918 Stephen White is promoted to 'Fitter Corporal' (marine). He had 'Debility - Trench Fever,' a moderately serious infectious disease caused by the bacterium Bartonella quintana and transmitted by body lice. It causes headache, pain behind the eyes, dizziness, back pain, sore muscles and joints and bodily stiffness.

He was apparently told by a Doctor that he had only 6 months to live,[146] with a total army service of 3 years and 91 days, and service abroad 2 years and 252 days. He was said to be 'full of shrapnel.' It was also claimed that he had experienced 'trench feet' or gangrene (which in 1914 had caused

20,000 British casualties).[147] He was discharged on the 11th October 1918, and went on to live for another fifty years.

Locally, the significant number of men from Glanville who died during the war were remembered in a ceremony led by the South Australian Governor Sir Henry Galway in 1918, with the unveiling of the Glanville War memorial. Every year former members of the 18th Battery marched in the ANZAC day parade followed by a drink at the Gresham Hotel (until it was demolished in 1965[148]), which was on the corner of North Terrace and King William Street, near Gresham Lane. The 18th Battery Men's Club held their main annual function on the 22nd November, the date they had disembarked from Australia.[149]

Casualty Form - Active Service.

Regiment or Corps 6th.Field Arty.Brigade.

Rank Fitter Cpl. Surname WHITE Christian Name Stephen William

Date	From whom received	Report	Place of Casualty	Date of Casualty	Remarks
4/3/18	E.Suffolk R. aff.Mil.Hpl. Colchester.	Adm. TRENCH FEVER	England	4/3/18	[illegible]
21/3/18	3rd.Aux.Hpl. Dartford.	Tfd. from E.Suffolk Hpl.	"	21/3/18	
[illegible]	" "	Disch.to No [illegible] C.D.	"	[illegible]	
[illegible]	No [illegible] C.D.	M/1 from 3rd.Aux. Dartford	"	[illegible]	
12/6/18	[illegible]	Returned to Australia per "D11" for Change.(STERILITY FLLG. TRENCH FEVER)	"	[illegible]	[illegible]

LIEUT.
For Officer i/c Records.
Admin.Hdqrs. LONDON.

Image above: An extract from WW1 Service Records of Stephen William White (no 1850441), Source: NAA.

Photo above: Hospital near Boulogne, France Source: Australian War Memorial, P00156.047 Photo below: 3rd Australian Auxiliary Hospital at Kent, where Stephen White stayed in 1918. AWM, P10997.033

Photo above: Returned soldiers marching along King William Street, Adelaide after WW1, 1918, State Library of SA [PRG 280/1/15/506]
Photo below: War memorial unveiling at Glanville by Sir Henry Galway (Governor), 1918, State Library of South Australia [PRG 280/1/15/289]

It is well known that the enduring Western Front battle was one of the bloodiest of all and the majority of allies, including Australian soldiers of the war died or became casualties there.[150] A total of 46,000 Australian soldiers perished on the Western Front, the highest number of casualties for WW1 (14,000 died elsewhere).[151] A total of 313,000 (out of 4.5 million in Australia) had volunteered for military service. There is the Australian National War Memorial in Villers-Bretonneux, France where Anzac day is still commemorated! There are also a series of other Battle of the Somme war memorials in this region.

The Thiepval Memorial to the Missing is the largest of all memorials and carries the name of 73,357 unknown British (including Australian) and South African soldiers[152]. At Menin Gate there is now an impressive memorial carrying the names of over 6000 Australian soldiers killed there[153] with no known grave and a total of 54, 896 soldiers with unknown graves.[154]

Post war experiences

Shortly after Stephen White returned from the war, he married Margaret Ethel Holman on his thirty sixth birthday (18th November 1919) at the Congregational Church in Port Adelaide, with his bride being 10 years his junior. He is seated during the wedding photographs, incredibly aged since his photograph as a new soldier taken just five years earlier, whilst his wife stands and his sister and brother-in-law are best man and woman (Auntie Ethel and Uncle Jim).

Photo above: Marriage of Stephen William White and Margaret Ethel Holman (centre) with Ethel Mary Graham (nee White) and Jim Graham 18th November 1919, photographers Walter J McNeill Port Adelaide (S. Battams)

After marrying, Margaret White had a stillborn baby. The couple continued to try to have children unsuccessfully for several years. It was reported anecdotally that it was Stephen who could not have children due to his war experiences.[155] Finally, the couple answered an advertisement in the newspaper to adopt a child in 1926.[156]

Stephen White was given a war service home/state bank loan in 1919 and lived at Cheltenham and then Minnipa on the West Coast of South Australia (from around 1924). However, he may have lost this house in 1927 in the lead up to the Great Depression (which first hit South Australia and Port Adelaide very hard, as described in the historical fiction book *Hunger Town*[157]).

Photo above: Former Independent Order of Oddfellows (IOOF) Lodge Hall, 94 Dale Street, Port Adelaide, circa 1920s. The IOOF also owned numbers 90-92 Dale Street, Port Adelaide (formerly Portland) (S. Battams) Below: Stephen William White's photograph of the Semaphore Angel Memorial (S.Battams)

Soldier Settlement Land at Minnipa

Stephen White worked on land under the Discharged Soldiers Settlement Act at Minnipa (9km east of Minnipa), where he is also described as a blacksmith and wheelwright. He obtained this land in 1921. Over 3000 soldiers were allocated Soldier Settlement land in South Australia between 1917 and 1931, and approximately 100 of these were in the Wudinna-Minnipa area, with James Head of Section 23 of Minnipa being the first settler in the region.[158] David Edward White lived opposite Stephen and Margaret White at section 16.

There was extended family around, with David White and Linda Cox, nephew Joseph Maguie who married a local, Merial Merle (Millie) Smart in the public hall at Minnipa in 1932, and nephew Bill Surman, along with siblings visiting.

Social activities in the small town of Minnipa included the monthly visits from the 'Cleve pictures' which included separate sessions of movies for the children and adults.[159]

For Margaret White, there was the Country Women's Association, with people often visiting from different regions for social activities, such as the Annual Strawberry Fete, where on the 1st December 1936 Margaret won a cake in a competition.[160]

Photo: Post office and general store at Minnipa, circa 1923, State Library of South Australia [PRG 280/1/41/249]

Share Farming

At one stage Stephen White is share-farming with his nephew Michael Joseph (Joseph) McGuire, his older sister's son. In 1927 Stephen was given 28 days' notice to pay up his debts or else he would be forced into bankruptcy. He must have approached an MP (the Hon J Kerr MLC) complaining about the decision, and it was then reversed. By 1929 he was trying to sell the farm, to no avail. But a JF Quick from Ceduna later wrote to the Soldier Settlement Superintendent asking to buy the farm.[161]

Nephew Michael Maguire went bankrupt with the public examination for bankruptcy held 28th May 1936 at the Local Court House (number 47 of 1936) at Minnipa, and the first meeting of creditors on the 11th June 1936.[162] The stressors of farming life over periods such as the great depression and the physical and psychological effects of Stephen White's war experiences were evident as he had been injured in the hip with shrapnel remnants causing some difficulty and pain walking, and he would only talk about the war in later years.[163]

In 1936, Stephen White had 27 sheep stolen, as reported in the police gazette:[164]

> *HUNDRED OF MINNIPA – Between the 30th June and 21st July 1936, from paddocks, 27 fat ewes in the wool, branded PK on off ribs in red paint, value £20 5s, the property of STEPHEN WILLIAM WHITE, identifiable.*

With such theft and drought, Stephen White eventually found farming a difficult existence and he went bankrupt in April 1937.

The experience of bankruptcy was not uncommon for returned soldiers who received land under the Discharged Soldiers Settlements Acts which began in states from 1916-17.[165] Even the government's experimental farm at Minnipa was a failure. The following are some anecdotal stories about the failure of this initiative:

> *The Commonwealth had guaranteed to meet the cost of settlement, but it was a debacle only equalled by the effect on the men who had tried to make a living from the acres. With many others my parents had taken up 'a block'..Within three years they had 'lost' it. "We couldn't keep up the payments," my father said. "And we had no money to stock it, or put up a proper house or fences or anything. Your mother and I worked hard enough at it, but that's how it goes I suppose". When she was caretaker of Nowingi railway siding in Sunset Country, beyond the Little Desert, my mother was approached by one of the soldier settlers from that wasteland. "if you'll give us a ticket south from here for the missus and kids and me you can have the things in our house – we're leaving them there anyway."*
>
> *A soldier…lived a few miles across the desert with his wife and babies, in a tent. She was a lovely woman. The babies were born in that tent. The family were in an awful way and he was a terribly*

sick man, wounds and shell shock made him often useless, but they both struggled on trying to make a go of it until the place was seized for debts. It was a rotten scheme. (No man today farms those desolate acres that had been sold as 'land fit for heroes'.)

Patsy Adam-Smith (2002), The ANZACS

Sale at Minnipa

White's 'blacksmithing and wheelwright' plant equipment was for sale in the *West Coast Sentinel*, July 1939. A 'Clearing Sale' was announced by auctioneers Goldsborough, Mort & Co Ltd, indicating that he was selling the Blacksmith Plant, along with a range of furniture and household effects. The local hotelier came around to purchase furniture from him that he had made (he was a carpenter and excellent craftsman, having done two replica mini churches, one of St Peter's in North Adelaide).[166]

Return to Port Adelaide

The family returned to Port Adelaide (Portland) in August 1939. It is uncertain whether this move was also related to the impending outbreak of WWII, which was 1st September, 1939, or due to the difficulties of farming life. When they returned to the city, Stephen White who was now 54 years of age, obtained a job on the wharves as a 'foreman stevedore.'[167] The 1930s and 40s was a period where there was a lot of political activity surrounding waterside workers. In one case in 1946[168], waterside workers threatened to strike over double -dumped wool, where wool bales were compressed into smaller packaging to allow more wool to fit into the container and reduce shipping costs.[169]

GENUINE

CLEARING SALE

MINNIPA

TUESDAY, AUGUST 8, 1939.

At 11.30 a.m. sharp.

Goldsbrough, Mort & Co.,

LIMITED,

will offer by auction on behalf of Mr. S. W. WHITE, who is leaving the district, the whole of his BLACKSMITHING PLANT and FURNITURE, as under:—

BLACKSMITHING & WHEEL-WRIGHT EFFECTS

116 sheets good Galv. Iron; 200 sheets old Galv. Iron; 3½ H.P. International Engine, good order; 5½-in. tyre English Waggon; Power Blower; Electric Blower; Forge; Anvil; Grindstone; Punches; Hammers; Swedges; Tongs; Sun and Massey Drill Parts; Binder, Stripper and Harvester and Plough Parts; Stocks and Dies; Binder and Header Knives; ½ cwt. Shoes; 3 tons Scrap Iron; quantity Timber, etc.

HOUSEHOLD EFFECTS

New Sideboard; Refrectory Dining Table, new; 7-piece Blackwood Leather Suite; Oak Kitchen Cabinet; Cool Safe; 3-piece Oak Bedroom Suite; Double Bed; Folding Bed; Stretcher and Bedding; Dressing Table; Chest Drawers; Copper and Stand; 90ft. ½-in. Hose; Garden and Carpenters' Tools; Linos for 3 rooms; Bike; 5-valve Astor Wireless Set, with 2-V. Battery; Sundries, etc., etc.

TERMS CASH.

Light Luncheon at sale. ea4

Image: Port Lincoln Times (SA : 1927 - 1954), Thursday 3 August 1939, page 4

Photo: Stephen White & Margaret White with brother Clarry White and his (grand?) son circa 1945, Glanville or Portland, Source: S. Battams

The White family appeared to have ongoing ties to the Independent Order of Oddfellows (IOOF), as there was a photo of the lodge building at Dale Street, Port Adelaide that belonged to my grandfather.

Margaret White spent time caring for her father-in-law David after his spouse (Linda White) died at Port Adelaide in 1935. However, Margaret died suddenly on the 25th July 1948 just short of Ray White's 22nd birthday, and the year before David died. She was only 54 years of age. At this time the family were still living at College Street, Portland. Stephen was to live for another 20 years and see his son marry and most of his grandchildren born. Margaret White's sister Ellen, or 'Nell', lived at Port Adelaide with Stephen after Margaret died, and was always knitting jumpers and the like for the White grandchildren. Stephen White reportedly enjoyed seeing his grandchildren, and would look after and buy presents for them. Before he died, he lived with his son and daughter-in-law and grandchildren, in a granny flat at the back of the house on the train line at 104 Day Terrace West Croydon.

Stephen White was remembered as being very 'British' in accordance with his generation who were brought up with British imperialism and patriotism[170], which would change somewhat as a result of WWI. He was also remembered in private reverie listening to old records with his favourites including 'American's singing sweethearts' Nelson Eddie and Jeanette McDonald , songs by Hammerstein and Kern and Mitch Miller, and Harry Belafonte.[171] Stephen White would also go on pub crawls with Alec White.

Stephen White died in 1968, and would have been 85 years that year, not bad for a man who had been given a sentence of '6 months to live' fifty years earlier. The death and funeral notices in *The Advertiser* on the 20th May 1968 read:

> *White – On May 19 at his late residence, Stephen William, beloved husband of the late Margaret Ethel, loving father of Stephen Raymond, daughter in law Val, grandpa of Lynette, Margret, Cheryl and Raelene and beloved brother of Ethel, Dave, Clarrie and Alex. In his 85th year."*
>
> *White – The friends of the late Mr Stephen William White (late 18th Battalion, 1st A.I.F.) are advised that his funeral will leave our private chapel 290 Greenhill Rd, Glenside on Tuesday after a service commencing at 3pm for the Cheltenham Cemetery.*

Amongst the things he left behind was his Digger Smith Trench Series from which the following lines come:

"Do you think us blokes Over There
When things was goin' strong,
Was keepin' ledgers day by day
An' reck'nin wot the crowd would pay?
Pull off! Yeh got it wrong
Do you think all the boys gone West

Wants great swank 'ead-stones on their chest?

"Beauty", sez Digger, sudden-like,
"An' love, an 'kindliness;
The chance to live a clean, straight life,
A dinkum deal for kids an' wife:
A man needs nothin' less...
Maybe they'll get it when I go
To push up daisies. I dunno.

"Dreamin'" sez Digger Smith. "Why not?
There's visions on the hill"...
Then I get up an' steals away,
An' leaves 'im with the dyin' day,
Dreamin' an' doubtin' still...
Cobber, it's up to me an' you
To see that 'arf 'is dream comes true"

from Digger Smith, C, J Dennis 1918[172]

The Mystery Caller – Who was Bill Surman?

In the 1980s someone from the White family contacted my mum Val (when we lived at Aldinga Beach) and asked about Dad, Stephen Raymond White - this could have been 1984 when David White junior died. The person talked about Bill Surman growing up on the West Coast with Dad. At the time it was a bit of a mystery to us who called, but mum said the person was 'Bill Surman.' (There was also said to be an earlier approach of someone contacting our family by knocking at the door at West Croydon after our father had died, asking about Bill Surman). It does not appear that Bill Surman had children – so this mystery caller may have been one of the younger siblings or nephews of Stephen William White.

Stephen Raymond (Ray) White grew up with William (Bill) Stephen Surman (1916-1941) on the West Coast, 'as brothers'. Bill Surman was the nephew (by marriage) of David Edward White snr, as his wife Linda (nee Cox) sister Charlotte Cox had married John Stephen Surman. Bill Surman was born in 1916 and over 30 years younger than his first cousin Stephen William White, but only 10 years older than Dad (Ray). Poor Bill Surman's mum Charlotte died in 1917 when he was only 1 year old and his father died in 1925 when he was 8 years old. Finding out about him was one mystery solved.

Bill Surman was engaged to Mavis Aubert in 1940.[173] He enrolled in the army in WWII on the 10th January 1941, when he was living at 9 College Avenue, Portland (Grandpa Stephen White's house).[174] He lists his Uncle David as next of kin, who at the time is living at 9 Old Port Road, Queenstown (now a retirement living place). He was an unemployed Labourer at the time, and it stated that he could ride a horse and drive a horse team, a motor car and a lorry. He was discharged to the Australian Infantry Force on the 26th March 1941. He married Mavis Aubert on the 10th May 1941, and they lived at 89 Dale Street, Portland (this may have belonged to the IOOF – as 90-92 was). Sadly, Bill died of an illness 5 months later in Port Adelaide on 21st October 1941, when he was only 25 years old and Dad was 15 years old. Mavis was also hospitalised at the same time for 9 days but survived, and she remarried in 1943.

Photo left: William (Bill) Surman aged 24 years, WWII enlistment photo, NAA, B883, SX11977, Item ID: 6397385

1856: Holman and Vierk families

Margaret Holman had an English, Cornish and Prussian background. She was born 29th March 1894 in Port Adelaide, to Elijah Holman and Annie Vierk.[175] Her grandfather Joseph Holman was born in Somerset, England but worked as an Agricultural Labourer and lived with his wife Alice Whitmore in Probus, Cornwall, England (where she was from). The family (Joseph, Alice and children Thomas, Catherine and baby Alice) departed Plymouth on the 20th December 1856 and arrived in Port Adelaide on the 27th March 1857 on the ship *Royal Albert.* Their religion was Church of England.The family lived in Probus (Cornwall), Leslie Place, Portland, Crafers, and Alberton.

Tragically, Margaret's mother Annie Vierk died of typhoid fever in 1899 aged 32 at the Adelaide Hospital, just a week after her eldest daughter Frances Alice Holman died of the same disease. Annie Vierk was the daughter of Wilhelm Friedrich Christian (William Frederick) Vierk and Frances Anne (Fanny) Trotter. William's brother Ernst married Ellen Mary

Trotter, Fanny's sister. The Vierk family was from Nurioopta (originally from Prussia), whilst the Trotter family (from England) had settled in Adelaide. William Vierk had won the tender to build the road at Hanson Street South, Adelaide in 1880.

Margaret Holman was one of seven children. With both her mother and eldest sister having died by the time she was 5 years of age, her grandmother Fanny Vierk would have played an important role in the surviving children's lives, especially as their father Elijah was working as a Porter on the railways at Port Adelaide.

Sadly another daughter, Grace Annie, died in 1904 aged just 7 years (the funeral procession left from her grandmother Fanny Vierk's house). That left just Edith (aged 14) Ellen (Nell) (13 years), Margaret (10 years), Joseph junior (9 years) and Fred (6 years).

Interestingly, when Joseph and Fred Holman both enlisted in WWI, they state Margaret as being their mother rather than their older sisters – Fred enlisted 12 April 1916, one day after his 18th birthday at Adelaide. At the time he lived in Peel Street, Yatala (Alberton -where Margaret Holman and Stephen White also lived). Like his father, he was a Porter with South Australian Railways. He returned to Australia 29 July 1919 per the *Omonde*. He also served in WWII and died shortly after his return from overseas on the 16 November 1945 aged 47, less than two months after the WWII ended. He is buried in a Commonwealth War Grave.

Fortunately, Fanny Vierk nee Trotter lived to the age of 88, dying in 1933. She is buried with her sister Alice J. Kroemer, who died aged 77 in 1927 (she was a widow whose husband had died aged 34 years at Dawson in 1887, northeast of Peterborough).

Photo: Fred Holman, brother to Margaret Ethel Holman, seated in front, second from left. 10th Battalion, Signalers (Source: NAA)

Travelling Back to Europe

Visit to Ypres, Belgium

Eighty years after World War I, in August 1997 I had the opportunity to visit the former Western front battle fields in Belgium, Flanders fields, the Menin Gate Memorial and around Ypres, and was extremely moved. It certainly put into perspective the shock of hearing the death of Princess Diana of Wales announced on the tour bus early that morning. My diary[176] extract from this visit reads…

> *Aug 1997*
> *We went to the battlefields around Ypres where Grandfather White fought – Passchendaele, Messines – There were many trenches, pill-boxes, cemeteries, shells/ammunition left – so much active ammunition is still buried underground – around 3-4 fatalities per year still occur through farmers hitting some live shells with a plough or similar. So much more keeps being found or is dug up. The Belgian [tour] guide's two uncles were in the war – his grandmother gave birth to his father in a refugee camp. He was passionate about it – he tried to give us a picture of what conditions were like – hell on earth. How does a human survive these conditions? We saw a trench that was '4 star' – an underground hole with beds packed in – it would have been rat and flee infested – they called the rats 'trench rabbits' they were so huge. The Aussie diggers – sewer-rats – dug massive underground trenches – as the Germans fought on top of them – many died by drowning in mud. The Tyne Cot cemetery is huge – but there are so many others full of white stone graves.*
> *At first gas was combated only by dipping a hanky or sock in water – or urine – then women's sanitary pads were sent over for the gas.*

We read stories of people who dragged mates out of mud and had to leave them – had to kill them to put them out of pain and go on. How did they survive this bloodshed? I can't understand – but if Grandpa White hadn't survived – hadn't gone home with trench fever and '6 months to live' – hadn't survived being blasted with shrapnel– I wouldn't be here today.

Photo: Menin gate, Ypres, Belgium 1997 (S. Battams)

Visit to Marseille, France

I have visited France many times but in 2011, when I lived in Geneva, Switzerland, I was visiting Marseille and felt drawn to visit a museum, La Vieille Charité, a beautiful architectural building. It was only when I arrived that I realised it was probably the place that Grandpa White stayed after he got off the boat and before he took the train to the Somme region – the railway station in Marseille being a place he definitely was in 1915 as the Australian soldiers took the train from Marseille to Le Havre. The museum was used by the French Foreign Legion in the early 20th C until 1922, and was used during WWI to house soldiers arriving in the port.

Trips to Brussels

I went to Belgium a few times for work and leisure when I lived in Geneva (European Commission, a conference, and travelling with Lyn and Robert), and once to the Netherlands for a conference. At the *International European Union in Global Affairs III* in Brussels (2012) I presented on the European Union's role in global health and the reform of the WHO, and I remember a question from a German member of the audience who questioned why I, an Australian, would be interested in the European Union! I remember thinking (but not saying) - why wouldn't I?! My family were heavily impacted by the First and Second World Wars which started in that part of the world. So many lives in Australia have been erased because of these wars, including in my parents' families discussed in this book.

Fifteen family members to have **served during WW1**, with six killed and never to return were:

***Rumbelow family*:**

Great Uncle **Frank Harris Rumbelow** (Grandma Stella's brother) **killed 12th October 1917 buried in the Buttes New British Cemetery, Polygon Wood, Zonnebeke, Belgium**.

Herbert Victor Rumbelow served and returned to Australia (he married great-grandma Ada Heading's younger sister Hilda Heading). Other Rumbelows who served are on the Rumbelow and descendants website: https://www.rumbelow.net/

Heading family:

Sir James Alfred Heading (1884-1969) and his brother:

Alf Vaughan Heading (1898-1918) (Killed WWI in 1918 and is buried in Dernancourt Communal Cemetery, FRANCE).

Holman and Vierk family:

Great Uncle Fredrick (Fred) Thomas Christopher Holman (Margaret White's brother) Service no 6265 Private 10th Battalion, Signallers, Born 11 April 1898 at Glanville, SA. Served WWI and WWII. Also his brother:

Great Uncle Joseph George Holman, (Margaret White's brother), Horse Driver. Enlisted 20th March 1915, fought in the 10th Battalion, including in Gallipoli.

George John Vierk (Uncle to Margaret Holman) **(Killed 7th July 1918, aged 38yrs, buried at Adelaide Cemetery,** (Plot I, Row B, Grave No. 5), **Villers-Bretonneux, FRANCE.**

Harry Frederick A. Dixon, **(**Cousin to Margaret Holman and nephew to George Vierk)**, Cabinetmaker, (Killed 8th July 1918 and is buried at Crucifix Corner Cemetery (Plot X, Row B, Grave No. 10), Villers-Bretonneux, FRANCE.**

Battams family:

Their lives were heavily influenced by the First and Second World Wars. Altogether there were **seven** Battams men in close family relationship who went to this war or served in the army. These included brothers:

1) William Alfred (jnr) Battams (my stepdad Len's grandfather – his father served at Loveday Internment Camp)
2) Henry Gordon Battams
3) Joseph Wesley Battams **(Killed 5th April 1918 aged 23, buried FRANCE 196 Ribemont Communal Cemetery Extension, 4 ½ miles south-west of Albert)**
Also, the sons and nephews of some of these men:
4) William Henry Battams (son of William Alfred jnr)
5) Frederick Alfred Roy Battams (son of William Alfred jnr)
6) Leslie George Battams (son of George Albert and nephew to William Alfred jnr). Interestingly, was initially rejected due to 'deafness' but later accepted, and released as went progressively deaf.
7) Frederick Stanley Battams (son of Daniel Potter Battams - grandson to Daniel Battams who first arrived in Australia) **(Killed 18th July 1917 aged 23, buried BELGIUM 70 Ploegsteert Wood Military Cemetery Warneton).**

Chapter 3: Our father's adoption and going back to Minnipa

5th Generation in Australia

When the adoption laws changed in South Australia around 1997, I obtained my first bit of evidence about my father's biological family. The adoption file indicated that he was named 'Jack Fahy' at his birth in 1926, as my mother had always claimed. His birth mother's name was Iris Marie Fahy, and she had 'Jack' when she was only 17 years of age, in the Queen's Home, Dequetteville Terrace, Adelaide (later the Queen Victoria Hospital).

The year Dad was adopted (1926) was the first year that adoptions were legal in South Australia – *The Adoption of Children Act* was passed in December 1925.[177] The Queen's home was the first state institution to take unmarried mothers. Iris was almost certainly forced to give up Dad through adoption because she was an unwed Catholic teenager. The single mother's pension (later the single parent's pension) was not introduced in Australia until 1973, and state and commonwealth payments available prior to this could not support a child.[178]

It was interesting that Iris (or her family) chose the 'government home' (Queen's Home) to have her baby, rather than one of the Catholic homes for unmarried mothers. This may have been due to the stigma in the close Catholic community and higher chance of privacy in a government institution, or because there were reports at the time of the poor conditions and high death rates of babies born at these Catholic homes.

Jack Fahy was officially adopted out on Saint Valentine's Day 1929, when he was 2 ½ years old, although the adoptive family (the White family) had him since he was just 3 weeks old. It was recorded that Stephen and Margaret White had answered an advertisement in the newspaper regarding adoption. At the time, many unmarried mothers (or perhaps those in the

Church) would advertise in the daily newspaper seeking a 'kind lady to adopt a baby,' and those seeking children would also advertise. The third advertisement below which states 'entirely given up – In September' could have been about 'Jack Fahy.' At the time, the adoption law was also informed by the view that it was best if the biological mother of a child was separated as early and completely as possible from her baby (the 'clean break' theory).[179]

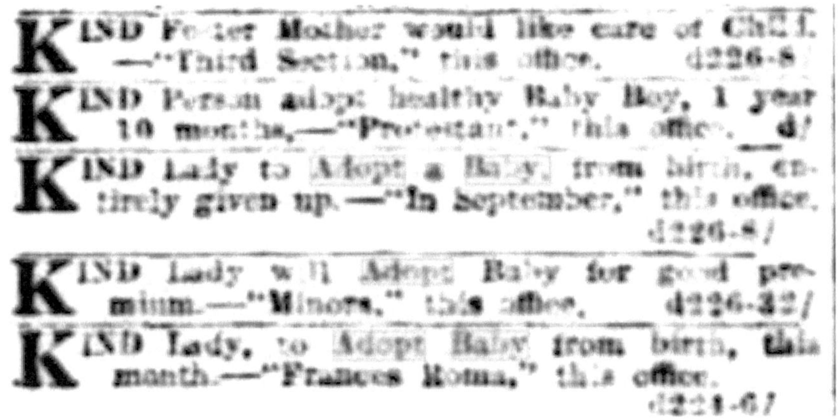

KIND Foster Mother would like care of Child.—"Third Section," this office. d226-8

KIND Person adopt healthy Baby Boy, 1 year 10 months.—"Protestant," this office. d

KIND Lady to Adopt a Baby, from birth, entirely given up.—"In September," this office. d226-8

KIND Lady will Adopt Baby for good premium.—"Minors," this office. d226-32

KIND Lady, to Adopt Baby from birth, this month.—"Frances Roma," this office. d221-6

Adoption Advertising, The Advertiser, 14th August 1926

The official adoption process was quite a long one with a 'police report' for a character reference on the prospective parents required by the state Children's Welfare Department. The request was first sent to the Commissioner of Police in South Australia, then to the Inspector at Wallaroo before being passed on to a local police officer at Minnipa.

Both birth mother Iris and adoptive mother Margaret changed their names on forms used for the adoption process, with Iris switching her first and second name and Margaret taking on the first name of her husband's sister (either this occurred or their names were reported incorrectly). Ray White would be the only child of Stephen and Margaret. She was reportedly a very loving mother and they were both remembered as good parents.

The story passed down to my grandfather was that Iris had fallen pregnant to a Protestant, and her Catholic father disapproved of the couple getting married. However, this was also the story of Iris's parents, as Irish Catholic Mick Fahy had himself married Helena Schulz, a Protestant Lutheran, who had to convert to Catholicism. At the time, it was custom for a wife to convert, so Iris would have had to convert to a Protestant religion.

Stephen White would say he brought up a 'poor little rich kid' who hailed from a publican family.[180] Our family is biologically related to the Fahy family from New South Wales (Orange region) who were publicans. It appears that Michael Fahy who settled in Orange who was a Publican was likely Edmund Fahy's brother (due to the DNA links of descendants to my family), and Patrick Fahy from Orange was also a Publican.[181] Stephen White would have been surprised to learn that his adopted child had also descended from the first boat load of Germans to come to South Australia in 1838 and a famous winemaking family (the Gramps).

The processes of first finding out about the birth family of Ray White and the adoption process itself was rather complicated, as described below:

First discovery of adoption information

In May 1997, I sent a letter from my then home in Hobart to South Australia's 'Births, Deaths & Marriages' government office and received some information which indicated that Ray White was adopted when he was 2 ½ years of age, however the family had known that he had been with his adoptive parents since birth. Later I sent a letter to the Department of Family and Community Services (DFCS), South Australia to find out more about his birth relatives.

31st January 1998, Adelaide

After settling back to Adelaide and phoning DFCS, I received some information in the post. There is a photocopy of the adoption card, titled Legal Adoption (Parents), listing the adoptive parents: Mabel Ethel (actually Margaret Ethel White) and Stephen William White, Connor Street, Glanville (Stephen White's parents' address). Then on this 70 years old piece of paper the government department wrote my name – Samantha Battams - and 'Daughter of Deceased Adoptee, new registration 23/5/97.' Underneath is 'Vide', Latin/French for 'void', and next to it Dad's birth name: John Fahy, illegitimate born 21st September 1926, legally adopted 14th February 1929.

2881

LEGAL ADOPTION (Parents)

M. White, Mabel Ethel

F. " Stephen William

Address Connor Street,
Glanville.

daughter of decd adoptee N/Reg 23/5/97
(Samantha Battams) R 5808

Vide Fahy, John
Illegte bn 21.9.26
Legally adopted 14/2/29.

Photo: Adoption card Source: S. Battams

Adoption Files

Also with this adoption card were photocopies of other information. Name of child: Jack Fahy, Name and address of parents: Marie I. Fahy, 189 Henley Beach Road, Torrensville, Place of Birth, Queens Home, Rose Park. Then the name of foster mother: Mabel E. White. Both birth mother (Iris Marie Fahy) and adopted mother (Margaret Ethel White) changed their first and second names for this process.

Also on the adoption file is information about the placement with foster parents, but this time there was listed Marie Iris Fahey [sic], 'Singlewoman'. There is also Margaret Ethel's name, Minnipa, West Coast, and her husband's name, Stephen William White, farmer, about 5 ¾ miles from Minnipa at Minnipa East. Married 7 years, no children. Answered an advertisement. Sent for police report 1st October 1926. John Fahey [Fahy], legally adopted 14th February 1929 to Mr & Mrs White, Connor Street, Glanville.

Religion— Meth CHILD WITH LICENSED FOSTER-MOTHER. FILE 2881

Name of Child Fahy, Jack Legitimate or Illegitimate Ill

Name and Address of Parents Marie I. Fahy, 159 Henley Bch Rd, Torrensville

Date of Birth 21 9 26 Place of Birth Queen's Home, Rose Park

Date.	With whom Placed.	Date of Leaving.	Visits made by Inspectress
1/10/26	White, Mabel E. (Mrs Stephen) ~~Minnipa, W Coast.~~ Connor St, Glanvill		Legal adoption 14 2 29

daughter of deco adoptee New Reg 23/5/97 (Samantha Battams) R 5808

Extract from adoption record, Source: S. Battams

Police Report

In the early days, police at a senior level were involved in the adoption process. Details about the process include:

- 'White, Mr & Mrs Stephen W. Sent to Inspector O'Connell for enquiry and report – *M Heartly, Pro Commissioner of Police*. 4/10/26.
- Forwarded to M.C. Judd for careful enquiry and report, Wallaroo - *G. Clark M. C. for Pro Inspector O' Connell (absent on duty)*. 6/10/26.

- Returned to Inspector O'Connell, with report attached, Minnipa 12/10/26 - *P. B. Judd, M. C.*
- Respectfully returned to the Commissioner of Police. -*M. D. O'Connell, Inspector 15/10/26.*
- Returned to the Secretary, State Childrens' Department, for his information - *M. Heartly, Pro Commissioner of Police.* 18/10/26
- Received 19th October 1926, State Children's Department.

Police Report, Minnipa Police Station, October 12th 1926.

To Inspector O'Connell, Wallaroo.

Re: Mr & Mrs S.W White, applying for State Child. Attached correspondence.

I beg to report that...

1. *I have known Mr & Mrs Stephen W White of Minnipa for the past 2 ½ years.*
2. *In my opinion Mr & Mrs White would be a very good couple to adopt a child.*
3. *I know from personal knowledge they are both very fond of children and they are in a position to give a child a good home if one were placed with them.*

P.B. Judd M.C.

Court Documents

The Port Adelaide Local Courthouse documents read:

> *Application for legal adoption by Stephen William White and Mabel [sic] Ethel White of Connor Street, Glanville, to adopt John Fahey [sic], an illegitimate child born on the 31st [sic] day of September 1926. Application set down for hearing at Pt Adelaide on Thursday, 14th February 1929. Application granted by above court. C Marin.*

Inspector L. F. W. Children's Welfare Department. Notified Mr Byrne.

Photo: Port Adelaide police court, circa early 1870s, now the Tourist Information Centre Source: SLSA [B1874]

As a young child, Stephen Ray White, known as 'Steve' at school and later 'Ray' as he insisted on being called as a child, was brought up at Minnipa on the Eyre Peninsula. He went to Minnipa East school, a tiny school – just a wooden building in the middle of a paddock, with one teacher and 10 to 13 students across all grades. The poor children were very vulnerable to a cruel teacher, as we later found out.

In November 1935, Dad was staying with his family at 1 MacKinnon Parade, North Adelaide. This may have been for The Ashes cricket series, Remembrance Day and the John Martin's Christmas Pageant (which all occurred that month). He also seemed to have an accident on a bike whilst there: his bike collided with a car and his head hit the windscreen and he was 'lacerated' and in hospital for 10 days (name recorded there: Raymond White).[182] In the school picture from circa 1936 (second school picture below), it appears that his head has been shaved, possibly associated with an operation/accident.

Photo: Stephen Raymond White circa 1928 on the 'Soldier Settlement' farm at Minnipa. Note one of the sheds with Red Cross cartons behind. (S.Battams)

Photo: School children at Minnipa East school, circa 1935. Stephen White is kneeling, second from right. The girl in the middle is Jean Kammerman. and the girl at right is Fay Bignell[183]. Below: Stephen White is standing, just right of teacher, Mrs Neave, Minnipa East school, late 1935 or early 1936. Jean Kammerman is standing behind Dad (left in the picture). Fay Bignell is kneeling in front. (J. Kammerman)

After his father's bankruptcy (in April 1937), the family moved to Port Adelaide when he was 12 years of age (in August, 1939). He did not like what he felt was the 'rough' culture of his new school at Port Adelaide, and the teacher said he would do well if he attended regularly.[184] However, he was an avid reader of books and journals (I have a copy of his '*The Quarterly Review* 1938' from when he was 12 years old, which has interesting facts about the situation of various European countries pre WWII).

As a teenager, Ray worked at the Port Adelaide cinemas selling ice-cream/lollies (lolly boy), where he was reportedly very popular amongst the young women, and where Val first noticed him. He was over 6ft tall, with green almond eyes and dark hair (taking after the German ancestors), he was exceedingly shy, with a low gentle voice.

Ray was a friend to Val's brother Len Miller, and he met Val (my mother) on his 22nd birthday party, less than 2 months after his mother's death. She had been invited by her brother. Ray married Valma Jean (Val) Miller in October 1950, with Uncle Alec/Alex (really his cousin) the best man and Auntie Marjorie (Miller) the chief bridesmaid and witnesses to the wedding.

As an only child who had come from the quiet country life, Dad's life experience and personality contrasted with that of his wife Val who was from a boisterous family of twelve. Val's Dad nicknamed him 'Silent Night' as he was so quiet and reserved.

Photo above: front of 9 College St, Portland (S. Battams) Below: Ray (on motorbike) and his father Stephen white at Portland (S. Battams)

Photo above: Ray as a young man, circa 1945 (S. Battams), Below: Val at Semaphore circa 1945 (S.Battams)

Photo: Valma Miller aged 18, as a bridesmaid at her sister Gwen's wedding, 12th June 1948 (S.Battams), Below: Wedding photo of Ray & Val White, October 1950 (coloured in the original) (S.Battams)

Photos: Ray and Val in the early years of marriage (early 1950s), College Street, Portland (S.Battams)

Ray and Val White had the following children:

Jennifer Dawn White (b. 26th May 1951, stillborn)

Lynette Jean White (b. 21st August 1952) (married Robert Parsons)

Margret Lillian White (b. 27th August 1954-d. 1st Oct 2002) (married Ken Harris)

Cheryl Leslie White (b. 11th March 1957-10th April 2014)

Raelene Joye White (b. 21st February 1962) (married Tony Linden, divorced)

Samantha Jane White, later Battams (b. 27th May 1971) (married Pierre-Alain Wulser, divorced)

The stillbirth of their first child was a very tragic event, with grieving mothers of stillborn babies at the time cruelly put in wards with new mothers. Val did not see the baby, although Ray did and said that she was perfect except for she wasn't breathing. At the time, stillbirth was four times more common than it is today, with around 29 deaths per 1,000 live births in 1950, compared with 7.2 per 1000 in 2021.[185] This was a significant event for mum, and when she died I found her keys on a keychain with a tiny baby's foot which was commemorating a baby's premature birth.

The young family lived in three places together: with Grandfather White's house at Portland, at Wingfield and at the beautiful bungalow they purchased at Day Terrace, West Croydon in 1956. This is where the White family lived for around 23 years, at the time were many new migrants from Greece, Italy and later former Yugoslavian countries amongst neighbours. Ray was actively involved in the Kilkenny Primary School committees where all of his five children went (and four of their children were tertiary educated, the first generation of university graduates). He was a great believer in public education as a means for social mobility. Ray was a dedicated family man and knew some of his many grandchildren, including Lyn and Margret's children.

Ray was a skilled tradesman (toolmaker) and had only 4 jobs throughout his life. Firstly he worked at Robin & Le Messurier's (Timber Yard and Steam Saw Mill) at Port Adelaide where he did his apprentice training as a toolmaker/fitter and turner.

He then worked at Gibb & Miller Limited Engineers at Port Adelaide which manufactured cranes, fuel tanks, a press for motor vehicle builders T. J. Richards and Sons, lifting jack units for the automative industry, trailers, spray pump equipment, conveyors, steel balls, rotary shears (used for cutting sheet steel), boilers (supplying the Royal Adelaide Hospital), girders (steel beams supporting floors, roofs or other structures), ammunition during WWII, a wind tunnel for weapons research and carried out work on naval ships,[186] machine tools,[187] and built a manufacturing plant for power station equipment at Whyalla,[188]opened by Premier Sir Thomas Playford.[189] Playford had a vision for Whyalla becoming one of the great industrial centres of Australia.[190] In 1953 A. J. Gibb, managing director, was appointed to a national advisory committee on defence production.[191]

In 1952 there was a claim for wage increase at the firm, which appeared to be awarded. The same year the firm pushed for a reduction in the basic wage and an increase in standard working hours from 40 to 44 (with other employers) through the Federal Arbitration Court, claiming that manufacturing costs had outstripped wage rises.[192] In 1954 the firm was involved in a pay dispute with metal trade unions, with a stop work meeting to discuss wages and the claim for increased margins refused by management, with the dispute going to the Trades and Labor Council.[193] This was the same year the first part of the Whyalla industrial site the firm had been contracted to build was opened. Dad did a brief 3-month stint working for the Municipal Tramways Trust around 1956, which must have been during the time he worked for Gibb and Miller. In 1958 there was a significant stop work meeting (for 2 and a half days) for wage demands; the management had paid a wage bonus of 7.5% but on grounds of paying for service leave this was cut to 5%, which meant 8/- less per week for tradesmen. As management stood firm after a meeting with unions, the men rejected the bonus system.[194] It appears that Dad worked for the company until around 1958 or 1959 when Alfred Gibb died and the business became a subsidiary of Perry Engineering.[195]

B 17416

Photo: Robin & Le Messurier's Timber Yard, Port Adelaide, SLSA B17416

This was followed by 18 years working at Rubery, Owen Holdings (ROH) Australia – Rubery, Owen and Kemsley Pty. Ltd. (it evolved into ROH Wheels)[196] which operated at Finsbury, a British engineering company that expanded to South Australia in 1946. The Playford government offered incentives to firms to use the Finsbury site post WWII in order to develop industry in South Australia (the empty site with saw-toothed roof had been used as an ammunitions factory during WWII and it was where my maternal grandfather worked as a fitter during WWII).[197] Rubery, Owen and Kemsley Pty Ltd established in 1950 for 'auto and agricultural wheels and rims, chassis members, tractor and car pressing and precision and pressed parts for various engineering industries.'[198] At this firm Dad was primarily a Toolmaker using a lathe and also operated/set the press machinery. This was precision work, with mum saying that 'he wasn't allowed to be a thou out' (one thousands of an inch out). He was a supervisor at work and also belonged to the trade union. Dad received more in salary due to his extra responsibilities, something which fellow unionists had complained about.

Photo: Aerial photo of Finsbury Park, SLSA BRG 397/2/90/5

Although he had a motorbike when he was younger and worked in a heavy industry closely associated with motor manufacturing, Ray never learnt to drive a car. Mum reported that he was concerned that if he had a 'health episode' when driving it would endanger his children, and he took the bus to work at ROH every day. He had been hospitalised on more than one occasion as a child, including from colliding with a car when on his bike, and had occasional dizziness that was linked to a piece of wheat embedded in his ear as a child that was only expelled many years later.

Ray only found out he was adopted around 1956 when he asked his father for his birth certificate when he was 30 years of age (and had three children of his own), as he needed it for a new job at the Tramways. This is when his father told him about his adoption. Later Dad reflected to my mother that he thought it a bit strange as when he was growing up he overheard his parents say, 'he hasn't turned out a bad lad, has he?' According to mum, my father didn't wish to find out about his birth family, since he felt that his parents who adopted him were the ones who had cared for him and brought him up, and were good parents. Around that time, adoption wasn't spoken about, and finding one's birth family was not a common thing to do. My father's best man at his wedding was 'Uncle Alec.' (really his cousin) who was also secretly illegitimate.

Photo left: Margret, Lynnette and Cheryl circa 1959 Right: Cheryl, Lyn, Margret at the zoo circa 1961 (S. Battams)

Amongst his friends were Val's considerable number of siblings and their partners, particularly Len Miller. One of them said that he was always well dressed when going out, even to the enormously popular at the time beachside Semaphore it was shirt and slacks. He also had a good friend John, an English immigrant and workmate at Rubery, Owen Holdings. Dad was a keen supporter of the Port Adelaide Football Club, regularly attending games with his friend John, and sometimes his daughters, and watching playbacks on television when he returned home.

Ray was often found reading in the evenings, and when his daughters were older, there were often discussions around the kitchen table in the evenings. Although a shy man, he apparently had a very dry sense of humour. He was also a very practical man.

In Dad's pocket diary from 1963 he has various jottings revealing some of his activities and personality. Within it are measurements and modifications for tools (utility web tool, welding jig, rim tool, welding adaptor, shaft break press) and either hours worked or the timing necessary for the tools (jottings related to his work). There are also mathematical equations and sums. There is also family budgeting (although Val was the money manager!), and what appears to be sketching for practical projects around the home (cupboards, scales, 'golf tees'). There is the agenda for the 'welfare club' (either a school or work committee). There are curious facts – a picture of an iceberg with the proportion below water ('check up for Florie' it says beside it) – and the mineral component of money. Also in the back are contacts of people (the neighbor, my mother's youngest brother Stanley). Then in the same diary there are the later scribblings of my older sisters – to record the progress of a child's game (between cousins). There is also a drawing of myself 'Samantha, our new baby' it says beside it (drawn by my 10 year old sister Raelene). Curiously, there is only one page missing – the 3rd June, the day he died (in 1977).

There are some nice photos of my family from the time when my eldest sister was married (from 1978). Ray looks a very proud man in these. Lyn was married to Robert Parsons, a farmer from Minlaton on the Yorke Peninsula (who also served in the Vietnam War – my birth was announced to him via telegram to Vietnam!). As there is a considerable age difference between the eldest and youngest White girls from the sixth generation (nineteen years), I grew up with my niece and nephews (Lyn's children) and at just 1 year of age became an aunt!

One of the great tragedies and sources of grief for our father was my older sister Margret developing a chronic mental illness as a teenager, at a time when there was no adequate and timely support for people with such conditions and their families, and a lack of education and understanding of it.

Ray died of lung cancer and a cerebral stroke, aged 50 years. His working conditions in the factory may have contributed, as other workers reportedly had respiratory problems due to ventilation issues, but Dad was a heavy smoker (which caused or contributed to the problem, along with a hereditary tendency to respiratory problems through his mother's side). His workmates had been generous in a collection for the family after he died, and the manager at Rubery, Owen and Kemsley would only sign the monetary payout directly to the family rather than through the lawyer. His close friend John left the workplace shortly afterwards; he had commented that he had the feeling that Ray was still around.

I have faint memories of Dad even though he had died when I was 6 years old, mainly of evenings of looking forward to the time when he was getting home from work, of being bathed, being read to in a slow calm voice and me eagerly turning the pages of books, generally I felt that I was very close to him when I was young. I remember the last time I saw him, holding his hand in the hospital bed at the Royal Adelaide Hospital, for what seemed like an eternity. One of the nurses at the hospital was Kay Price (nee Maidment), Auntie Marjorie's (mum's sisters) daughter, who was a young 19 year old nurse in training at the RAH at the time.

Photo: The White family at the zoo. Back: Lyn, Val, Ray. Front: Raelene, Cheryl, Margret (circa 1966) (S.Battams) Below: Cheryl and Raelene with much loved dog Rascal (circa 1967)

Photo above: Lyn and Robert's wedding photo, with their parents (Ray and Val White and Merle and Allan Parsons) (S.Battams) Below: Ray and Val at Lyn and Robert's wedding, 1972 (S.Battams)

Photo, top: Ray and Val with Sam, 1971 (S.Battams) Below left: Sam and Lyn, sisters born 19 years apart, 1971 (S.Battams) Below right: Margret and Sam, 1972 (S.Battams)

Above left: Cheryl and Sam with dog Rascal, circa 1975 (S. Battams) Above right: Sam, Val, Raelene, circa 1975. Below: Lyn and Robert with their family (Leslie, Calli, Jeremy, James and Adam)

Photo above left: Sam with Father Xmas, 1976 (S.Battams) Above right: Sam with Graham and Shaun at Aldinga Beach, circa 1980 (S. Battams) Below: September 1976, Ray White's 50th Birthday (less than 9 months before his death) (S.Battams)

Back to Minnipa: 2020

My sister Raelene Linden, niece Jessica Carr and I visited Minnipa and Wudinna in July 2020 and we found out more information about the White family's time in Minnipa. We visited the soldier settler farm that Stephen William White had owned (2047 acres, section 21 Minnipa). We found out that the only picture we had of Dad as a young child (as a 3 year old) was probably of him in front of a government shed that was one of two built on the properties of WWI soldier settlers – one shed was used to live under, the other used for storage.

Fred Bignell (born at Minlaton) was a soldier from the 50th battalion that was a neighbour living on section 22 at Minnipa (the adjacent farm where the Minnipa East school was) – his daughter Fay Bignell went to school with Dad, and is the girl often closest to Dad with pigtails in photos. Coincidentally, we found out that Fay Bignell was first cousin to Allan Parsons, the father of my brother-in-law Robert Parsons.[199] Fay's mother was Jesse Poole, sister to Edith Emily Poole who married into the Parsons family at Minlaton.

On the advice of (the late) Doug Elefsen, the former owner of the Minnipa Hotel, we visited Jean Kammerman (nee Kwaterski) at Wudinna in 2020, who went to the Minnipa East School with Dad (Doug had gone to the Minnipa central school). Jean showed us three photos from the Minnipa East School and one of a group in front of the brush shed which was at the school, including photos with Dad which we had never seen before. The Kwaterskis were not soldier settlers - their father John Kwaterski was Polish and had been interned during WW1 and sent back to Europe. He came back to South Australia and set up farm near Pildappa Rock. The Kwaterski children made up half the school at Minnipa East.

The Minnipa East School was a wooden building at 'Kings Corner.' The teacher Mrs Neave (who married Bill King) was said to be cruel and hit children with sticks found around the paddocks, with the children having to find these sticks of punishment themselves. Jean Kammerman reported how an adult saw her injuries from one beating and told the local police officer (who in told reprimanded the teacher) and the following week the 'children copped it.' Jean also told of how at one stage when our Dad was 8-9 years old he wagged school for a whole week and was later caught when the teacher asked about his whereabouts. Dad had to walk a few kilometers to the school.

The following is a blog I wrote about the experience of visiting Minnipa:

Postscript: Back to Minnipa: a family history pilgrimage

In July 2020 I visited Minnipa with my sister Raelene and niece Jessica, for a family history pilgrimage, where our grandfather Stephen William White had received Soldier Settlement land following WWI. I had discovered that he moved to Minnipa in 1921 after (presumably) losing his (state bank/soldier) house in Cheltenham which was sold in May 1921 (he had been renting it out to a returned soldier with a large family), and in November 1921 he was allocated land, section 21, at Minnipa East.

The story passed down was that Margaret White (nee Holman) had lost her fiancé in #WWI, but further research showed that her uncle and cousin also died in WWI and are buried in #VillersBretonneux, France. Her brother Frederick Holman also went to war (both WWI and WWII).

Unable to have children, Margaret and Stephen White adopted a baby (our father) in 1926. They lived in Minnipa for 18 years, but none of us had been to Minnipa before, and we didn't know what to expect.

I asked our eldest sister Lyn what she remembered about our grandfather before we left for Minnipa. She was sixteen when he died, but I was born a few years after his death – he knew 4 of his 5 grandchildren. Lyn said she remembered him playing music in the back granny flat where he lived at our house, such as Harry Belafonte. I listened to some Belafonte songs, including his popular 'Island in the Sun,' before I left.

We stayed in Minnipa for three nights, and #MtDuttonBay for two nights. On the long drive to Minnipa we briefly stopped at Port Augusta (Wadlata Outback Centre) and #Kimba, at the painted siloes and the #BigGalah.

On the first night we met our friendly host at the Minnipa Hotel, Rick Elefsen, whose family had managed the hotel since my grandfather's time. Rick's father was one year older than our father would have been. Rick's Grandfather's story was interesting – he was a twin who had arrived on a boat from Norway with his twin brother, and they both jumped ship at Port Pirie. Sadly, as the twins separated and changed their names in order to remain hidden from the authorities, they never found each other again.

I had a prior phone call with Rick, as a work colleague from Ceduna knew him. When we arrived, Rick showed us a map of the land parcels in Minnipa, and showed us which one Grandpa White owned, section 21 (his son and two of his grandchildren were born on the 21st!). We saw from the map that it had a large bit of granite on the land, and #TchardulkuRock next to it, with the old Minnipa East school on an adjacent farm. We could see that another member of the White family (David Edward White, our great grandfather) had the farm just opposite 'White's Farm,' Section 16. Dad also had his older cousin (actually his Dad's cousin) on the adjacent farm, Bill Surman (whose parents had both died when he was young, so he was cared for by his maternal Auntie, Linda White nee Cox). Minnipa was also the site of the 'Minnipa Experimental Farm' established by the government.

At dinner we met some locals, including Bruce Heddle and his wife/family and Jack Gosling and his partner. We were told that the large granite rock on the White farm had been completely destroyed, fissured by a mining company during mining in the 1990s so now it could not be mined (as it lost its value due to the fissure). One of the Sydney shopping centres is paved with 'Desert Rose' granite from that very site.

We were advised us to have a look in the archival room behind the Wudinna Council offices (where we later found many local history pictures and archives – which require better protection from the weather!).

We were told something interesting about the farm leases – due to the #GreatDepression, many farmers engaged in share-farming to try to survive, so the land became partially owned, by a bank, or by groups of farmers. Tennis player Pat Cash's grandparents had owned the land that Jack, a Poochera local, now owned and the land had a $1500 debt on it that he had to pay before it became freehold. The region has created some great sporting talent – the Phillips family, well known in football circles (Greg Phillips), also came from the tiny town of Minnipa (a Kwaterski daughter, Mary, married a Phillips).

As members of the #PortAdelaideFootballClub, it was good to see that the town strongly supported the club in the AFL, with the #PortPower flag proudly flying high outside some of the houses. The second evening Rick Elefsen organised for the live footy to be on the TV in our rooms, but we were driving around that day in Wudinna – listening to the exciting match on the radio, where Robbie Gray kicked the winning goal after the siren.

From Bruce we found out about 'Climate App' where you can check the climate and rainfall of each year. We saw that there had been good rainfall just before our Grandfather left Minnipa in August 1939 to go back to Port Adelaide to become a 'foreman stevedore'. We knew he had become bankrupt in 1936. The years 1927 to 1930 were tough on the farm, with Stephen White being threatened with foreclosure and in 1930 he started share-farming until the bankruptcy. He was keen though, with one newspaper reporting he was the first to harvest his wheat and deliver it to the train that year. Perhaps the rainfall in the years leading up to 1939 meant the family were able to 'pay up' and finally had enough money to leave. Our grandparents may have wanted our father to have better opportunities in the city. Life on the land at that time was extremely harsh. I could not stop thinking about how tough their existence would have been in Minnipa, especially during the #GreatDepression. It was reported that it was costing more to produce the grain than what they were receiving for it!

It was also an isolated, lonely existence, and there would not be a lot of opportunities for socialising. However, they were surrounded by their family and the tiny school community. Grandfather White would also have had the Freemasons (although the hall was not established until 1936) and Grandmother had the Country Women's Association which, from newspaper reports, she was keenly involved in. Interestingly, there was a returned soldiers' group established, which it appeared our grandfather chose not to belong to (although he later was an active member). There were also Red Cross events, church events, picnics, school activities and the local hotel.

At that time, they had to travel everywhere by horse and cart, although the Elefsen family had a chauffer service. To get to Minnipa, one usually took the 'Minnipa' boat from Port Adelaide to Port Lincoln, and then the train from Port Lincoln to Minnipa. It took nearly a day to get there, with the boat trip being an overnight journey.

On the first full day we were in Minnipa, we firstly went to #PildappaRock, which is stunning. We climbed the large rock (one of the largest of its kind in Australia) to see the undulating crop fields and #GawlerRanges in the distance. We thought about how our father/grandfather likely climbed the rock and had picnics around the base. One of the nearby family's was the

Kwaterski family. The Kwaterski girls planted geraniums at the base of the rock, and there is a plaque to mark the site.

After this we got the opportunity to visit our grandfather's farm, which was still known locally by the Elefsen family as 'White's farm,' after our family – it had been over 80 years since their departure! We saw the ruins of an old farmhouse, just some old stone rubble in the middle of a paddock, a house built on sand. They had 2000 acres which seemed to be the standard size for the soldier settlers in the area. This was ten times what a pioneer farmer had in the city at the start of European settlement in Adelaide. At the back of the property we saw the large granite quarry which had been destroyed through mining in the 1990s. Sadly, the site was destroyed as had been described, and it was horrible to think what it would have been in the past compared to what it is now. It now makes for a kind of 'amphitheatre' and picnic site. The farm site had beautiful views of the Blue Sturts in the background.

We only had one photo of our father from when he was young, he looks about 2-3 years old and there is a shed behind him with some Red Cross boxes. We were trying to make out on the property where the shed might have been in relation to the house. It was amazing to be on the property where the White family lived, where Dad had grown up.

After visiting the farmhouse, we visited Tchardulku Rock, which is just adjacent to 'White's Farm.' Jessica and I climbed the beautiful rock and soaked up the amazing views, including a good view of 'White's Farm' and of the 'Blue Stuarts,' mountains in the background. This was a rock we know that our father would have been on. At the base of the rock is a small old shepherd's cottage, which an Aboriginal couple lived in for many years, Tom and Tilly. They would have been the closest neighbours to the 'White's'.

The following day, we visited the Gawler Ranges and Wudinna. Despite it being the middle of winter, it was very dry. There was no water at the stone dam. We visited a little cottage farm, some lonely graves, and Policeman's point. On the way back to Wudinna we visited Wudinna Rock.

That night we finally met Mr Doug Elefsen, the father of the current hotelier who previously managed the hotel. He was 95 years old, a year older than our father would have been. He said he remembered visiting White's farm once as a child (when he was 8 or 9 years old), as Grandpa White was selling some furniture. Doug said that Grandpa White was a 'good cabinet maker.' He was in fact a carpenter by profession who made furniture, and also the local blacksmith, aside from trying to keep the farm during the Great Depression. He was a 'bridge carpenter' prior to the outbreak of war. He made at least two miniature wooden replicas of St Peter's Cathedral at North Adelaide, which was built during his lifetime. Like many farmers, Grandfather White went bankrupt and had a large bankruptcy sale when he left Minnipa in 1939, which included blacksmithing equipment and an eight-piece leather lounge.

Mr Elefsen said he remembers meeting Dad 'at the pictures' when young, as the Cleve pictures would travel around the towns monthly, with one movie for children showing in the afternoon (with about 80 children attending) and a film for parents showing in the evening. He said that he had been to the Minnipa School, but our Dad had been to the Minnipa East school, so we needed to speak to a few of the other surviving members who went to the school, including one Jean Kammerman (nee Kwaterski), who now lived at Wudinna.

Doug told us that the government built the soldiers two sheds on their farms, one which they initially used to live under (some would put hessian around, and lime on the hessian to create 'walls'), and one which was a 'storage shed.' There were no walls around the sheds that they lived in initially. Little did we realise that the only photo we had of our father could have been of him in front of his 'house,' rather than a 'shed'! The children walked around 5 miles to schools in those days. Doug also proudly told us that he had been an aircraft mechanic during WWII and a 'bush pilot.'

The next day I rang 95-year-old Jean Kammerman and we visited her at Wudinna - she remembered our father well. She showed us some old school photos which included at least two with our father in them, and others with members of the White family! Our father is next to Jean Kammerman (nee Kwaterski) and his neighbour Fay Bignell in two of them (Dad is just right of the teacher in the first photo below, and between the two girls at front in the middle photo, below). The next farm over was owned by Fay's father Fred Bignell, also a returned soldier.[200]

The Minnipa East school was only open for 12 years, and was very small, with one class of 9-13 students of different age groups in the whole school, depending on the year. The children included the Kwaterski, Spencer, Bignell and Hillier siblings and our father who was an only child. The school was just one portable wooden building. There was also a hay 'lean-to' on the property, with photos of the parents from the school in front of this construction..

Jean told the story of how our father wagged school for a whole week once when he was 8- 9 years old without being caught, until the teacher asked his parents why he had not been at school. He would leave home in the morning at school time and arrive back when he could see the kids were returning from school (perhaps from the granite outcrop at the back of the farm). It was a few kilometres walk each way, and his family did not own a car (nor would he ever drive or own a car). According to Jean, the children feared the teacher who was cruel and used to hit the students with sticks that she would make them find in the paddocks. The teacher got in trouble with the local police officer once after one of the other parents noticed an injury on a Jean's leg. But then the next week, according to Jean, 'boy did we really cop it!'

Jean said that there was a picnic once a year at #TchardulkuRock and they used to take the horse and dray to the #GawlerRanges for picnics (quite a rough journey in those days!). Jean described how they had lime over hessian for walls in their 'house.' They used to bathe in a copper pot and had to collect the water from outside for their bath.

Jean told us an interesting story about how her Polish father, John Kwaterski (from Solec), was interned at Torrens Island during WWI after he jumped ship. Despite that, he liked Australia so much (with an abundance of things such as 'wood') that after the war he returned with his wife Anastasia and set up house near #PildappaRock. Her father befriended a well-known Adelaide University geographer who took an interest in Pildappa Rock. Her father had a role in saving the granite '#MurphysHaystacks' at Streaky Bay, among the oldest rocks in Australia, by enlisting the support of the same geographer in lobbying to save the 'haystacks.' The granite was going to be broken down to be used/make way for a road. Jean also told us that she had once worked at Koonibba Children's Home (Koonibba Aboriginal Mission, Eyre Peninsula) and on an orchard in Horsham, Victoria before she was married. Her family had once cared for a young Aboriginal boy (nicknamed Sonny), who Jean said had been left with their family by their father (after his mother had died).

It was such a delight to meet Jean Kammerman, and so exciting to see the photos of our father as a child. After meeting Jean, we travelled to Coffin Bay and at lunch we messaged our older sister Lyn, to tell her about the photos we now had of our Dad. She said she had seen one of the photos before, and we found this hard to believe. My sister Raelene then rang her to find out more, and it turns out that she had seen one of the photos as Fay Bignell from Minnipa was the first cousin to Lyn's husband's father (Allan Parsons). Fay had showed Lyn one of the photos many years ago and asked her if she thought her father was in it! Small world! That night we stayed in the beautiful #MtDuttonBay.

On the way back driving on my own into Adelaide after our long trip (we had taken separate cars), I was listening to the local ABC radio when Peter Goers, the announcer said that he was playing a song that he hadn't heard for a while – Harry Belafonte's 'Island in the Sun,' one of our Grandfather's favourite songs! I wondered if that was a little acknowledgement from 'up above' of our little trip to Minnipa!

After our visit, I sent Jean the book 'Captured Lives' by Professor Peter Monteith, about internment camps, and she sent me a card with a photo of her and her young sister at the Pildappa geraniums she planted. The long-awaited trip back to Minnipa was a wonderful journey that we appeared to make 'just in time,' given the ages of the cohort of people our father went to school with.

After our trip, I left feeling a great admiration for Grandpa White and reviewing my thoughts about the little house they owned at Port Adelaide. I felt sorry for him and other returned soldiers experiencing and surviving all of the horrors of war, only to come home and experience so much hardship once they got back. It was quite shocking to realise that the soldiers were provided sheds without walls, and they brought young children into that environment, and later built their own houses. Our Grandfather was always trying to adapt to earn a living and support his little family. It would have given him a sense of pride to purchase the tiny house in College Street, Portland, where he lived before he moved in with our family. Sadly, his wife died age 54, only 9 years after he returned to the city. His cousin Bill Surman also died in the Second World War. Some memorabilia I have from him includes the WWI issue bible where he has written the death dates of his mother and wife, as well as the original Roll of Honor from his battalion, an RSL badge, and his 'Digger Smith' trench series book, as well as his WWI medals.

Photo above: Raelene Linden, Samantha Battams & Jessica Carr at Minnipa, section 21, at the ruins of the White farmhouse. More than 80 years since they left, it was still known as 'White's farm' to those in the region

Part 2: Paternal (Biological) Ancestry

1857: The Fahy Family - Irish Catholic Outsiders

Chapter 4: The Fahy from County Clare, Ireland to Kapunda, South Australia

Introduction

The Irish Fahy ancestors came directly from County Clare to Kapunda and Mount Gambier, South Australia in the 1850s. Great great grandfather Edmund Fahy was sponsored by Prankerd, Stuckey and Rogers (friends of Edward Stirling) to work at the Kapunda mines. The Irish community appeared to be very close knit and continued their Celtic traditions and cultural heritage through songs, recitations, music and of course celebrating St Patrick's Day! The second generation in Australia played a key role in establishing institutions at Moorak near Mount Gambier. The name Fahy has the following meaning:

> *Fahy in Irish is Ó Fathaigh, probably from fothadh meaning "base" or "foundation."*[201]

1st Generation to arrive in Australia

Edmund Fahy was born in 1832 or 1833 to Patrick Fahy[202] and was from County Clare, Ireland,[203] according to the *Lady Ann* shipping record bound for South Australia. My Irish ancestors travelled to Australia with friends and relatives, in a ready-made and closely knit community.

Origin of the Fahy family, and links to the Graney and Geoghegan families

My great great grandfather Edmund Fahy was living in Attyslany South, Kilkeedy Parish, Corrofin, Inchiquin Barony, County Clare in the Griffith's Valuation index of 1855. This index was a survey of landowners and lessees to determine the amount that should be paid to the Poor Law System.[204] Edmund's landlord was Patrick Geoghegan, who sponsored several relatives and others to come to Australia, on the same boat as Edmund. They all came to South Australia on the *Lady Ann* on the 11th October 1857. Edmund Fahy was 24 years old and travelling with his siblings Mary, aged 20, and Bridget aged 10.[205] Also arriving on the *Lady Ann* was his future wife's brother, Michael O'Leary.[206]

Patrick Geoghegan sponsored Michael Geoghegan, and John and Roger Graney, to travel on the *Lady Ann* with Edmund (who was a cousin to John and Roger Graney). Thomas Geoghegan also travelled on the *Lady Ann.* The sponsor for Edmund Fahy and Thomas Geoghegan were South Australian entrepreneurs D. Prankerd, R. Stuckey and William Rogers.[207] The sponsor (or 'Purchaser of Land') for Mary and Bridget Fahy was Edward Stirling.[208] Edward Stirling had purchased land in Kapunda, the place Edmund was bonded to.

Prankerd and Stuckey had laid out the township of Stirling in the Adelaide Hills, in honour of their friend Edward Stirling, MLC. Edward Stirling senior (1804 - 1873) was a Scotsman, pastoral pioneer, politician and establisher of the Moonta and Wallaroo copper mines in 1855 through Elder, Stirling & Co of which he was partner. He was also a director of the South Australia Banking Co. His wife was Harriet Taylor, close friend of the famous Catherine Helen Spence. Edward Stirling's eldest son was the famous doctor and parliamentarian Sir Edward Charles Stirling, co-founder of the University of Adelaide and Medical School, Professor of Physiology, and founder of the museum and women's suffragist who introduced the women's suffragist bill into the South Australian Parliament.

John and Roger Graney and others were bonded to the Southeast of South Australia (Mt Gambier), and Mary and Bridget Fahy went to Mt Gambier, with Hanorah Graney nee Fahy, who was likely their auntie. Some of these family voyages from Ireland to Australia were sponsored by Hanorah Graney. Hanorah was a widow when she came to Australia on the *Magdalena* in 1855.

The family history passed down within the Graney family in Australia and New Zealand[209] was that they were originally from Loughrea, Galway, which is close to County Clare. There were a John Graney and Patrick Grany recorded in the villages of Knockaunkeel and Pollaturick in the parish of Addergoole, Galway, which is not far from Athenry[210] There were also a number of Grany and Fahy families who lived in the parish of Castlegar, County Galway, which is adjacent to Addergoole, and both were within the Civil Parish of Ahascragh, County Galway.[211] In the Griffith's Valuation index (1857) there is also a record of Edmund Fahy leasing 380 acres from John Bagot, with Hugh Ward and Ferdinand Keely in Loughrea, Galway.[212] Also in the Valuation Records (to 1856) 'house books' is a record of Edmund Fahy leasing houses in the Townland of Doonally East, Loughrea; adjacent are Ferdinand Keely, Hugh Warde. And Patrick Keely.[213] A Patrick Fahy is also leasing from the Marquis of Clanricarde in Cosmona Townland, Parish of Loughrea, Galway.[214] In 1860 Patrick Fahy of Loughrea was fined at the Athenry court for *'a breach of the Sabbath by driving his horse and cart through the public street of Craughwell (near Loughrea) on Sunday 29th.'*[215]

Why did they leave Ireland?

Charles Bagot, who lived in Kilkeedy Parish, County Clare, Ireland, was actively involved in encouraging emigration to South Australia, and was said to have handpicked those who came.[216] Arriving on the Birman in 1840, he had been given the right to manage 4000 acres, in exchange for owning a quarter of it.[217] His son Charles, along with Francis Dutton, discovered copper in Kapunda in 1842:[218]

> *Emigration [from Ireland] to South Australia only began in the 1840's and was much encouraged by Charles Bagot, land agent for Bindon Blood who lived at Rockforest, Kilkeedy and who was supervisor of the Burren road system...He chartered a boat, the Birman, which arrived into Adelaide in 1840. His son discovered*

copper at Kapunda. Several North Clare families, probably prompted by Bagot, settled in the district - Kerin, Canny, Linnane, Davoren etc. and all have descendants there today. Dr Blood, first medical doctor in Kapunda and first Mayor of the town, emigrated from Corrofin in 1844. The Clare Valley, the great wine-producing area in South Australia, and the town of Clare are named after the County of Clare in Ireland.[219]

In the lead up to mass emigration, the potato famine and occupation and ownership of the land by the British caused a great deal of poverty, unemployment and homelessness in Ireland. Under the *Corn Law Act* 1845, crops and their profits were forced to be transported to England whilst the local Irish population starved. Thousands of people became evicted and homeless as they could not afford to pay the high rents of the Kilrush Union Landlords (and their homes were actually destroyed in the process of eviction). The Kilrush Union of which County Clare was a part, was the poorest in Ireland, and half the population was receiving relief. Twenty-four thousand working farmers out of a total of eighty-two thousand perished.[220]

The parents of the Fahy's may have died during the potato famine, given that their 10 year old sibling traveled with them. There is no record of a Fahy family being evicted in the evictions of the Kilrush Union in County Clare. However, a number of Fahy children died in the Kilrush and Ennistymon workhouses in 1850-51 (of measles, dysentery, starvation and croup).[221]

The people lived on the potato because they were poor; and they were poor because they could not get regular employment. This want of employment seems in great measure to have arisen from the state of the law and the practice respecting the occupation and ownership of the land.

Society of Friends 1852, in History of Clare, Rev White.

There was considerable emigration from County Clare to South Australia, in particular the Kapunda region, from 1854. The fact that Edmund Fahy was bonded to the copper mining area Kapunda[222] may suggest that he was a Labourer at the copper mine like most of the Irish working around the mine, although he could have been a miner (which his son Michael became).

Wedding Bells

Edmund Fahy and Margaret (O') Leary were married in South Australia on the 4th Feb 1860 at St. Patrick Church, Adelaide, when Edmund was 27 and Margaret was 26 years old.[223] Margaret was from Kilkenny, Ireland, born around 1833 and her father was James O'Leary. She came to Australia as a single woman on the *Octavia* in 1855.[224] Sponsors at the wedding were John Graney and Anna Colbert. Edmund and his wife were illiterate, as indicated by their 'X' to mark the spot on their wedding certificate.

The need to transport ore from the Burra mine led to a number of small settlements developing on the route back to Adelaide: during 1857-1860 ore was taken to Gawler via Riverton, Forrestor and Templers, as the railway line to Burra was not established until 1870. The Fahy family lived at Templers which is half-way between Gawler and Kapunda. They were living there in 1870 when Edmund Fahy was a subscriber to *The Irish Harp and Farmers' Herald.*[225]The family later moved to Kapunda.

A few of the Edmund and Margaret's children were baptised at St Peter & Paul's Church, Gawler Town. There were five children, with Michael (my forebear) being the fourth child: he was the namesake of baby Michael who died in 1866 in Adelaide, after only 16 days. Any local illnesses at the time may have been treated locally by an unregistered 'Dr' - Dr William Carmichael who served in Kapunda and Freeling. Edmund and Margaret Fahy had the following children:

Painting of "North Star" Hotel at Templers, ca 1850. Hotel was run by William and Martha Templar from 1846-1870, State Library of South Australia [B37187]

Alice May (1864-1950) (died 23rd October 1950, aged 86 years at the RAH. Alice never married.

Michael (1866-1866) Michael aged 16 days died 13th February 1866 at Adelaide.[226]

Edward John ('Ted') Fahy[227] (1868-1921).[228] Baptised 11th April 1868 at St Peter & Paul Gawler Town (sponsors at his baptism are Michael Leary, (Margaret's brother) and Bridget Fobb or Foff. Edward John Fahy was a railway guard/porter, like his brother James/Jim Fahy.

Michael Patrick ('Mick') Fahy (1870-1934). Born at Templers and baptised ('Patrick') 18th January 1870 at St Peter & Paul Gawler Town (sponsors are N or W Broderick and Catherine Rohan,[229] see picture of church below). Died 15th July 1934, aged 64 years. (Known as 'Mick')

James Joseph Dominic ('Jim') Fahy (1877-1930). Died 12th February 1930.

The fortunes of Edmund Fahy improved, and he quickly went from being a Labourer to a Farmer at Kapunda. The family lived on Hill Street, Kapunda.

Drawing: Catholic church of St Peter & Paul, Gawler Town, 1851, the local catholic church where Michael Patrick Fahy was baptised, State Library of South Australia [B11519]

Edmund Fahy was admitted to the Royal Adelaide Hospital on the 7th March 1864 due to 'contusion' – case of emergency – and discharged the same day. He died many years later, on the 21st June 1890, aged 58 years, of 'paralysis.' (stroke).[230] At this time 'Mrs E. Fahy' put a notice in the newspaper to thank the community for their condolences.

> *Mrs E. Fahy begs to return her SINCERE THANKS to Friends for their kind enquiries and expressions of sympathy during her late bereavement. June 27th, 1890*[231]

Daughter Alice Fahy, spinster, was the sole executor of his will, to whom he left all of his money and property.[232] The money from his will included payment from Forester's Lodge and Government Compensation.

Daughter Alice lived at Kapunda with her parents at the time of her father's death. She also lived at Railway Terrace Mile End, and in the city where she had a shop in the West End at 250 Wright Street, Adelaide (near the corner of Lowe Street),[233] just across the way from the Prince Albert Hotel. Her shop was broken into in 1933, with 22 pounds and 6 shilling stolen. Alice is mentioned in Adelaide's social pages, including when she attends the Mayoral Garden Party in 1906[234] attended by the Governor, and goes on a six month tour of the South East in 1910 (where her brother Mick Fahy and family lived at the time).[235] She was a subscriber to the St Francis Xavier Cathedral building fund, and regularly donated to catholic causes (gifts to Saint Teresa) and institutions (St Patrick's Church renovation fund, St John's Boys' Town, Brooklyn Park).

Margaret Fahy went on to live another 20 years after her husband's death. She died on the 11th January, 1910, aged 78 years, during a heatwave.

> *FAHY. -In loving memory of our dear mother, Margaret Fahy, who died at Kapunda, on January 11. 1910."Sweet Jesus grant her eternal rest." -Inserted by her loving children.*[236]

An article read:

> *The recent heat wave proved particularly oppressive to old people, infants and those not enjoying good health, and an unusually large number of deaths have been chronicled in "The Advertiser" since the beginning of the year.... Mrs. Margaret Fahy, Kapunda, 78. She is buried in St John's cemetery, Kapunda.*

The Advertiser, 13th January 1910

The family put an 'in memoriam' notice in the newspaper the following year with the same message, whilst her daughter Alice placed 'in memoriam' notices in the newspaper until 1913.

Margaret is buried with her husband and brother Michael O'Leary at St John's Catholic Cemetery in Kapunda.

Margaret's brother Michael O'Leary died on the 2nd July, 1869 in unusual circumstances. He was the person responsible for looking after horses (an ostler) at the Sir John Franklin Hotel, Kapunda (a place which is still operating). He died in his bedroom, which was off the stables, and an inquest was held into his death. The Jury at the inquest (held at the hotel) determined that he died of 'a fit of apoplexy.' This could have been a cerebral hemorrhage or stroke. It was claimed that two months earlier he had fallen down suddenly and was unconscious for 2 hours afterwards. It was also reported that he had a mark on his cheek when he died.

Photo: A bullock dray outside the Sir John Franklin Hotel, Kapunda (circa 1900), where Michael O'Leary died. The trip from Burra to Port Adelaide took 8 to 10 days, SLSA B16395

Mr. J. O'Leary attended Iris Fahy's sister Dorothy's wedding in 1924 (likely to be either James jnr or Joshua O'Leary). A James O'Leary (Father Bartholomew O'Leary) born around 1854 arrived in South Australia on the 'Hesperus' in 1878 and was a Labourer and Hawker[237] in Templers. His wife was Sarah Anne Hatch (married in Gawler Catholic Church, 1882). He was admitted to the Adelaide Hospital for middle ear disease and phthisis pulmonalis (pulmonary consumption), which he died from aged 50 in the Adelaide Consumptive Home on the 7th February 1905.[238] He was buried in the Catholic Cemetery, West Terrace. When his daughter Molly (born 1889) married on the 27th October 1909 in Kapunda it is said that her father is the 'late James O'Leary of Templers.'[239] Molly's brothers included James junior (born 1887) and Joshua.

DNA discoveries

I have DNA links to Irish people on the myHeritage website who have Fahy ancestors from Athenry, Galway. The Fahy family also appears to be DNA linked to the Rohan family who went to the US around the time my Fahy family came to Australia (Catherine Rohan was the sponsor at Edmund's son Michael Patrick Fahy's christening). Based on DNA links, it seems that Michael Fahy who came to Australia in the 1860s and settled in Orange, New South Wales, was a brother to Edmund Fahy, and he became a publican. There are DNA matches to a number of people from Canada who have O'Leary ancestors, so some of the O'Leary family went to Canada around the same time that Margaret O'Leary (Edmund Fahy's wife) arrived in Australia.

Chapter 5: Michael Patrick Fahy, Pioneer Settler of Moorak, Mt Gambier

2nd Generation in Australia

Great grandfather Michael Patrick Fahy was a proud Irish Catholic man and founder at Moorak, Mt Gambier. He was key in establishing the first school building and first public hall there. He was one of the first dairy farmers in the region and secretary of the Mt Gambier Agricultural Bureau. He set up an annual community picnic and the first tennis and football clubs at Moorak. There wasn't much that happened in Moorak without M.P. Fahy having a hand in it. He was an energetic leader and organiser determined to serve and develop the local community. Throughout his life he was a miner, dairy farmer, confectioner and fruiterer with his own shop, and hawker. Perhaps his greatest achievements were those he made in Moorak as a pioneer settler. He was a family man and community minded, frequently described as energetic and a 'live wire,' described as 'modest' even though he was also a showman who had acted in comedy and theatre and had a love of singing and performing recitations in front of an audience. He also loved sport, including football and coursing/horseracing, and was likely competitive.

As an 11-year-old, Michael Fahey [sic] from Kapunda was admitted to the Royal Adelaide Hospital due to 'strumous glands' (a tuberculous swelling of the lymph glands) and discharged 19th September 1881. His parents would have been extremely worried as at the time tuberculosis was the main cause of death for adolescents and young people.[240] However, he survived and thrived, was active in sport, including coursing races, and played football for Kapunda in their first match in 1893.

Horseracing and the Kapunda Coursing Club

In 1891, aged 21, Mick Fahy was involved in horse racing or hunting through the Kapunda Coursing Club. Coursing races involved hound dogs or greyhounds hunting a live hare, with men following on horseback around a 'course' with jumps, and included financial stakes. In one day, the men could do up to 48 courses, and there always appeared to be a few falls or kicks from horses. There was a paid advertisement for Coursing in the Kapunda Herald on Christmas Day 1891, in the form of a song, which gives a picture of the bloodthirsty sport:

DEDICATED TO JOHN MOYLE, ESQ., KAPUNDA AND HIS TRAINER, MICK FAHY, BY AN ADMIRER

Oh, list while I sing about the dog Ring,
Whose owner was famed Johnny Moyle,
He won a fine race at an elegant pace
As he bounded o'er Australian soil.

Chorus – Long life to John Moyle, may he
live a good while,
He's a man you don't see every day,
He likes a good dog, also a good prog[241];
Call and see him when you go that way.

His trainer, Mick Fahy, who made a display
With the hound that he trained for John Moyle,
I'd have you know, he made a good show
At Auburn, and brought home the spoil.

Chorus

He was the great gun at Auburn, he won –
He beat thirty dogs and jumped like a deer,
They were beat like a hack by Mr Moyle's black –

Here to his owner in Palmerston beer.

Chorus

Should you go to Kapunda, don't make a blunder,
Palmerston pub with your friends you should go,
Then Moyle you will see, he will talk very free
About coursing and dogs you all know.

Chorus

Sool 'ems[242] *are dead, from Kapunda are fled,*
John Moyle and his friends are glad, I suppose.
They are a blood-thirsty lot, and hunt for the pot,
They disgrace our town everyone knows.

Chorus

The course with no slips, but let their dogs rip –
A dozen or more, we hear people say;
To them it's great fun, some carry a gun
To shoot puss if she comes in their way.

Chorus

They rush all around the poor hare to the ground,
A sool 'em then makes a grab for her tail,
Another her leg, another her head,
And some try hard to get a toe nail.

Chorus

I think it is time I did end this rhyme.

I give you all thanks for lending your ear,

I wish no encore, but I'll give you some more

When coursing commences next year.

Chorus

December 23 1891[243]

In 1892 Michael (Mick) Fahy was involved in the Kapunda Coursing Club's annual meeting being held at Dutton's Anlaby Estate, in front of 300-400 spectators.[244] Mick was the 'slipper,' or the person who officiates the event and is responsible for releasing two greyhounds at once from a set of slips (leather leads with collars), once they are at least 100 metres from the hare.

> *Mr M. Fahy performed his part of the proceedings very creditably, but was occasionally blocked in too much by the crowd, and was kicked by a horse on the leg, fortunately without doing him serious damage.*[245]

In 1893, Mick Fahy is described at the Tattersall's Café on the night before the Adelaide Cup.

> *THE NIGHT BEFORE THE ADELAIDE CUP AT TATTERSALL'S THEATRE ROYAL, 1893 [BY DAMPER]*
>
> *It is now twelve months since my last communication. I then said, that owing to ill-luck over the Adelaide Cup, I would have to retire to saltbush country for twelve months, which I did. I have now returned with the intention of seeing the 1893 Adelaide Cup run for……By appointment we met at Tattersall's Café the night before the Adelaide cup was run for. We had some refreshments at a small table that stood in a commanding position, enabling us to have a good view at this wonderful gathering of all conceivable grades of society and nationality…Horse owners were numerous in this crush, and there was only standing room in this large hall. The Kapunda*

push, Silver-King James, Cleary and the modest slipper (Mick Fahy) were present.

Kapunda Herald, 9 May 1893

Copper Miner and Footballer

In 1893 and 1894, Mick Fahy was playing for the 'Kapundas,' the local Kapunda football team. In the opposing North Kapunda team was A. Geier.[246] It appears that aged 26, Michael had a child with Agnes Geier (likely the brother of 'A.Geier'). This could have been Bridget Agnes Geier (born 1874), whose mother was Irish. The Prussian Geier family had settled in Greenock. On October 31st, 1896, Agnes Geier had a son to Michael Patrick Fahy, at St Leonards (Glenelg), which she called Harold Edward Fahy.[247] There is no record of a marriage between Michael Patrick Fahy and Agnes Geir.[248]

There is no other record of Harold Fahy in SA, and no death record, so perhaps he was adopted out. However, in 1921 a 'Harold Fahey' aged 23 years sells a bike stolen from Mile End to a store.[249] Bridget Agnes Geier stayed in Greenock and married in 1942 at the ripe age of 68 years. Her older sister Sophia Agnes Geier (born 1866 in Kapunda, married 1885) went to Western Australia and died in 1905 (Mick Fahy also went to WA and married Helena Schulz there).[250]

In 1896, when Mick Fahy was 24 years old he was working on the copper mines at Kapunda. Around this time, he was charged by police for 'riotous behaviour' at Hamilton, 23km north of Kapunda, and attended the Magistrates Court at Kapunda. He pleaded guilty, saying that he was sorry that he had broken the law, but that he was provoked. As it was his first offence, he was fined 1 pound and avoided jail. Hamilton was a stop for mining carts going from Adelaide to Kapunda and back, so the riotous behaviour was likely in relation to work.

An Amateur Actor

In 1899, M. P. Fahy plays a minor part in a 'farcical comedy' by the Celtic Dramatic Club, called 'Turned Up.' Its season at the Bijou Theatre (97 King William Street, Adelaide) is advertised in *The Advertiser.* The review of the play was favourable, with the reviewer saying that:

> *'Turned Up,' a sprightly little comedy, was staged at the Bijou Theatre by the Celtic Dramatic Club on Saturday evening. The members of the company had already acquitted themselves well as amateurs, and in this piece...again created a favourable impression...the minor characters were well sustained by Messrs. W. Higgins, M.P. Fahy and J. Brown and Master A. Sheridan.*
>
> *South Australian Register, 13th November 1899*

Photo: Inside of The Bijou Theatre, 97 King William Street, Adelaide, SLSA B13272

Michael met Helena Marie Schulz, known as 'Lena' some time at the end of the 1890s or early 1900s. Helena was from the Tanunda in the Barossa Valley, the granddaughter of pioneer winemaker and farmer, Johann Gramp.[251] Johann Gramp was a hardworking and self-made pioneer, and perhaps a role model for Michael Patrick Fahy.

Mining in Western Australia

Michael and Helena travelled to Western Australia, where Michael was a gold miner at Boulder City, Kalgoorlie. They travelled there in 1900 without being married,[252] when he was 30 and she was 23 years of age. There was a trip back to South Australia in 1901, when an entrepreneurial Mick Fahy established a stand at the corner of Wakefield and Pulteney Streets for the Royal Visit (of the Duke and Duchess of Cornwall and York, later King George V and Queen Mary), selling tickets at 3s per seat (advertised in the *Kapunda Herald*).

In 1903, Helena's grandfather Johann Gramp died, and the following year Michael (then 34) married Helena at Guildford, WA. Marrying a Catholic would make Helena a 'black sheep' in her family of origin,[253] although she continued to regularly visit them in the Barossa Valley throughout her life, and when her mother was dying Helena 'nursed' her.[254]

Mick and Lena had the following children:

Dorothea (Dorothy) Alice Fahy (born WA 7th December 1904-1981)
Married James Denis Nash

Edmund Wilfred 'Bob' Fahy born 10th Jan 1907 Tanunda (b 777, p 408)[255]
Married Mary Morissey

Iris Marie Fahy born 1st May 1909 Adelaide, died 1967 (b 821 p 381)
Married Henry J. "Jack" McDermott

The photograph of the couple taken with baby Dorothea (born 1904) says on the back 'from the real Boulder City.' They were living in Kalgoorlie-Boulder in 1906, but by 1907 Michael and Helena were back in the Barossa

Valley, where their son was born. They also lived at Kangarilla (where Mick was working) at one stage, with Helena's sister's family (Clara Brookman nee Schulz). At the time of his youngest daughter Iris' birth in 1909, the Fahy residence was 20 Myers Street, Adelaide (Grey Ward), where they still lived in 1912. Auntie Alice Fahy lived around the corner in Wright Street, Adelaide.

As well as being a miner, Michael Fahy was variously listed in the Sands and MacDougall directories as a Contractor, Fruiterer and Confectioner, Canvasser, and Carrier. Brian Nash (son of Dorothy Nash) had remembered going out on the cart with him when a child. In 2008, 20 Myers Lane (East side) where the Fahy's lived still existed; it was a large old stone free standing building with extremely high ceilings and was then used as a music recording studio (it has since been demolished).

Helena Fahy had come from 'good German stock' and had many practical skills that would have been useful during the Depression years, such as fruit drying and making clothes.[256] She also catered for the large events (sometimes with up to 1000 people!) organised by her social husband and had good organisational skills.

Photo on previous page: Michael Patrick Fahy, Helena Fahy (nee Schulz) and baby Dorothy 'From the Real Boulder City' (Kalgoorlie-Boulder, W.A), where Patrick was a miner, circa 1905 (Photo: S. Battams, care of the late P. Nash).

Pioneer of Moorak, Mount Gambier

Michael's mother Margaret died in January 1910. He likely received an inheritance, as the same year he purchased land at the newly subdivided Moorak Estate, Mount Gambier. There he would become a founding pioneer dairy farmer, one of the first two people to set up a farm there, along with his friend and cousin Roger William Graney (John Graney's son). Land at Moorak (section 906, which costs 30 shillings) was allotted to him in 1911 by the Land Board, and the Fahy family moved there around 1912 and would stay there until 1921.

Many families of Irish origin settled at Moorak, and Celtic motifs can still be seen on gates and houses around the region. Aside from Fahy and Graney, Irish names around Mount Gambier and nearby Millicent (many of which intermarried with the Fahy and Graney families) included Barry, Casey, Gleeson, Guerin, Nash, Naughton, O'Connor, O'Toole, Ryan, Skehan, Sutton and Thompson, just to name a few. Anthony Sutton and David Power were two of the first Irish settlers in the South East region.[257]

Moorak School and Public Hall

Michael was secretary of the Moorak School Committee, through which he was involved in establishing the first school building. Eldest daughter Dorothea Fahy described the beauty of Moorak and also the harsh conditions for farmers when in 1915 she wrote to 'Aunt Dorothy' of the newspaper:

> *Dear Aunt Dorothy*
>
> *I haven't written to you before. Please will you accept me as a new niece? I go to the Moorak school and I am in the second class. My teacher's name is Mr. Mitchell. The school is a nice new building. The children have a little garden each. I walk to school about a mile. My age is 10 years and 5 months. Moorak is four miles from Mount Gambier. When we drive to Mount Gambier, we pass the*

Blue Lake and the other three lakes, the Valley, the Leg of Mutton and Brown's Lake. They are very pretty lakes. The season is very dry, the paddocks are very bare, and a lot of stock is dying. I am sending 3d in stamps for Minda. I hope the little children a Minda are well. With love to you and Uncle George – I remain, your loving niece,

Dorothea Fahy

The Chronicle, 22nd May 1915

Photo: Moorak School Committee, 1916. M. P. Fahy is seated, second from left, Les Hill Photographic Collection, Mount Gambier Public Library

In 1916, there was a very active day at the Moorak school, where the school committee (when MP Fahy was secretary) and parents and friends were involved in digging and planting a hedge and a range of trees. This was *'the work that the government had placed in their hands.'*

Cypress plants were put in for a hedge on the windward side, and flowering gums and pines were also planted on the other side of the

ground. The children also planted some shrubs. The ladies kindly attended to the creature comforts of all present...An excellent tea was served around indoors, after which the children were treated to lollies...Mr. W. H. Taylor, Chairman of the Committee, read an interesting address..(and) thanked all present...Mr. Mitchell, on behalf of the children, thanking the Committee and friends for their assistance and sympathy. The children then saluted the flag and brought the proceedings to a close by singing the National Anthem.

Border Watch, 26th July 1916

Mick Fahy also supervised the building of the first public hall at Moorak, with some dispute over where it would be built in the process. There had originally been a plan to build a hall at Moorak, but then a decision was made to amalgamate with the O.B. Flat district to build the hall, a decision that was rescinded as the O.B. Flat residents wanted the hall built on the former O.B. Flat cattle station – further away from Moorak. As Mr Glynn said at a meeting

At first it was decided to build a hall on Moorak. Now you want to build the Moorak hall on O.B. Flat. (Laughter).

Border Watch, 5th November 1913

A proposal was made that the public hall be built at the crossroads, where it now stands, but a decision could not be arrived at, as many Moorak settlers were unwilling for it to be built there. The Chairperson and committee members all resigned, and it was decided that the money and books could be handed to a responsible party to take up the question of where the hall would be built. Finally, Mick Fahy took charge and got the Moorak residents on board with the hall being built at the crossroads and then supervised the actual building of the hall.

The Red Cross and Welcoming Home Returned Soldiers

In 1915 a Red Cross concert was organised at Moorak, held at the shelter room at the schoolhouse.

> *A Red Cross concert took place last Friday evening, and despite the adverse weather conditions it was a pronounced success. The enthusiasm of the residents was proof against rough weather, for the large shelter-room of the school house…was filled. The room was appropriately decorated with red, white and blue streamers, and with British and Australian flags. A large red cross was conspicuous between a Union Jack and Southern Cross at the back of the stage. …Mrs. R. Telford kindly lent her piano for the occasion, and Mrs. Meller played the various accompaniments. Songs were rendered…recitations were given…Little Miss Elvie Meller executed a Scotch dance to a mouth-organ accompaniment, played by Master Lennie Stafford. The same boy treated the audience to the popular tune 'Tipperary' on a mouth-organ. Both children were heartily applauded for their contributions…A half hour farce entitled 'Our Aunt from California' comprised the second half of the programme…The singing of the National Anthem brought the concert to a close.*
>
> *Border Watch, 3rd Jul 1915*

Michael Patrick Fahy was chief among the singers and deliverer of recitations that evening. He was described as a 'live wire' and 'lively' member of the community, and you can just imagine his spirited partaking in such events. He regularly did recitations and took every opportunity to sing at such events, with many examples at farewell events. His wife Helena would regularly cater for social events in their home and orchard.

In March 1919, Mick Fahy was involved in a meeting to decide how the Moorak community would welcome returned soldiers to the district –

presentations of certificates were suggested, but Mick Fahy proposed welcome home socials for every returned soldier, with leftover funds raised being used to build a memorial, and a committee being established to plan the socials. As some opposed this plan, he reported on the meeting to the local newspaper, to the horror of some meeting attendees. He then wrote a letter to the editor stating that he was a press correspondent when he reported on the undertakings of the Red Cross meeting, which was denied (although he appeared to regularly speak to the press about various events). Mick Fahy got his way and a welcome home social was organised by the Red Cross in May 1919 for three returned soldiers.

Moorak Coursing Race

Mick Fahy continued coursing at Moorak, with the coursing race going through the Fahy property, among others in the district.

> *The Hounds at Moorak*
>
> *Residents of Moorak are looking forward to the hunt on Wednesday, June 14. They are taking a lively interest, and have erected some fine jumps. The public will be able to see each jump from Yell's road, and the Moorak ladies will provide afternoon tea at the Moorak Cheese Factory.....Much interest is taken in the coming event, and the local young men are trying their steeds.*

Border Watch, 10th June 1919

> *At the invitation of the Moorak residents the usual weekly run with the Mount Gambier hounds took place in the vicinity of the Moorak Cheese and Butter Company's factory on Wednesday last....As the day was fine there was a large crowd to witness the sport. The onlookers fairly took possession of Yell's road, which was lined from end to end with vehicles of very description, including many motor cars and drags. The school was closed at 2.30pm and the children had a great time. Spectators who arrived on foot took*

possession of every vantage point, all the straw and hay stacks being well occupied...Never before had such excitement been witnessed at Moorak....Eleven horses took part to the check, and 12 from the check to finish....The only local rider was Mr. A. Stafford. He was mounted on a pony (Stiff Luck), and the Moorak people rejoiced that he never left it from start to finish. They cheered at each jump. It is only a pony, and is driven in a dray each day. The public were surprised to see it go the course. Mr. Stafford's mount caused a lot of merriment, and was the chief Moorak attraction...

The Moorak ladies were known far and wide for their energetic work. They had shown that day their kind hospitality by providing afternoon tea to such a large gathering, and it was very much appreciated...

Mr. M. P. Fahy was pleased to see the hounds at Moorak, and was sure the gathering that day proved that the residents were pleased also. Hunting ought, in his opinion, to be encouraged, as it was the means of bringing out many a good horse, who afterwards won classic events. One thing that marred that day's outing was that he was unable to don the red coat himself and follow (laughter), but he had a boy coming on, and perhaps in the near future he would join the gentlemen in the red coats. He thanked them for their kind remarks on behalf of the ladies. (Applause)...

Mr. F. J. Butler said that although he was not a privileged landowner he would like to make a few remarks...It must be a great honor to present day huntsmen to ride over the same country as the famous Adam Lindsay Gordon had ridden over. There was a certain amount of risk in the sport, but it made them brave and fearless.

Border Watch, 5th July 1920

It seems that the laughter was due to a double meaning about donning the 'red coat' – as an Irishman, Fahy could not bring himself to don the 'red coat' of the English, but he may also have been injured and unable to participate in the race.

There was another poem in *The Register* in the 'Coursing Notes' section mentioning Mick Fahy in 1928, however the romance surrounding these races would soon cease as attitudes towards, and treatment of, animals improved. Coursing races were banned from the Parklands in 1937 (as they were dangerous to other small animals).[258] Moves to ban live hare coursing were made in New South Wales in 1928,[259] but the RSPCA was continuing to lobby for the banning of coursing in South Australia from 1947 due to animal cruelty, supported by churchmen,[260] and also raised concerns about speed racing with greyhounds due to cruel practices used when training.[261] However the coursing ban debate continued throughout 1953[262] and beyond, and coursing using a live hare was not banned in South Australia until 1986. Cruel training practices used in greyhound racing have continued to be an issue up until the present day, and there are still calls for greyhound racing to cease permanently.

Moorak Annual Picnic

Mick Fahy was a popular member of the community, organising the annual picnic as secretary of the Moorak Picnic Committee. His children, especially youngest daughter Iris, were often winning running races at the event, although Helena had won the married women's race, and Mick had won the 'committee men's race' along with the 'milk-cart horse race' in the first division, with his horse 'Daily Bread.'

The Moorak Picnic was a huge affair. In 1919 there were around 1000 attendees, with donations of money and cordial received from the local Bellum Hotel, and four pipers attending. Ten women were in charge of the luncheon and refreshments for the day, with Helena Fahy at the helm.

The annual picnic organised by the Moorak people was brought off successfully on Wednesday last. The picnic is usually held near the school house, but this year the ground for the gathering was under crop, and as no suitable ground was available the committee approached Mr. T. C. Ellis, who readily consented to the settlers having the use of the homestead paddock. It proved an ideal spot for the gathering, and as the day was beautifully fine a large concourse assembled to see the sports and partake of the settlers' hospitality. Long before noon on Wednesday the picnickers began to arrive, and by the time luncheon was announced several hundreds were present. In the afternoon the crowds must have increased to quite a thousand...Mr. M. P. Fahy made an efficient and courteous hon. Secretary. It was due to the energy and good management of the committees, both ladies and gentlemen, that the gathering proved such a success.

Border Watch, 9th November 1919

After the festivities took place, the Moorak Picnic Committee honoured its secretary:

Mr. F. J. Butler, the hon. Treasurer, presented a balance sheet, which showed that when all accounts were paid there remained a credit balance of 10/10/ It was resolved to hand that to the school committee, who will easily find a good use for it. Mr. Taylor then, on behalf of a large number of appreciative residents, handed to M. P. Fahy (who had been hon. Secretary of the picnic committee for several years, and to whose energy and zeal in the performance of his duties much of the success of the picnics had been due) a handsome gold Elgin hunting watch and an Onoto fountain pen, in recognition of his work in connection with the picnics over a series of years. Messrs. Butler and C. Kennedy supported the remarks of Mr. Taylor in the heartiest of terms, and spoke of the pleasure they had in being associated with Mr. Fahy, who put his whole heart into anything he undertook. Mr Fahy made a suitable reply.

Border Watch, 18th November, 1919

By 1919, in the above report of the Moorak Picnic, Dorothea Fahy had already left school as she partakes in the 'old scholars' race; she was only 15. By 1921 the Moorak reunion and picnic had grown to such an extent that they established a separate children's picnic and sporting event.

Celebration of St Patrick's Day annual was also a big event, with a St Patrick's day Carnival held in Mount Gambier. Mick Fahy also became chair and founding member of the first football club and founding member of the tennis club at Moorak.

Agricultural Bureau and Dairy Farming

Aside from being a dairy farmer, Mick Fahy grew kale, potatoes and flax, among other things. He was also secretary of the Mt Gambier Agricultural Bureau and was often proposing new farming strategies and facilities for the district, as well as new business strategies. He gave a paper on raising dairy cows at the Agricultural Bureau, which was well written and printed in the local newspaper, *Border Watch*. Dairy farming began in Moorak in 1917, with the encouragement of the government. Mick Fahy played a central role in its development:

Dairy Bull for Moorak. – At a meeting of men interested in dairy farming at Moorak, it was decided to get the number of guarantors required for the leasing of a bull, and write to the dairy expert (Mr P. H. Souter) for the bull. So far 18 cows have been guaranteed at 11/6 per cow. Mr M.P. Fahy will look after the animal for six months for the sum of 7 10/. It was also decided that the bull should be here and ready for service by June 1.

South Eastern Times, 16th March 1917

The bull was provided, but it did not sire, and the Moorak group returned it to the government. At the May meeting of the Mount Gambier Agricultural Bureau, Mick Fahy presented a paper on 'herd-testing,' in order to improve the dairy stock. In the ensuing discussion it was mentioned that the government had offered to subsidise contributions for herd-testing pound for pound, but at the time there were record prices for milk, so that this was less of an urgent matter.

In June 1919, a meeting of the Moorak branch of the Agricultural Bureau was held at Mr. M.P. Fahy's residence, with 18 attendees and Lena providing the catering. At this meeting, the Government Orchard Inspector Mr Harris gave a 2-hour demonstration on pruning, whilst the weather was described as 'boisterous and bitterly cold, with heavy showers.'[263]

In September of 1919, there was a large Farmers Congress in South Australia. The dairy industry was then struggling, and Dairy Expert Mr Souter stated that it was *'urgently necessary that greater stimulus be given to production in this industry.'* Michael Fahy moved that:

> *'In view of the limited area available for grassing at Moorak Closer Settlement, and the consequent slaughter of young calves which would otherwise grow into valuable stock, we request that the Government allot some suitable space as commonage.' This was carried. Mr. Fahy also moved – 'That in the opinion of this congress it is desirable that the Government should provide suitable, efficient, and proved dairy bulls to be loaned to various dairying districts.' After discussion the motion was rejected.*
>
> *The Chronicle, 20th September 1919*

In 1919, general farming conditions were also challenging, and the local newspaper reported on the sale of some local farms.

> *Moorak is very dry, and grass is going off. An inch of rain would do a power of good. The farmers are cutting their grass hay. The crops*

are on the light side. The milk supply is going off fast, and hand feeding will soon have to be sorted to. The summer fodder is holding its own, but sadly needs moisture. There are several large plots of summer fodder growing, and the dairymen are realizing that they must keep the green food up to the cows to get milk. The early potatoes look well considering the dry spell, and the farmers are busy planting the late varieties.

Border Watch, 25th November, 1919

In December 1919, there was an annual tour of the Mount Gambier Branch of the Agricultural Bureau – it was fixed for that date to be able to meet with the experts from the government's Agricultural Department, who inspected Moorak, O.B. Flat and Mount Gambier East. When they toured through Moorak, it was reported that:

After they entered on that road [McIntosh's or Palamountain's Road] there was a fine display of farming and dairy effort. Fine crops of miscellaneous sorts were observed – chow-mollier [kale], oats, peas, barley, maize, onions & c. The potatoes, which were in every stage of growth, appeared vigorous, but were it was feared, living on their capital – the seed – and would be benefited by heavy and immediate rain. Hay was lying in stocks or heaps on many fields and stack-building was actively going on. The stock – mostly dairy cattle – were in fine sleek condition. The grass everywhere was quite dry, and some paddocks that had been apparently over-grassed seemed absolutely bereft of herbage. The question of how people were going to feed their cows in summer and autumn was a problem which was discussed. Of course, people are growing a large quantity of hay, and growing chow-mollier, Lucerne and other green fodder, but if the season continues rainless some of the dairy people may find their provision run alarmingly short. The barley crops looked good, but both they and the oats were on the short side as far as the straw goes.

Mr R. W. Graney's Ensilage –
Mr. Fahy piloted the party through Moorak, and from MacIntosh's road he directed them along Yell's road to Mr. Graney's ensilage, which was in a far corner of his property. Mr. Graney has no silo and merely heaps up his green stuff in the form of a stack, and places a quantity of heavy timber on it to press it down. In appearance the heap seemed like a low grass haystack, with logs on it. Alongside there was a big heap of black stuff that looked like an old, uncovered stack on which the rains of many winters had fallen. That was an experiment in ensilage making that Mr. Graney made a season or two previously.

Professor Perkins pointed out how wasteful and ineffective such a system really was. In the case of the newer heap, he considered the stuff had been cut too late in the season to make ensilage of. He pointed out the advantages of a silo, which saved trouble, made the best ensilage, and absolutely without waste.

Mr. Fahy remarked that even with the rough and ready system Mr. Graney adopted they got three times the amount of feed from it than they got if it were made into hay. Mr. Graney had 25 cows feeding on his block, and they received a good deal of this sort of ensilage. In this case he had the grass given to him.

Border Watch, 5th December 1919

The Professor insisted on the need for silos and said that under the 'Loans to Producers' Act' the government would advance the money for the silos. They continued along the tour until they came to Michael Fahy's property:

After the inspection of the ensilage…they proceeded along Yell's Road, the Port MacDonnell Road, and a narrow road running west, to Mr. Fahy's 30-acre block, every square foot of which is put to some profitable use. On the way they passed some fine potato fields…and some small Lucerne plots which were in a fine state considered that they had not been irrigated. Mr. Fahy said he kept 15 cows, 2 horses and a bull, besides calves on his block, and they were all in good fettle. On the block he had some 5 acres of chow-mollier growing strongly, some of it nearly ready for plucking, and 6 acres of potatoes, besides some fallow ground. The potatoes are Carmens, and they looked well. Having inspected Mr. C. Janeway's, in whose barn it was arranged they should have luncheon. In the absence of a public hall this is the hall in which most of the dances and other functions are held at Moorak…After luncheon the visitors had a short look through the cheese and butter factory. The hands were busily cutting up curd in the vats by machinery. It was said that the daily intake of milk at present was about 1,900 gallons.

Border Watch, 5th December 1919

The family left Moorak in April 1921 to go back to the city, and lived at Torrensville. A turning point was the drought and struggling farms. Additionally, Mick was not elected to the Board of Directors of the Moorak Co-operative Dairy and Produce Co Ltd at the end of February 1921. He had been the honorary secretary of the company for the previous two years (when J. H. Buck first came to the meeting as a visitor)[264] and was elected to nominate for the Board as a Director. There were two positions available, with existing retiring directors renominating, with J. H. Buck receiving 47 votes and J. W. Barry 43 votes, whilst M. P. Fahy received just 22 votes. Subsequently J. W. Barry became the Chair of Directors.[265] Sometimes Mick did not make himself popular when pursuing what he believed was best for the community, however perhaps there was no room for the two Irishmen on the board. John Henry Buck (Johann Heinrich Joachim) coming from a (Lutheran) Protestant background (born in Denmark) may have helped his votes to the board, whilst Mr J. W. Barry was 'a trustee of the Friendly Society Dispensary representing the Hibernian Lodge [an Irish Catholic Fraternal Association].'[266] Mick would have been disappointed as he had pushed for the community co-operative, which had led to the establishment of the company.

At the same meeting, there was much discussion about shareholders taking more than their share of produce, and fiddling with the 'disc' system that was used to denote they were a shareholder and enable them to take produce. There was also an amusing aside about cheese wrapping:

> *Mr Tarrant suggested that rolls of white paper should be purchased for the wrapping up of cheese at the factory. They were tired, he said, of reading [news]papers backwards on the outside of their cheese.*
>
> *Border Watch, 1 March 1921*

Upon Mick Fahy deciding to resign from the Mt Gambier Agricultural Bureau and to leave the District, the Bureau report stated that:

> *The President spoke with regret at Mr. Fahy, the hon. Secretary, tendering his resignation and leaving the district. As president he knew the value of Mr. Fahy's services to the branch. He had brought the branch to what it is. He was full of energy, and his departure would be a great loss to the branch and the district also. Personally, he was very sorry he was leaving, and accepted his resignation with regret. Mr. W. A. Palamountain supported the president's remarks, and assured Mr. Fahy that it was with sincere regret they had accepted his resignation. He said the secretary was a tower of strength to the branch. In different matters from time-to-time Mr. Fahy had shown his ability and energy. As ex-president he knew the value of Mr. Fahy's services to the branch. Mr. J.F. Nicholls supported. The secretary, he said, had carried out his*

duties in a business-like manner. He was always to the fore and up to date, and what he did take on he made a success. He wished Mr. Fahy good luck and prosperity in his new sphere of life, and trusted they would be able to meet him again before leaving the district. Mr. T. Barry said he was very sorry Mr. Fahy was leaving the district, but he could rest assured he had the good wishes of the Moorak branch of the Agricultural Bureau. He hoped before Mr. Fahy left the district they would have the pleasure of meeting him again. Mr. H. S. Tarrant supported the remarks of the previous speakers. The secretary was the live wire of the branch, and he carried out the secretarial duties with credit to himself and the branch. Moorak would lose one of its best and most industrious settlers. While Mr. Fahy was secretary of the school committee, he proved himself industrious. The Moorak Union picnic grew to such an extent through Mr. Fahy's influence that the committee decided to have two picnics a year – one for children and the other for settlers. The school grounds would stand as a district monument to Mr. Fahy's energy. He moved that a record be placed on the minutes of Mr. Fahy's valuable work to the Moorak branch of the Bureau. Mr. J. Mahoney seconded, and the motion was carried.

Mr. Fahy thanked the members for their kind expressions and appreciative remarks. He had done what he thought was the best for the branch and district.

The president then asked the secretary to retire for a few minutes, and when he was recalled the president asked him to meet the members of the branch in the Cave gardens in town at 3.30pm on Saturday afternoon, March 26, when he would receive a presentation from them.

Border Watch, 5 April 1921

There was a big farewell party for the Fahy family's impending departure from the district. On reading his farewell presentation, one gets a picture of Michael Fahy's high energy, sociable characterful, good management and him being a stalwart of the local community.

> *On Wednesday evening last, a large number of friends (about 50) of Mr. and Mrs. M. P. Fahy met at their residence in the form of a surprise party to pay a tribute to the respected settlers and to make a presentation. Councillor J. T. Kerin presided. Singing, card playing and dancing was indulged in until the early hours of the morning. Songs were rendered...and a humorous recitation by Messrs. M. P. Fahy and J. F. Boardman. Music for dancing was supplied by Messrs. A. Leggett and A. J. Janeway (accordion) and J. Jones (violin). Mr. T. Jones acted as M.C. During an interval in the proceedings the Chairman referred to Mr. and Mrs. M. P. Fahy as most popular residents, and Mr. Fahy had been a lively man on the settlement. Mr. H. Tarrant, in supporting, said that as secretary of the Moorak School Committee and the recently appointed secretary of the Agricultural Bureau, he could bear out the speakers' remarks. His work in connection with the School Committee would stand as a memorial to his energy for years to come. The Reunion picnic, under Mr. Fahy's influence as secretary, had also grown to a large extent. Mr. Fahy's good work in connection with the Agricultural Bureau, fighting on the commonage question and various other important matters, would always be remembered, and Mr. Fahy was to be congratulated on the present position of the Bureau. The speaker thought it a difficult matter to replace such a man, but as he had been elected to the position, he would do his utmost to keep up the already good reputation of the branch. He wished Mr. and Mrs. Fahy and family happiness and prosperity for the future. The sentiments of all present were expressed by acclamation. Mr. J. F.*

Boardman then presented Mr. Fahy with a silver-mounted shaving outfit, on behalf of the residents of Moorak, and Mrs. Fahy with a marble-mounted clock. Miss H. Stafford presented to Miss D. Fahy a silver candle stick from her girl friends. Mr. Fahy in responding said he was leaving Moorak without an enemy. During his stay on the settlement he had met with much help from the people which he appreciated. As a settler he had tried to do his best in the interests of the place, and felt that evening that he had been amply rewarded by their kind and generous gifts, which they would always treasure. 'For they are jolly good fellows' was sung, and supper concluded a most pleasant evening.

Border Watch, 12th April 1921

East End Market

In 1926, M.P. Fahy, Fruitier and Confectioner, lived at 189 Henley Beach Rd, New Mile End (later Torrensville).[267] He traded in a shop at the East End Market for 7 years. Alos living in Mile End was Mick's brother James Joseph Dominic Fahy. Nephew Leo Fahy (son of his brother James Fahy) was a footballer for West Torrens around 1926-27 (and one-time secretary of the Torrens B Club).[268] He also worked as a court correspondent (was a 'deposition clerk,' Senior Associate Clerk in the local Court department[269] and Supreme Court senior official shorthand reporter).[270]

In 1926 Michael and Helena Fahy travelled back to Mount Gambier for the 'Back to Mount Gambier' festivities. It was a greatly anticipated and large event, reported on in *The Register* newspaper (along with everyone who had purchased a ticket to travel back for the festival).

When Michael Fahy sold his shop in November 1927 (at the time it was said for retirement), employees of the fruit merchant firm A.E. Pitt and Son at the East End market, recognised him 'as they motored down' and paid a visit to his shop.[271] This was a large firm also in NSW, that had chaff and grain stores. Mr Ryan made a presentation in which the firm acknowledged the high esteem he was held in, and gave him a silver mounted pipe, and his remarks were supported by Mr Dunkley and Mr Percy Miller. He left the firm as the family was moving from Torrensville to Marion Road, South Plympton (more than a year after Iris Fahy had given birth to Jack Fahy).

In 1928 Mick Fahy obtained a Hawker's license when he was living at South Plympton. In 1930, M.P. Fahy is a 'Carrier' (transporter of goods) and in 1933 he is a 'Canvasser' (seller).[272] However times were difficult as it was the Great Depression, and in 1930 the house at Marion Rd, Plympton was forced to be sold. This must have been a crushing blow to such an enterprising character. Fortunately, the family was able to live in the same house. Sadly, in 1930 Mick's brother James or 'Jim' Fahy, who was a railway guard, died suddenly on the Adelaide Railway Station platform aged 57 years.

M.P. Fahy is last listed in the Sands and MacDougall directories 1934. He died on the 15th July 1934, at the Royal Adelaide Hospital, aged only 64[273], and is buried in the Catholic section of the West Terrace cemetery, along with his wife and daughters. There is an obituary recounting his pioneering days of Moorak, and of his great energy and organisational skills:

Photo: A.E.Pitt and sons delivery lorry at the East End Market, State Library of South Australia [PRG 280/1/15/835]

Original Moorak Settler

Death of Mr M. P. Fahy

Played Leading Part in Early Progress of Settlement

The death of Mr M. P. Fahy at the Adelaide Hospital, on July 15, at the age of 64, removes one of the original no 2 Moorak settlers. It will be remembered by many older residents that when Moorak Settlement was allotted some 28 years ago, the late Mr Fahy, with Mr. P. E. Graney, was living in a tent on the site of the present Moorak Hall, and many a pleasant evening was spent at that camp until his house was erected on the block now held by Mr. F. Greve. The untiring efforts of the late Mr Fahy as the original honorary secretary to the Moorak School Committee will also be long remembered. Assisted by an energetic committee, the pioneering work at the school as carried out with much hard work, involving horses, drays and wheelbarrows. A very large portion of the low-lying ground was filled by working bees under his supervision, and the response was always a tribute to his good management. When the first Moorak settlers picnic at which horse events were introduced, was held in Messrs Ferguson Brothers' property opposite the school, many will recall the thrilling incident that occurred in the Moorak Hack Race for horses caring milk to the Moorak Factory. The late Mr Fahy, riding Daily Bread, the old grey, who was handicapped on the limit mark, kept front position until the straight was entered. When Mr A. Cambers, on Blue Gum, challenged the leader, he was much surprised to be met with the continual flash of a long buggy whip in front of his horse's face, which kept him back until the willing post was reached, and cheers were forthcoming from the crowd for Mr Fahy's popular win. A protest was survived, and Mr Fahy was awarded his first race at Moorak.

When a critical vote was taken as to whether the site of the Public Hall should be on the present position, or amalgamated with the O. B. Flat district, it was through his able guidance that the matter was settled. There was an even vote of 46 each way, and the Chairman of the Picnic Committee (the late Mr W. H. Taylor) wisely withheld his casting vote. It was not long before the first load of stone was placed on the ground where the present hall stands.

After disposing of his Moorak property, Mr Fahy, with his wife and family, went to Adelaide, where a mixed business was taken over at Torrensville. After spending a few years in business, Mr Fahy lived practically a retired life. Mr Fahy paid a few visits to Moorak to renew old acquaintances, and always received a hearty welcome.

Border Watch, 19 July 1934

From 1935 to 1957 Lena Fahy lived at 468 Marion Road, South Plympton,[274] a house that was shared with her youngest daughter and son-in-law. A connection grew between the Fahy and Schulz families, as in Mr and Mrs Vic Schulz, Tanunda, were guests of Mrs E. Fahy at Glenelg (Iris's sister-in-law).[275]

Helena lived at Marion Rd, Plympton until her death (from cancer) in 1957, but at one stage stayed with Brian and Pat Nash. She was buried on the 25th March 1957 at West Terrace Cemetery, Catholic section, site 212. A Lutheran Minister came to the funeral although she had converted to, and brought up her children in, the Catholic faith.[276] She is buried with her husband, two daughters and a son-in-law.

3rd Generation in Australia

Iris Marie Fahy was born on the 1st May 1909 at 20 Myers Street, Adelaide, (Grey Ward) where her family lived. She grew up at Moorak, Mt Gambier from 1911/12 to 1921, before the family moved to Torrensville, followed by Plympton. The family also briefly lived at Kangarilla.

Iris was an athletic child, participating in running races at the 'Moorak Picnic' from a young age (7 years),[277] coming second in the '8 to 9 years' Girls Race in 1917 when she was 8 years old,[278] and winning the '10 years' Girls Race aged 10.[279] In 1920, she won the Girls Race at the Nelson Rowing Club's Annual Regatta and Land Sports meetup (in neighbouring Victoria)[280] and in 1921, she won the '10 and under 12 years' race at the Moorak Reunion and Children's picnic.[281]

Iris also did public recitations (of poetry or drama), and when she was 9 she did a recitation at the farewell party for the Mitchell family (Mr Mitchell was the teacher at the Moorak school) who were leaving Moorak.[282]

Iris was a bridesmaid at her sister's wedding on Monday 29 December 1924, at the Queen of Angels church, followed by a wedding reception breakfast held at the Masonic Hall in Torrensville. It was reported that Iris

> *frocked in apricot crepe de chine. She wore a black hat, and carried a posy of autumn tints…Mr and Mrs Fahy entertained a number of guests at the Masonic Hall, Torrensville, where the wedding breakfast was held.*
>
> *The Observer, 10th January 1925*

Iris was also bridesmaid at her cousin Doris Bruckman's wedding to Clement Clayton at Kangarilla on 23rd May, 1931:

> *Miss Iris Fahy, bridesmaid, wore a frock of blue crepe de chine of ankle length, and carried a bouquet of pale pink flowers with pink streamers. A black lace hat and silver shoes completed the toilette. Mr Colin Smart was best man.*
>
> *Advertiser and Register, 27th May 1931*

Between these two weddings, the conception of our father occurred (around Christmas 1925) when Iris was only 16 years of age, and she gave birth to John or 'Jack' Fahy when she was 17, at the Queen's Home, Rose Park, later part of Queen Victoria hospital. The Queen's Home was a private maternity hospital officially opened on the birthdate of Queen Victoria in 1902, but it was not until 1917 that unmarried women were admitted to the hospital. The building now stands as a lovely old sandstone building on Dequetteville Terrace, with 'Queens Home' on the facade.

B 27285/3

Photo: Queen's Home, Rose Park, 1918, State Library of South Australia [B27285/3]

There were mysterious stories about Dad's birth mother and her family, i.e. that the family had 'always kept an eye out for him', that 'she didn't want to let him go'. Anecdotally, Iris, a Catholic, become pregnant to a Protestant man much to her father's disapproval, set in the context of societal sectarianism.

This story seems slightly strange because although her father was of Irish Catholic stock, he had married a German Lutheran woman. Being unmarried at 17 and of the Catholic faith may have been reason enough for adopting out a child in the 1920s. It was only in Iris Fahy's grandparents' generation that there was a scandal in their tiny settlement of Klemzig, of an unmarried mother accused of killing her baby and serving time in jail (the woman later married the father of the stillborn child).

After Iris gave birth to an 'illegitimate' child in 1926, the Fahy family moved shortly after the birth, from 189 Henley Beach Road, New Mile End, to 468 Marion Road, Plympton where they would stay until their deaths. Iris was 27 years of age when she married, although she never had any more children – perhaps, raised as a Catholic, she may have seen that as a punishment - or at least her fate.

Iris married Henry J (Jack) McDermott, 11 years her senior, at the Church of our Lady of Victories, High Street, Glenelg on the 25th January 1936, around a year and a half after the death of her father Mick Fahy. After Mick died, Jack posted a memorial that read 'to my dear friend…ever remembered.'[283]

I visited the Church of our Lady of Victories in the late 1990s, amazed to think that my biological grandmother Iris regularly visited there. When she married, her occupation was a Machinist, and she worked in North Adelaide. The officiating minister was Thomas M O'Rourke and two witnesses were: J Richardson, Machinist, North Adelaide (a cousin of Jack, and the child of his Auntie C.S. Richardson who he had lived with in Railway Terrace, Croydon) and Iris's sister Dorothea Nash (nee Fahy), Domestic Duties, South Plympton.

Jack McDermott, born 26th September 1898 in Broken Hill, New South Wales, had served in both the First and Second World Wars. When enlisting in WWI in 1917, he was an 18 year old Boilermaker's apprentice, and listed his next of kin as his Uncle Francis McDermott, Railway Terrace, Ridleyton (and later listed his Auntie C. S. Richardson, Railway Terrace, Croydon). He had to sign an oath stating that he had no legal guardian. His mother was deceased and Jack says that his father 'left home about 1906 and had not been heard of since.'

Jack was a Private in the 10th Battalion (25th Reinforcement), Australian Imperial Force. His brother Private Walter J. McDermott also enrolled in 1915, and served in the 12th Battalion before being killed in action near Pozieres, France, between the 19th and 22nd August 1916. Jack was able to receive a pension due to his brother's death, until he enlisted in the war about a year later.[284]

Jack had to reapply for his discharge letter from WWI, as in 1926 his home was destroyed by a fire, when he was away from Broken Hill. In the Second World War, Jack served as a member of the 10th Battalion again (and has an Australian Army Grave at Centennial Park).

Photo: Church of our Lady of Victories, 1927, SLSA [B4491]

There was a bit of excitement in 1939 when Iris ('Mrs H. J. McDermott") won 10 pound 10 shillings in a state-wide competition, out of nearly 3000 entries, for choosing the best slogan to promote sport. The competition was organised by an Adelaide sporting goods manufacturer, with the judges being Mr Chapman of radio station 5AD and Mr A. Martin of Martin's Advertising Agency. Her winning slogan was '*Fitness is a National Asset – Play Sport.*' The winning slogan was to be used by various sporting goods firms in their advertisements, and it was proposed that the slogan be printed on window stickers and streamers to be distributed throughout the state.

Much was made of the fact that the slogan came from a woman – 'Best Slogan Written By Woman' stated *The News*.[285] However, when Harris Scarfe Ltd used the logo in their advertising, they congratulated 'Mr H. J. McDermott for the winning slogan![286]

Photo: Iris & 'Jack' McDermott, (S. Battams, courtesy the late P. Nash)

Like Iris, each of her two siblings only had one child each. Dorothy's son Brian Nash, became a politician and secretary of the Wayville Branch of the ALP (a Catholic right member, he was expelled from the Labor party along with three other members for acting on his 'Catholic conscience' and refusing to support an endorsed candidate for Boothby, Rex Matthews, as he was on a list of communists).[287] Bob Fahy's child became a well-known Doctor in South Australia (the late Dr Carlien Kimber).

Iris's sister Dorothy spoke to her daughter-in-law Pat Nash of knowing 'someone else' who had experienced an ectopic pregnancy (apart from herself - that is why she could not have any more children), and Pat wondered in hindsight whether she was referring to Iris.[288]

It appears that Jack and Iris were family and community minded, as an example they were involved in collecting money for the Ashford Community Hospital Appeal.[289] Being originally from Broken Hill, Iris and Jack regularly flew back there, probably to visit Jack's siblings. Iris was considered to be a 'fun' person by Pat, who had been good to her and made the 'frocks' for her wedding to Brian Nash.

Iris had bad emphysema which Pat attributed to Iris smoking when she was younger,[290] however she was also a railway employee, which is linked to higher rates of respiratory problems and chronic obstructive pulmonary disease.[291]

Photo: James & Dorothy Nash, Jack & Iris McDermott taken outside of the house at Plympton Park. (S. Battams, courtesy Pat Nash)

Iris died aged just 58, on the 26th August 1967, at the Royal Adelaide Hospital, with the list of ailments including: respiratory failure, pneumonia

(60 hours), congestive heart failure, severe asthma, bronchitis and emphysema. On her death certificate she is registered as being a 'Railway employee' and still living at 468 Marion Rd, Plympton Park, where she had lived for over 40 years. She was buried in the Catholic section of the West Terrace cemetery, with her parents, and the grave next door being her sister and her brother-in-law (all paid for by Helena Fahy). Two graves away on one side there is someone by the surname White, and one grave away on the other lies another by the surname White. There were three notices of her death in the Adelaide Advertiser on Monday, 28th Aug 1967, one from her husband, one from her sister and family and one from her brother and his family (who at that time were residing in the United States).

Visit to Ireland 2002

In 2002, I had an opportunity to travel to Ireland and spent a wonderful two weeks there, visiting Counties Dublin, Donegal, Clare (Ennis, Cliffs of Moher), Sligo, Mayo (Croagh Patrick, Clare Island, Achill Island), Galway (Galway, Connemara), the Aaran Islands (Inishmore), Kerry and the Dingle Peninsula (Tralee, Ardfert, Fenit, Ballyheigue, Ballybunion, Listowel), Cork and Kilkenny. Whilst mostly travelling alone, I was fortunate to find a travel companion and we drove around the Dingle peninsula together. I also met a lovely Irish woman called Margaret who showed me around Achill Island (and introduced me to the singer Eva Cassidy).

There was so much joy and 'craic' to be found in Ireland, in the spontaneous playing of music and singing of songs, with memorable experiences at the high energy 'The Crane' in Galway and soulful singing and playing in many places on Achill Island.

I was extremely moved by the national famine memorial in County Mayo along with other stories of the hardships endured, and it brought me closer to the experiences of the Irish ancestors. I felt Ireland to be an extremely spiritual place, particularly the Aran Islands. During the trip I also picked up and read the book 'Anam Cara' (John Donohue)[292] on Celtic spirituality. Some extracts from my diary from the trip read:

28th August 2002

During the tour at Donegal we went past the area where people waited for the boats to Canada and North America to collect them during the famine. They waited up to a month there for boats to come, with little food, and many died waiting, so there is a nearby graveyard. Also, only 50% of passengers made it to their destination due to the conditions on the ships….On a hills of Donegal tour we stopped near Errigal, the highest mountain and went through some great rugged and remote places full of peat bogs. Also stopped at Glen Neagh National Park where we walked up to the castle…more stories about the famine, some of these areas were deserted during it. The area between Dunleavy and Dungloe was particularly desolate and beautiful. Lots of pink weed, orange flowers, craggy fields, stone ruins'

29th Aug 2002

Caught a bus to the beautiful Croagh Patrick, a holy mountain associated with St Patrick, also the national famine monument is there because Mayo was most affected by the famine.

1st Sept 2002

Yesterday I walked to Keem Bay [Achill Island], up a mountain and then down into the beautiful beach. It was a gorgeous sunny day…Today I walked to Slievemore, where a whole town used to be, but it was deserted around the time of the famine.

Yesterday, as we were travelling to get the ferry, some people hopped on the bus as they are making a DVD to promote 'Ragus', a traditional Irish song and dance performed on the Aran Islands in summer and they also tour. They got us to sing the chorus of a song! Later, they were also at the pub filming, and we had to sing the same chorus again! The Irish songs were beautiful, and beautifully sung.

4th Sept 2002

Just went for a fantastic ride to Dún Aonghasa, [an old stone Celtic fort by the sea] on Inis Mor island [one of the Aran Islands], then to Hallig Carriage and back. Beautiful cliffs and stone forts and residents of monks/hermits..

Now on the way to the Cliffs of Mohor…which were spectacular – you couldn't walk to Hags Head due to the dangerous cliffs, but I walked on that side anyway. Clare is very green, especially compared to Inis Mor, which was treeless. Apparently there was originally no soil, they used seaweed as the basis for soil and dug under the rocks for it. It seemed to me that Dún Aonghasa, was just as dangerous as the Cliffs of Mohor, but there are no barriers or signs around there…Spanish Point Beach is nice, just passing through.

7th Sept 2002

We met a nice American guy who looked like Tom Hanks on the Dingle Peninsula, who gave us a map of the Ring of Kerry. He said he was in the Gallarus Oratory [an ancient stone chapel that dates ack to the 8th to 12th centuries] with another woman, a stranger, when he heard 'Te Ra' said to him. He mentioned this to the stranger who gasped and told him that was the name she was given by an Eastern religious person to mediate to!

8th Sept 2002

The Atlantic yesterday was fantastically wild. The Blasket islands looking wonderful, lashed by the sea. There was this excluded little beach at the end of Slea Head…

Photo: Cliffs of Moher, County Clare, 2002 (S Battams 2002)

1837: The Gramp Family: Winemakers of the Barossa Valley

Chapter 6: Johann Gramp, founding a dynasty

Introduction

The Gramp story in South Australia started when Johann Gramp, a teenager from Bavaria who was orphaned at a young age, travelled to Hamburg and was selected as a Labourer contracted to the South Australia Company. Gramp first settled on Kangaroo Island working with the Company, before moving to Adelaide, Hope Valley and the Barossa Valley where he became the first commercial winemaker in the area, planting the first grapes in 1847. Gramp would become a prominent pioneer South Australian, acknowledged on one of the North Terrace (Adelaide) jubilee plaques which commemorated 150 years of South Australia.

1st Generation to arrive in Australia

Johann Gramp was just 18 years of age when he came to South Australia with the South Australia Company (the Company) on the *Solway*, one of the first boats from Hamburg to the new Colony. There had been an earlier struggle in getting non-British subjects to South Australia.

> *Among the departures for the New Colony of South Australia we observe the Solway, with a large number of German emigrants. It is well known in the Colony, that at the time of Dr Lang's departure [Reverend Dr John Dunmore Lang], it was his intention to introduce at least one shipload of French or German Vine-dressers*[293] *to the Colony, and the leave of the Colonial Government to introduce such emigrants on the Government bounty was obtained before his departure. With a view to affect this purpose, that gentleman traversed the greater portion of France and Germany and had entered into the necessary arrangements to procure a supply, when the British government interfered, refusing to sanction the appropriation of the Colonial land fund to the*

introduction of any other than British subjects, the scheme was quashed. It is difficult to conceive why the Home government have interfered in the one case and not in the other.

The Sydney Gazette and New South Wales Advertiser,

31 October 1837

What kind of person was Johann Gramp, and why did his family and friends leave Europe? There is a picture of the man publicly available, perhaps due to the prominence he achieved in his life. I was curious to find out that he was from Bavarian origin and in one enduring photo, he proudly wears his German smoking cap. Why did he come to South Australia from Bavaria when most of the early German speaking arrivals were Prussian? There appeared to be multiple reasons to leave the region.

Gramp's parents were Johann Ehrhardt Grampp and Elisabeth Hahn, who married in 1796. Elisabeth was 17 years when she married, whilst Johann Ehrhardt Grampp was 33 years older than his bride. Their first child was born in 1798, and they would go on to have 10 children. Three of their children died at a young age in the year 1807.[294] Around this time, Bavaria was at war, fighting with the French in the wars of the second, third and fourth coalitions.

Johann Gramp was the youngest child in the family, born on 28th August 1819, in Aichig,[295] Kulmbach, Bayreuth, Upper Franconia, Bavaria, close to the Czechia border. Aichig is around 400 metres above sea level and in 1818, was a very small town, with only 86 residents, 16 houses, and no church.[296] Johann was baptised in the St Petri Lutheran Church (Petrikirche) in nearby Kulmbach on the 19th September 1819. The imposing Plassenberg castle, hailing from 1835, sits above the church.

Photo: Johann Gramp, wearing a German embroidered smoking cap, toward the end of his life.[297] A smoking cap was popular in the late 19th and early 20th centuries and a symbol of sophistication, designed for wear during leisure and especially whilst smoking tobacco pipes or cigars, to keep the head warm and prevent hair and clothes from smelling of tobacco[298]

Johann's father was a mature 74 years of age at his son's birth, whilst his mother was 41 years old. His father died in 1823 of tuberculosis when Johann junior was just 4 years old. Sadly, Johann's mother died just 3 years later in 1826 of 'dropsy.'[299] After his parents died, Johann may have been cared for by his older sister Anna (27 years) or brother Friedrich (26 years).

By 1830, emigration from what would become Germany (in 1871) had increased dramatically, with the main destination being the United States (US). In 1832, 10,000 Germans arrived in the US but in 1854 this figure was 200,000.[300] Johann Gramp's sister Margretha Schmidt (later Smith) was one of the early emigrants, arriving in New York in 1834. Living next door to her was August Gramp and family, John Gramp and his wife and 'John Sweet,' all from Bavaria.[301] Emigration was accelerated by revolutions which commenced across Europe from the 1830s, associated with industrialisation, poor working conditions and failed agricultural crops.

Protestants (such as Gramp, a Lutheran) were being oppressed in Bavaria in the 1830s. In 1818, a new constitution was established in Bavaria, with equality of religions recognised and the rights of Protestants in place. However, in 1837, with the rise to power of Prime Minister von Abel and the Ultramontanes, a Catholic political group, Protestants were oppressed and stripped of their rights. [302] Von Abel was later ousted due to his attitude towards King Ludwig's (the 'Mad King') much younger Irish mistress, the much written about dancer, actress, seductress, lecturer and author 'Lola Montez' - the stage name of 'Marie Dolores Eliza Rosanna Gilbert' (Eliza Gilbert), who was pro liberal and anti-Jesuit.[303] Von Abel pushed to have her naturalised, and objected to the King making her a Countess. The King abdicated and Lola fled from Bavaria to Switzerland during the 1848 revolutions.[304]

Avoiding army service may have been a reason for some emigrants to leave, as there was compulsory military service, and Bavaria had been the centre of conflict during French wars with Austria, resulting in the loss of many lives. The region in Bavaria that Gramp was from had historically transferred hands many times. From the Andech to Thuringian counts, to the House of Hohenzollern, from the Prussians to the French via Napoleon, Kulmbach eventually became part of the Kingdom of Bavaria in 1810. Bavaria was reliant upon and fought for Napoleonic France, and during France's invasion of Russia in 1812, the Bavarian army was slaughtered – losing around 29,000 of 33,000 troops.

One story explaining Gramp's departure from Germany was that Johann met 38-year-old Wilhelm Milde, a baker, and his family at the local Lutheran Church (in Kulmbach), who became a friend and persuaded him to try to join them on the trip abroad. Another story was Gramp's taste for reading and adventure led him to leave Bavaria.[305]Whatever the reason for his departure, he did not do it alone. Johann Gramp travelled to Hamburg and boarded the *Solway,* bound for Kangaroo Island, South Australia, along with his friend Milde and 50 other German passengers (70 in total), including 27 people contracted to the South Australia Company.[306]

Johann would have been literate due to compulsory education laws,[307] but not English speaking, however he learnt English quickly. In early 1837 he obtained a contract with the South Australia Company, and was paid in advance from 29 April to 31 October 1837. He would be bound to the Company for 3 years upon his arrival in the Colony.

The Company had employed Dr Dreschler as an interpreter and to conduct business on behalf of the Germans, with the company's Colonial Manager (McLaren). Gramp was one of the youngest adult male passengers on the *Solway*. The boat left Hamburg on the 3rd June, 1837 and first went to London before passing through the Canary Islands, stopping at Rio de Jenaro, Brazil and the Cape of Good Hope (for food and water) on its way to South Australia.[308] A newspaper later said that it was an

> *eventful voyage during which they were nearly wrecked in the North Sea whirlpool, and for days were becalmed on the fringe of the Dead Sea.*

The Leader (Angaston) 28 October 1937

It was also tragic for some, as Gramps' friend Kleemann lost his wife and one of their children on the journey.

The South Australia Company was established in 1835 by George Fife Angas and other merchants. Angas was on the South Australian Association along with Wakefield, Torrens and Gouger, which lobbied to form the new Colony of South Australia. Angas was also on the South Australian Colonisation Commission, established following the *South Australia Act* 1834, but resigned to form the company.[309] The company's purpose was to encourage the sale of land in the new Colony. The Company purchased land not sold under 'advance sales,' (which was required to be sold as stipulated by the British Parliament in order to support the colonisation venture) which amounted to 2/3rds of the land. Thus the Company effectively saved colonisation plans.

George Fife Angas equipped four ships to sale to South Australia as part of the Company's ventures, which left in advance of the SA Colonisation Commission's ships. These ships included the *Solway* – which unfortunately would not last long, as shortly after its arrival in the colony it was shipped to Encounter Bay and wrecked there.[310]

The Company played a pivotal role in the establishment of the new settlement, not only buying land but also building wharves, harbours, roads and bridges. Labour was required for this venture, and the company turned to Germanic regions for recruitment, influenced by the long association between Hamburg and the Dutton family of South Australia. Patriarch Frederick Dutton (1768-1847) had been the British vice-consul in Cuxhaven, Hanover – part of Hamburg. All of his children, including Frederick Dutton of Anlaby (1812-1890), were born in South Australia.[311]

On July 12th, 1836, in London, the Company provided instructions to agent Mr Mengl to select the best agricultural land in South Australia. The *Solway* arrived in Kingscote on the 16th October 1837, its passengers first settling there. On Kangaroo Island they planted mulberry tree cuttings,[312] with one old mulberry tree still there at Reeves Point, Kingscote, Kangaroo Island, now a tourist attraction.[313]

Gramp, along with his friends Milde and Kleemann, prepared land for sowing crops to supplement their wages from the Company. Oral history states that the productive German settlers were treated unfairly by the jealous British settlers on Kangaroo Island, and their successful crops may have been one reason for the jealousy.[314] Gramp stayed in Kangaroo Island temporarily to support Kleeman due to his personal loss (of his wife) on the voyage to Australia.[315]

In 1838, Gramp left Kangaroo Island and assisted Colonel William Light to survey the Port River, [316, 317] just before Light's death in 1839, and worked on the construction of the South Australia Company's first Wharf at Port Adelaide,[318] with the old landing place known as 'Port Misery.'[319] At the time, William Jacob was Assistant Survey to Colonel Light, surveying the north side of the River Torrens,[320] so it is likely the two men knew each other. Jacob's Creek (where Gramp ended up) was named after William Jacob, who had come to South Australia in 1836 on the *Rapid* with Colonel Light. After pastoral interests in the northern Flinders waned, Jacob settled at Moorooroo (Jacob's Creek) in the Barossa Valley.[321]

Johann Gramp may have witnessed both the *Prince George* and *Zebra* arriving in Port Adelaide in 1838, and so may have met his future wife's family when they arrived on the *Zebra*. Johanne Nitschke was born 25th November 1825 in Lochau, Brandenburg, Prussia and was 12 years old when she arrived in South Australia.[322]

In 1840 Johann Gramp worked as a baker, for Bremer and Bauer who had travelled on the *Solway* and started up a bakery in Currie Street, Adelaide.[323] Gramp then resided in Gilles Street, Adelaide. Also working at the same bakery were good friends Gottfried Nitschke (his future brother-in-law),[324] and Edward Kalleske.[325]

Gramp and Kalleske left Adelaide in 1841, to take up sections 175 and 175 in the Hundred of Yartalla (Yatala),[326] which in 1842 was called Hope Valley. It was there he built a log cabin,[327] and engaged in farming. In late 1846 he purchased 83 acres of land at Jacob's Creek, where he soon settled. Gottfried Nitschke also purchased land and settled in the same area, as he later told a South Australian newspaper.[328]

> *Mr Nietschke[329] spent about seven years at the [bakery] trade, and settled at Jacob's Creek in company with the late Mr G. [J.] Gramp. They acquired land opposite his present homestead, and some years later another section was bought on the other side of Jacob's Creek, on which Mr Nietschke now resides. The land at that time was very heavily timbered, and hard work from dawn till late at night was the order of the day. Wheat was sown on the portion cleared, but many difficulties had first to be overcome in clearing the ground which had to be levelled and ploughed with the aid of oxen.*
>
> *Mr Nietschke well remembers the funeral of Colonel Light, which he attended. A few years ago he visited Light's grave in Adelaide. The late Mr. Giles of the South Australian Land Company was also well known to him, and many others, including Colonel George Gawler and Captain G. Grey (Governor of South Australia in those early days). It seems a pity that Mr Nietschke has never attended the Glenelg Commemoration Day festival. He has always been a good supporter of the mission societies in many ways, and is a member of many years standing of St John's Lutheran church, Tanunda, of which he is also a trustee, and formerly was a lay reader. His wife has been an excellent helpmeet [sic] to him. Both are highly respected throughout the district.[330]*

Apart from successively buying tracts of land in the Barossa Valley, Gramp acted as mortgager in the land purchases of other Germans, such as members of his wife's family.[331]

Gramp was already partnered with Johanne Eleonora Nitschke when living in Hope Valley and, unusual for the time, the couple had four children before they were married on 26th December 1851. His bride was six years younger than him. They were said to have ten children (six survived Gramp), and at least one was adopted. His children included:

Louisa Mathilde Gramp (1843 Hope Valley -1929)
Anna Dorothea Gramp (4th May 1845 Hope Valley - 1932)
Johann Friedrich Gramp (1847 Rowland's Flat -1853)
Gustav Gramp (1850 Moorooroo – Rowland's Flat 1927)
Johann Hermann Gramp (1852 Rowland's Flat -1919)
Maria Caroline Gramp (1854 Rowland's Flat -1941)
Johann Ehrhard Gramp (1856 Rowland's Flat -1928)
Emma Helene Gramp (1860 Jacob's Creek -1903)

Having children before he was married was to the chagrin of the local Lutheran pastor, who urged the couple to get married. One initial reason Johann may not have married straight away was because Johanne was only 18 years old when she had their first baby and if under 21 years of age, a couple had to obtain the signed written consent of the parents (if they were around).

When Eleanor's sister Johanna Mathilde Emma (Mathilde) Nitschke[332] died aged in 1880 aged 50 years, she had three young children (with her second husband Richard Garrett, who was 26 years older than her, and had pre-deceased her three years earlier). Eleanore and Johann Gramp brought up at least one of these three orphan children, Edward Garrett (1872-1969), and Johann Gramp was listed as his guardian upon his school admission in 1880.

Edward Garrett's sister Emma Lomman Garrett was raised by her maternal uncle (Nitschke) whose property was across the creek from the Gramps.[333]

Photo: Jacob's creek, c1900, State Library of South Australia [B49268]

The Barossa Valley was named by Colonel William Light in 1837, after Barrosa in southern Spain, where he fought under his friend General Graham (later Lord Lynedoch) in the Battle of Barrosa (1811), with the British victors over the French.[334] The Barossa Valley was identified by German geologist and mineralogist Menge (who also worked for the South Australia Company) as being an ideal spot for flourishing vineyards and orchards.[335] It was here that Menge made his home in a makeshift shelter (partly rock, partly hut).

The first surveys of Tanunda were undertaken by Flaxman in 1839. George Fife Angas (South Australia Company) held huge tracts of land in the Barossa Valley, much of which was sold to Prussian share farmers at considerable interest.[336] Angas's agent Flaxman purchased much fertile land in the North East of the Barossa, either borrowing money from Angas or purchasing it on his behalf without Angas's permission (using Angas's account, but purchasing the land in his own name). After meeting financial troubles, he offered the land to Angas for sale. Angas and Flaxman eventually reached an agreement on the land sale which was much to Angas's advantage.

One sad story in the history of the Barossa Valley is that of Hoffnungsthal, literally the 'Valley of Hope'. Hoffnungsthal was the first Lutheran settlement in the Lyndoch Valley, established in 1847, and was flooded in 1853. Susan Marsden describes the fate of those Germans that settled here, who had not heeded the advice of the local Aboriginal people:

> *Aboriginal residents in the valley, the Peramangk ['s]*[337] *...understanding of the natural environment was far greater than that of the newcomers. This is revealed by the fate of Hoffnungsthal. The settlers did not heed the [Aboriginal People's] advice against flood-prone land and in 1853 the lagoon flooded the area. The settlement was abandoned. Now, only the recent monument on the site of the church, some scattered foundations and the lagoon-itself mark the site.*
>
> Marsden 2004

The Trinity Lutheran Church at Rowland Flat was formed by members of the former Hoffnungsthal congregation.[338]

Gramp and Sons is hailed as the first commercial winery in the Barossa Valley. Whilst Johann Gramp planted his first vines at Jacob's Creek around 1847, it was not until three years later (1850) that he made his first octave of table wine. In 1853 there is a record of Johann exhibiting his wine, 'Vineyard of the Empire,' and grapes at the Lyndoch Valley Agricultural and Horticultural Society Show, for which he was awarded first prize for both. Later in 1880 it was stated that:

Mr Johann Gramp, of Barossa, Jacob's Creek, states that his vineyard was planted in 1848 to 1858, in a red clay soil. There are six acres under cultivation, the best yielding variety being the Cheres. Yield this season about 2,150 gallons. The vines are very healthy. There are 6,000 gallons of light dry wine in stock.

South Australian Chronicle and Weekly Mail, 22nd May 1880

In 1848, the year of political upheavals and revolutions in Europe, Johann Gramp became a 'naturalised British subject,' along with many other South Australian Germans. Some of the first Germans had sworn their allegiance to Queen Victoria in 1839, grateful for their religious freedom, however, formal naturalisation was not enabled until 1841 following an Act of parliament.[339]

In July 1860, Gramp became councillor for the Barossa East Council, serving on the council for 20 years, including as Chairperson, and helped support building of the Rowland Flat school. He was on the Council in July 1879, when his son Gustav was also on the council.

Johann Gramp became a successful farmer and gardener (his main crop being wheat). The *Land Tax Return of 1885* showed that he owned three large parcels of land in the Barossa Valley including 83 acres, 235 acres, and 135 acres, and in nearby County of Light (at Jacob's Creek) he owned 82 acres.[340] He went from six to eight acres of vineyards from the 1870s to 1890s and produced around 2000 gallons of wine per year (around 7570 litres). The main grapes or styles were Syrah or Shiraz (Hermitage style), Mataro, Verdelho, Blanquette (Mauzac) Sherry (Albillo), Malaga (Moscatel), Black Portugal (Tinta Amarela or Trincadeira), Madeira and Pedro Ximines.[341]

In 1890, amidst a period of severe economic depression in Australia, a terrible tragedy took place in Angaston, and Johann was a key witness. A woman tried to drown herself and her four children in a well. Johann was in a nearby paddock and heard the children crying out. He came to the rescue of three of the children and their mother, not knowing there was a fourth child drowned until after they were walking away, when the mother asked him to get this child, a baby, from the well. An inquest was held, and it was declared that the mother was mentally unwell.[342, 343] (There were many similar crimes around the same period in Australia, and I have written about this in *The Secret Art of Poisoning*, although I knew nothing of my ancestor's connection to the above tragedy when I wrote that book).

Johann Gramp died on the 9th August 1903, aged 83 years, leaving a large estate of £10,650, and land including 535 acres. He appointed his 'dear wife' Johanne Eleanore and his son Gustav as executors of his estate, along with good friend Wilhelm Altmann[344] – at that time a gardener, but also a tanner, tinsmith, plumber, shearer and employee of Gustav Gramp.[345] His wife Johanne Eleanore died in 1919, aged 93 years of age. They are both buried at the Rowland Flat Cemetery.

Gramp founded a dynasty and left a great legacy to winemaking in South Australia. From his humble beginnings in Bavaria, he took every opportunity available to him throughout his life and lived unconventionally at times. His eldest surviving son Gustav Gramp continued the winemaking business and transferred from the original winery at Jacob's Creek to Rowland Flat, became a limited (incorporated) company under G. Gramp and Sons (in 1912)[346] and at the same time had its operating name changed to Orlando Winery.[347] In 1918, a Maxwell 22.5 horse power car was registered to Gramp and Sons Limited, Rowland's Flat.[348] Later, grandsons Hugo and Fred Gramp managed the winery, whilst Bern Gramp managed the original Jacob's Creek property.[349] They were to grow Gramp and Sons and Orlando into a significant, internationally renowned wine brand.

Louis Hugo Gramp sadly died in the famous Kyeema airplane disaster in 1938, where 18 people including a delegation of winemakers (including Thomas Hardy and Sidney Hill Smith), pilot and crew (18 in total) crashed into Mount Dandenong. As a result of the Royal Commission and an Air Accident Investigation Committee investigating the crash, new safety regulations were introduced, including flight officers monitoring flights and advising on position, weather and alternative landing options and planes being fitted with a radio range system to advise pilots on their course.

'Teetotaller' Premier Sir Thomas Playford IV GCMG commemorated the 100th year of Orlando in 1947,[350] and when 150 years of Orlando was celebrated in 1987 through *The Orlando Way* book, a foreword was provided by the then Governor, Sir Donald Dunstan, KBE, CB,[351] whilst Sir Eric Neal provided the foreword for the 1997 book *A Heritage of Innovation: Orlando Wines 1847-1997*.

In 1971, the family winemaking business was purchased by Reckitt and Colman,[352] and in 1986 it was part of their multi-national parent company. Orlando was purchased back in 1989 and then sold to French company Pernod Ricard, along with the Jacob's Creek label, in 1989.[353] In 2024, Pernod Ricard agreed to sell the company to Australian Wine Holdco (owner of Accolade Wines),[354] and in 2025 Vinarchy emerged from a merger of Accolade Wines and Pernod Ricard Winemakers.[355] The 'Jacob's Creek' brand is still carried.

Photo: Aerial view of Gramps Orlando in 1946, Source: SLSA, BRG 397/2/84/1

Women in Winemaking

One historian claims that women in the Gramp family initially had a significant role in the winemaking business, but this waned across time:

> *It seems clear that the women in the Gramp family, during the second half of the nineteenth century, made significant contributions to the work in the vineyard in the developmental phase of the family business, and they may well have provided support and some input into other aspects of management and production in the winery. However, by 1910, when the Gramp business had prospered sufficiently to be converted into Orlando, a limited company, it was evident that women's participation in the business was no longer deemed necessary.*

Tolley (2004)[356]

The photo below shows many women in the family actively involved in a late 19th century vintage. Gustav Gramp's daughter Olga Regina Gramp (who never married) 'spent her life in the service of G Gramp and Sons, holding the position of Secretary to her late father and her late brother, Hugo.'[357]

Photo: Gramp family during vintage, late 19thC. The person standing up on the wagon with the two children appears to be Hermann Richard Schulz, who worked for his Uncle Gustav Gramp for many years. The young man standing with the horses appears to be his brother Heine Schulz. The man standing at right appears to be Gustav Gramp, with his wife Louise (nee Geue) seated at his feet. Other people in the photo appear to be Gustav's children, whilst others are unknown members of the Gramp family.[358]

German Lutheran Aboriginal Missions

Little discussed in winemaking histories of the Gramp family is the relationship between the local Aboriginal communities and the German Lutherans in the Barossa Valley. It is well known that the South Australian German settlers established missions in an attempt to convert Aboriginal people to Christianity. It appears that the Gramp and Schulz families, had strong links to the Koonibba Aboriginal Mission (or Koonibba Lutheran Mission established in 1901 near Denial Bay, West of Ceduna), with these names associated with those working at and visiting the mission.

Gustav Gramp of Rowland's Flat (Johann Gramp's son) was treasurer of the Lutheran Synod[359], where the main item of discussion at the Lutheran conference in 1914 was the Koonibba Aboriginal Mission, and a 'Miss Gramp' was a cook at the Koonibba mission. In 1914 it was reported that J. G. Gramp (Rowland's Flat)[360] was farm director on the Lutheran Mission Committee. They were also involved in the Hermannsburg Mission Northern Territory, Killalpaninna Mission (Bethesda) near Coopers Creek South Australia and Point Pass in the mid-North of South Australia. In 1911, the Lutheran Mission proposed that the Preparatory College be moved from Point Pass to Tanunda.[361]

Koonibba Mission

In September 1914, *The Chronicle* reports on the Lutheran Mission Committee delegates visiting Koonibba mission station to make a recommendation to the mission committee of the Lutheran Synod. It describes the harsh conditions on the station and unforgiving weather, along with its productivity, with Aboriginal people both living on and nearby the station, and working intermittently or on a regular basis, with a children's home and school on the station.

> *The mission has 38 horses, 50 cattle, 15 pigs and 40 head of poultry. The station consists of 12,000 acres (leasehold, with right to purchase at 5/ per acre), and 4,500 acres (perpetual lease) at Davenport Creek. The latter country is fit only for cattle, and is 25 miles from the station, having water to be obtained at a depth of a few feet in the sand. The station has a church with seating for 200 persons, which was built in in 1910, and a missionary's residence of seven rooms, also a children's home, erected in August 1913, where nearly 50 [Aboriginal] children are housed [ranging from 2 to 8 years].[362] The home is under Miss A. von Einem, as matron, and Miss M. Eckermann as assistant matron. In a schoolroom, measuring 33 by 24 ft, 51 [Aboriginal] pupils were being instructed by Mr W. Linke and Mr S. Rudolph (assistant teacher). The school was built about 11 years ago by J. Richards, one of the [Aboriginal*

men], and was originally used as a church. Other buildings are a teacher's residence of six rooms, the six roomed house of the farm manager (Mr A. Schmidt), a ...dining-room [for Aboriginal adults and children], where about 70 [Aboriginal people] receive food, Miss Gramp being in charge of the kitchen, four (Aboriginal people's] houses, a store under the control of Mr Rudolph, and a second-hand or donation depot, administered by Miss B. Schmidt, who is also tailoress in charge of the manufacture of clothing for the [Aboriginal population]. Miss H. Schmidt teaches the white children. Adjoining the mission station are the properties of Messrs G. Schultz [Previous farm manager at Koonibba][363]*, J. Foggo and H.E. Gersch. The mission farm is well supplied with sheds of every description, substantially built of iron. The stable has sufficient stalls for all the horses on the station. There are implement, chaff, and wheat sheds, blacksmith shop, oil and paint shop, and timber shed. Koonibba Mission Station is built on a plain called by the [local Aboriginal people*[364]*] 'Koorapuny' (magpies nest)...There are on the station about 150 [Aboriginal people], of whom a number still live in camps nearby, receiving employment and maintenance from the station. The wurlies number about 40, and are built with mallee ribs covered with tea-tree and bags, the whole being fastened with wire. The [Aboriginal people] work by the week, but in some instances by contract. When employed at a distance from headquarters they take a supply of food with them, but can go a long while without a renewal of water supply, as they satisfy their requirements from a particular kind of mallee root...*

Several attempts have been made on Koonibba station to bore for water, but no fresh supply has been obtained. There are 70 [Aboriginal people] on the station, who have been baptised, and 30 are members of the Lutheran Church.

On the Sunday morning divine service was held in the Koonibba Church...There were present about 80 [Aboriginal people], 29 of whom received the Lord's sacrament. About 40 white people also attended, including the delegates.[365]

The crops at Koonibba are exceedingly poor, and unless rain falls soon will not return seed. Feed for stock is very short, and horses and cattle are in low condition. One farmer in the neighbourhood has lost 17 horses, but fortunately none have died at the mission station, but many are more or less affected with 'sand.' One station owner near Fowler's Bay we were told, has lost 20,000 sheep this year.[366]

The mission was managed by the South Australian government from 1963 and the Koonibba Aboriginal Community Council from 1975.[367] The 1997 *Bringing Them Home* report identified this mission as an institution housing Aboriginal and Torres Strait Islander children who had been removed from their families,[368] contributing to intergenerational trauma.

1838: The Schulz Family, part of 'Kavel's people'

Chapter 7: The Schulz Family, from Klemzig, Prussia, to Klemzig South Australia and the Barossa Valley

Introduction

The Schulz family came to South Australia as part of 'Kavel's people', refugees fleeing religious persecution with Pastor Kavel. They were sponsored by George Fife Angas from the South Australia Company along with the whole of Pastor Kavel's group. The Schulz family was the first boatload of Prussians to arrive in South Australia in 1838 on the *Prince George* (the second ship was the *Zebra*). The first group would settle just outside of Adelaide in the suburb of Klemzig – including my forebears. They would then turn towards the Barossa Valley. In Klemzig, South Australia there is a memorial to the Prussian emigrants identifying the exact place of residence of each family, including our Schulz ancestors.

1st Generation to arrive in Australia

Johann Gottfried Schulz (born 3rd February 1812, died 1869 aged 57 years) and **Johanna Eleonore Schulz** (nee Rau) (born 4th February 1814, died 1873 aged 59 years) were from Klemzig, district of Zullichau, Provence of Brandenburg, Prussia.[369] This is now Klepsk, district of Sulechow, Poland (due to a change in borders), not far from present day Berlin. Also travelling on the same boat (and also from Klemzig) appear to be Johann's parents (Georg) Friedrich Schulz/Schultz[370] (1785-1858) (thresher-gardener) and Anna Elisabeth Woidt (1782-1848), and four other children.[371]

The left Klemzig on the 8th July 1838 via Plymouth and arrived at Holdfast Bay on 18th November 1838. Johann Gottfired and Johanna Eleonore Schulz travelled with a son, Johann Friederich aged 1 ½ who died at sea from severe skin disease and dropsy.[372] Johann Gottfried Schulz was a 'servant, coachman, agricultural labourer.'[373]

Pastor Kavel had arranged with George Fife Angas – founder of the South Australia Company - for the Prussians to emigrate. Angas ended up giving them money from his own pocket as the SA company said their priority was for people from British stock. They were later required to pay back Angas at considerable interest rates.[374] Angas was sympathetic to the Lutherans, being a Freechurchman who had to leave France for religious reasons.[375]

The Schulz family first settled at a place they named Klemzig (after their homeland) in South Australia and later moved to Light's Pass, Barossa Valley.[376] Even though they were fleeing persecution, and known as industrious by the British settlers, the pastor at Klemzig was concerned that his flock was more interested in earthly than spiritual endeavours. This included my ancestor Schulz.

> *Incidentally, one would be very much mistaken to suppose that the emigrating adults were all shining lights as Christians…Most of the adults were spiritually dead or did not have an understanding to give an account of their faith. Some of these sought earthly fortune, earthly freedom, and earthly well-being. Most went along because one or another of the family was leaving. The servant Schultz [sic], the wheelwright Petras, a drinker and a gambler, the day-Labourer Schubert, an idler, the wife of day-Labourer Honke, a thief and a liar, the wife of day-Labourer Christian Rau, a bad tempered woman, and similarly several others, were completely without special merit; they were easy to replace. Klemzig, 1838, W Kauffman, Pastor*
>
> *Iwan (1995, p. 76)*

Johann Gottried and Johanna Eleonore Schulz had the following children:[377]

Johann Friederich Schulz (born 1837 died 26th Aug, 1838, at sea, 1 ½ yrs)

Johanna Caroline Schulz (born 5th Dec 1840, Klemzig, SA)

Johann Gottfried Andreas Schulz (born 8th April, 1843, Klemzig, SA)

Friedrich Wilhelm Schulz (born 3rd Jan, 1846, Klemzig, SA)

Carl August Schulz (born 7th Sept, 1848, Rowland Flat, SA)

Johanna Mathilde Schulz (born 2nd October 1850, Rowland Flat, SA)

Johanna Luise Schulz (born 31st May 1853, Rowland Flat, SA)

Maria Elizabeth Schulz (born 28th May 1856, Rowland Flat, SA)

Photos of sisters of Friedrich Wilhelm Schulz: Above left, Louisa Schulz (Johanna Luise Schulz, b. 1853) (courtesy the late Clive Schulz) Right: Johanna Caroline Schulz (b.1840) (Moad family history)

These children would inter-marry with other German emigrants, contributing to building large German communities across South Australia.

Painting: Klemzig, SA, Angas George French, courtesy National Library of Australia 7342551-v

PRG 280/1/40/72

Nixon Drawing; Klemzig, German Village on the Torrens, South Australia, 1845, State Library of SA [PRG280/1/40/72]

2nd Generation in Australia

Friedrich Wilhelm Schulz was born on the 3rd of January 1846, the middle of eight children, and was a farmer in Schreiberau, near Tanunda, and later of Lyndoch. On the 3rd August 1870, he signed an oath to become one of the constables for the Tanunda region, but he would soon be on the wrong side of the law.

Friedrich married **Anna Dorathea Gramp** (born 4th May1845 at Jacob's Creek, and died 2nd October 1932 Rowland Flat).[378] Anna Gramp was the second child of Johann Gramp and Johanne Eleonore Nitschke. Anna and Friedrich Schulz were the first couple to be married at the Trinity Lutheran Church at Rowland Flat, which had just been built before their marriage. Friedrich's father Johann Gottfried Schulz played a key role in the establishment of the church:

> *J.G. Schulz a member of the congregation offered as a donation the piece of land where the church stands today. The foundation stone was laid on 14th May 1867. The dedication service took place on 25th August 1867. A porch and vestry were added later and a Saturday School was established in 1899.*[379]

Friederich and Anna Schulz had ten children, two of whom died young:[380]

George William (Bill) Schulz (born 9th May 1869 Halletts Valley, married (Ida) Emma Kleeman 29th April 1898 in Tanunda, died 1906)

Clara Louise Schulz (born 1871 Halletts Valley, married Alfred Ernest Rudolph Bruckkman 1893, lived in Kangarilla, SA)

Anna Amanda Schulz (born 24th September 1874 Hallets Valley, died 28th March 1884 in Tanunda, aged 9 years)

Herman Richard Schulz (born 29th November 1872, married Anna Louise Geue, died 22nd October 1939)[381]

Helena Marie Schulz (born 10th June 1876 at Schreiberhau, married Michael Patrick Fahy, died 23rd March 1957)

Mata Maria Schulz (born 26th June 1878 Halletts Valley, married Ernest Gottlieb Graetz 1896, lived in Henty, NSW and died there 31st December 1934)

Ben Schulz (married Millie Floss and lived in NSW)

Anna Elisabeth Schulz (born 17th October 1880 Hallets Valley, died 11th February 1914 Tanunda, aged 23)

Emma Bertha Schulz (born 23rd May 1887, Tanunda, married Friedrich Wilhelm Koch (Fred Koch) 4th July 1912 – have photo of marriage, died 20th April 1965)

Heinrich (Heine) Bernhard Schulz[382] (b 22nd May, 1889 Halletts Valley, married Clara Seidel, died 13th April 1973)

An Alcoholic in the Barossa Valley

Unfortunately, Anna Gramp had not chosen wisely in Friedrich Schulz as he was a violent alcoholic who had appeared in court for assaulting his wife, and all local winemakers were ordered to not serve him any alcohol for 12 months. Not all was well between Friedrich and Anna.

> *MAGISTRATES' COURT. TANUNDA: FRIDAY, JANUARY 8. [Before Mr. J. Rudall. S.M.] F.W. Schulz, of Hallet's Valley, was fined 20s. and 15s. costs for committing an assault on his wife on December 28. The same defendant was also proved to be addicted to the habitual use in excess of intoxicating liquors, and an order was made prohibiting licensed victuallers and wine dealers to supply defendant with intoxicating drinks for twelve calendar months.*

South Australian Register, 11 January 1886

Friedrich Schulz died at Lyndoch on the 6th November 1902 and was buried at Rowland Flat. Anecdotally, as told to my sister by a member of the Schulz family, there was a suggestion that Friedrich died suspiciously over a dispute with the Gramp family. There was a family rumour passed down that Friedrich had left Anna for another woman, taking a large sum of money resulting from the sale of some property, and that he was separated from Anna at the time.[383] The money from the sale of land was allegedly not present with him when he died. Friedrich was living at Lyndoch, and his wife Anna was living at Hallet's Valley at the time of his death. The original will of 1883 was read to F.W. Schulz and acknowledged, with witnesses Friedrich Ludwig Richter (Medical Practitioner), Lyndoch, and Johann Ehrhardt Gramp, Farmer, Jacob's Creek (one of Anna's younger brothers).[384] Anna was the sole executor of Friedrich's will, and it was proven in the Supreme Court of South Australia on the 19th March 1903. The estate was worth £840. There was also said to be a coronial inquest into Friedrich's death, however, there is no record in the Coroner's reports 1900-1910[385] or inquests 1800-1942.[386]

Photo: Great grandmother Helena Marie Schulz (Lena Fahy), (daughter of Anna Schulz (nee Gramp) and Friedrich Wilhelm Schulz) circa 1887, (courtesy the late Clive Schulz)

Photo: Brothers Heine Schulz (left), George William (Bill) Schulz and Herman Richard Schulz, Greeve Photographic Studio, Tanunda. This looks to be taken for a wedding – prior to 1906 (courtesy the late C. Schulz)

Image: Memorial Card from the funeral of George William (Bill) Schulz (tinsmith), who died age 37 years, on September 18th, 1906, probably of some sickness (courtesy C. Schulz). The verse reads:

'Father is gone but not forgotten, Nor is the good advice he gave, Sweetest thoughts shall ever linger, Around our darling father's grave, Long days and nights he bore in pain, To wait for cure was all in vain, But God alone, who thought it best, Did ease his pain and gave him rest,

DEEPLY MOURNED.'

The Schulz family also appeared to be involved in missionary or at least Sunday School teaching in the Lutheran faith (Immanuel Synod). I have a photo taken circa 1905 of William (Bill) Schulz (who is pictured standing with his two brothers seated on a previous page), who died aged 37 in 1906 (as per the funeral card on the previous page), with a group of six Aboriginal children. This was possibly taken at a Sunday school in the Barossa Valley, as Bill was a Sunday School teacher (the photo was given to our family by the late Clive Schulz). I have not been able to use this photo in this book as I have been unable to meet with and get advice from Ngadjuri Elders regarding the inclusion of the photo in this edition of the book.

Photo: Marriage of Emma Schulz to Fred Koch, Rowland Flat, SA, 4th July 1912. Helena Fahy nee Schulz is seated at left with her daughters seated on the ground (photo courtesy the late Clive Schulz)

Photo: Marriage of Heine Schulz and Clara Seidel (it was said that Heine took on his bride's name) (courtesy the late Clive Schulz)

Photo: members of the Schulz/Seidel family - the person on the left appears to be Heine Schulz and the person with the baby could be his wife Clara nee Seidel) The two young girls dressed alike appear to be twins. (courtesy Clive Schulz)

Photo: Ben & Millie Schulz and family (lived in NSW). Children include (oldest to youngest) Rita, Norma, Jean, Joyce, Ken and Beau (the youngest appear to be twins) (courtesy the late Clive Schulz).

In the Supreme Court
Testamentary Causes Jurisdiction

This is the last Will and Testament

of me Friedrich Wilhelm Schulz of Schreiberau in the Province of South Australia Farmer After payment of all my just debts funeral and testamentary expenses I give devise and bequeath all my real and personal estate whatsoever and wheresoever unto my Wife Anna Dorothea Schulz formerly Gramp for her absolute use and benefit And I hereby appoint and nominate my said wife Anna Dorothea Schulz Executrix of this my will And hereby revoking all wills by me heretofore made I do declare this to be my last Will and Testament. In witness whereof I have hereunto set my hand this eleventh day of June One thousand eight hundred and eighty three.

F. Wm Schulz

Signed and acknowledged by the said Friedrich Wilhelm Schulz the Testator by a Mark after being read to him as and for his last Will and Testament in the presence of us both being present at the same time who at his request in his presence and in the presence of each other have hereunto subscribed our names as witnesses

Theod. Ludwig Richter Med. Pract. Lyndoch
Johann Ehrhardt Gramp Farmer Jacobs Creek

The above Will of Friedrich Wilhelm Schulz formerly of Schreiberau in the State of South Australia in the Commonwealth of Australia but late of Lyndoch in the said State Farmer deceased who died at Lyndoch aforesaid on the sixth day of November 1902 was proved in the Supreme Court of South Australia on the nineteenth day of March 1903 by Anna Dorothea Schulz of Lyndoch aforesaid Widow the relict of the said deceased the sole executrix therein named.

Dated this 19th day of March 1903

(S) Alex. Buchanan
Acting Registrar

Estate sworn not to exceed in value £840

Extracted by R. B. von Bertouch Solicitor Mutual Life Chambers 44 Grenfell Street Adelaide and also at Mount Barker.

Image: Will of Friedrich Wilhelm Schulz proven in the Supreme Court of South Australia[387]

Anna Schulz may have been too busy managing her own farm to be involved in the Gramp family winemaking business. When her husband died nearly thirty years before her, she took a prominent role in successfully managing (with eldest surviving son Herman Richard Schulz) her own farm at Halletts Valley (outside Tanunda), until the farm was handed down to him. They made a significant economic contribution through the management and development of the farm. Anna led a long life with a number of challenges, including a violent alcoholic spouse and the early deaths of two children, but died a woman much loved by her family. Her obituaries are as follows:

> *Mrs Anna Dorothea Schulz, of Hallet's Valley, who died recently at her residence, was born at Hope Valley on May 4, 1845. She was the second daughter of the late Mr and Mrs Johannes Gramp. On November 6, 1867 she was married to Mr Friedrich Wilhelm Schulz in the Lutheran Church at Rowland's Flat. This was the first wedding the church, which had just been completed. Mrs Schulz remained a member of the church all her life. After their marriage Mr and Mrs Schulz moved to Hallet's Valley, where farming and gardening pursuits were successfully carried out. Her husband died in 1902, and Mrs Schulz, with her children, carried on the farm for another 20 years, and then handed it over to her eldest son on the share system. The deceased, who was 87, lived at Hallet's Valley for 65 years. She leaves three sons. Messrs Richard Schulz, of Hallet's Valley; Ben Schulz, of Walla Walla, NSW; and Heinrich Benjamin Schulz of Tanunda; and daughters, Mesdames Alf Bruchmann of Kangarilla; Mick Fahy of Plympton, Gottlieb Graetz of Urangeline East, NSW and Friedrich Koch, of Stockport.*
>
> *The Advertiser,*[388] *October 1932*
>
> *ANNA DOROTHEA SCHULZ (nee Gramp)*
>
> *The deceased was born at Hope Vally on May 4th 1845. She was baptised by Pastor Kavel and confirmed by Pastor Muecke. In 1867 the departed entered holy wedlock with Friedrich Wilhelm Schulz, and resided at Hallett's Valley. The issue of the marriage was four*

sons and six daughters. On Sunday, October 2nd, she peacefully fell asleep in faith in her Saviour. Her mortal remains were laid to rest on Rowland's Flat cemetery on October 4th, Pastor J. Georg officiating. Texts: 2 Cor. 5: 1-3 (German) and Is 53:5 (English).

Peacefully sleeping, resting at last;

Life's weary trials and suffering past;

In silence she suffered, in patience she bore,

Till God called her home to suffer no more.

-Inserted by her loving children and grandchildren.

Australian Lutheran, 9th December 1932[389]

When son Herman Richard Schulz died in 1938 his obituary described his early life farming and working for his Uncle's Gustav Gramp's winery:

Death of Mr Hermann Richard Schulz, nearly 66, of Hallets Valley, near Tanunda...he had been in good health until recently; the last illness being very brief. He was the second son of the late Mr and Mrs Friedrich Wilhelm Schulz, and was born at Hallets Valley on November 29, 1872. He was christened, confirmed and married in the Rowlands Flat Church, where also his funeral sermon was delivered.

He attended Tanunda school, but at an early age had to stay home and help his father. Later he was employed for many years by his uncle, Mr G. Gramp, at Rowlands Flat Winery, and on February 19, 1900 he married Miss Anna Louise, elder daughter of Mr and Mrs Aug. Geue, of Lyndoch: Pastor Ey officiating. The couple lived at Lyndoch until about 24 years ago, when Mr Schulz took over the old family home at Halletts Valley, and looked after the farm and garden property. Although not prominent in public affairs, he was a man of quiet understanding who made his years full of usefulness and service.

George [Pastor Johannes Wilhelm Georg] ministered at the funeral in Rowlands Flat Cemetery on Monday, the bearers being Messrs C. Zerk, G. Haese, F. Zerk, P. Koch, B. Liebich and G. Braunack. District esteem was indicated by the large collection of floral tributes, including a beautiful wreath from Tanunda Welfare Club, and another from Mr Guerin[390]*, scholars and the staff.*

Surviving with Mrs Schulz are four sons and eight daughters: Messrs Hugo, Adolph, Glen and Master Cliff Schulz, all of Halletts Valley; Mrs A. Sonntag, Keyneton, Mrs E. H. Dutschke, Karoonda; Mrs O Wuttke, Glenelg; Mrs Aug. Milde, Rowlands Flat; Mrs F. Heinrich, Miss Edna Schulz, both of Halletts Valley; Miss Ruby Schulz, Tanunda; and Miss Lorna Schulz, of Halletts Valley. There are two brothers and three sisters surviving; Mr Ben Schulz, Walla Walla NSW; Mr H. B. Schulz, Tanunda; Mrs A. Brookman, Kangarilla,; Miss M. Fahy, South Plympton; and Mrs F. Koch, Stockport.

Leader Angaston, 27 October 1938

Visits to Germany

I have been to Germany four times, as part of two longer European trips in 1997 (Colbe, Munich) and 2002 (Weimar, Berlin, Postdam), and when I was living in Geneva (end of 2010-beginning of 2014). I went to Berlin twice for work (Global Health Forum 2012 and 2013) and joined that with a holiday with friends. I have a lifelong German friend I met when I was studying my undergraduate degree at Flinders University in Adelaide (Berndt), whom I have stayed with in Colbe and Weimar, and we have caught up in Berlin as well as Basel when I lived in Switzerland (as well as Hobart and Adelaide!). I have also been to Bavaria where the Gramp family is from – the capital at least (Munich) but have not been to the place where the Schulz family was originally from Klemzig, which is now Klępsk in Poland (the closest I have been is Berlin). I have also had two visits to Austria (1997 and 2002), travelling around the country with Austrian friend Michael whom I met when I lived in Hobart.

It was amazing to think that whilst my grandfather Stephen William White fought against Germany in WWI my friends' grandfathers (German friend Berndt and Austrian friend Michael) were fighting on the other side – and my grandfather would come home to adopt a child whose descendants hailed from Germany! My friends have generously shown me around their cities or countries and that includes deep dives into historical places (especially as Berndt is a sociologist), some of which have been extremely moving (such as Buchenwald) and I hope we never repeat the horrors of the past. Berlin is such a vibrant, cool city and I have really enjoyed my time there.

Photo: Sam with friend Diana with Marx and Engels Statue in Berlin, October 2012 (S.Battams)

Part 3: Mother's Maternal Ancestry

1854: The Seafaring Rumbelow Family of Encounter Bay

Chapter 8: The Rumbelow Family of Encounter Bay

Introduction

The Rumbelow family of Encounter Bay are a well-known fishing family, with the place once known locally by European settlers as 'Rumbelow Town.' Encounter Bay was named following the encounter between French explorer Nicholas Baudin (who was advanced in his attitudes towards First Nations people at the time) and English explorer Matthew Flinders. The traditional owners and custodians of the land are the Ramindjeri people, part of the Ngarrindjeri. There are different theories of the origins of the name Rumbelow: one theory is that it is an Anglo-Saxon name which refers to a person who lived near three hills,[391] mounds or barrows, a kind of ancient burial mound; another that it derives from a sea shanty; whilst others claiming it has French/Norman (de Romylou) or German (Rumbold) origins.[392]

First Generation in Australia

My great-great-great grandfather **Malin Rumbelow** (1812-1884), his wife Alice (nee Pitches) (1812-1890) and family were from Mildenhall, Suffolk in the United Kingdom, and travelled to South Australia, arriving at Port Adelaide on 5th October 1854 on the *Pestonjee Bemanjee*, on a long 114 day journey, with 350 emigrants. Malin senior left his twin Thomas (both baptised 29th March 1812), in the UK[393]. Malin was thought to be named after his mother's maiden name (Mayling) and his name was spelt 'Maylin' on the baptism, however it soon became Malin (which means 'clever,' 'cunning' or 'devious' in French).

The ship the Rumbelows travelled on had an eventful life and was built in Dumbarton Scotland in 1834. In 1838 it brought the second Governor of South Australia, George Gawler, to the state. In 1841, the master of the

Pestonjee Bemanjee was murdered by Chinese villagers in the Chusan (Zhoushan) islands. From 1845 to 1849, the ship was a convict ship transporting convicts to Van Dieman's Land (Tasmania).

There were eight Rumbelow children who travelled on the ship, with their children including:
Godfrey Rumbelow (1832 – 1855)
Alice Rumbelow (1833 – 1920)
Samuel Rumbelow (1836-1837)
Sophia Rumbelow (1838-1895)
Mahalia Rumbelow (1840-1879)
Caroline Rumbelow (1843-1935)
Malen 2nd Rumbelow (1846 -1905 -spelling changed from Malin to Malen)
Emma Rumbelow (1849 - 1938)
Sarah Rumbelow (1852 - 1923)

Alice senior was pregnant on board the ship, and she gave birth to **David Godfrey Rumbelow** on 8 March 1855. Alice was lucky to survive the trip and not to have given birth on board, as another woman died whilst giving birth on board, and diarrhoea was common on the ship. However, shortly after they arrived in South Australia, eldest son Godfrey died aged 23 years. Another child, **Hannah Rumbelow**, was born 3rd February 1858.

Following the marriage of Alice Rumbelow to Cain Jelliff in January 1855, the family travelled directly to Victor Harbor by bullock dray, settling at Encounter Bay. Later he acquired land, and was a farmer and contractor:

> *Council Assessments for 1856-66 show that Malin Rumbelow owned part section 82 of 3 acres with house and garden...section 11 of 40 acres (eastern side of Tabernacle Road, part of the Lake Development) part sections 173 and 174 of 50 acres (in the angle formed by the Inman Valley Road and Swains Crossing Road) and lot 33 in section 17 of 1/2 acre*[394].

They settled in a small stone cottage in Beach Street (now Maud Street), at Newlandtown, named after Reverend Ridgeway Newland. Reverand Newland was an early European settler in Encounter Bay.

> *Reverend Ridgeway Newland and his party (of 34) left Staffordshire, England in January 1839 aboard the Sir Charles Forbes. On arrival at Port Adelaide, he sent five men overland [three settlers and two Aboriginal men who guided them]*[395] *with stock [a cow, four bullocks, some sheep and goats]*[396] *and the rest of the party travelled on board the Lord Hobart to Encounter Bay where he had already taken up land. They were recognised as the first European settlers in Encounter Bay. However, two boys, William and Alexander Honeyman, were living in Victor Harbor before European settlement in Adelaide. They had travelled to Sydney with their widowed mother* [Jane and sisters] *on the Castle Forbes Bay in 1822; William was then 15 and Alexander 9 years* [their father was an escaped convict who had died on the run].
>
> *The boys were escaping from their strict step-father John Lander,*[397] *and to get away joined a whaling boat [which mainly worked in Tasmanian waters but also went to the South Australian coast]*[398] *which proved to be very unseaworthy and when it pulled into Victor to do some repairs they jumped ship and swam ashore. [It was claimed they lived with the local Ramindjeri people] until they were told [by them] of the landing at Holdfast Bay. Both boys then walked to Adelaide [where William worked as a chainman for Colonel Light when he was surveying Adelaide]*[399] *but later returned to Victor, and their descendants are still there today.*[400]

Malin senior, Malen 2nd and his brother-in-law Cain Jelliff (a sailor) founded a fishing business in 1864. Malin Rumbelow (1st) had no prior experience with the sea, being a farmer and Agricultural Labourer in England. The women in the family had roles in scaling the fish caught ready for market, along with selling the fish. Malin had sight in only one eye and was quite disabled for the last 20 years of his life.

Photo above left: Malin and Alice Rumbelow, Source: https://www.rumbelow.net/
Right: Maud Street Cottage, home of Malin and Alice Rumbelow (M. Miller)
Below: Malin and Alice Rumbelow, Source: https://www.rumbelow.net/

Edward Robert Bolger married three Rumbelow Sisters

Edward Bolger was a significant person in the family as he married three Rumbelow sisters! He claimed that he was 'descended from an Irish lord,' although there is no proof of this, and as he was born 30th November1845 in Tasmania[401] this made me believe he could have descended from convict stock. His parents were Anna Maria Geary[402] and Robert Bolger,[403] who travelled from Launceston to Port Phillip, Victoria in 1841. They married in a Presbyterian church in Geelong, Victoria, 1st February 1842 and had three children: Emily,[404] Edward Robert[405] and Mary Ann.

Robert Bolger was a publican in Corio, Geelong in 1841[406], and Master of the Cutter *Shamrock* that sailed between Launceston and Victoria.[407] In 1841 he challenged his barman to a duel, which never eventuated, much to the disappointment of the 'good people of Corio.'[408] Being a Mariner, Robert was highly mobile and in 1845 he sailed with his wife and three children from Melbourne to Port Adelaide on the boat *Mary*.[409] In 1849 Bolger's five-oared whaleboat *Kate* participated in the Tasmanian prize race for the Hobart Regatta.[410]

On the 18th March 1850 Bolger was listed as a crew member of the *Lady Denison*, going from Adelaide to Hobart Town.[411] It was said that the boat went missing whilst sailing between Port Adelaide and Hobart, and sank near Church Island, North West of Tasmania.[412] However, there is no newspaper report of a wreck of the *Lady Denison* or a wreck near Church Island in the 1850s. Additionally, on 20th July 1850 Robert Bolger travelled from Hobart Town to Port Adelaide on *The Punch*,[413] although some state that only Mrs Ann Bolger and her 3 children arrived in South Australia from Hobart. The *Lady Denison* brig also continued to operate between Australia (Hobart) and New Zealand (NZ) in the 1860s, and between Adelaide and Hobart.[414] It was wrecked at Wanganui (NZ) in 1865,[415] however was still operating and sailing to Wanganui in 1867.[416]

It is uncertain when Robert Bolger died or if he was still active in the whale business.[417] In October 1850 a Robert Bolger travelled from Hobart Town to Port Jackson,[418] on the *North Esk*.[419] A Mr and Mrs Bolger also left from Adelaide for Melbourne on the 20th December 1851. A publican named Boulger was involved in a court case regarding the Clarendon Hotel in Victoria in 1857.[420] In April 1851, Robert and Ann's 18-month-old daughter Mary Ann died. Ann was said to be widowed and remarried, but her second husband also died shortly after in Port Elliot.

Edward Bolger became an upstanding and responsible citizen who was a former chairman of the Victor Harbor District Council and a council member for many years. Bolger marrying three of the Rumbelow sisters (!) was only made possible due to the *Deceased Wife's Sister Act 1870*[421], a first in the commonwealth colonies. It was made necessary due to a shortage of women in the Colony. Firstly, Edward married Mahalia Rumbelow in 1866 after her first husband Henry Weymouth died. When Mahalia died, Edward married her sister Alice in 1879 after her husband Cain Jelliff died (Alice and Cain had been together for 23 years). Edward and Alice were married for over 40 years,[422] with Alice bringing up her sister Mahalia's children. Alice was a strong woman in the family, who played a key role in hawking the fish caught by the family, and taking it to the market. After Alice died, Edward married Emma Rumbelow in 1921 after her husband Thomas Watson died. Bolger Way in Encounter Bay[423] is named after Edward Bolger.

2nd Generation in Australia

Malen Rumbelow (2nd) (1846-1905) married Mary Glassenbury (1845-1923). Their children included:

William Henry (Henry) Rumbelow (1864 - 1928)

David 'Malen' Rumbelow (1866 – 10th April 1905)

Godfrey (2nd) Rumbelow (1869 - 1942)

Alice Hester Rumbelow (1871 - 1957)

Rose Mary Rumbelow (1875 - 1955)

Cain Jelliff Rumbelow (1877 - 1952)

Maria Jane Rumbelow (1880 - 1960)

Samuel Rumbelow (1881 - 1886)

Grace Emily Rumbelow (1885 – 1973)

After their wedding, Malen and Mary initially lived in a basic wooden cottage on the foreshore with a shingle roof, dubbed 'The Crystal Palace' by visitor Captain Parkes. They later had their house 'Yeltanna' (cool place) built next to the cottage around 1880 from granite chips obtained from West Island near the Bluff (whilst the good quality stone was reserved for (Old) Parliament House, Adelaide).[424] The men who supplied the stone would row across to the island every Monday, whilst the building contractor Mr Oliver would come back to collect the men the following Saturday morning. The workers lived on the island in shacks and tents whilst cutting the granite. It appears that all did not go well with the building contractor, as one at least two occasions there was fighting reported between Oliver and Edward Bolger in 1876.

In 1886, Malen and Mary's son Samuel Rumbelow died on the 13th December 1886, aged 5 years, from a congenital condition associated with spina bifida.

An article from 1907 describes the Rumbelow family in Encounter Bay, when Henry Rumbelow left to farm in Narrung. It describes Godfrey (my great grandfather) being unsuited to the fishing life as he became seasick, 'oftentimes to the point of bringing up blood.' He had a close encounter with a 10-foot-long carpet shark when fishing as a youth with his brother Henry, and he just managed to scramble back into the boat before falling prey. He instead took the fish to the market in Adelaide and sent consignments of fish to Ballarat, had a milk run in Victor Harbor, and farmed at Waitpinga.

Photo above: Malen (2nd) and Family at Yeltanna. Back: Alice, Godfrey, Jane, Cain, Rose. Front: David Malen, Malen (2nd), Mary, William and Grace (on the ground) Below: Malen 2nd at Yilki with crayfish. Source: Rumbelow and Descendants: https://www.rumbelow.net/

The following article also describes a funeral pyre and ceremony of the local Ramindjeri people – sorry business – seen by Alice Rumbelow. At the time cremation was not commonly practiced amongst the Europeans. Cremation was a topic of public debate in the 1890s in Australia, with it first being officially introduced in the Colony of South Australia in 1891 (the first place in Australia). The Aboriginal cremation practice was referred to in the article in a disrespectful way (not repeated here) as was probably done locally at the time by non-Aboriginal people. The whole ceremony was a practice very different from that of the Europeans, and was likely to be sacred and extremely moving.

> *THE RUMBELOW FAMILY. REMARKABLE FISHERMEN AND BOATMEN.*
> *[By our Victor Harbour Correspondent.]*
>
> *—Whaling Days and Corroborees.—*
>
> *Then the whaling industry was in full swing. Every visitor to the Bluff has viewed with interest the old jetty, and the old shed has been painted by many artists.*
>
> *Mr. Rumbelow did not take an active interest in whaling, but for a time worked at the old shed, and assisted in the boiling down of one monster of the deep. At this time there were many people living near the Bluff, whalers and their families, but these and even their cottages have long since disappeared. There were many [Aboriginal people – Ramindjeri-Ngarrindjeri] residing at the bay in those days, and numerous corroborees were witnessed by the family. The Rumbelows witnessed ... [an Aboriginal cremation pyre and ceremony] which was enacted not far from the Bluff...the [Aboriginal women] who sat round anointed their bodies with the dripping oil and wailed piteously...Mrs. R. E. Bolger, who was Miss [Alice] Rumbelow, and is still living at the harbour, witnessed this gruesome scene. On another occasion a[n] [Aboriginal man] who had gone out in a whaling boat died, and when the body was*

brought to shore the scene made by the wailing [Aboriginal women] over the dead brave, and the mournful procession to the scrub, made a harrowing spectacle never to be forgotten.

—An Historic Partnership.—

Mr. Rumbelow and his son-in-law decided to enter on a fishing business. A boat was purchased from a whaler named Long, and the historic partnership of Rumbelow, fishers, began. Mr. Jeliff had been a sailor, and so trained the others in the business, but it soon became apparent that the Rumbelows were boatmen by nature. During this time the lad of eight years who had come with the family had grown to young manhood, and he, too exhibited the natural aptitude of the father to boating. These men were really the pioneers of the local fishing industry, which they put upon a sound business basis. They were so careful in seamanship that mishaps were rare. The only losses recorded against the whole partnership were a cutter, which sank at its moorings at the Bluff and the original Ferret was sent ashore during a storm of great severity one night at the bay.

—Fish for Adelaide.—

The fish caught was taken in carts to Adelaide, and Mrs. [Alice] Jeliff did most of the hawking in the early days. Schnapper and crayfish were captured in large quantities.

Meanwhile young Rumbelow had married, and in course of time five sons and four daughters were born to the family—the sons Henry, Malin, Godfrey, and Cain.

From early infancy these boys became toilers of the sea, and helped grandfather and father in the work. Mr. Jeliff, the original partner of the Rumbelows, while fishing near Goolwa fell from the boat one dark night, and was drowned. As the boys grew to manhood, all save Godfrey showed in various ways their aptitude for a seafaring life. Godfrey was placed in charge of the hawking of the produce, travelling to Adelaide in a van with loads of fish, and frequently crayfish. When train service was available Godfrey tried the fishing and boating again, but it had become distasteful. He entered other pursuits, and is now a principal milk vendor to the harbour.

—Boatmen by Nature.—

The father and son Malin were boatmen by Nature, and as visitors began to make the bay a holiday resort they devoted themselves largely to catering to the boating pleasure parties. The father became a veritable institution with the visitors. At regattas in the district his management of sailing boats and his cleverness as the "duck" will long be remembered. Malin [2nd] —almost a giant in proportions—a boatman of unequalled skill, in whom even the most nervous had the utmost confidence, was of a genial, good-natured disposition, which endeared him to all—tourists, residents, and family. For many years father and son catered for the ever-increasing "visitor" business. Henry was the fisherman par excellence, not only of the family, but of the district. None knew better than he the best places for schnapper and mullet. Many magnificent hauls he has recorded—on one occasion 230 dozen mullet, and on another 300 dozen. He has also had battles with sharks, and succeeded in killing a large number.

— Exciting Experiences.—

... While Godfrey and Henry were keenly engaged in bringing to land a large haul of mullet a few seconds of great peril came. Godfrey was standing breast deep in the water when he noticed a huge shark. He called to Henry, who brought the boat with a vigorous push to within jumping distance. As Godfrey landed with one huge jump into the boat the horrid jaws of the shark just passed by—one second more and it would have been all over. Subsequently the brothers killed the monster, which measured 10½ ft. Another great feat was the successful battle which Malin had with a huge

shark near to the Bluff. The monster attacked the young fisherman. A terrible fight ensued, and Malin succeeded in killing the shark, which measured 12 ft. 6 in.

The boys all married and settled near each other at the bay. Soon a little village of Rumbelows grew, and has been named Rumbelow Town. About 18 years ago the grandfather of the young fisherman died. He had lived the whole time at Encounter Bay, and had never left it—not even on a visit to Adelaide. Meanwhile Mrs. Jeliff had married again, and she (Mrs. R. E. Bolger) is still living—one of the old pioneers of South Australia, and highly respected by all the neighbourhood. Over this happy village of happy, contented people a heavy blow was soon to fall—a blow that really has just shown its final effect in the breaking up of a partnership of over 40 years, in which three generations had participated, and which had become a highly treasured institution of the district.

—Giant Cut Off.—

Malin [3rd] was brought home one bright day dead. He had expired suddenly while in charge of a pleasure fishing party. Even the lifting of the body from the boat was attended with pathetic interest. He was so giant-like in size that he had to be hoisted from the cabin with ropes and the cutter's tackle. This tragic end created a profound sensation. The blow fell heavily on the father [Malen 2nd], who sank beneath it, and within three months he, too, was borne to the grave.

—Henry and Cain.—

Henry and Cain carried on the business, but the former never seemed to recover his usual vivacity. This, combined with indifferent health, at last decided him to retire from the business and seek other avenues. Therefore during the last fortnight the partnership was dissolved. Henry is moving with his family to Narrung.

Cain is still determined to continue business of fishing on his own account. Charles (son of Malin 3rd) and his mother have also begun business in The Spray, which was built by his late father. The mother of the boys [Susan Rumbelow nee Pearsons] and two sisters are keeping a boarding house at Encounter Bay [Ocean View guest home]. This is a favourite house with visitors who love fishing and boating.

But the old order changeth, yielding place to the new.

One cannot meet the Rumbelow family without admiring the genial, cheery dispositions of all and their sturdy manhood — traits that have distinguished each generation. Henry Rumbelow and his family carry with them the esteem and regard of all who know them, and it is hoped success and renewed vigour will crown them in their new sphere.

The Observer, 15 June 1907

As described above, Malen 2nd and Mary Rumbelow's son David Malen Rumbelow (also known as Malen 3rd) died on his boat on the 10th April, 1905. Malen 2nd died just over 2 months later, on the 1st July, 1905, whilst wife Mary (nee Glassenbury) died on the 27th July, 1923. Even though David Malen Rumbelow had died in 1905, in 1922 there were still 'In Memorium' notices placed by the family in his memory.

RUMBELOW – In loving memory of our dear husband and father, Malen, who passed away 10th April, 1905

We are thinking of you today, dear,
Thinking of the past,
Picturing you, in memory,
Just as we spoke to you last.

- *Inserted by his loving wife and children, also mater*

The Chronicle, 15th April, 1922

1840: The Glassenbury Family of Goolwa

Malen Rumbelow 2nd married Mary Glassenbury of Goolwa. Her parents were William Glassenbury and Esther (nee Mansfield, later McDonald), who arrived in the Colony in 1840 on the *Fairlie*, from Gloucestershire (with William, Ann, Em, and Emanuel[425] – Mary and Fred were born in the Colony).

> *They sailed from Liverpool in the ship 'Fairlie' and after a nine months' trip arrived at Adelaide on July 6th, 1840. On the trip out very rough weather was experienced, and the ship also caught fire, but only little damaged was caused. The only building at Adelaide then was an iron shed; used as Government stores, and the new arrivals had to camp in it for the first night after landing.*
>
> *Wangaratta Chronicle, 24th July 1918*[426]

Esther Mansfield had married Robert McDonald in England, but her spouse died, and she was left with a child to care for (Ann McDonald), who came to Australia.[427] Esther remarried William Glassenbury in Stroud, Gloucestershire, England, in 1837.

An *Advertiser* article of 7th July 1909 called 'The WONDER OF THE WORLD'[428] describes the interesting and dangerous life of Mary Glassenbury's brother Fred Glassenbury, along with the early pioneering days of father William who had worked as a gardener for explorer Captain Charles Sturt at Reedbeds, whilst his wife Esther took in washing and ironing for employment. They saved enough money to buy a bullock dray, bullocks, an old wagon, and horses and with son William then became involved in carting food to the Burra copper mines, and copper from the mines back to Adelaide for treatment.

Photo: Explorer and Surveyor General Captain Sir Charles Sturt, whom William Glassenbury senior worked for at Reedbeds, SLSA, B6847

Mr Glassenbury's first occupation was as a gardener for Captain Charles Sturt, the great explorer, on a block of land at the Reedbeds, and his wife took in washing and ironing, as food was a terrible price then. Both being hard toilers, they got together enough money to buy a bullock dray and ten bullocks, with a very old-fashioned wagon, and six horses. These cost a lot of money. Mr Glassenbury aided by his eldest son, William, began carting on the road from Adelaide to the Burra Burra copper mines. He carted foodstuffs from Adelaide, and brought copper back to Adelaide to be treated. The [Ngadjuri] was very vicious, so that Mr Glassenbury and his son had to take turns in watching the teams by night. The [Ngadjuri people] who were numerous, would steal the horses unless care was taken, and guns had often to be fired over their heads to keep them off. One day an Aboriginal [person] threatened to kill Mr Glassenbury with his waddy, but [an Aboriginal] police [officer] thrashed the culprit. Mr Glassenbury was very kind to the [Ngadjuri people],and carried provisions to distribute among them. They were not particularly grateful. A few would come to get food, and then a large number would gather and threaten to take food meant for the mines by force if it was not given to them. Several years of this work disheartened Mr Glassenbury, and he removed to Bald Hills, in the south.[429]

Due to this tension between settlers and Ngadjuri peoples, William senior turned to farming at Bald Hills (where Fred was born) with Mr Gibson of Victor Harbor, however the farm and house was burnt, and William senior was severely burnt whilst rescuing son Fred from the flames. Shortly after, both Fred and his sister Mary contracted diphtheria, but survived.

Fred's account tells of the freedom of the children on the farm but also of the dangers and their high level of responsibilities at a young age. In one event, Fred and Mary were crossing the Inman River to bring in the cows on the farm, but when they returned the river was in flood. Older sister Mary was leading Fred by the hand when her feet slipped, and whilst she recovered, Fred fell into the river, and caught hold of the wires that crossed the river 60 metres downstream, and clung on until his sister rescued him.

Other near death scrapes throughout Fred's life included two more near drownings, encountering a few snakes and being bitten by one snake and attacked by another, being rushed by a bull, being thrown from a horse and dragged from the scrub, being kicked by a horse, and meeting a 'savage horse' that had 'killed a man in its temper', and an employer that threatened to 'thrash him.'

Fred's story also tells of local Aboriginal people (the Ngarrindjeri) rescuing him when he was a child and adult at Goolwa (or later offering advice and support on traditional medicines).

He [Fred] removed to Goolwa, and one nice moonlight evening went for a bathe in the Murray. He undertook to dive further than the best man in the crowd. He dived so far that he struck the cross currents, and when he came to the surface he was carried half a mile downstream to a sand pit, not far away from [an Aboriginal] wurlie. The [local Aboriginal people, Ngarrindjeri people] saw him float ashore and thought he was a big fish. He was wrapped in their blankets and given over to a policeman, who brought him back to consciousness.[430]

Fred was a driver for Reverend Ridgway William Newland of Encounter Bay (driving him to Bald Hills for religious service fortnightly), who was father of Mr. Simpson Newland CMG, pastoralist, politician (one time SA Treasurer)[431] and author of the novel about pioneers *'Paving the Way: A romance of the Australian bush' (1893).'* At one stage Fred broke his toe when a horse stood on his foot, and Reverend Newland had to drive him to a Doctor. When working for Mr Edward Ernest Dutton (1863-1944) at the 'Ardune' property at Lucindale, he was galloping a horse to get other horses into the yard, when he slipped and he fell under it, and was confined to a bed for some time. In another near-death experience, Fred Glassenbury was almost buried alive:

> *Whilst sinking a well with Mr. A. M. Childs, of Goolwa, the earth slipped at a depth of 14 ft., and buried Mr. Glassenbury up to his neck. His mate cleared the dirt and tied a rope round his waist and four men pulling at the end of a long pole they tried to lever him out like a bullock. Mr. Glassenbury is 6 ft. in height, and did not think it a joke to be stretched any taller. However, they managed to rescue him just before the well collapsed and filled up within 2 ft. of the surface.*[432]

Fred had a spine disease that had caused him to be temporarily paralysed in both legs. George Pantonie, a local Aboriginal man, advised him on Aboriginal medicine treatments and he restored back to health through this advice.

> *Mr. Glassenbury went to Nhill, Victoria, and started work for a farmer, but was taken ill and sent to the hospital, suffering from*

influenza, bronchitis, and inflammation of the lungs. He was six months in the hospital. He returned to work, but whilst carrying wheat he strained his back. He went back to the hospital, after being there three months was paralysed in both legs. He was advised to return to South Australia at once, as he could only live a few years, as he had spine disease, caused by the accident in the well, and was incurable. He returned to Goolwa, and whilst going home one day he fainted and fell. The doctor not being at home, the chemist advised him to enter the Adelaide Hospital without delay. He was sounded by the doctors, and a galvanic battery was adjusted to strengthen his spine, but his nerves and heart were too weak to stand the strain, and he fainted. He was insensible for five hours. He awoke suddenly and saw men with a stretcher by his bedside waiting to carry him away, as the doctor pronounced him to be dead. But he cried out, "I'm not dead; take that stretcher away." He went home to Goolwa but was weak for several years. Then he met [an Aboriginal man] named Pantonie, who told him to try a native shrub cut in pieces and applied to the seat of the pain between two cloths. Now he is a new man, practically speaking. He is known in Goolwa as "the wonder of the world." At 58 years of age, he carries ten scars, which will remain until his death. He has been a great athlete. Once he cleared 5 ft. 7¼ in. in a high jump, and he was a splendid runner. He has a wonderful constitution and never indulged in alcohol or spirits of any kind. He is staying with friends in Narrung and feels quite strong and healthy. He returns home to Goolwa shortly.[433]

George Pantonie was a well-known Aboriginal man whose obituary appeared in various Adelaide newspapers, in January 1919.[434] George had grown up at the Port McLeay Mission Station in Ngarrindjeri country, on the south banks of Lake Alexandrina in 1859, and was described as a lay preacher with excellent biblical knowledge. He was a member of the

Salvation Army and had sung before Queen Victoria at Buckingham Palace at the Diamond Jubilee with officers of the Salvation Army, before visiting other parts of Europe. He was well known to those on the Coorong (Kurangk), guiding and participating in duck shooting expeditions, he accompanied the Duke of Edinburgh on a shooting excursion on the lakes (Coorong region), and when he died he was described as a 'guide, philosopher and friend.'[435]

Fred Glassenbury's older brother (William junior) tried his luck on the goldfields, setting out to the Victorian goldfields in 1852 with many others, but he was unlucky. He turned to 'teaming,' or transporting goods via bullock and dray, with the drivers known as 'teamsters,' it was extremely hard work in the early days. He later settled in Wangaratta, Victoria in 1863. William Glassenbury junior…

> *well remembered Captain Sturt setting out from Adelaide on his exploring trip. In 1852 he heard of the rich finds of gold in Victoria...He tried mining at Bendigo and McIvor, but not meeting with success he decided to go in for teaming. ...When he passed through Wangaratta 64 years ago its few buildings were composed of slabs, bark and shingles. The teams crossed the Ovens river by means of a punt... Naturally the unformed roads were a source of great trouble to the teamsters, several of whom travelled together so that they could help each other when boggy pieces of road were met with. The teams consisted of the old two-wheeler bullock dray and from 8 to 10 bullocks, while the average load carried was 2 ½ to 3 tons. The journey from Melbourne to Beechworth and return occupied from 8 to 12 weeks, according to the seasons of the year. In the wintertime, it was not unusual for a team to only travel three or four miles in a day, and sometimes a driver camped two nights at the one spot. The prices per ton varied from £80 to £110, and good money was made...*

He had vivid recollections of the great floods of 1867 and 1873, but believed the 1917 flood was a record. During the 1867 flood the road from Wangaratta to North Wangaratta was covered with water, and the mail contractor (Mr Pratt) refused to carry the mail…Mr Glassenbury with others helped to save a number of [Chinese men] who were marooned by the waters of the 1873 flood, and even assisted to take the council boat to Evertone where they rescued a Mr Johnstone, who had been in the flood waters all night…For some time he conducted a coach building and blacksmith shop at the Ovens bridge.

Wangaratta Chroncile, 24th July 1918

Chapter 9: Third and Fourth Generations of the Rumbelow Family

3rd Generation in Australia

Great grandfather Godfrey Rumbelow, born 2nd January 1869 was the third child of Malen Rumbelow 2nd. He was said to be a keen sportsman and good at running, cricket and football. His grandson Kenneth 'Peter' Rumbelow played for Norwood in the SANFL (1959/60).[436] Godfrey Rumbelow was also a good singer, belonging to the local church choir, touring with the choir and winning a singing competition. He and his wife Ada endured hardship through their life through the early loss of two of their sons.

Central Fish Market and East End Market

Godfrey Rumbelow married Ada Heading in Adelaide in 1890. Ada was the daughter of Martha Ann Lomman and John Heading. Godfrey and Ada may have met through the church, or because Godfrey was selling fish at Edwin Daw's Central Fish Market in Adelaide[437] (he also sent consignments of fish to Ballarat[438]). This was next to the Metropolitan Ice Works in the vicinity of the current Adelaide Central Market (facing west near the corner of Gouger and Grote Streets), where Ada may have worked at one stage as her family were market gardeners mainly selling produce at the East End Market (known then as the new market).

Godfrey, who grew afraid of fishing after his near death encounter with a large shark, took over the selling of the fish from his Auntie Alice Rumbelow (Jeliff/Bolger). Rumbelow's Fish Market was later a well-known stall within the Adelaide Central Market precinct.

Godfrey Rumbelow

Photo Above: Godfrey Rumbelow as a young man, at Encounter Bay (Rumbelow and Descendants website), Below: Edwin Daw's Central Fish Market, Adelaide, 1922, SLSA, B1082

B 1082

Above: Godfrey seated below right with the Newland Congregational Choir, Rumbelow and Descendants website

Eventually Godfrey and Ada moved from Campbelltown to Waitpinga where the family had a dairy farm and milk run, and then Victor Harbor. Godfrey was a lay preacher and part of the choir in the Congregational church. Although a Methodist-Congregationalist, in 1940 it is reported that Ada was playing bridge as a fundraiser for the local St Joan of Arc Catholic church.[439] Ada and Godfrey had the following six children:

Ada May (May) Rumbelow (2nd May 1891-22nd Dec 1970) (married Herbert Reid)

Samuel Godfrey Rumbelow (27th December 1893 – 24th April 1920) (married Ruby Freda Lemon)

Frank Harris Rumbelow (26th March 1895 – 12th October 1917, Died WWI)

Stella Lillian Rumbelow (2nd April 1898-1972) (married Leonard Albert Miller)

Kenneth Stanley Rumbelow (30th July 1902 -1998) (married Reta Hentschke) (served WWII)

Dulcie Gwendoline Rumbelow (2nd March 1909-1961) (married Vernard Swain)

In 1912, after all of their children were born, Godfrey and Ada moved back to Adelaide and were living at Maylands. This is where their son Frank Harris Rumbelow lived when he enlisted in WWI in August 1915. He served in the 48th Battalion on the Western Front and was killed on the 12th October 1917 at Passchendaele Ridge - the very same day that Ada's cousin Sir John Alfred Heading took charge at Passchendaele Ridge. Frank Rumbelow is buried in the Buttes New British Cemetery, Polygon Wood, Zonnebeke, Belgium (a place I visited in 1997). It was claimed that our grandmother Stella could not stand the sound of 'the last post' due to her beloved brother Frank's death.

Photo: Ada (nee Heading) and Godfrey Rumbelow, Rumbelow and Descendants website Source: https://www.rumbelow.net/

Frank's cousin Herbert Victor Rumbelow also served in WWI (in the 50th Infantry Battalion) and returned to Australia, marrying Ada Heading's younger sister Hilda, who was 27 years younger than Ada.

Extraordinarily, I was in a Strathalbyn antique shop in 2019 and recognised a framed picture of Frank Rumbelow with three other pictures. I opened the back of the picture frame and there was Frank's writing *'To Auntie Hilda'* – discovered 102 years after his death! The other three framed pictures in the set were almost certainly members of the Heading and Rumbelow families that I had not previously seen.

Photo above: Great Uncle Frank Rumbelow, who died in WWI and is buried in Belgium (S. Battams)

Samuel (Sam) Godfrey Rumbelow also died just a few years after his brother Frank, in 1920 when he was aged 27 years. Sam had set up one of the first tourist businesses in Victor Harbor, driving tourists around in his charabanc (see photo below), between Encounter Bay, Victor Harbor, Port Elliot and Middleton. On the 19th April 1920, Sam had taken a tourist, Miss Meryl (Merle) Duall (or Duell), down to Port Elliot so she could photograph 'The Nature's Eye' at Geen Bay.[440] Suddenly she became dizzy and fell off the rocks. Sam attempted to save her by diving into the sea, but a wave swept away both of them. Other visitors pulled Meryl (Merle) out of the sea to safety, and she finally regained consciousness after 45 minutes of resuscitation by Dr S. J. Douglas. When the first wave came, he was seen standing up to his waste in water, he threw off his coat and clambered onto a rock and stood for a moment, but another wave broke over the rock and he was swept out to sea.[441] His body was later found in Green Bay. The story of Sam's death was widely reported on across Australia (in QLD, NSW, NT, SA, TAS, WA). Samuel was described as follows:

> *He gave his life in attempting to save a fellow creature from a watery grave. It was a heroic sacrifice and worthy of the one who made. ...He always had a cheery word and smile for all whom he came into contact with, and lived a life that would be a pattern for others. When his cup was overflowing with joy he enjoyed seeing others sip from it, but he bore his sorrows and cares silently and alone. For several months past he drove his own charabanc, catering for visitors, and every one of his patrons liked him for his gentlemanly manner and happy disposition. Only a few weeks back he drove a number of bandsmen to Strathalbyn and was eating his dinner there when he learnt that another charabanc with a load of band boys was stranded on the Ashborne road. He left his meal unfinished and drove back for them...He was a member of the Congregational Church Choir and possessed a rich and pleasant voice, and four members of the choir (Messrs. J. Wilton, S.D. and D. D. Bruce and H. Smith) acted as pall bearers. He was a staunch follower of the football club and was always a good loser and generous winner. The large number of folks who attended the*

service in the congregational Church prior to the funeral was a striking testimony to the popularity of Sam.

Reverend Stevens said that:

> *He has covered the name of his family with a glory that shall not die. The sea has been at once the home, the friend, and the ever-present enemy of the men of his race, and knowing its terrible power, as he and the men of his race have reason to know it, yet he dared the monster, and died in the midst of a fine and splendid deed.*
>
> *The Victor Harbor Times and Encounter Bay and Lower Murray Pilot, 23rd April 1920*

Samuel Rumbelow was married to Ruby Freda Lemon (later Hyde), and they had a daughter Doris Ada Rumbelow (born 1914) – who was just 6 when her father died. She was sent to the Methodist Ladies College (now Annesley College) for high school. Doris had a slight cognitive disability (described by her mother as 'slightly below normal mentality') and went missing in her early twenties, and despite her cognitive abilities and the unflattering description of her in the *Police Gazette*, was married twice (after having an affair on her first husband named Dowdy, she married Withy) and lived in Sydney. A year on from the tragedy, there were a number of memorial notices of Sam's death, including from the Duell family:

> *RUMBELOW – In sad and grateful memory of Samuel Godfrey Rumbelow, whose life was sacrificed in an heroic attempt to save another at Port Elliot on April 19, 1920. A tribute from Mr and Mrs Thos. Duell, and daughter Merle.*
>
> *RUMBELOW – A tribute of love and honor to my brave husband, who gave his life for another at Port Elliot, April 19, 1920 – Inserted by his loving wife and little girl.*

RUMBELOW – In loving memory of our dear son and brother, Sam, who lost his life trying bravely to save another at Port Ellliot on April 19, 1920.

> *So dearly loved, so sadly missed,*
> *Some day we will understand*

Inserted by mother, father, sisters, May, Stella and Gwen, and brother Ken.

RUMBELOW – In loving memory of our dear grandson and nephew Sam. Brave deeds never die.

Inserted by grandmother, grandfather, and Aunty Hilda, Heading.

The Chronicle, 23rd April, 1921

Above: Great Uncle Samuel (Sam) Rumbelow with his tour car, circa 1919-1920 (the same year he died) - he died just three years after his brother Frank (S. Miller)

Photo: Stella Rumbelow as a young woman circa 1912 (S. Battams)

Photo above: a mother and her daughters: Ada May Rumbelow (May Reid), Stella Rumbelow (Stella Miller), their mother Ada Rumbelow (nee Heading), Dulcie Gwendolyn (Gwen Swain) circa 1918.[442] Photo Below: Siblings May, Stella and Ken (late M. Miller)

Above: Godfrey Rumbelow and Ada Heading on their 50th Wedding Anniversary, 1940 (Source: M.Miller). Below: the surviving members of the familyincluding Ada, Godfrey, May, Stella, Ken and Gwen (S. Miller)

100 Years of Age

Godfrey died in 1942, two years after his 50th wedding anniversary. Ada lived to see 100 years of age, outliving her husband and most of her children. The celebration of this milestone read:

> *100 YEARS OF AGE*
>
> *Mrs. Godfrey Rumbelow, of 12 Victor Street, Victor Harbour, will celebrate her 100th birthday anniversary on Thursday next, 24th September. Mrs. Rumbelow was born at Campbelltown, S.A., in 1870, and was the eldest of 13 children of Mr. and Mrs. John Heading. She was married eighty years ago and, with the exception of 12 years in Adelaide, has resided in Victor Harbour since her marriage. Her husband, the late Mr. Godfrey Rumbelow, died 28 years ago at the age of 73 years. Surviving members of the family are Mrs. Bert Reid, Mrs. Len Miller, and Mr. Ken Rumbelow. Two sons, Sam and Frank, and one daughter, Gwen, are deceased. Relatives and friends are invited to afternoon tea at the Newland Memorial Church Hall on Thursday to help Mrs. Rumbelow celebrate this most important occasion.*
>
> *Victor Harbor Times, 18 September, 1970*

Another report on the celebrations described the event:

> *VICTOR HARBOR WOMAN IS 100*
>
> *On Thursday of last week seventy relatives and friends gathered at the Newland Memorial Congregational Church hall to join in the birthday celebrations. A birthday cake was made by a grand-daughter, Mrs.Ted Fisher, and iced by a great-niece, Mrs. Eric Lang. On it were the words: '100 years, happy birthday, 1870-1970.' Mrs. Rumbelow received congratulatory telegrams from Queen Elizabeth, the Governor-General (Sir Paul Hasluck) and the Premier, Mr. D. A. Dunstan. Altogether more than 130 cards,*

telegrams and messages were received from well wishers. The Mayor of Victor Harbour congratulated Mrs. Rumbelow on attaining 100 years and other speakers were Mr. Ken Rumbelow (son) and the Rev. Gordon Branson. Surviving members of Mrs. Rumbelow's family are Mr. K. S. Rumbelow, Victor Harbour, and Mesdames May Reid, Seacliff, and Stella Miller, Brooklyn Park. Two sons, Sam and Frank, and a daughter, Gwen, are deceased. Mrs. Rumbelow has 21 grandchildren, 60 great grandchildren and 39 great great-grandchildren.

Victor Harbor Times, 2 October 1970

Ada died the following year, on the 29th April, 1971.

Chapter 10: Women in the Rumbelow Family

Caroline Rumbelow, the Women's Suffrage Petition (1894) and Paving the Way (1893)

Those that signed the women's suffrage petition of 1894 in the Rumbelow family included Caroline Cakebread nee Rumbelow (1843-1935). Caroline Cakebread was known as a strong figure in the family. The character of Petrel (named after Petrel Cove at Encounter Bay) in the book about the pioneering life '*Paving the Way: A romance of the Australian bush*' (1893) was said to be portraying or was inspired by her, as the author Simpson (Sim) Newland (1835-1925) and Caroline were said to be 'sweethearts' in their youth,[443] but it should be noted that Caroline was 8 years younger than 'Sim' and was married by the time she was 17 years old (to John Rymill Cakebread). One family story passed down was that when John and Caroline went to Ballarat to the gold diggings, Simpson Newland followed them there and asked Caroline to leave John for him.[444]

The character of Roland Grantley in *Paving the Way* was associated with Simpson Newland, whilst David Cleeve was inspired by Malin Rumbelow.[445] A description of Petrel in the book is as follows:

> *Altogether she is as fair a girl as one could wish to see, and gives promise of attaining a beauty so perfect as rarely falls to the lot of women. Of music as taught in the schools she knows nothing; but her voice is as sweet as the native warblers that sing around her in the antipodean groves. Unversed in the usual feminine accomplishments, she can shoot well, and no disciple of the famous Izaak ever handled rod and line more deftly.*
>
> *Simpson Newland, Paving the Way*[446]

It has been claimed that Caroline Rumbelow virtually grown up with the local Ramindjeri people and knew several well including one person referred to as 'King Pole.'[447] Similarly, it is said that Simpson Newland *'valued the education he had acquired as a child from the Ramindjeri people of Encounter Bay.'*[448]

However, there was a rather brutal interaction between Caroline and a local Ramindjeri man the locals gave an unflattering name, who came begging for food:

> *I remember an encounter a cousin of mine had with [a Ramindjeri person]. 'She was left home alone and "Swell Face Jack," a huge [Aboriginal man] came along and demanded flour. He was told there was no flour, but noticing a small quantity in the corner of the kitchen strode into the room and took it, despite the threat of my cousin that she would shoot him if he did so. As he was striding away through a field of wheat, carrying the flour, she peppered him with shot from a shotgun. He dropped the flour and ran. On another occasion [an Aboriginal person] was shot in much the same way, and actually came back and asked for a pin to pick the shot out with.*
>
> *The Mail, 4th Dec 1926*

The *Paving the Way* (1893) novel opens with apparent reference to the 1840 'Maria massacre,' where the Brig *Maria* was shipwrecked on the Coorong near Kingston and its 26 survivors were killed by some of the Milmendura clan of the Tanganekald people of the Ngarrindjeri nation.[449] Ngarrindjeri oral history passed down indicates that the killing was in retaliation for some of the sailors on board trying to sexually assault the Aboriginal women.[450] This led to punishment via hanging of two Milmendura men (without fair trial), and the lack of fair trial was one of the reasons for the dismissal of Governor Gawler.[451]

Caroline married John Rymill Cakebread in 1861, and they went to the Victorian goldfields during the gold rush (1859-61) before returning to Encounter Bay. Simpson Newland married Jane Isabella Layton in New South Wales (where he was a partner in pastoral stations) in 1872 and came back to South Australia, where he entered politics and was a member of the House of Assembly for Encounter Bay in state parliament.[452]

Lady Mayoress Mahalia Philps (1889-1968)

Lady Mayoress Mahalia Alice Philps (nee Honeyman) was the great granddaughter of Malin Rumbelow 1st and granddaughter of Edward Robert Bolger and Mahalia Rumbelow. Fraternising with royalty and dignitaries, Mahalia came a long way from her Tasmanian convict ancestor William Honeyman who escaped in 1820 and died whilst on the run. Mahalia made a significant contribution to Adelaide in her time as Lady Mayoress and wife of Mayor of the City of Adelaide, John Scott Philps (Lord Mayor 1954-1957).

John Philps hailed from the tiny town of South Kilkerran, near Maitland on the Yorke Peninsula. He arrived in Adelaide in 1902 and from an office boy at a timber mill, he became chairman of the directors of the furniture company Malcolm Reid and Co (the façade of Malcolm Reid's Emporium is the beautiful building 187-195 Rundle Street, Adelaide, with the sign still visible).

John Philps had been egged on to become a councillor by the well-known Bert Edwards, councillor of Gray Ward known as the 'King of the West,' whom John had known since he was a boy.[453] *The News* said of John Philps *'his is a kind of Dick Whittington[454] story, but he needed no bells to tell him to turn again. He found a job, and kept on doing it.'*[455]

Mahalia married John Philps on the 9 April 1914 at the Newland Congregational Church at Victor Harbor, a few months before WWI commenced. Sadly, their first child, a girl named Yvonne Mahalia born 2nd February 1915, died just a few weeks after she was born and is buried in the West Terrace Cemetery. They had two more children, both boys, John and Donald. The couple had a farm at Waitpinga and also lived at South Terrace, Adelaide, Magill Road, Tranmere and Henley Beach Road, White Park.

Whirlwind of Events

Mahalia Philps was a hardworking woman, an allrounder, public speaker, extremely active in civic life and community affairs during her time as Lady Mayoress and president or chair of many charities. Being Lady Mayoress was more than a full-time job; in her first year in the role (1954) there were 54 reports of her in social and community engagements.

> *A busy week is ahead for the Lady Mayoress ...In addition to official engagements at the Town Hall she will: - Open the Convent of Mercy fete at 2.30pm today [Saturday]; attend with the Lord Mayor...the Festival of Music in Adelaide Town Hall on Monday; visit Estcourt House [a home for the elderly and children with disabilities, ,later the Strathmont Centre][456] with the president of the SA Hospitals Visiting Committee (Lady McEwin) on Wednesday; open Finsbury Park Baptist Guild fete next Saturday.*[457]

The main event of that year was entertaining Queen Elizabeth II – the first reigning monarch to visit Australia (a cousin, Vera Watson, was a floral artist who founded the Mt Gambier Floral Art Club and presented a floral bouquet to the Queen on her visit).[458] Mahalia was an art appreciator who opened Adelaide Art Group's show in 1954, cake maker, making the cake for the Royal Naval Friendly Union's 15th birthday party in November 1954, and a keen gardener, preparing a massive 'floral carpet' for the visit of the Queen Mother to South Australia (1958). As reported in the newspaper:

> *The Field Naturalists are specially thrilled to have the Lady Mayoress (Mrs Philps), who is a very keen gardener and fervent flower-lover, open their wildflower and nature show.*[459]

With her husband she was a guest at many events, including a dinner dance at Mt Osmond for the Royal Automobile Association of SA, the centenary of Wendts Jewellers, the Air Force Association ball at the Palais Royale, and Citizenship ceremonies:

First to congratulate 20 new Australian citizens after the naturalisation ceremony in Adelaide Town Hall yesterday were the Lord Mayor and Lady Mayoress (Mr and Mrs Philps). After the ceremony they provided refreshments in the Queen Adelaide Room to the excited and vigorously hand-shaking new citizens.[460]

Most of the articles on Mahalia Philps during her time as Lady Mayoress in the social pages of the daily newspapers focused entirely upon her clothing rather than details of events, their messages or causes, and her interests and service. When the Lord Mayor and Lady Mayoress hosted the English men's cricket team, it was said that '*The Lady Mayoress ..combined her favourite colours in trim black suit, white lapel posy, and little white hat. She sat with Mrs. T. Playford, wife of the Premier, in muted blue.*'[461] *The Advertiser* newspaper launched a 'Sound Shell' in Elder Park in December 1954, at which *'The Lady Mayoress...wore a pretty petunia-patterned improve and a soft orchid shaded cartwheel hat, with a shadowed brim.'*

Chair of the Red Cross and Baptist Women's Board of Australia

Mahalia was President of the Baptist Women's Board of Australia, board member of Iloura home for the aged at Norwood and Chairperson of the Red Cross in 1955.[462] Mahalia intimately knew the importance of the Red Cross, as her son Donald had been a Prisoner of War (POW) in Germany during World War II. He wrote home and explained conditions as a POW:

Bdr. D.C. Philps ...gives the day's routine and diet as follows: "Up at 5.45. Breakfast of mint tea at 6.15. Check period at 6.35. I go out to work (in camp) once or twice a week, starting at 7.30. Lunch at noon of cabbage soup and potatoes. Tea at 5pm of a slice of mettwurst and tea, and three times a week we have margarine. Lights out at 9.30. Unless you are working, you are free all day."

Bdr. Philp's letters also show clearly what the Red Cross parcels mean to men living under these conditions. He adds: "I have

> *received three Red Cross parcels and four cigarette issues. From now on I hope to receive a parcel every 10 days and cigarettes every five or six days. My last parcel contained ovaltine, tea, milk, sugar, jam, honey, chocolates, sultanas, meat loaf, pilchards, and biscuits. It sounds a lot, but they were small tins. Nevertheless, it was great to receive them." It is to help to send these weekly parcels that Prisoner of War groups are being formed.*[463]

When he returned home in 1945, Donald spoke of the bitterness of released POWs, who were in no mood for mercy towards Germans after they had enslaved so many millions. He spoke of seeing something of conditions in the concentration camps at Dachau and Belsen, marching past on a 900-mile evacuation trek, after the Russians had charged into Germany. He saw the gaunt figures behind the wire, '*and we could smell them. Most of the poor devils had not washed or changed their clothes for months.*' He said that German authorities must have been fully aware of the horrors of the concentration camps, and that German guards were known for their inhuman indifference towards the suffering of others, and that their sadism must have been sought out by those who chose the guards. All returning prisoners spoke of the importance of the Red Cross Society during their own imprisonment and after their release, and how parcels sent by the society prevented starvation and malnutrition.[464]

Health, Education, Disability and Social Service Charities

Mahalia Philps was deeply interested in the then called 'Home for the Incurables'' (which was later the Julia Farr Centre, closed in 2020). She also supported fundraising for the then named 'Crippled Children's Association' (now Novita Children's Services). Mahalia Philps was often working closely with Lady George (wife of Governor Sir Robert George), Lady Constance Jean Bonython and Lady Margaret Rymill (former Lady Mayoress). In October 1954 it was reported that:

The Lady Mayoress (Mrs Philps) will distribute prizes won in competitions arranged by several stalls at the SA Council of Social Service Spring Fair in the Adelaide Town Hall at 2.30pm on Friday. Lady George will open the fair, convened by Lady Bonython at 11.30am.'[465]

Image: Lady Mayoress Mahalia Philps, The Advertiser, 20 November 1954.

The caption reads *'Happy picture of the Lady Mayoress (Mrs Philps) with Mrs William Boyd (otherwise Tripalong, petite wife of 'Hopalong Cassidy' star William Boyd). The Lady Mayoress wore cocoa organza frock and black picture hat for the civic welcome given by Mr and Mrs Philps in the Queen Adelaide room Town Hall, for Mr and Mrs Boyd, in honour of their fundraising visit for the Crippled Children's Association.*

Other events opened by Mahalia Philps or where she attended as guest included: the St Aloysius (Sisters of Mercy) Mothers Association fete and St Aloysisus College fete to raise funds for a new science room, the Aquinas College building fund fair (for which she judged the best dressed doll competition), St Andrew's Hospital women's auxiliary fete, the Children's Mannequin Parade (raising money for the Mothers and Babies' Health Association (MBHA) and Women's Service Association), the Sailors, Soldiers, Airmen and Nurses Relatives' Association, a film matinee to raise funds for the Red Cross and District and Bush Nursing Society (DBNS) (of which the Mayor was president), St Andrews Presbyterian Hospital fete, the Field Naturalist's Second annual Wildflower and Nature Show, the New Pounds for Pensioners Appeal, a Red Cross Drive held at the Palais Royal, the Royal Navy Friendly Union (RFNU) fete, (with her husband) the annual meeting of the Australia Nursing Federation, the annual meeting of the Lady Victoria Buxton Girls' Club in Whitmore Square (a home for young girls in distressed circumstances), and the Good Neighbour Council conference.

Women's and Girl's Associations

Mahalia took a special interest in charities and initiatives associated with the welfare and progression of women and girls. However, when Mahalia hosted a party for delegates of the Australian National Council of Women in 1954, the newspaper reporting almost exclusively upon her clothing, and that of the other delegates:

> *Mrs Philps was hostess in a self-printed heavy coffee silk organza, with wide lapels on the V neckline. Her pillbox massed with tiny pink hyacinths was as bright at a birthday cake.*[466]

In a party to welcome Chief Commissioner of the Girl Guides, it was said:

> *The Lady Mayoress (Mrs Philps), very trim in silver grey self-patterned faille suit with pearly sequins twinkling demurely on her white pillbox hat, made one of her best speeches in the Queen Adelaide Room, Town Hall, yesterday afternoon.*[467]

At the Royal Agricultural Show Ladies Day Reception meeting in 1954,[468] the newspaper stated that '*rhinestones sparkled discreetly on the emerald hat worn by the Lady Mayoress (Mrs. Philps) with an anthracite wool tailleur.*' At another art exhibition opening:

> *For the Lady Mayoress (Mrs. Philps), a sandstone coloured coat was flecked in tiny tufts of white. Buttercups, pinned to the lapel, toned with her little polished straw hat.*[469]

Mahalia seconded a motion by the Minister of Health Sir Lyell McEwin regarding the important work that the Mothers and Babies Health Association were doing, declaring it work of national importance. This was at the time when a substantial grant was made to the government by the association.[470]

Visiting the American Women's Association, it was reported that:

> *The Lady Mayoress (Mrs Philps) chose a specially [sic] good time for her first visit as official guest of the Australian American Association women's committee. This was at the committee's informal and, as it turned out, highly informative tea for visiting American lawyer Miss Sally Butler*[471] *yesterday...Mrs Philps wore a little white variety felt pillbox with her black tailleur accented with frosty white accessories.*[472]

Amidst the ongoing media scrutiny on her appearance, and social and fundraising whirlwind, there were more serious matters about women's status and political role being discussed Miss Sally Butler had been sponsored on a world tour by the US State Department. Her message was entirely lost in the local Adelaide newspapers, but was reported in Sydney. Butler, herself over 50, was advocating for women's employment in older age, women being politically independent and becoming influential through affiliation with clubs:

> *'age is no handicap to a business woman in America...There is a decided trend towards employing the older woman, because she doesn't have the home or social responsibilities of a younger girl.'* Butler also observed that *'Australian women do not yet 'realise their own power...in America, American women from the President's wife to the milkman's wife belong to clubs. It is the fact that these clubs have a central organisation, the General Federation of Women's Clubs, that makes them so effective in influencing the political and social life of the country.'* She also said that *'the*

American woman's vote is more effective than her Australian sister's because she is more ready to vote against her husband.. She thinks for herself...But don't think I'm advocating a militant feminism...Only men and women working together will ever achieve anything worthwhile.'[473]

In October 1954, the New Zealand Women's Club were similarly visited by the Lady Mayoress at the Queen Adelaide room in the Town Hall. She was a special guest at the Soroptimist Club's Christmas luncheon, of which she was vice president. The soroptimist association aims to transform the lives of women and girls and help them to realise their aspirations and have a voice in creating strong, peaceful communities. In 1956, the Lady Mayoress presented the oscar for the 'sportswoman of the year', on the Women's Sports Memorial Ground, near Shepherds Hill Road.

Her husband said at one Adelaide town hall event which welcomed delegates of the triennial conference of the Australian Federation of Women Voters:

The devotion and tenacity of our women in public service should be an inspiration and a challenge to our men... there was no doubt that the work of the women of Australia in public life had been of immense benefit to the country as a whole."[474]

When the founder of the federation – Mrs B. M. Rischbieth – and the vice president Miss Ruby Rich spoke, they emphasised that '*the federation was concerned with matters of social, political and economic importance, in relation to the welfare of humanity as a whole.'* Miss Ruby Rich *'warned the Lord Mayor that after the last triennial conference in Perth the first woman councillor was elected in that city. Perhaps, she said, the same result might follow in Adelaide.'*

In fact, the first woman councillor in Adelaide had been appointed much earlier, in 1919 - Susan 'Grace' Benny, at the Brighton Council, who became the first woman councillor in Australia. Her lawyer husband Benjamin had earlier been Mayor of the Brighton City Council (1903-1905), and was in the Australian Senate in 1919. Leaving due to health reasons, he was later charged and convicted of fraudulently converting treasury bonds and other trust funds and sent to jail. Grace Benny established the Elite Employment Agency to support her family through the Depression. After her husband died, she married a tramway worker 20 years her junior.[475] A bronze bust of Grace Benny was unveiled at Brighton in 2017.

Freda Rumbelow (1907-1982)

My grandmother Stella (born 1898) had first cousins, Ruby and Alfreda (Freda) (Godfrey's brother William 'Henry' Rumbelow's daughters), sisters who both gave birth out of wedlock. Ruby Alice Rumbelow (born 1892) had a daughter, Dulcie Helena, who was born in 1909, when Ruby had just turned 17 years of age. Dulcie was raised in the Rumbelow family and appears in the Rumbelow family history book.[476] Ruby married two years later in 1911, to John Willis Bottrill.

Ruby's younger sister Alfreda (Freda) (born) 1907) went to school at the same time as her niece Dulcie. Freda gave birth to a child when she was aged 20, Mora Dawn Rumbelow, who was born at Rose Park (Queen's Home) on 16 September 1927[477] and died on the 16 October 1927 at Woodville.[478] This child was also 'illegitimate.'

Freda Rumbelow had a career as a registered surgical nurse (1931) (Adelaide Children's Hospital) and midwife (1939). She became a nursing Sister, working as a midwife at the Memorial Hospital and Calvary Hospital (1946-47), with family notices in the newspaper thanking 'Sister Rumbelow.'[479] She also ran a 'nursing' home at Parkside – given she was a midwife, this was likely a maternity and babies home.[480]

Unusual for the time, Freda did not marry until she was aged 40 (in 1947, to veteran Victoria Park horse trainer named Ernest Birchall McKeon),[481] with their impending marriage announced in various newspapers, including *The News.* When he was asked his age by a journalist, Ernest said that he had 'lost it.' He was in fact 55 years old.

Photo: Freda and Dulcie Rumbelow at Loveday Bay School, circa 1923, Rumbelow and descendants website[482] Below: Ernest McKeon and Alfreda Rumbelow, *The News*, 12th June 1947

To Be Married

E. B. McKEON, veteran Victoria Park trainer, and Miss Alfreda Rumbelow, who will be married at Pirie Street Methodist Church on Saturday, June 28.

1840: The Lomman Family in Paradise and Athelstone

Chapter 11: The Lomman family of Paradise and Athelstone

Introduction

Henry Lomman came to South Australia from Devon along with siblings Eliza, John and Thomas Lomman. Henry's life was one of mixed fortunes, with a largely successful farming and market gardening business, he had trouble with alcohol and mental health, and became one of the first residents of the Parkside Lunatic Asylum, which we know as Glenside. There is a crossover between the Lomman (on mum's side) and Nitschke families (on Dad's side), as Henry's brother John Lomman married Johanna Mathilde Emma Nitschke, the sister of Johanne Eleanore Nitschke, Johann Gramp's wife. When Johanna Mathilda died, one of her children was cared for by Johanne Eleanore and Johann Gramp.

Henry and Martha Lomman's daughter Martha Ann Lomman married John Heading, who were also market gardeners at Campbelltown.

1st Generation in Australia (1840)

The Tragic Tale of Henry Lomman, Pioneer of Paradise, and the Adelaide Asylum

I saw it in a newspaper on Trove many years ago and had an inkling that it was an ancestor, but I wasn't ready for researching it – it was an article on Henry Lomman who went to court for attempted murder in 1860. He was my great-great-great grandfather, a pioneer settler in South Australia. His wife Martha Strong was strong in both name and nature as she, along with Henry, experienced a great deal of trauma throughout her life.

Henry Lomman, born in 1812 in Pitminster, Somerset, the eldest son of John Lowman and Ann Lenthall. The Lowman family has deep roots in Devon,

Southwest of England, where there is the Lowman River and several towns named after it. Henry's father John Lowman was listed as a 'Pauper-Agricultural Labour' in the 1851 census, when he was 69 years old. Four of his six children (Henry, Eliza, John and Thomas Lomman) headed to South Australia in search of a better life.[483, 484]

Henry Lomman married Martha on 13th August 1839 in the Church of England in the Parish of North Petherton in the County of Somerset. He was a 27-year-old Labourer, and she was a 23-year-old Servant - the marriage certificate said they were both 'full age.' Henry was literate and signed his name, but Martha left an 'X' mark on the marriage certificate, indicating she was illiterate. Her father was a Carpenter, whilst his was a Labourer.

Just two days after they were married, Henry and Martha applied for assisted passage to South Australia. They departed Gravesend, London, England on the 12 September 1839 and arrived in Port Adelaide, South Australia nearly five months later on 5 February 1840, travelling via the barque, *'John'*.

There are two diaries of the trip from Richard Ellis (State Library of SA) and Elizabeth Archer (in the Mitchell Library). The diaries report much drama and tragedy on board, including quarrelling and fighting, an accidental poisoning, deaths, wild weather and ceremony. The ceremony for crossing the equator was thus described by Elizabeth Archer:

> *7th Nov 1839: At eight in the evening a shout was heard from the forecastle of a boat ahead which we were informed contained his majesty Neptune, whose awful voice I soon heard enquiring 'What ship is this??' The officer on duty answered 'the Barque John from London.'...'Have you any of my sons or daughters on board?' roared the King of the Seas...in affirmative being given he informed us he would come on the morrow to initiate us on the mysteries of crossing the line [the equator]. Neptune's car, a tar barrel, was then lowered in the water and passed along emitting bright flames. This*

was the signal for giving shower baths to the curious, bucket after bucket of water was poured til every person on deck was drenched, even we who were on the poop [stern deck] did not escape a sprinkling, and the Captain who was with us venturing too near the watery regions, had a complete dousing, which he took good naturedly...8th Nov 1839: after breakfast we went on the poop to see the grand sight, a band of musicians struck up 'See the conquering hero comes' and amid deafening shouts Neptune and his Queen made their appearance on the gun carriage drawn by three constables, at the side of the chariot walked the bear (a sailor covered with our poor ram's skin) and bear keeper, behind the barber carrying a tar pot for leathering the sections, admirably dressed beside him his mate bearing the razors. The Doctor, no insignificant personage, watched the proceedings through a large hoop in lieu of a quizzing glass. As soon as they had taken their respective stations beside the bath, Neptune, who held a large book, called for his son Ratford (the… third mate). The constables immediately came in search of him and the young man wisely made no resistance but accompanied his frightful guides their dresses and the paint which besmeared their faces and bodies made them look like savages. Being seated on the edge of the bath with a cap over his eyes, Neptune enquired if he had ever crossed the line before, a negative was given. 'What will you give me not to punish too severely?' was the next demand, a sum being mentioned. The doctor stepped forward and offered a powder, which after tasting was refused, a bottle containing a draught was then presented, but the contents were not relished, a smelling bottle was placed under his nose which contained either a pin or needle - the patient started back, the barber next [with] a paint brush gave him a daub of tar on the cheek. Neptune telling him at the same time never to eat brown bread when he could get white. Not being answered, the tar brush

> *was popped into his mouth, after a scarping with one of the notched razors he was thrown backwards into the bath to be well ducked by the bear and his keeper who were in the water to receive him. The doctor watching the proceedings through his quizzing glass hoop. With few exceptions, all passengers were shaved or had a little tar on their faces, by giving money came off without too much scraping, we could pretty well tell what the gift was by the degree of punishment inflicted. The ladies were exempt from paying the fine. The performers were treated with a glass of spirits by the Captain and amidst great cheers, Neptune and his Queen were carried off the scene of action.*[485]

In 1841, the *John* was reported lost at sea: a whale boat arriving in port reported that it had foundered 700 miles to the west of Swan River, Western Australia. The crew had embarked from the ship in four boats, only one of which was rescued after being ten days at sea. The John may have been rescued, or it was a different boat at that time, as the emigrant barque *John* was wrecked on Manacles Rocks (reef), Cornwall in May 1855, with 196 lives lost, in one of the worst shipwrecks on the Cornwall coast.[486, 487]

Martha was 7 months pregnant when she arrived in South Australia, and had her first child, **James Strong** Lomman, on the 4th April 1840 (died 1862).[488] They next had twins **Hannah (or Anna) Maria** (1841-1927) and **Eliza Ann** (1841-1920) on the 15th May 1841 at Beaumont Grange, baptised on Christmas Day 1841, along with older brother James.[489] At the time, Henry was a Labourer at Beaumont Grange, a farm at Paradise. Martha then had **Joseph** in 1845 (died 1924) and **William** in 1846 (died 1847). At this time, Henry worked at Richmond Hill Farm (now Wadmore Park, Athelstone). **Thomas** (1847-1848), **Thomas Henry** (1849-1932), **<u>Martha Ann</u>** (1851-1924), **Louisa** (1853-1924), **William** (1855-1877) and **Harry** (1858-1928) were their other children (born at Shepley, Paradise).

At their deaths, it is reported that Henry and Martha had three surviving sons and four daughters. In total, they had 11 children that were born from 1840 to 1858, two died in their infancy (William (1st) in 1847 and Thomas in 1848) and two died as young adults. These tragic events may have contributed to Henry's his first 'attack' of mental illness (at 37), when he went to the Adelaide Asylum and was released after a short period.

Henry Lomman had sizeable portions of land at Paradise, Fifth Creek and Athelstone. There were sizeable pieces of land owned at Fifth Creek and Black Hill (around 390 acres). The South Australian Colony was selling land to raise funds, with limited structure or legal requirements for landholders. In 1849, Henry Lomman purchased 84 acres of suburban land lots for £84 and 1 shilling (section 816).[490] The following year in 1850, he bought section 817, 100 acres for £201 and 1 shilling. This was in the 'County of Adelaide – Fifth Creek.[491] These parcels of land are at Athelstone, section 817 being right on the Torrens River. In 1850, Henry purchased another 103 acres (section 999) in the County of Adelaide at Black Hill (near Athelstone), for £103 and 3 shillings.[492] In 1854 Henry bought another 103 acres 'Near Black Hill, Hundred of Adelaide' – these may have been sections 335 and 336. He warned potential trespassers about crossing his land in 1860:

> *Notice – All persons found TRESPASSING ON or making a thoroughfare through Sections Nos 817, 816, 999, 335 and 336, Hundred of Adelaide, will be PROSECUTED: and all CATTLE and HORSES will be IMPOUNDED after this notice.*
>
> *HENRY LOMMAN*
>
> *Adelaide Observer, 26 May 1860*

In 1859 he was granted a timber license by the East Torrens council, likely obtained to clear land. Henry also donated half an acre of land to the Athelstone Gorge Primitive Methodist Church to build the church on the site (foundation stone laid 1861). The Athelstone Gorge Methodist Church celebrated its 50th jubilee on the 29 January 1915.[493] The original trustees of the church included Henry's eldest son John Strong Lomman of Torrens.[494]

Henry and Martha's daughter Hannah Maria Lomman (later Austin) spoke about seeing, when growing up in the 1840s, 500 Aboriginal people from the Kaurna plains holding a corroboree on the banks of the Torrens River, known as Karrawirra Pari to the Kaurna people. The corroboree was held where the Paradise bridge (also known as the MacDonnell Bridge) was later built in 1857. She also spoke about 'wild dogs' (dingoes) causing destruction for farms, and the family travelling to Glenelg in bullock drays for holidays.

> *Her parents settled on the section now known as Paradise Park. She used to narrate interesting stories regarding the [Aboriginal people] and she remembered having seen as many as 500 holding a corroboree on the banks of the River Torrens, where the Paradise Bridge now stands.*[495]

In 1844 in a letter to *The Register*, a European settler reported on words supposedly translated from a song sung at a corroboree:

> *Adelaide no more good since the white men came – now the road has tired me – throughout Yeona there is a continuous road – what a fine road this is for me winding between the hills...*
>
> *South Australian Register, Saturday 16 March 1844, page 3*

Colonisation had a devastating impact upon the Kaurna people and their culture. Food sources were depleted through the purchase of land and farming practices. In 1847, an Act was introduced which also restricted the movement of Aboriginal people, the 1847 *Vagrancy Act*. Diseases from Europe brought untimely death.

Gold fever struck South Australia in the 1850s, leaving the colony in jeopardy as people fled for Victoria. In 1852 Henry Lomman contributed to the Tolmer Testimonial Fund, which involved a group of businessmen fundraising for payment of Police Commissioner Tolmer and a group of South Australian mounted police troopers in a police escort. This police escort was protecting gold being transported from the diggings in Mount Alexander, Forest Creek and Bendigo, Victoria back to South Australia. This was partly to ensure the return of the diggers and their gold back to South Australia, to ensure the ongoing economic operations of the fledgling colony. The escorts of the gold (18 in total) would save the colony from bankruptcy and ensure the livelihood and welfare of its European residents. From 1853 to 1856, England was involved in the Crimean War, and collections were being taken in South Australia for the War Relief Fund.

In 1856, Henry Lomman placed an advertisement in the Melbourne *Argus* newspaper every day for two weeks, searching for James Fort, formerly a dairyman of Adelaide (from Government Farm, Coromandel Valley), who had likely gone to the gold diggings in Victoria (James Fort had not had a lot of luck in SA, losing a mare in 1853 and then being robbed in 1854, he left SA in 1855). At that time Henry was living in Paradise.

In 1860 things start to unravel for Henry. He was admitted to the Adelaide Asylum on the 25th March 1860 and discharged on the 2nd May 1860, after 39 days. On the 13th December, 1860 Henry was remanded in custody in the Old Adelaide Gaol and accused of murder for attempting to shoot his eldest son James, and committed to jail on the 14th December 1860.[496] Henry went to the Supreme Court and it was revealed how he had abused his son and threatened to kill the whole family whilst drunk (and likely during a mental illness episode), then came outside with a shotgun whilst James fled towards the house. Henry shot at the door of the house and left a hole the side of a hand.[497] James went out the back door to get help from his Uncle Thomas.

Although Henry pleaded guilty, Judge Boothby stated he would not pass sentence. It was said that he committed the offence when 'under the excitement of drink.' There was also commentary about him 'not appearing to be in his right senses' when the case was first heard. He was released from custody in 1861 with a £100 bond. It was stated that he entered into the bond with the understanding that if he made such an attempt again, he would be brought to the court and receive a very severe sentence.

There was a story passed down the Lomman family that earlier Henry had got into a fight with a neighbour and was hit on the head with a shovel, which caused a brain injury that resulted in his admission to the asylum. However, there is no other evidence of this in records or newspapers.[498]

On 4th January 1862[499] Henry and Martha's eldest son John Strong Lomman died, aged 22 years, from measles. This was only shortly after John had married Susan Skinner at Ferryville (part of Largs Bay). Later the same year, on the 18th December 1862, Henry Lomman and John Loller (his brother in law, married to his sister in Eliza) applied to have Henry's land recognized under 'The Real Property Act' (sections 999 and 816 and part of 817).[500] This Act was developed to provide a clear legislative framework for property rights and ownership, to ensure that land was not being wasted, and to bring some order to the chaos of private sub-divisions that was occurring.[501] In 1865, Henry Lomman and John Loller attempted to sub-divide land as allotments in the Village of Thorndon Park (part of section 298, Hundred of Adelaide).[502] There was also reference to a residence, 'near Roseworthy.'

Henry and Martha's daughter Hannah Lomman married John Austin on the 4th April 1866 at the Trinity Church. Shortly after this event, on 15th June 1866, Martha Lomman 'charged' her husband Henry with being of unsound mind at the Police Court of South Australia, and he was removed for medical examination. He was sent by the authority of Samuel Beddome, Police Magistrate at the Police Court. Henry re-entered the Adelaide Asylum on the 15th June 1866, the medical certificate was signed by George Mayo on 14th June 1866. The patient file said that he had his current attack for 10 days.

Dr George Mayo was the honorary medical officer of the Adelaide Hospital and President of the Medical Board at the time. His granddaughter was Dr Helen Mayo, women's health pioneer. It is said that Henry had 'dementia and unsound mind.' His 'diagnoses' included 'mania' and 'dementia.' At the time, there were only three main diagnoses: mania, dementia and melancholia,[503] and schizophrenia was known as 'dementia praecox.'[504] It is likely that he had psychosis and a chronic mental illness. Henry would spend the remainder of his days at the Adelaide and Parkside Lunatic Asylums, and he died at the Adelaide Asylum in 1900.

Photo: The Parkside Lunatic Asylum (Glenside) 1880-1910, SLSA B 72111/19

Henry Loman, Case notes from Parkside Asylum (F19)

By whose authority sent: Samuel Beddome JP

Date of admission: June 15th 1866

Name of patient, and Christian name at length: Henry Loman

Married, single or widowed: Married

Sex and Age: Male 53 years

Condition of life, and previous occupation (if any): Farmer

The religious persuasion, as far as known: Church of England

Previous place of abode: Paradise

Whether first attack: No

Age (if known) on first attack: "1848"

When and where previously under care and treatment: Adelaide Asylum

Duration of existing attack: 10 days

Supposed cause: Not Known

Whether subject to epilepsy: No

Whether suicidal: Not Known

Whether dangerous to others: Has used threats

Name and Christian name, and place of abode of nearest known relative of the patient and degree of relationship (if known): Martha Loman, wife of the said Henry Loman

Degree of Education: [never completed]

Previous habits: [never completed]

Date of Medical Certificate, and by whom signed: 15th June 1866 Geo. Mayo

State on Admission

May 7th Has a cough. Examined Chest. Right lung, Heart sounds consonated [sic], dullness and want of elasticity in upper part. Cough is not natural but more the result of habit. It sounds like clearing of the throat. Examined specially for aneurism but could detect no symptoms of the existence.

May 18th 1870 – Removed to Parkside Asylum [day first male patients relocated there]

Jan 1885 Health Good. Mental condition dementia.

July 1885 Health frail. Mental condition senile dementia

Jan 1886 Health improved. Mental condition dementia.

August 20th 1900 Transferred to Adelaide Asylum

Suffering from hemiplegic weakness from a stroke

Dec 3rd 1900 Died of Senile decay & dementia.

In 1868, there was a report on the building of the 'New Lunatic Asylum' (Parkside, now known as Glenside). It was reported that '25 or 30' inmates would be moved from the grounds of the Adelaide Lunatic Asylum to Parkside, to trench and plant the ground, so that in 2-3 years when all 'inmates' were there, there would be flower and fruit trees. Initial apartments were built at Parkside to accommodate the first patients.

In 1869 there was a Parliamentary Inquiry into the Lunatic Asylum, whereby a Select Committee examined a number of allegations including the drunkenness of the attendants and cruel treatment of so-called 'inmates' by Resident Medical Officer Dr Alex Patterson and attendants. Eight of the attendants were seen drinking a bottle of brandy by members of the Gas Commission. At the time there was a 'Board of Visitors' who provided information to the inquiry, in particular Mr Fuller. Two discharged attendants and two current attendants who were denied promotion (according to the *Adelaide Observer*) also provided evidence 'for the prosecution.' Evidence included patients being physically assaulted or denied water, and there were allegations that Dr Patterson received food and beer from the store.

Dr Patterson's statement about the allegations were printed in full in *The Express and Telegraph Newspaper,* and it makes for extraordinary reading. In response to accusations of misappropriating supplies, Dr Patterson argues that it was the 'ordinary custom of an asylum' to take vegetables for himself and his family, and for his washing to be done at the asylum. He did, however, take 15 pounds of pork, a major focus of the inquiry. He also claims that the 50 chickens on the site were his own, which he bought from his predecessor. He was accused of giving away plants from the asylum, but claims that they were his personal property, having been given 300 to 400 plants by his friends. He claims he gave them away to prevent them from being destroyed. He also broke in two colts on the asylum grounds – but says that these horses had always been available for public purposes, saving government expense. He argues that he broke the horses in there for his own entertainment, and not economy, and that 'the excitement of riding a young horse is a relaxation from the monotony of constant intercourse with diseased minds.'

Dr Patterson was also criticised for allowing patients outside of the asylum, but he claimed that asylum residents were allowed excursions out of the asylum as part of testing their fitness for discharge. Dr Patterson describes giving leave to a resident so that he could work at his brother-in-law's boot shop in Rundle Street, so that he could give the proceeds to his wife and young children, who were in a 'starving state.' He responds to concerns about the escape of a patient by saying that the asylum was not a prison, but attendants slept with 'master keys' under their pillows. He also answers to the 'illegal incarceration' of a patient.

Dr Patterson also makes reference to waiting for the 'new building' to open (at Parkside), and that he was managing both the new asylum and the existing one, without any additional remuneration. Dr Patterson was also accused of unfairly dismissing staff. The Doctor refers to one attendant being responsible for 130 residents across six corridors. He refers to asylums in Victoria having 2 medical superintendents for 250 people, but complains he is on his own with 257 patients (daily average). Another article states that there are 270 patients, and 33 attendants, in addition to the medical doctor. It is a wonder that he broke in the horses on the hospital grounds and planted trees!

Dr Patterson boasts a higher recovery rate and lower death rate than any of the English asylums. Regarding the quality of the attendants, he states

> *It is worse than useless to erect too high a standard by which to judge of the attendants in a Lunatic Asylum; the reality will inevitably fall far short of the ideal. The model attendant can be easily sketched. He should possess courage, presence of mind, self-reliance, a quiet, but firm and gentle manner, the greatest forbearance and patience, sobriety, a good preliminary education, a stout muscular frame, and, above all, a fair share of that moral force which gives man power over his fellows. To secure a combination of these qualities in any one man or woman is difficult, or rather I should say, impossible; their possession would command a prominent place in the race of life, and the fortunate owner, especially at the present rate of remuneration, is not likely to apply his energies to the care of lunatics.*
>
> *Dr Patterson, The Lunatic Asylum Inquiry, 1869*

Dr Patterson mentions the risk of physical assault that attendants are subject to and claims that *'modern treatment of insanity forbids the use of all restraint or coercion.'* If this was the case, perhaps conditions were better then than now!

The *Adelaide Observer* declared their public support for the Resident Medical Officer (who did not appear to be, in fact, resident but did daily visits) and ridicules the Lunatic Asylum Committee and the central question of 'who appropriated the pork?' It questioned how the Select Committee was ever able to be established in the first place. At the time the newspaper was owned by a group of wealthy shopkeepers and merchants, likely in support of the government.

Henry Lomman was one of the first male patients to move from the Adelaide Asylum to Parkside and arrived at Parkside on the 18th May 1870. The final buildings at Parkside were intended to accommodate 800 residents.

Whilst Henry was a faithful husband with a devout wife in Martha, the same could not be said for his siblings. His brother Thomas bolted for California in 1850, just five weeks after he was married, leading to another court case where his wife Louise nee Brachel ('a respectable looking girl') sued. Thomas's daughter Louisa Ann Loman was only 15 years old when she got pregnant. The father of her first child was aged 30 and also disappeared. Louisa had her child in the Destitute Asylum in 1872 when she was almost 16 years old, and was picked up by the police when she was almost 19 years old for prostitution in the Parklands in 1874,[505] before she married (Oscar Franke) aged 22, and had four more children.

Henry's brother John arrived in South Australia in 1840, on the *'Dauntless.'* John married Johanne Mathilde Emma (Ann) Nitschke, but in 1864 she left him, and he advertises that he will not be responsible for any of her debts and that her leaving has been done 'without just cause.' John appeared to have a violent and volatile nature, and a problem with alcohol. In 1851, he was taken to court as he was accused of assault by a nurse who was taking care of his pregnant wife. In 1866, John and his son Samuel went to the Police Court as they were charged with assaulting John's brother Thomas, and both were fined.

Henry Lomman would have missed the 1871 'Old Colonists Dinner' attended by his brother John, as he was in the asylum. John is pictured in the Old Colonist's banquet dinner mosaic (misspelt Lowman), with the dinner being held at the Adelaide Town Hall on 28 December 1871. His daughter from his first marriage, Matilda Lomman, ended up in the Destitute Asylum in 1880 *'confined on June 3rd 1880 of a female child'*[506] and gave birth to Elizabeth Ann Lomman Frelter in the asylum (father of the child, Carl Frelter, had disappeared). In 1881 aged 19, Matilda entered the asylum again with her 8 month old child Elizabeth, from a refuge at Norwood. She stated she had a stepmother and father John Lomman at Campbelltown, who was paralysed. They stayed in the asylum from the 27th January to the 14th May 1881. Matilda married Otto Moritz Matthes in 1883, and went to Sydney.

Photo: John Lomman (Henry Lomman's brother) at the South Australian pioneers' dinner 1872 (Townsend Duryea), SLSA B7865/11K. Forebear Henry Lomman was at the Parkside Asylum at the time.

Despite Henry's location in the Parkside Asylum, whenever his children were married their notice in the newspaper always refers to their father as 'Henry Lomman from Athelstone' or Paradise.

In 1876, Martha and Henry's youngest daughter Louisa Lomman married Gordon Bilney, at the time both were living at Athelstone. Two of the sons married sisters (maiden name Semmens) from McLaren Vale (Harry in 1881 to J Semmens).

In 1877, Henry and Martha's son William (2nd) was fatally shot at Caltowie, aged 22 years. There was an inquest into his death, held at Ingram's Hotel, Caltowie. He was with his brother Harry and other friends at the time shooting kangaroos and rabbits, and it appears as though he accidentally shot himself in the left groin. He was walking with a crutch under his right arm and was carrying a gun powder flask around his neck with a string, and holding the gun by the barrel. He died in his brother Harry's arms. That was the fourth child that Martha had to bury, likely alone as her husband was by then already institutionalised.

Henry's wife Martha did well to manage the land and farm, with the support of her oldest surviving son Thomas. Details of an application in 1882 for Martha and Thomas Henry to take over Henry's affairs are held in the SA Archives - *Lunacy petition 48A/1882*. Henry's land section 335 was exchanged with Mary Ann Wright and Emma Wright for a plot on section 336 with right of way to 336 from Alders (or Allen) Street. The petition mentions that Henry had been suffering dementia and unsound mind for 16 years. His estate papers give his address as Parkside (the location of the Lunatic Asylum).[507]

Martha Lomman died in 1897; at the time she lived at Campbelltown. There were two death notices, which stated she was a 'colonist of 58 years' and that 'another pioneer passed away.'

LOMMAN.—On the 18th August, at Campbelltown, of heart disease, Martha Lomman, aged 81 years, leaving 3 sons, 4 daughters, 36 grandchildren, and 7 great-grandchildren. Arrived in the old ship John, in the year '39. Another pioneer passed away. Gone to her rest.[508]

Henry Lomman died at the Adelaide Asylum in 1900 (he had been transferred there in August 1900), aged 87 years. His death notice mentions that he was a colonist of 61 years and states *'sweet rest at last.'* He had spent his last 34 years in the Adelaide and Parkside Asylums, at a time when mental health care was highly restrictive for patients, with the use of archaic instruments such as 'straight jackets' and other physical forms of control. Henry's son Joseph Lomman also died at the Parkside Asylum, spending only his last four months of life there, dying from senility and heart failure.[509]

***

Women's Suffrage Petition 1894

The women's suffrage petition was signed by members of the Lomman family, including Harry Lomman (Henry and Martha's youngest son) and Jane Lomman of Gawler South, and T.H. Lomman (Henry and Martha's 7th child) and his wife M. Loman/Lomman (nee Woodcock) of Walkerville.[510] This may have been influenced by seeing their mother Martha Lomman nee Strong running the farm but not having the same political rights as the 'unsound' Henry (see the story in the Lomman chapter). It was wonderful to see these male ancestors on the suffrage petition, probably influenced by the experience of their mother in battling with the government to manage land after her husband went to the asylum. They were also probably influenced by the temperance movement as they were devout Methodists and there appeared to be problems with alcohol addiction in their father's generation.

Chapter 12: The Heading Family of Campbelltown

The Heading family came to South Australia on the *Joseph Rowan* in 1854 from Cambridgeshire, England, United Kingdom. The ship left Liverpool 20 March 1854, and arrived at Port Adelaide 15 June 1854. On board were **William Heading** (42) and his wife Anne[511] (38) (nee Brooks), and children: **Elizabeth (Betsy)** (18), **Anne** (16), **William** (10), **John** (8) (our forebear), **Simon** (5) and **Charles** (2). Youngest children **George** and **Mary** were born in the Colony of South Australia. Two children died young in Cambridge (**James Keep Heading** and **John Heading** 1st).

The Heading family were farm Labourers and market gardeners around Campbelltown. Son Charles Heading owned a farm at Klemzig, and there are many photos of this farm in the State Library of South Australia. There is a photo of the five Heading brothers on Ancestry.

2nd Generation in Australia

Henry and Martha's Lomman's third daughter Martha Ann Lomman (1851-1924) (my forebear) married John Heading (1846-1935) in 1868, and they had a long marriage with 15 children (including my great grandmother Ada Heading). John was a market gardener at Campbelltown. John and Martha were active members of the Methodist Church, with John being the Superintendent of a Sunday School. John was also sworn in as a Constable for the Athelstone area at the Campbelltown Council, 13th August, 1870.

John and Martha Ann had the following 15 children:
Ella Ann Heading (1868-1870)
Ada Louisa Heading (1870-1971) (married Godfrey Rumbelow)
Frank John Heading (1871-1948) (married Margaret Mortimer)
Alice Mary Heading (1873-1948) (married Joseph Mitchell)
Martha Amy Heading (1875-1967) (married Herbert Farnham)
Ellen Ann Heading (1876-1954) (married Ross Herbert Stevens)

Edith Maria Heading (1878-1951) (married Richard Martin)

Bertha Eliza Heading (1880-1963) (married Frank Henry Edwards)

Joseph Henry Heading (1881-1956) (married Florence May Reid)

Emily Selena Heading (1883-1974) (married William John Woods)

Maud Betsy Heading (1885-1975) (married Wilfred Pitt Bray)

Walter Thomas Heading (1887-1961) (married Nellie Noble)

Harold Reginald Heading (1889-1941) (married Elizabeth Sadler)

Leslie Charles Heading (1891-1980) (married Helena Triffie Mathews)

Hilda Blanche Heading (1897-1980, married Herbert Rumbelow, nephew to Godfrey Rumbelow)

There is little information about Martha Ann Lomman and John Heading, except for what is available in the newspaper reports of their wedding anniversary and obituaries. They appeared to lead a pious life and had little contact with the law or other institutions (unlike other relatives!).
John and Martha lived at a homestead at Campbelltown where they celebrated their golden (50th) wedding anniversary in 1918.[512] This anniversary was reported on in the local newspaper as follows:

> *The golden wedding of Mr and Mrs John Heading, of Campbelltown, took place on Feb 18. There was a large gathering at the homestead in which the old couple have resided during the 50 years of their married life. The eldest son, Mr Frank Heading, on behalf of the other members of the family, presented them with a purse of sovereigns. Mr Heading was born in Cambridgeshire in 1846, and came with his parents when eight years of age. He has been an ardent worker in the Methodist Church, and for many years was superintendent of the Sunday school. In 1868 he married the third daughter of Mr Henry Lomman of Paradise, and has a family of nine daughters and five sons. There are also 42 grandchildren and six great-grandchildren. The old people are in remarkably good health.*

The Observer 2 March 1918

The years seem to hang lightly on the aged couple, who are both hale and hearty, early risers, and able to follow their occupation as well as many much younger people.

The Express and Telegraph, 22 February 1918

Photo thought to be of John Heading (S. Battams)

The obituary of Martha Ann Heading read:

Mrs. John Heading who died on Good Friday at her home at Campbeltown, was one of the oldest and most respected residents of the district. She was 73 years of age and was a daughter of Mr. Lomman of Athelstone. She married in 1868 Mr. John Heading, of

Campbeltown where she had resided in the same house during the whole term of her married life, 56 years. Here she saw grow up around her a family of five sons and nine daughters, all of whom survive, together with fifty grandchildren and fourteen great-grandchildren. Mrs. Heading was a devoted member of the Methodist Church. And until illness prevented her she was a regular attendant, at the morning service.

The Advertiser, 22 April, 1924

John Heading died 11 years later, and his obituary read:

Mr. John Heading, who died at his home at Campbelltown on November 7, was in his 90th year, having been born at Borne, England, in 1846. He arrived in Australia with his parents and brothers in the ship Joseph Rowan in June. 1854. The family first lived at Marden. but shortly afterwards moved to Campbelltown, where they carried on gardening and farming.

In 1868 he married Martha Ann Lomman, of Athelstone, and struck out on his own account on a small holding at Campbelltown, where he lived for the rest of his life. He was a devoted churchman and regularly attended church every Sunday. For a number of years he was superintendent of the Campbelltown Methodist Sunday school. His wife died eleven years ago. Fourteen children (nine daughters and five sons), 57 grandchildren and -42 great-grandchildren survive him.

The Chronicle, 5 December 1935

Sir James Alfred (Jim) Heading (1884-1969)

The Honourable Sir James Alfred (Jim) Heading CMG DCM was the son of William Heading and Rhodda Sarah Cook, and born at Payneham, South Australia. He served in WWI, where he took charge at Passchendaele following the death of three officers:

> *On 18 September 1915 Heading enlisted in the Australian Imperial Force. He joined the 47th Battalion in Egypt and in June 1916 moved with it to the Western Front. His service was interrupted by long periods of convalescence in England as a result of wounds to the leg and the shoulder. In June 1917 he was promoted sergeant. On 12 October at Passchendaele Ridge, Belgium, after all the officers of three companies had become casualties, he took charge. Disregarding personal danger, he placed outposts and connected the flanks; for these actions he was awarded the Distinguished Conduct Medal. At Dernancourt, France, on 5 April 1918 his platoon commander was killed. Heading again took charge and established control of no man's land in the immediate vicinity; he won the Military Medal and was promoted warrant officer. Transferring to the 45th Battalion in May, he arrived home in August 1919 and was discharged on 14 October. On 2 October that year he had married Ruby Jeanie Thomas at the Methodist Church, Clarence Park, Adelaide.*
>
> *Australian Dictionary of Biography*[513]

Sir James (Jim) Heading moved to Queensland in 1909, farmed (including cattle farming) at Cobbs Hill, near Murgon, and became a conservative politician, first being appointed to the local Council and then to the Legislative Assembly of Sir Francis Nicklin's Queensland government, representing Wide Bay, he also became a Minister for Public Works and Local Government and Immigration from 12 August 1957 to 9 June 1960, and was knighted in 1961. Sir James Heading Memorial Park in Murgon, Queensland is named after him.[514]

Heading's Cliffs Lookout

Heading Road, Murtho and the stunning Headings Cliff Lookout outside of Paringa, Renmark are also named after descendants of the Heading family, who were significant landholders at Murtho (section 17, Hundred of Murtho) and have been farming for 4 generations in this area, and introduced irrigation on a large scale in the 1950s. These were the descendants of John Heading's son Joseph Henry Heading.

Photo: Headings Cliffs, Murtho, 2025 (S. Battams)

Part 4: Mother's Paternal Ancestry

1859: The Heslop Family from the United Kingdom to Aotearoa New Zealand

Chapter 13: The Heslop, Miller and Abbott Families in New Zealand

Introduction

Whenever I visit Melbourne and wander along the Yarra River, I sometimes think of the only photograph I have of my great-great grandmother Elizabeth Abbott and her family. It shows them having a picnic on the banks of the Yarra around 1911. Shaded under a large drooping willow tree, a small wooden boat is moored nearby, suggesting they arrived at the picnic spot via it. Elizabeth is the matriarch of the group, surrounded by her children, grandchildren, and friends. Her second husband Pastor Albert James Abbott is noticeably missing from the photo, although he was still alive at the time.

I was surprised when I first saw this photo, as there is an air of wealth and refinement about the group. Its characters are well dressed: men in suits with pocket watch chains visible, women in dresses or blouses with long skirts, and a range of hats on show. Perhaps this was the influence of Elizabeth's family background in the clothing and shoe industry – or of her second husband Abbott who had described himself as a 'Gentleman' upon their marriage, suggesting that he need not work for a living. Elizabeth's brother became a Doctor in the US, her son Albert a Dentist, and her grandchild Hepburn was a Lawyer. I later found out that Elizabeth's grandfather George Heslop was a naval officer with the British Royal navy - which required one to be a landholder at the time.

My grandfather Leonard Miller, Elizabeth's grandson, is standing apart at left of the group in the photograph, with his hand on his hip and bowler hat, aged 21. He looks quite cocky and would soon disappear from the Melbourne scene altogether. Another photo I have of Leonard as a baby (on the front cover of this book) sees him clothed in velvet and frills - a far cry from his later letter to the daily Adelaide newspaper complaining of a gardener's meagre salary and harsh working conditions. These photos made me curiouser about the origins of this family and what had happened since their arrival to the Antipodes. Who was Elizabeth, and what kind of family did she really come from? And why had Leonard left Melbourne?

Photo: The Miller-Abbott family on the banks of the Yarra River, Melbourne, circa 1911. Back Row, standing from left - Leonard Miller age 21, unknown man and wife (friends), Percy Miller (with bowler hat) aged 19, Edith Miller nee Thompson, George Miller, and standing at right Clayton Abbott. Seated, from left: Two children (girl with hidden face is Dorothy Miller, twin to Grace), two unknown children, Edith 'Elsie' Miller aged 18 years, Grace Miller (seated front), Ethel Abbott (Clayton's wife), Elizabeth Abbott nee Heslop, Albert Malcolm 'Albie' Stevens (child seated front), Mabel Stevens (with handkerchief on head), Tom Stevens, unknown child) (courtesy the late M. Miller)

A life of excitement and upheaval was the ordinary way for great-great grandmother Elizabeth Heslop-Miller-Abbott. Elizabeth lived in three countries (England, New Zealand and Australia) and was an alleged bigamist who played a central role in some scandalous legal cases that featured prominently in early 19thC Victorian newspapers. Elizabeth's second husband Pastor Abbott was one of the greatest charlatans in Melbourne and Sydney at the end of the 19th and early 20th century and became involved in shonky spiritualism. Sir Arthur Conan Doyle, writer of the Sherlock Holmes series, weighed in on his views on Abbott's associate, psychic Mrs Annie Turner, when he toured Australia, in support of her mediumship skills and their role in solving crimes!

Elizabeth was no victim of fate, as she appeared to flee misfortune and seize opportunities where she saw them. During one legal case Elizabeth was described by a journalist as a piteous figure. This certainly did not fit the picture of her picnicking happily along the Yarra River with her family surrounding her, her daughter Mabel Stevens leaning on her mother, signifying a close relationship. However, the description does point to some of the challenges she faced throughout her life with the man missing from the photograph.

1st Generation in New Zealand

The Heslops bound for Canterbury, New Zealand

Elizabeth Heslop was 19 years old when she arrived in New Zealand with her parents George and Jane (nee Kitchener) and siblings on the *Zealanda* which left London 11th August 1859. There were 360 people in total on the ship, with the Heslop family being government assisted migrants. New Zealand had been colonised only three years prior.

The Heslop family was from Durham, north-east of England, a pretty town with a Norman castle that overlooks the River Weir, from where the town name Auckland, New Zealand comes. Durham was known for its carpet making and weaving trades. The connection between Durham and New Zealand was through the First Earl of Durham, John Lambton, who was Governor of the New Zealand Company (1825) and the New Zealand Association (1837). The latter was founded by Edward Gibbon Wakefield in 1837, the same man who planned the colonisation scheme for South Australia. Wakefield had withdrawn from the South Australia initiative after conflict with colleagues including Robert Torrens and turned his interests towards New Zealand. Wakefield and Lambton were colleagues who spent time in Canada together, Lambton being made Governor General of Lower Canada, employed to introduce responsible government to the nation. Wakefield and Durham had something else in common: both had eloped with young women. Wakefield had been imprisoned for kidnapping a young woman for the purpose of eloping, during which time he developed the colonisation scheme.

George Heslop senior was a currier, a specialist in the leather processing industry, and a boot and shoe merchant. Theft from George Heslop's boot store was not uncommon, and it had great consequences. In 1854, Mary Frazer was charged with stealing four pairs of boots from George, and she was committed to Durham Gaol for her crimes, lucky to be spared from transportation to the colonies.

In November 1857, it was reported in the *Shields Daily Gazette* that the wife of George Heslop, of 7 Bedford Street, North Shields (boot and shoemaker) had given birth to a daughter. Travelling was part of the trade - in February 1859 it was reported that 'the barque Minna with Heslop of Shields, was departing for Cadiz, Spain.

George Heslop was originally from Yorkshire whilst his wife was from Brighton, Sussex. Jane was born into a family who were part of the 'Countess of Huntingdon's Connexion', who were evangelical travelling Methodists. It was also rumoured that she was related to Lord Kitchener, who was from the same region (Brighton).

Elizabeth was the second of five children on the boat to New Zealand; there was also older sister Maria (24), younger brother James (18), sister Charlotte (12) and brother Alfred (10). Sons George William Heslop (22) and Mowbray Heslop (21) had already arrived in the Colony.

Elizabeth, Maria and Charlotte were all dressmakers whilst James was a painter. The Heslop girls were among the few females with a skilled trade on the ship, although there was a female cook, dairy maid and 27 domestic servants. Men on the boat were agricultural Labourers, Tinmen, Carpenters, Butchers, Brickmakers, Masons, Joiners and Plumbers, all required trades in the new Colony. On arrival, Charlotte is listed as a single woman despite being only 12 years old, but Alfred is listed as a child travelling with his parents. In England they also had a servant from London, Isabella Robinson.

As Elizabeth stepped onto the *Zealanda*, she likely felt excitement and trepidation, with the day of departure being long awaited. She would head down into the depths of the ship to her primitive quarters, to see that her living arrangements for the next three months were not fancy. Her bed would be made of rough wood, with a thin mattress pulled over, and she would be sharing a bunk with one of her younger sisters. She likely wandered up to the deck to observe the ship's departure and wave to anyone on the dock. I can imagine her breathing in the icy cool sea air in winter, pulling a shawl tight over her shoulders and hearing the seagulls squawking overhead, amidst the bellows of the ship's crew. Some would be jealous that they were not chosen for the journey toward a new life and would continue to try to leave England. The family would be proud that they had been selected for emigration. Elizabeth may have imagined exciting adventures ahead of her that would keep her hopes up through the three-month journey. Elizabeth must have wondered about her marriage prospects in New Zealand, or her chances of meeting a future husband aboard the ship. She would have been too busy packing up and travelling in preparation for emigration to go to many dances prior to her departure. Elizabeth Barrett Browning's sonnets had just been published, which may have fueled her imagination. Elizabeth would quickly acquired her sea legs, with many more journeys by sea ahead of her.

Many had perished in ships travelling to the Antipodes. Only a few years earlier, the immigrant ship *Polar Star* had caught fire in the South Atlantic whilst travelling to New Zealand, with all of the passengers and crew put to work with pumps and buckets fighting to control the fire. It was not until two days later that a passing ship rescued them. In 1859, the ship *Burmah* along with all passengers and livestock disappeared without a trace, her wreck never found. One theory was that the boat travelled too far south and struck an iceberg in the great Southern Ocean.

One thing Elizabeth could look forward to was seeing her brothers again. Her family were likely introduced to the idea of travelling to New Zealand through the letters of brothers George William (22 years old) and Mowbray Kitchener Heslop (21 years old) who had already arrived in Auckland, New Zealand with their wives. George William was an Engineer in Auckland, whilst Mowbray was a photographer.

Arrival in Lyttelton

The Heslop family arrived in the Port of Lyttelton in November 1959 and would be met with stunning beauty: the intense blue waters of the volcanic basin, surrounded by steep hills. The frantic arrival activity of the sailors on deck provided a bookend to the scene of the departure. When the anchor was finally dropped and ropes tied to the dock at Lyttelton, all the passengers would be lined up for the departure name call.

Front of mind for the families aboard upon arrival was finding a place to live and settle. The Heslop family found a residence on Canterbury Street, Lyttelton, not far from where they had arrived. George started off as a Leathermaker and Merchant and then was also a Draper. In 1861 he (along with his accountant) took over the estate of a man named Henry Inwood, a Tanner who was 'assigned' to him but could not pay his bills.

However, George would also have his fair share of bad luck and changing fortunes, although he was the type of person to take things into his own hands. Moving his family to a new country for a better life, he endeavoured to ensure that conditions were acceptable in his new place of residence. In 1864 George complained to the Lyttleton Council of an 'intolerable nuisance' from a stable near his residence, the smell of which was 'endangering the health of his family': the Inspector of Nuisances was called to investigate and gave notice to the occupier of the stable. In 1866 George wrote to the Council asking for a street lamp to be erected near his house.

In 1866 George acquired a boat; initially co-purchased with a man by the name of Joseph Hobbs, it was later owned by Heslop, David McKay and Mr Moir. The boat, a 17-ton ketch, was named *Maid of the Mill*, and frequently travelled the short distance from Kaiapoi River to Lyttelton Harbour and back, transporting goods for sale, and sometimes it went up to Napier. This was the same year that a flax mill had opened in Kaiapoi. The purchase of the boat would be a turning point for his daughter Elizabeth. In October 1867, the Captain of the Maid of the Mill, Thomas Carter, had got into trouble by getting the boat on the 'south spit of the Kaiapoi bar.'[515] A new Captain was soon found.

On 24th October 1870 a large fire in Lyttleton started in an empty house between the Queen's Hotel and a boot and shoe salesman's shop, most likely George Heslop's shop, and spread to the entire business part of the town of Lyttelton. The fire led to the damage of much of George Heslop's drapery stock. He placed an advertisement in the paper titled 'Lyttleton Fire', to the effect that he had rented out two shops in London Street West to 'dispose of the goods saved from the wreck. They will be cleared out at low prices, more or less injured.' During the 1870 fire, a number of items were also stolen from his drapery business or home – in 1872 he sued a woman for having his 'punch bowl' but the case was dismissed and the woman given the benefit of the doubt. In 1870 the 'Maid of the Mill' was listed for the ketch's sale or hire (by David McKay, Leithfield; George Heslop, Lyttelton or Mr Moir, Central Hotel, Christchurch).

George's son Mowbray rushed to take photographs of the blaze, and the photos can now be found online. This would not be his first experience of taking photographs of a fire. In 1877 *The Star* newspaper reported that Mowbray Heslop took an excellent photo of the ruins of another fire that had occurred in Gloucester Street, immediately after that fire.

It has been assumed by family members that the 1870 Lyttelton fire was associated with the bankruptcy of George Heslop, but this was not filed until 5 years after the Lyttelton fire, in October 1875, when he was living at Papanui Road, Christchurch. George Heslop had reestablished his drapery business at Yorkshire House, Whately Rd, Christchurch. A month after he filed for bankruptcy, his son George William Heslop of Auckland (engineer) also filed for bankruptcy.[516] Son John George Heslop, a Draper from Greymouth, had earlier become insolvent in 1869. George Heslop senior sold by public auction the entire goods of his drapery business in October 1875 and the lease of his shop at Yorkshire House was auctioned in January 1876. From March 1876 a new owner or lessee (R. Gabites) occupied this drapery business, advertising millinery, ladies underclothing, babies' linen and fancy goods.

Mowbray Heslop, Photographer, Surgeon, World Traveller and Bigamist

Mowbray joined his family in Christchurch where he set up one of the colony's first photography businesses, M. Heslop & Company. His first photography studio was in Litchfield Street, 'three doors from Colombo Street,' Christchurch (until March 1870), and then around the corner at 'Imperial Studio', Colombo Street.[517] His old photography can be seen on historical websites about Aotearoa New Zealand. In 1869, Mowbray advertised that he was a photographer looking for 'a situation,' declaring himself to be a first-class operator from the United States.' It may have been where he had learnt photography, and he later travelled back to the US.

Mowbray later established his business and said it was 'the most extensive establishment in the Colony.' He was involved in the Good Templars lodge (IOGT), taking portraits of prominent lodge members in America and New Zealand, and publicly displaying life-sized portraits of the characters at lodge meetings. Many of Heslop's photographs can be found in the Aotearoa New Zealand archives and online.

Mowbray had questionable integrity and abandoned his first wife in New Zealand in 1878, with no forwarding address. She became ill and sadly died only a few years later, and shared the name of Mowbray's sister Elizabeth:

> *Heslop – Died, after a long and painful illness, Elizabeth, wife of Mowbray Heslop, Photographer, late of Auckland, Christchurch and Port Lyttelton, who is earnestly requested to forward his address to Mrs Alice Chissell, 2, the Green Mistley, Manningtoll, Essex, England – Newspapers please copy*
>
> *New Zealand Herald, 17 October 1881*

Mowbray had already remarried a second, much younger wife in Melbourne, Victoria (Emily Jane Bowern, 24 years his junior) in 1878 (as a bigamist) before fleeing to America and then abandoned his second wife in the US and married a third. His brother Alfred also left his wife.

Mowbray would reinvent himself as a Doctor/Surgeon in America before resorting back to photography. In 1880 Mowbray is recorded as Physician/Surgeon in the US census, living in the Corvallis Precinct in the County of Benton, State of Oregon. Exactly how he came to reach this lofty status from his background as an apprentice bootmaker in the UK and a photographer in the US and NZ is unknown. The period appeared to enable one to be self-proclaimed in their chosen profession, however some training was obviously required for these professions! There is a story (passed down from American descendants) that he learnt surgery whilst in the military

(American Civil War)[518], although there is no record of his service there. Mowbray died in Spokane, Washington in 1913.

Coincidentally, when I was travelling through the Rocky Mountains, Canada in the US in 2002 my camera suddenly stopped working at the beautiful Lake Louise. A lovely American lady called Margaret offered to take photos of me and send them back to me in Adelaide. My sister Margret had just died, so I thought this friendly stranger's name was a coincidence. When Margaret sent me the photos of me at Lake Louise, she also sent a number of postcards from Spokane, Washington, where she was from. It was only much later that I discovered a Great Uncle Mowbray who had lived and died in Spokane, Washington, and was a photographer by trade!

Above: Mowbray Heslop (D. Porter, Ancestry). Below: Advertisement for Mowbray Heslop's Photography Studio. He would be one of the first photographers in New Zealand. The Star, 2 November 1876.

PER 10s DOZEN.

FOR CARTE DE VISITE PHOTOGRAPHS, First-class work only, at the Largest and Coolest Studio in the Southern Hemisphere. To avoid having to wait, come early in the day.

Large PICTURES equally reduced in price, and beautifully finished. These Prices will only be continued for a short time.

M. HESLOP & CO.,
COLOMBO STREET,
OPPOSITE THOMPSON'S SEWING MACHINE DEPOT. 254

Star, Issue 2684, 2 November 1876, Page 3

2nd Generation in New Zealand

Elizabeth Heslop and Captain Charles Miller

Seven long years after her arrival in New Zealand, Elizabeth finally found a suitor. On 18 September 1866, Elizabeth was 26 years when she married in the home of her parents, to 28 year old Charles Miller, a 'Master Mariner.'[519] Miller had become the captain of her father's boat, *Maid of the Mill.* Family history claims that Miller was born in Scotland (and was from Aberdeen).[520]

Charles was a widow who had previously married Amelia Emma Ashton, in the house of Mr. King (his mother in law's father) at 61 Montreal St. Sydenham, Christchurch in 1865. Amelia died shortly after from pneumonia, leaving behind a young baby, Amelia Emma Magdalene Ashton,[521] who was left behind with her grandparents, Charles's in-laws (mother-in-law Eliza Ashton, nee King).

One year and three months later when Charles was still in 'half mourning' period over the death of his first wife, Charles married Elizabeth Heslop. But less than 8 months later, Charles placed an advertisement in the *Press* newspaper of 6 May 1867 that indicated that Elizabeth had left him:

> *My Wife Elizabeth Miller nee Heslop, having been induced to leave her home without cause, I hereby give notice that I will not be responsible for any debt she may incur, either in her own or my name.*
>
> *Charles Miller, May 3, 1867*

Elizabeth must have left Charles for good reason, especially as she was 6 months pregnant. She had a son, **George Heslop Miller**, on 21st August 1867.[522]

The reasons for Elizabeth fleeing may have been that Charles committed a crime. In October 1867, George Heslop was taken to court by 'Fleming's

Estate,' with them claiming £8 7s, contracted by Captain Charles Miller, for goods supplied to the *Maid of the Mill.* Were these goods stolen or resold by Captain Miller? This case may have led to difficulties for transporting goods in the *Maid of the Mill*.

It appears that Charles Miller initially stayed in Lyttelton and became Captain of the ketch *Margaret* (26 tons), which he owned. In 1878 the *Timaru Herald* reported that the *Margaret*, captained by Charles Miller and 'engaged in the firewood trade' was missing and later found; it came into trouble when its headsail was damaged by heavy gales, and had to be towed back to shore. The crew of the *Margaret* were entirely without food for 5 days, and prior to this had limited food for 10 days.

Also in 1878, Charles Miller, captain of the *Marguerite* [sic] was witness to a violent crime aboard his boat when two men from another boat that he had invited aboard (after spending time with them at the Wharf hotel) got into a fight. In 1879, Charles Miller was captain of the 'schooner' *Margaret* when it was dragged ashore from the river and caused a great deal of damage.

Finally, the *Margaret* was sold August 1879 at Lyttelton by public auction.

> *Mr John S. Willcox is instructed by Mr Charles Miller to Sell by Public Auction on August 12th , 1879,*
>
> *At his Rooms, London Street, LYTTELTON,*
>
> *The well-known ketch MARGARET, 25 tons register, with all her gear, sails, anchor and chains, kedge, double-purchase windlass & c., complete, in good working order. Sale at 1pm precisely.*

It is difficult to establish where Charles Miller came from, or where he went to after this, as there is no clear trace of the death of Elizabeth's first husband in New Zealand.

A Charles Miller, Mariner, was residing in Napier in 1882-1884, 1887 and 1898-1899.[523] He lived on Stafford Street, Port Ahuriri, which is right on the harbour. As this was the main harbour in New Zealand at the time, Charles Miller may have moved to Napier after he sold the *Margaret* in Lyttelton.

There is another Charles Miller, who was a seaman, a Dane and a known thief, who disappeared from New Zealand around 1876, and was thought to be in Sydney. He later died in 1908 in Cobden, Greymouth, New Zealand – but appears to be around 10 years older than the Charles Miller who married Elizabeth. This Charles Miller was a 'seaman' and not 'Master Mariner,' although men greatly exaggerated their claims at the time.

Another candidate with the same profession, was Charles Miller (Master Mariner), who married in Hobart, Tasmania in 1857, aged 23 years, and was with the British Royal Navy. He was born around 1834 – so four years older than 'my' Charles Miller. Charles married Elizabeth Hackett in Hobart and separated from her without divorcing (as my Charles Miller did with Elizabeth Heslop). Elizabeth Hackett was later looking for him when it was said that he was last known to be in Lyttelton, New Zealand.

Elizabeth Hackett had inherited money from her father that she could not claim, as she was still married to Charles Miller – money that, it was said, Charles Miller intended to claim. Later, in a Hobart court case, a lawyer states that Charles Miller is known to be in Melbourne (where my Charles Miller had relatives at that time - his daughter Amelia Emma nee Ashton and son George Heslop Miller). In 1889, a Charles Miller is staying at Barry's Marine Hotel in Melbourne.

Master Mariner Charles Miller is as elusive in death as he was in life! Did Elizabeth Heslop ever go back to Charles, spurred on by her father's bankruptcy and inability to financially support herself and her child? Charles popped up again in 1876, and about six years into Elizabeth's new marriage.

Chapter 14: Elizabeth and Albert James Abbott

By June 1876, eleven years after Elizabeth Heslop married Captain Charles Miller, Elizabeth was pregnant with the child of another man, Albert James Abbott. Albert would later say that he met Elizabeth when he was thrown from a horse when riding near her family property, after her brother offered assistance to him and brought him back to the Heslop family home.

However, the Heslop family lived on the same street (Papanui Rd, Christchurch) where Abbott's father Thomas Abbott had his nursery business and where Albert Abbott worked– so they could have met if Elizabeth was a clientele of the nursery. Elizabeth's younger brother Alfred was also part of the St Albans community, Christchurch (where he lived 1874[524] -1876)[525], which Albert was also a part of (and St Albans borders Papanui Road).

At the time in New Zealand, one could legally remarry if their spouse had been continually absent for 7 years.[526] It had been more than 9 years since Charles Miller had placed the advertisement saying that he would no longer be legally responsible for Elizabeth. Elizabeth was already living with Albert James Abbott – they resided together two months before their marriage – so perhaps Charles Miller briefly re-entered the scene, discovered his wife with another man and confronted her. On the 11th August 1876, Charles Miller was charged with assaulting his wife at Lyttelton, with the case being 'dismissed with a caution.' Earlier, on the 22nd June 1876 in Napier, Charles Miller was named in a criminal case at the Supreme Court, charged with indecent assault against a woman. The case did not proceed as the woman did not attend the sitting.[527]

Just weeks after the assault, on the 25th September 1876, Elizabeth remarried the much younger Albert Abbott 'a gentleman' at Timaru (south of Christchurch) – she was 36 and he was aged just 22. Elizabeth states that she is a Spinster on the marriage certificate, although she had not obtained a divorce from Charles Miller. She was now three months' pregnant (with Albert's child) when she remarried. It was said that Albert's parents strongly opposed the marriage between Elizabeth and Albert twice (perhaps as they knew that she was already married). Banns were published in the Avonside Anglican Church, Christchurch. Then the couple were married by a Baptist Minister, but the marriage and its registration was declined upon the advice of the Bishop of Christchurch and a registrar. The couple finally eloped to marry in Timaru with a Baptist Minister officiating.[528] Elizabeth was likely friends with Phillipa Thompson (nee Parsons) from Timaru, who like Elizabeth was a Dressmaker. Her child George Miller would later marry Phillipa and George Thompson's child Edith.

Exeter Nursery on Papanui Road was known for its 'choicest roses' and was a highly successful business. Thomas Abbott advertised in 1874 that he was 'By appointment to Sir James Ferguson, Governor of New Zealand,' with the endorsement of the Royal Emblem for New Zealand, and he later produced 'A general catalogue of plants' (1886). Albert Abbott was not just a 'Nurseryman' at his father's nursery business in Christchurch, he also called himself a 'Botanist'. There is no sign that he had science or botany training at a university, but this may not have been required at the time.[529]

Christchurch is known as the garden city, and the Abbott family played a central role in the development of its horticulture. The Christchurch Horticultural Society was formed in 1861, breaking away from the Christchurch Agricultural, Botanical and Horticultural Society to focus on horticulture. Albert spoke in public from an early age and became a senior member of the Christchurch Horticultural Society. As a teenager, in 1869 he received a special commendation for a bouquet of 24 cut roses at the Christchurch Horticultural Show. In 1873 he was elected a member of the St Albans Young Men's Christian Association and in the same year he gave a public recital called 'The Parting Hour,' deemed to be 'good,' according to one review.

Aside from having George (Miller), Elizabeth and Albert Abbott had the following children of their own:

Albert Lancelot Abbott (changed his surname to Miller), born 23rd March 1877 Christchurch, died 6th February 1953 South Melbourne

Hector Alfred Heslop Abbott born 21st April 1878, died 7th June, 1894 (aged 16 years)

Clayton Mowbray Abbott born 26th October 1880, Woolston, New Zealand, died 29th August 1963, Parkville, Victoria

Mabel (May) Violet Abbott was born in 1885[530], died 18th May 1974, Brunswick, Victoria. She married Thomas McWhinney Stevens, who served in WWI.

In November 1880, Mr Gimblett announced that A. J. Abbott of Exeter Nurseries 'with a well-known ability and acquaintance with the requirements of the public' would be managing Gimblett's nurseries. It is interesting that Albert decided to move away from working for his father's successful business, and this may have been due to his marriage to Elizabeth, which his parents strongly disapproved of.

In 1881, Albert was elected to the committee of the Papanui Educational District Board, resigning to move to the Heathcote district (Woolston) to take up his new job managing nurseries, where he became a member of the local council and United Ancient Order of Druids (a fraternal society). There he worked in Gimblett's nursery on Ferry Road, which was 20 acres, and managed the land in the Heathcote Valley also owned by Gimblett, another 20 acres.

The year 1882 was a highly eventful one. Work was going well and Albert sent ferns to the Great Exhibition of 1882 in Christchurch, the International Exhibition at Hagley Park. He also received a special prize for a bouquet exhibited at the Christchurch Horticultural Society.

However, tragedy struck the family the same year, as Albert's 8-year-old niece Ruth Harrison drowned in the Heathcote River. The coronial inquest at which Albert was a key witness was held at the Wharf Hotel, Woolston. Another witness told how the elder Harrison sister was allowed to go with her three younger siblings for a walk along the river (her mother and the children were visiting Albert and Elizabeth from Auckland); it was said a man gave her sister Ruth a fish and she was dangling it in the river on the end of a string when she fell in. It was noted by a juryman that the 'wires were broken down at the spot, where a great many children congregate.' No-one saw the child fall into the water, and when she was already in the water her older sister called out, and Albert ran and jumped in to save her, to no avail as the child was already drowned and could not be saved.

Albert may have felt responsible for his young niece's death, or for not being able to save her. The young family may have wished to avoid reminders of their loss, as the following year, in 1883, Albert and Elizabeth moved from the district of Lower Heathcote and away from the scene of the awful tragedy.

***

In February 1884 Albert and Elizabeth Abbott were living back at Papanui Rd, Christchurch (perhaps with his in-laws), but Albert was still not working with his father. He advertised in the *Lyttelton Times* that he was looking for 'a situation' as a nurseryman, florist or head gardener. The following month, Albert advertised that he was selling specimens of native and exotic ferns, carefully dried, mounted, and named, and at lower price than any other person in the profession.

In 1887 Albert was exhibiting and judging at the Christchurch Horticultural Society's flower show and read a paper titled, 'Narcissi.' He spoke regularly at the society, and in March 1888 gave a talk on 'Exhibition flowers'. His full talk covered the topics of roses, chrysanthemums, carnations and picotees, dahlias, gladioli, pansies, penstemons, verbenas, auriculas, phloxes, asters and zinnias. He is very knowledgeable about his subject and speaks in great detail, but he starts with a false humbleness:

> *In coming before you tonight, with the subject I have chosen, I feel I have undertaken a task too large, and one that requires greater talent and tact that I can possess. I feel I cannot address you with that confidence which is the outcome of greater ability, though I have been very successful in the cultivation and exhibition of almost every class of flower.* [531]

He also makes disdainful commentary on the New Zealand approach to the classification of certain flowers:

> *I need say very little about asters. The English and Continental growers have a great many classes of this flower, but we are not so highly civilized yet, for in our exhibitions we only recognize them as "quilled" and "not quilled." However, they are an important feature in our shows.*

In July 1888, Abbott gave another talk on 'Exhibition Blooms' to the Christchurch Horticultural Society, and along with his father and brother, he was also a judge of floral exhibitions.

Suddenly in September 1888, there is first mention of 'Professor Abbott' giving a talk at the Belfast Library[532], Christchurch, with his 'Professor' title likely to have been self-proclaimed. Albert's standing in the community, with the help of self-promotion, was about to rise. It appeared to be a time when one could declare themselves anything, or say they could do anything, without requiring proof and charlatans were free to roam. Whilst his horticultural experience and status in the industry was blooming, Albert's interest in spiritualism was also flourishing.

***

John Alexander Dowie, the Father of Pentecostalism and Faith Healing, arrives in New Zealand

Despite being raised as a Baptist, Albert became the Secretary of the Christ Church Divine Healing Association on 12 April 1888, at an inaugural meeting of 100 people This was the night after a talk at the Theatre Royal in Christchurch on faith healing by forceful and persuasive Evangelist Reverend John Alexander Dowie, titled 'The Sanctification of Spirit, Soul and Body.'

The same night of the inaugural meeting, Reverend and Mrs Dowie left for Auckland before heading to America. Dowie had arrived in Christchurch from Melbourne on the heels of an arson scandal that burnt down his Tabernacle church in Collingwood. He set up another healing centre in Fitzroy, but was a highly controversial figure in Melbourne, and was essentially fleeing Australia.

Faith healers such as Dowie were against the rapidly developing fields of medicine and pharmacy and believed that the earth was flat. Faith healing is the belief that (frequently Christian) prayers and other gestures (such as placing hands on the body) can lead to divine intervention for healing physical health problems and disabilities. Faith healing is still prominent in some countries – and appears to be on the rise, along with 'flat earthers'. It is associated with Pentecostalism which is one of the few growing religions and said to be the fastest growing religion in the world. John Alexander Dowie is known by some as the 'father' of Pentecostalism.

Reverend Dowie was dubbed a 'rascally false prophet.' He was born in Edinburgh, Scotland and was first a religious Minister in South Australia, before changing to faith healing and settling in Melbourne. One of his written works, still for sale and published by the revival library, is titled *'What Should a Christian Do When Sick?'*

In America, Dowie first established a mail order faith healing business in San Francisco, before setting up another faith healing business in Chicago, and then eventually establishing the religious City of Zion, near Chicago, where he owned most of the town's land and businesses. Scandal followed Dowie, and in 1903 he was charged with libel and taking US$2000 (worth around $75,000 now) from someone by fraudulent means.[533]

Photo: Alexander Dowie, who first taught Abbott faith healing. He fled Adelaide, then Melbourne, then Australia and set up the City of Zion in America (Leaves of healing, 1904, Zion City, Illinois – Public Domain)[534]

A new life in Melbourne

In September 1888 there was a large earthquake in North Canterbury, New Zealand, with many buildings being damaged in Christchurch including the Durham Street Methodist Church where the Heslop family worshipped. This was the same year that Elizabeth and Albert went to live in Melbourne, and may have been one of the reasons why they left New Zealand. Forced evacuations arising from the large earthquake could have been seen as an opportunity to make a new start and to try and protect their family and children.

Other reasons why the family left may have included that people in New Zealand knew that Elizabeth was a bigamist. There is also no record of Elizabeth having divorced Charles Miller, or of his death, so Elizabeth may have been concerned that the law would eventually catch up with her.

Other factors spurring them along were a number of deaths in the family. Both of Elizabeth's parents, who had been living with her family (at Springfield Rd, Christchurch) had now died, her father (in his 79th year) on 24th March 1887 and her mother (in her 83rd year) on the 29th September 1888. It was said of George Heslop's death: 'his end was perfect peace.' George Heslop is buried in the Addington cemetery in Christchurch (along with nine other Heslops), which was the first public cemetery in New Zealand, established by Scottish Presbyterians.[535] Elizabeth's elder sister Maria Shrimpton (nee Heslop) also died on 3rd November 1888 at Hokitika, on the West coast of New Zealand's South Island. Maria had been married to the chief postmaster and senior member of the Presbyterian church, Jonah Shrimpton. She had named one of her children after her sister Elizabeth (a child that had died in 1873, aged 8 months).[536] Maria was just 55 years of age when she died.

Another factor compelling the Abbott's to leave New Zealand was the great Melbourne Centennial Exhibition (1st August 1889 – 31st 1889). Albert arrived in Melbourne in time for the exhibition and before the rest of his family, and he advertised himself in Melbourne as a self-employed premier show card writer, designer and price ticket manufacturer.[537]

Dowie's escape from Australia also left a vacant position as Head of the Free Christian Church in Melbourne, which Albert Abbott eagerly took up (around 1890).[538]

On the 11th December 1888, Mesdames Abbott and children (possibly Elizabeth Abbott with Albert junior, Hector, Clayton and Mabel) sailed from Lyttelton to Melbourne. A new life at 48 years of age. Elizabeth's son George Miller came with them, but went back to marry Edith Thompson (Elizabeth's friend Phillipa's daughter) in New Zealand. George Miller's half-sister Amelia Emma Magdalene Miller also lived in Melbourne, after marrying Walter John King in New Zealand in 1885.

***

In Melbourne, the Abbott-Miller family were co-located in the headquarters of the Free Christian Church, the Bethshan Faith Healing Centre, 156 Nicholson Street, Fitzroy. This place is still standing and a photo of it can be found on the website realestate.com

Son George kept his father's surname Miller, whilst the older Abbott child changed his name to Miller!

The Free Christian Assembly met at York Street, North Fitzroy and the famous Foresters Hall, Collingwood (corner of Smith Street, Collingwood and Gertrude Street, Fitzroy), where Pastor Abbott gave many speeches and public lectures. Troubles with the Free Christian Church began in 1891, when *The Weekly Times* reported on 'A Peculiar Parson.'[539] The problem was that Albert James Abbott was abusing his power as a Pastor by 'seducing' and sexually assaulting young women in the church, kissing and fondling them.

That first accusation (by Johnson) of this nature were not acted upon, but shortly after, in 1892, Elizabeth accused Albert of acting in an inappropriate manner towards other women in the church. Elizabeth and Albert would cease to live with each other from the 11th September 1892, the date when Elizabeth refused to copy and send a letter written by Albert to one of his alleged lovers. Elizabeth was 52 and Albert 38 years old at the time. In November 1892 an article in *The Herald* was headlined:

A Bethshan Scandal. Pastor Abbott on his Defence. Charges of Immorality Refuted

A Queer Story, A Queer House, A Queer Family, A Queer Religion

Descriptions of Elizabeth and Albert can be found in the article:

> *Mrs Abbott is a somewhat tall woman, whose face at present resembles a pathetically worried appearance, due to the domestic grievances of which she believes herself to be a hapless victim... She was dressed entirely in black. Her hair is tinged slightly with grey; her figure is angular; and she has every appearance of having a soul sick with grief, or else a poor deluded creature with the bells of her intellect "jangled out of tune and harab." ... Mr Abbott is a very ordinary looking man of about 35 or 38... He might be taken for a bank clerk or shopkeeper – anything but a faith healer.*
>
> *The Herald, 28 November 1892*

Elizabeth referred to another woman on Mr Abbott's knee, being fondled and kissed by him, who was seen leaving his bedroom at midnight. These accusations were supported by a Mr John L. Jonas, of 150 Barkly Street Carlton, who was described as 'the champion of Mrs Abbott,' fighting against Elizabeth's poor treatment. Elizabeth says to the reporter:

> *We have been married 17 years, and before this woman came between us there has never been a happier couple.*
>
> *The Herald, 28 November 1892*

Elizabeth was accused by Albert of being deluded, and he said to the reporter that her son (George) and other members of the church had made a statement saying that her claims were unsubstantiated. At a public meeting, Elizabeth discusses how she was being 'gaslit'.

The woman accused of being Albert's love-interest admitted to going to Abbott's room on a Friday night to drop off his mended trousers. John Jonas wrote to the Editor of *The Herald* to correct inaccurate reporting on the matter. In his letter he refers to a child of Elizabeth and Albert's being sick – Hector (but Abbott did not want to use traditional medicine for his illness). Mr Jonas is Elizabeth's hero, a do-gooder and upstanding member of society who stands up against the devious Albert. Mr Jonas was also assistant secretary of the Pioneer Society, which promoted the Star Bowkett system, a co-operative non-profit building society/financial institution providing interest free loans to members.

Another public meeting was held in December 1892 where Abbott speaks up in his own defence and answers the accusations of his wife and Jonas. He gives his life history, claiming he hails from the Abbotts of Canterbury, New Zealand. George Abbott (born in Surrey, England) was the Archbishop of Canterbury from 1612 to 1633, his brother Robert the Bishop of Salisbury and brother Maurice the Lord Mayor of London.

Abbott detailed his education in faith healing, under the guidance of Dowie on his brief stop-over in Christchurch. At this meeting he claims that his wife suffered from a 'malady' and said that she had 'mania' from several years earlier. He also said that it was she, not him who was having an affair, but he retracted the statement after the crowd's cries of 'shame.' Albert would do anything to divert attention from accusations towards him that he was acting sexually inappropriately towards young members of the church, including when he was undertaking 'spiritual healing.'

Abbott outrageously claimed that the woman whom his wife was suspicious of was his wife's own daughter in law – Edith Miller (nee Thompson), the attractive young wife of Elizabeth's eldest son George - and one defence was that it was customary to kiss family members good morning and good night!

One charge against Abbott was that he had forged the name of another 'Brother' (Howard), in an application for permission to celebrate marriages, and exaggerated the number of the Free Christian congregation. Whilst the

Law Department was willing to investigate this matter, Howard had not wanted to proceed. Meanwhile, Brother Carvis also had issue with Abbott, describing how he was seducing young women in the church, including his own daughters![540] Another 'Brother' James Brown had seen Mr Abbott acting in an improper way at a picnic at Mentone,[541] and stopped speaking to request that all ladies leave the room to discuss the charges. Brother Brown resumed his statement, which resulted in Pastor Abbott arranging to withdraw from his position in the Free Christian Assembly. Brother Brown's statement was backed up by Sister Philips, who had been a witness at the meeting on the 29th November. Brother Atcheson also joined the criticism of Abbott.

In a dramatic moment, a Mr W. H. Bilton arrived at the hall and came up to the platform to read a letter delivered from Abbott. A gentleman suggested that as Mr Abbott had not appeared in person, the letter should not be read, but the meeting decided to read the letter aloud. In the letter, Abbott denied all charges against him, with many of his statements met with laughter by the congregation. Abbott claimed that the Carvis girls had put their arms around him and asked if he loved them, which was adamantly denied by their parents.

> *Mrs Carvis briefly explained that she had disapproved of Mr Abbott, and had called him a 'villain' to his face. She appealed to parents to protect their daughters by putting an end to such disgraceful proceedings.*
>
> *The Argus 28 Dec 1893*

It was decided by vote at this meeting that the charges against Abbott would be brought forward in public. The Chairman of the meeting, who had supported Abbott's character a year prior, now said that he was *'staggered when he became convinced that the charges made were true.'* Pastor Abbott was asked to withdraw from his senior position with the Free Christian Assembly, however this did not occur.

Scandals and run-ins with the law were ongoing for Abbott. One incident occurred in February 1906, when it was reported that Abbott sued a young woman, Mrs Rebecca Haldane, for attacking him with an umbrella at the Temperance Hall. During the court case, Rebecca is described as *'a small and thin-built little woman, young, and neatly dressed.'*

The scene of the umbrella incident occurred just after Abbott had walked his new partner psychic medium Mrs Annie Turner into the church. As Mrs Turner was singing a solo piece on stage, Rebecca went up onto the stage and, aiming for Abbott's head, she instead struck his arm. Rebecca had accused Abbott of various things, and according to Abbott, called him 'vulgar and wicked names.' Rebecca had struck Abbott as a result of a threatening 'horrid letter' he had sent her. Earlier, Abbott had hypnotised Rebecca and then forced her to write a letter in which she said that all previous charges she had made against him were false.

Pastor Abbott was the first to report the umbrella incident, firing off a letter to the editor at *The Age.* He then proceeded to sue Mrs Haldane. Sadly, Abbott's lawyers, Mr Westley tried to make Rebecca out to be a lunatic, just as Abbott would his wife. Mr Hobday represented the defendant, with Mr Dwyer (Presiding Magistrate) wise to the case, and the minor impact it had on the victim. Mr Hobday asked Abbott whether Mrs Haldane had any cause for making the attack, perhaps aware that Mrs Haldane was the true victim.

Rebecca Haldane had been part of the Free Christian Church in Collingwood in 1895 when Pastor Abbott was using faith healing for unsound purposes. Rebecca describes becoming infatuated with the Pastor when he was performing faith healing and phrenology and *'pat oil on [her] forehead...over the bump of individuality'.* Haldane said that Abbott was a constant visitor at her home until May 1905. She had made charges against him and was initially willing to go to the church committee as a witness to report against him, but concerned it would ruin him, she agreed not to proceed with the charges – but in front of two witnesses, said she did not deny them either.

Albert claimed that Rebecca and his estranged wife Elizabeth were conspiring against him, and blamed Elizabeth for Rebecca assaulting him (although Rebecca claimed Elizabeth knew nothing of the matter). However, much earlier Rebecca Haldane visited Elizabeth Abbott 'incognito.' During the visit, Elizabeth expressed sorrow for Rebecca who soon revealed her true identity. Rebecca reported to the newspaper that the older woman convinced her to go back to her husband. Elizabeth warned Rebecca against Abbott, his philandering having gone on for at least 14 years by this stage.

Elizabeth made a statement to the press on these events, and Abbott retorted, claiming that she was a bigamist as her first husband was still alive. Abbott claimed that he had married Elizabeth in 1880 (it was in fact 1876) when she said that she was a widow, but that her husband, a seaman, 'reappeared' six years into their marriage before again leaving on a voyage. He claimed that he had only three children by Elizabeth (perhaps disowning his eldest son who had, by then, changed his surname to Miller!). He said that he was paying her an allowance to 'keep things quiet for the sake of the children.' He inferred that the separation was due to his discovery that she was a bigamist, and not his own scandals that were revealed in 1892-93 and beyond. Such 'umbrella hitting' cases involving affairs were normally dismissed as they were deemed 'provoked', but in this case, Rebecca Haldane was fined 5 shillings. Abbott's sexual abuse of many women in the church was not addressed through the law.

Abbott continued a business and romantic partnership with Annie Turner, now Foster-Turner. Annie Foster-Turner claimed that she had channelled the ghost of William Stead[1], and took his advice to establish a 'Julia Bureau'

---

[1] William Thomas Stead was an English newspaper man and editor of the Pall Mall Gazette, who was said to be the pioneer of investigative journalism and used the now common practice of using the press to influence public opinion and the law. He raised the plight of child prostitution in England, through unethical practices. He

which she established in Melbourne and Sydney. These were the 'Foster Turner Institute' at 110 Bathurst Street, Sydney (a building that still stands), and the 'palatial mansion' at Foster Court, St Kilda Rd (corner Commercial Road), Melbourne, which had a fancy roof with an electric globe upon it. *The Truth* newspaper would creatively title an article about Annie's collaboration with Albert (although by this time, it was said that Annie had remarried a German, who had taken on her surname and was fined for it). They presented in March 1916 at St James Hall, Phillip Street, Sydney, and a very rich and derisive description of Annie and the event was provided:

> *A number of strong, well-fed men who would be better in military camp or doing honest farm-work, were buzzing about with the two portions of a cane carry-all, collecting articles from which Mrs. Turner was supposed to give readings by the aid of second-sight and spooks. By the time the collections were finished, two tables and two chairs were heaped up with a miscellaneous assortment of women's bags, purses, gloves—black, white, and brown—blouses, bundles, men's hats, collars, neckties—probably Mrs. Turner*
>
> *DREW THE LINE AT SOCKS*
>
> *—photographs of all kinds and ages—many in khaki—and hundreds of letters in sealed envelopes. The articles were arranged—the medical readings at the table at the seer's right hand; the love, business, etc., at her left.*

---

was a 'spiritualist' who claimed he received messages from the spirit world and produced automatic writing (writing that had come directly from spirits). Stead founded a 'Julia Bureau' in 1909 in Mowbray House, London, for people wanting to experience communication with spirits in the after-life. The Julia Bureau was named after Julia A. Ames, an American temperance reformer and journalist whom Stead met in 1890, just before her death. Another friend and correspondent of Stead's was Sir Arthur Conan Doyle, who shared his interest in spiritualism and the paranormal. Stead appeared to predict the Titanic disaster through stories he wrote, one in 1886 and one in 1892. Stead boarded the Titanic voyage in 1912 to participate in the peace Congress at Carnegie Hall, as requested by President Taft, but went down in the Titanic.

The night was close, and the audience found Mrs. Turner so late in materialising that it signified its disapproval by clapping and stamping in the customary manner, so Mr. Abbott, who was busy arranging the articles—there were quite enough to stock a suburban shop—stepped forward on the platform, and holding up one white finger in a warning fashion, said, "My Guide tells me that he will prevent Mrs. Turner from reading the articles of those who stamp or clap." At the mention of

THIS AWFUL THREAT,

the gulls became silent as the grave, so Mr. Abbott went on to say that the new surroundings were so strange that the audience must have a little consideration. He is evidently the right-hand supporter of the spookist, and he looked a worn imitation of "Get-Rich-Quick Wallingford" in a grey frock-coated suit, grey hair, brushed nicely back from a "smart" brow, a sky-blue necktie, and a blooming pink bouquet in his buttonhole.

The curtains arrived at the back opened, and Mrs. Foster-hyphen-Turner arrived. My Colonial Oath! She was a great, gorgeous and gargantuan vision. Anything less spirtuelle and mystic it is impossible to imagine. To put the matter plainly, the spookist is fat, and as symmetrical as a beer-barrel; indeed,

ANNIE'S AVOIRDUPOIS

is amazing. She does not glide or float as a witch should – she waddles. The top half of her was decollette, and the immensity of her bare, beefy back a dream in these days of dear meat. Her skirt was of embossed purple velvet of royal tone and a long train tried to add majesty to her squat appearance. Her bodice – what there was of it – was cream lace, and on the place where her waist would have been had she been the possessor of one, was placed a bunch of roses. Her patent leather court shoes were decorated with paste buckles. Round her neck was a gold chain and pendant with sparklers. Her fat arms, with which she could doubtless give a good account of herself at a washtub, were bare, while her fat paws sparkled with diamond rings. On her head she had piled enough brown hair to stuff a bolster, several combs studded with brilliants, and a bunch of roses and foliage adorned the structure. Raising spooks and

CLAIMING TO CURE SICK PEOPLE

must be a paying game, for Mrs Turner is a splendid specimen of Mrs Newly Rich.

The performance consisted of alleged medical diagnoses of all the evils flesh is heir to, from the articles on the medical table, prophecies from the articles on the business table, interrupted by visions of spooks. She drawled out what she had to say, taking a very long time to say very little, and skimming off the danger signals by saying that if she spoke any plainer and said any more, she would have the law down on her.[542]

Annie Foster-Turner died aged 60 in 1921 at Foster Court, St Kilda Rd, Melbourne. An obituary followed which recognised her 'remarkable gift,' whilst it was also reported that she had to pay 150 pounds for giving police false information, but which later proved to be true. When author Sir Arthur Conan Doyle (of Sherlock Holmes fame) toured Australia, he commented on Foster-Turner's gifts and assistance in helping to find a missing person (who was deceased), which caused much controversy in the press.

Foster-Turner left a considerable amount of wealth and gave the farm at Trafalgar to her ex-husband George and other property to family and friends. Abbott may have inherited the 'Foster-Turner' Institute property at 110 Bathurst Street, Sydney, were he continued to work as a 'Medical Botanist', 'Botanic Herbalist,'[543] 'Spiritual Healer,'[544] Phrenologist,[545] and 'Psychological Expert' offering 'Vocational Guidance'.[546]

Photo: Albert James Abbott, 2nd husband of Elizabeth Heslop. Source: (M. Miller) Below: Love Rivals, At left, Mrs Rebecca Haldane, accused of 'assaulting' Pastor Abbott with an umbrella At right: Mrs Annie Turner, whom Abbott would have a relationship and business partnership with (Trove)

Abbott became more right wing in his views and broke with his spiritualist past. In the 1930s Abbott fiercely attacked the theory of evolution and in 1934 he also attacked radical theologian Dr Samuel Angus at a public forum in Sydney at the British-Israel World Federation (of which Abbott was President), where Angus critiques contemporary interpretations of the atonement. In the 1930s debate, Abbott declared himself a *'gold medallist in theology…[and said that] he had the record in Australia in marriages – he had celebrated 14,000; and that he refused to take money for preaching the gospel.'* He said that Angus was *'flying to idolatry, and [was] going astray.'* In 1932 he gave a speech as part of the New Guard Civil Unit (a growing fascist movement at the time) on *'God, King and Country'* and in 1935 he was involved in Empire Day with the Governor, giving a talk on '*The Ancestry of the British Throne.'* The same year, in an article titled *'Abbott Again,'* he vehemently denied accusations that he was ever a spiritualist.

***

Elizabeth Abbott worked to the end as a 'Warehouse Manager' to support herself, whilst Albert made for Sydney. Elizabeth died in 1920 at 174 Barkly Street, Brunswick, and is buried at the Coburg Cemetery.

Elizabeth seemed to have lied about her age during her lifetime, as her death certificate indicates that she was born in 1848, however the census of 1851, shipping records of the *Zealanda* and her baptism suggest she was actually 79 or 80 years old when she died, and born in 1840.[547]

Elizabeth died at her daughter (and son in law's) Mabel and Tom Stevens's house. A personal notice placed in the newspaper indicated that she was the *'dearly loved mother of G. H. and A. L. Miller, and Clayton M. Abbott, and Alfred (deceased)'*. She was very close to her surviving children when she died, as the photograph by the Yarra showed, and her death notice placed by them read:

We may be loved by others

But love like mother's never comes again.

When Abbott died in Melbourne in May 1941, there was only one funeral notice, placed by two of his students:

In loving memory to our late beloved Pastor and teacher, Professor A.J. Abbott…A faithful and true leader.

Albert had lived around 30 years in NSW and 20 years in Victoria at the time. He was not close to his children, and in one letter his daughter writes to him to complain about his infrequent visits and she was upset that she had not been invited to his birthday in Sydney, although she briefly cared for him when he was unwell until his death.[548] After his death, his legal firm tried to sell his herbal remedies and books.

Above: Two of Elizabeth and Albert Abbott's children. Mabel Violet Stevens (nee Abbott) and Thomas McWhinney Stevens, Ethel May Abbott (nee Walsh) and husband Clayton Mowbray Abbott, circa 1911 (late M. Miller)

Back to Aotearoa New Zealand

Aotearoa New Zealand is a favourite destination of mine, which I have visited on four occasions, in 2003 (Lyttelton, Akaroa, Christchurch, Kaikoura, Timaru, Queenstown, Dunedin, Invercargill and in between), 2008 for a conference and leisure (Auckland, Rotorua and Taupo), 2017 (Wellington, Napier and Hawkes Bay, Taupo and Whanganui River Road), and 2025 (Auckland, Whangarei and Bay of Islands). The place is stunning and feels like a second home, whilst Christchurch has a similar feel to Adelaide. Visiting Lyttelton and Akaroa was a must on the first trip, given that our ancestors first settled in Lyttleton and the Miller's house in Victoria was named 'Akaroa.' Seeing the Lyttelton harbour for the first time, it was easy for me to imagine the ancestors being captivated by the natural beauty of the place upon their arrival.

Photo: Piha Beach, west coast of Auckland, 2025 (S. Battams)

Chapter 15: The Miller Family in Victoria

3rd Generation in New Zealand and Australia

George Heslop Miller and Edith Elsie Thompson married in Christchurch in July 1889 (in the Wesleyan Church, Colombo St). Edith was born on the 3rd December, 1870 in Timaru, New Zealand. George's usual residence was Melbourne at the time of his marriage – he had come to Melbourne with his mother Elizabeth, Albert Abbott and family in 1888 and gone back to Christchurch to marry Edith. George and Edith Miller then travelled back to Australia after their marriage. Initially, they lived at 45 Turner Street Abbottsford (where Leonard was born) and for a time with Elizabeth and Albert Abbott at Nicholson Street, Fitzroy. They later lived at 31 Alice Street, Coburg, and the house was named 'Akaroa' after the beautiful town harbour town outside Christchurch in New Zealand (the house has since been rebuilt).

George was listed as a clerk in the Victorian Directory, and a Commission Agent – a person who makes money from directly selling goods or services on behalf of others. When he died a message was left in the newspaper by the Royal Victorian Liedertafel, a choral society with German roots, that regularly played in Melbourne saying: *A tribute to the memory of George H. Miller, from the members of the Royal Victorian Liedertafel Society, 'whom he served faithfully and well.'*. He was a Commission Agent for the Liedertafel society, making money from selling concert tickets. This may fit with the story that his son Leonard Miller insisted that all of his children learnt to play a musical instrument. This connection with music appeared to be connected with the Heslop line. A descendent of Elizabeth Heslop's sister Charlotte said that *'Charlotte was by all accounts quite a cultured woman, well versed in music and the arts (being an accomplished pianist and amateur composer), and always received a generous allowance from her father until her marriage in about 1865 to Henry Patterson Harrison.'*[549]

Photo: Edith Miller nee Thompson with baby Leonard Albert Miller (Grandfather) (late M. Miller). She died aged 41.

Photo: George Heslop Miller (late M. Miller)

George Miller and his wife Edith had seven children, but three died when they were young:

Leonard Albert Miller born 7th February 1890 at 45 Turner Street, Abbottsford, City of Collingwood, Victoria. Died 29th July 1954, Adelaide

Percy Clarence Miller 1891, Melbourne, died 14th August 1974, Kew, Victoria

Edith Elsie (Elsie) Miller 1893, died 1st December 1967 at Heidelberg (married Richard Lowe)

Stanley Wilfred Miller 1895 (died 28th August 1908 aged 13 of acute rheumatism)

Cecil George Miller born August 1899, died 1st January 1900 of gastro enteritis (aged 4 months)

Dorothy Parsons Miller and **Grace Heslop Miller** born 27th July 1901. Dorothy died aged 11 on the 20th December 1912 (acute rheumatic fever) at Heidelberg, Victoria. Grace died 2nd March 1967 (congestive heart failure)

Edith and George Miller would regularly travel back to New Zealand – there is evidence of them travelling together in April 1892,[550] June 1893[551] and of Edith on her own in January 1895.[552] I wondered if she stayed in New Zealand in 1895, as 'Mrs George Miller' won a prize for three pounds of butter at the Waimate Show in November 1895,[553] and our grandfather referred to spending some time in New Zealand growing up. There may have been good reason to travel back to New Zealand and escape from the confines of the Bethshan Faith Healing Centre in Melbourne, especially due to the scandals arising at the end of 1892.

In 1912, poor George Miller's wife Edith died in July – when she was just 41 years of age - and his daughter Dorothy died in December of the same year. Twelve years later George remarried Esther ('Essie') Amelia Hoyle in 1924 (there were no children from this marriage).

His son Percy Clarence Miller was a highly successful businessman; a knife, drop forge and die manufacturer / engineer who commenced companies such as P.C. Miller, The Australian Boot and Shoe Shank Company and

Miller Cyclone Forgings (with the Cyclone company), which is now known as Cyclone (still operating today).

Albert Lancelot Miller, half-brother of George Heslop Miller, became a dentist, and his children included twins Robert Hepburn Miller (known as Hepburn) and John Robertson Sheddon Miller, barrister, who died young at East Woodburn, Newcastle-on-Tyne, Northumberland, England. When Albert Lancelot Miller died, he left a few thousand pounds which was to be shared equally between the Prince Henry's Hospital, the Children's Hospital, Blind Institute and Lost Dog's Home. Another half-brother, Clayton Mowbray Abbott, married Ethel Walsh, whilst his sister Mabel Violet Abbott married Thomas McWhinney Stevens.

Photo above: Grace Heslop Miller, younger sister to Leonard A. Miller (M. Miller)

Thompson and Parsons Families in New Zealand

The Thompson family came over to New Zealand around the same time as the Heslops, arriving on the ship '*Lincoln*' on the 19th July 1**867**.[554] Phillipa Parsons (1837-1918) was from Cornwall whilst her husband George Thompson (1836-1911) was from Yorkshire. George was a Labourer, and his father was an agricultural Labourer. George and Phillipa were married at Soke Damerel, Devon in 1863, and lived for a time at Kent, where George was a gunner in the 5th Brigade of the Rifle Artillery at Woolwich, Kent (1866).

Phillipa was 29 years old when she travelled to New Zealand on the *Lincoln* in 1867 with George and three children; Harry (3), Mary Ann (2) and Emma (9 months). This was a perilous journey that took 5 months (15th February to 19th July 1867). The Thompsons would have five more children in New Zealand, including Maraquita[555] (1867), Thomas (1869), **Edith** (1870), William Parsons Thompson (1875) and Annie Thompson (1879). Their last three children were born in Timaru, New Zealand. The passage of George Thompson and his family cost £70, £62 of which was paid by George's father-in-law Thomas Harris Parsons in the Colony of New Zealand (in July 1866).[556]

Phillipa's parents, Thomas Harris Parsons (who owned a Foundry and was an iron founder, farmer and carter, Timaru) and Mary Ann Lang had already arrived in New Zealand in **1865** with youngest children Mary Betsy Lang Parsons (15) and William Moses Parsons (7) (who would become an engineer). Their trip was also paid by 'friends in the colony' – son-in-law Thomas Mills, the husband of their daughter Susanna Parsons. Other children in the Colony included Thomas Harris Parsons junior (contractor, New Plymouth – later went to Western Australia). Another son, James Parsons (Farm Labourer), travelled to New Zealand on the *Lincoln* with his wife and child in 1867, with his sister Phillipa and George Thompson and family.

The Thompson family lived and had a dairy farm at Okutu Valley, Little River, Canterbury on the Banks Peninsula, now about 45 minutes' drive from Christchurch. In February 1883 the entire family were forced to escape from a fire with just the night dresses that they were wearing, with their eight-roomed house destroyed. The premises were not insured, and a large quantity of dairy produce and equipment were destroyed, around £300 worth.

Tragedy again struck in June 1883 when a house on Sophia Street, Timaru (near the Timaru Harbour) owned by Thomas Harris Parsons senior (Phillipa Parsons' father) was burnt down during the night. The house had just recently been vacated by a tenant leasing the property. Thomas Harris Parsons was accused of arson for the insurance money (which he had recently organised). He was charged with willfully and unlawfully setting fire to the house in Sophia Street, Timaru with the intention of defrauding the Liverpool, London and Globe Insurance office, with a bail of £200 and two sureties of £150 being allowed 'as before.'[557] Parsons was accused of purchasing tar that was found about the burnt down house. In December of 1883 the Grand Jury of the Supreme Court found 'no bill' against Thomas and he was discharged.[558] Perhaps the two fire events were related, if Thomas Parsons was in fact guilty.

The Thompsons returned to the city of Christchurch and were living in Phillipstown, a suburb of Christchurch, when the following year their daughter Maraquita died aged 16 (on 26 March 1884). In 1883-84 there was a typhoid outbreak in New Zealand, and pertussis was also widespread. Measles, scarlet fever and diphtheria were also common. Maraquita was buried in the Addington cemetery in Christchurch, where many of the Heslop family are also buried. Sadly, older brother Harry Thompson died of typhoid just two years later (1886) in Sydney.

There are a number of wonderful old photos of the Thompson family in New Zealand, including of George and Phillipa Thomspon, their daughters with their mother at Little River, and of son William Parsons Thompson (on Ancestry).[559] Unfortunately I have not been able to contact the person who uploaded them to get permission to publish them here.

Chapter 16: A DNA Surprise – The Hazlehurst and Bird Families

The DNA testing turned up one unexpected surprise in this story, regarding a secret kept for 136 years! After more closely analysing my DNA results and matches it became apparent to me in October 2025 that we are related to the Hazlehurst and Bird families on our maternal grandfather's side. Thus we are not biologically related to the Miller and Heslop families, and our grandfather Leonard is not biologically a 'Miller.'

The person who offered to help through the DNA Angel network (Merrie Bott) who first assisted in 2021 to analyse Dad's DNA noted that the name Hazlehurst kept appearing in the DNA match results – but it was clear that this was on our mother's side. In 2025 the latest update indicated for me a strong percentage of DNA from Northern Wales and North West England (25%), but no known family members from there, so this led me to go back and check the Hazlehurst name, which was in fact from Cheshire in North-West England.

I then discovered amongst DNA matches two English trees which had a common combination of ancestors, and trees in New Zealand that had the same Hazlehurst names– to discover that I (as well as my sisters and my Uncle) am definitely a descendant of the couple John Hazlehurst (1811-1873) and Elizabeth Bird (1816-1890).

I then researched the name Hazlehurst on Ancestry and Papers Past websites to discover that some of the sons and grandsons of this couple (John Hazelhurst and Elizabeth Bird) had travelled to New Zealand and Australia.

Our great grandfather George Miller's family had just moved to Melbourne in 1889, and George came back to New Zealand to marry Edith Thompson.

Just before her marriage (in Christchurch) to George Heslop on 6th June 1889, Edith must have fallen pregnant to a Hazlehurst descendant.[560] Edith was born and raised in New Zealand, and came to Australia with George after her marriage. Our grandfather Leonard was born in Melbourne 7th February 1890, seven months after his parent's marriage.

Whilst we can identify the great-great grandparents on this side, it is more difficult to pinpoint the our great grandfather. Below are some possible candidates (sons and grandsons of John Hazlehurst and Elizabeth Bird).

Candidate: William Hazlehurst senior (1842-1910)

William Hazlehurst (1842-1910) arrived in Auckland, New Zealand, from Cheshire, United Kingdom. He was an apprentice blacksmith in the UK and became a Farrier in the No. 1 Troop, Colonial Defence Force and Auckland Militia, fighting in the second Taranaki war, for which he was issued a war medal (which he did not collect for many years).

William later worked as a Farrier for Mr James Blyth, a Blacksmith at Prebbleton, near Christchurch, Canterbury.[561] Blyth commenced business there in 1864,[562] and had advertised for another Blacksmith in 1870.[563] Blyth became bankrupt in 1874,[564] but did not sell his effects until 1877.[565] By 1872, Hazlehurst sought tenders for opening up a store at Prebbleton,[566] which he did and that became a successful business. He also got in trouble with the police for selling liquor illegally from the store, and leaving his horse unattended a few times! Notably, there was also a William Heslop who was a blacksmith at Prebbleton, who may have been related to our Heslop family (although this link has not yet been found) – this William also had a child called George Heslop (not our great grandfather George Heslop).

William Hazlehurst senior built the local community hall at Prebbleton, a swimming bath (open to the public through a private subscription), and was the agent for Government Life Insurance. He was also the distributor of a number of products (such as local newspapers) through his business. He was a member of the Oddfellows and Druids lodges and the Masons.[567] He was an active participant in the early development of the Christchurch, being on School Committees and Road Committees, commissioning the building of Prebbleton Hall, known as 'Mr Hazlehurst's Hall,' was on the All Saints' Church committee and part of the Friendly Societies (a mutual benefit society) and the Prebbleton Mutual Improvement Society, which in 1892 debated the issue of women's suffrage with William arguing in favour of it[568] - New Zealand being the first country in the world to enable women's suffrage.

William Hazlehurst senior was 'between marriages' at the time that Edith Thompson became pregnant. He married in 1870 to Isabella Henderson, but she died young, and he remarried Alice Wright in December 1889. In 1889 a Hazlehurst forebear (who could have been the same as ours) also got another woman pregnant by the name of Alice Schroeder (she went on to marry someone by the surname of Lawrence about 13 years later).

William Hazlehurst (Chairman) and a George Thompson (not my forebear but another George who hailed from Warwickshire, England) were on the Prebbleton School Committee in 1882.[569] William Hazlehurst was also involved in a 'plough racing' competition, with a George Thompson.

There was also a William Heslop, blacksmith, who worked at Prebbleton (his son was George Heslop) (but it is difficult to establish a relationship with our Heslop family).

Elizabeth's Heslop's father and brother Alfred Heslop also lived in the same vicinity as William Hazlehurst. William was on the same list of electors in 1868 with George Heslop, who were lobbying for the return of William Rolleston Esquire to office.[570] He was also in the Prebbleton Horticultural Society in 1881,[571] which may have later put him in touch with A. J. Abbott and Elizabeth.

William Hazlehurst owned a house and land at Heathcote (the continuation of Colombo St South) and was also a member of the Druids: Superintendents Roll – Canterbury 1873-74. Prebbleton was part of the Heathcote district (where Elizabeth and A. J. Abbott lived), and William Hazlehurst is listed on the Heathcote Electoral Role for 1880-1881.

In his older years, William had a 'Magnetic Healing' (an alternative therapying using pulsating magnetic fields) business at 57 Cashel Street, Christchurch. He died in 1910 aged 67 at 59 Cambridge Terrace, Christchurch.[572]

Candidate: William Hazlehurst (1874-1943)

William Mathew Hazlehurst born in New Zealand in 1874 was the eldest son of William Hazlehurst above. He is a possible candidate, and was just 4 years younger than Edith (he was only 15 in 1889 whilst Edith was 19 years years old).

Candidate: James Hazlehurst (b.1851)

James Hazlehurst was born in England in1851 to John Hazlehurst and Elizabeth Bird, a brother to William Hazlehurst senior (b 1842). He travelled to New Zealand, where he got Sarah Lewis pregnant, but they were unmarried. Sarah went to court to sue James, but James escaped jail as he stated that he intended to marry Sarah, which he did, and they went on to have several children. However, James abandoned Sarah, and Sarah resorted to prostitution in order to survive. Their children were fostered out, with one of them (John) dying at Woodend when he was just 9 years old, when living in the home of a foster carer. There was a large investigation into John's death reported in the New Zealand newspapers.

Candidate: Thomas Wesley (1870-1948)

Thomas Wesley was the son of William Hazlehurst senior's sister Elizabeth Hazlehurst (and William John Wesley). Thomas Wesley moved to

Melbourne, Australia, however appears to still be living in England in the 1890s. In 1915, Thomas Wesley, driver, was living at 118 Barkly St, Brunswick, the same street where Elizabeth Abbott was living when she died (174 Barkly St, Brunswick). Thomas Wesley died in 1948 at Parkville, which is around 8 kilometres from Coburg (where Edith Miller nee Thompson lived).

Candidate: William Henry Hazlehurst (1874-1902)

Another William Hazlehurst (nephew of William Hazlehurst senior, above), lived in New Zealand, but was killed in a work accident near New Plymouth in 1902. His father was said to be serving in the Boer War, South Africa at the time. Both George and J.E. Hazlehurst (either John or Joseph) served in the war, with J.E. Hazlehurst being a Farrier (shoe smith) in the second Boer War.[573] William Henry Hazlehurst was 4 years younger than Elizabeth. Based on DNA matches of the descendants of George Hazlehurst, this is a strong candidate.

Grace Roscoe

Through this newly discovered branch in the family tree, we have a famous ancestor by the name of Grace Roscoe (1715-1795), who was disinherited of a fortune as she refused to marry the man her relatives wanted her to, and instead married for love.

There are mixed accounts of her story, but the main thread was that her grandfather was James Hardman (1st) who had two children, Margaret and Richard Hardman. Margaret Hardman married John Roscoe, and Grace was one of their three children. Richard Hardman had two children, James (2nd) Hardman, Esquire of Rochdale, and John Hardman, who became nouveau rich merchants (their wealth was linked to the slave trade), and owned many properties in a large estate (land in Childwall, Woolton, Garston, Aigburth,

Liverpool and Allerton). John Hardman was also a Member of Parliament for Liverpool.

The eldest brother (James) had two wives, the second wife being Jane Leigh, whom he had six children with. Jane was related to the aristocratic Percival family and wanted Allendale Hall, Liverpool (now a pub) kept in Percival family hands. Richard Percival had purchased Allerton Hall and owned it from 1670 until 1736, when James Hardman purchased the land, reportedly at the insistence of Jane.

The family wanted Grace Roscoe to marry James Percival, an older cousin of Jane Hardman, and it was intended that she would inherit the estate on the death of the Hardman brothers. None of James's children were living – a daughter and three sons all died.

However, young Grace had fallen in love with a coachman, John Hazlehurst and they eloped and fled Allerton, marrying in Eastham in 1732. Grace and John Hazlehurst leased a farm, Brow Farm, situated off Hoylake Road, Birkenhead.

James Hardman (2nd) died in 1746, and rather than leave his inheritance to his niece Grace his estate was left to his brother John. When John died in 1755 without children, he left a will barring Grace and her descendants from inheriting the state for 99 years, and left his brother's widow Jane Hardman as his executor.

When Jane died in 1795, aged 93, there was a dispute over who would inherit Allerton Hall and the entire estate. It was said that a man named James Clegg removed Jane's body to Rochdale and buried her privately (with her husband) and then went to Allerton Hall, dismissing the servants and taking possession of the estate. Clegg was the owner of half of the property which he had purchased.

In 1799 the self-made historian, writer of children's literature, botanist, art collector, lawyer, M.P. and one of England's first abolitionists William

Roscoe purchased Allerton estate and became the occupant of Allendale Hall. He wrote 'The Butterfly's Ball and the Grasshopper's Feast,' books that I loved as a child, especially the beautifully illustrated versions (which I still have). It is unknown whether William Roscoe was related to Grace Hazlehurst nee Roscoe.

The estate was still meant to revert to the descendants of Grace after 99 years. In 1831, William Hazlehurst, a grandson of John and Grace Hazlehurst, attempted to make a claim for the estate. He was said to have found proof that the Hazlehursts were the rightful heirs, and that Jane Hardman was guilty of fraud. He intended to bring the case to court, entrusting the documents to a solicitor, however the solicitor was said to be found dead in Allerton and the documents proving the claim were missing.

In 1889 another claim was made by Samuel Hazlehurst, furniture broker, heading up a syndicate of Hazlehurst descendants. One of the sticking points for the claim was proof of Grace Roscoe and John Hazlehurst's marriage. There is reference to this marriage in the Bishop's Transcripts for Eastham. A more recent publication from 1911[574] claims that this reference is a clear forgery, with different ink and handwriting to other entries,[575] and it is stated that at this period a 'new year' commenced on the 24th March, so a 30th March wedding (when they were said to be married) should have been at the beginning of the year 1733.

There was a book of fiction written about this saga in 2022, titled *'Grace Roscoe: A True Love Story,'* written by another descendant, Ruth Welsby (Ruth has also written crime books).

Hoylake Boatmen – the Birds

Another ancestor was John Bird (1771-1810),[576] one of the Hoylake Lifeboatman, who aged 40 years, along with two of his children, Harry (18 years) and John (16 years) and his nephew Henry Bird (18 years) (son of William Bird) died in an attempt to rescue a sailing vessel called the

Traveller. The vessel got into trouble in a storm on the way to Liverpool, and was driven ashore via the Mersey River on 22nd December 1810.

Altogether, 8 men and boys died in the lifeboat, whilst two men including Captain Joseph Bennett survived and were able to swim ashore when the boat capsized. Amongst those who died was Joseph Hughes, 38, his brother Richard Hughes, 36 years and Richard's son Thomas Hughes (16 years old). The men were buried on Christmas Day and Boxing Day 1810 at St Bridget's Church in West Kirby, whilst an eighth member of the crew, Nicholas Seed, was buried in St Hillary's, Wallasey on Christmas Day 1810. At the time, the village Hoose would have only had around 100 people living in in. The newspaper at the time reported that:

> *The bodies were all found the same day, and carried to their respective homes, where a scene of piercing misery was witnessed which defies all power of expression. The deceased were all near neighbours, and lived in a small village called Hoose, near Hoylake, in the most brotherly kindness; these brave fellows were the flower of the Hoylake fisherman, and had always displayed the greatest promptitude and alacrity in assisting vessels in distress. They have left large families totally unprovided for.*[577]

In 2010 an impressive community funded memorial sculpture statue was erected on the seafront at Hoylake, Wirral, in memory of the Hoylake Lifeboatmen, depicting a coxswain at the helm of a lifeboat,[578] and a commemoration event was held 200 years after the tragedy.[579] A musical called *'Lessons from the Past'* was written by another descendant of the Bird family and performed in 2019 which included the story of a man discovering his family were involved in the Hoylake lifeboat disaster,[580] as I have just done!

Chapter 17: The Miller Family in Adelaide

4th Generation in Australia

Mum said that my grandfather Leonard Miller had spent some time in New Zealand growing up, that he was mostly raised in Melbourne and came to South Australia in his early 20s. Leonard became a 'seaman' who left his boat at Encounter Bay, where he met my grandmother Stella Rumbelow. He married Stella in Norwood on the 23 June 1914. Leonard was 24 years old and Stella was just 16 years old, and she gave birth less than 3 and a half months later. Their children's middle names indicate their links to names from the paternal line (Heslop, Parsons):

Dorothy Heslop Miller (4th October 1914-30th July 1991)

Frank Albert Miller (25th November 1917 Coburg, Victoria – 12th March 2004)

Edith Stella Miller (26th April 1919 Payneham– 3rd November 1988)

George Godfrey Miller (24th May 1920 Kensington – 11th August 1998) (served in WWII Citizens Military Forces)

Joyce Lillian Miller (11th February 1922 Richmond – 5th June 2003)

Audrey Mae Miller (10th February 1925 Richmond – 29th September 2011)

Daphne Joan Miller (7th November 1926 Clarendon – December 2017)

Gwendoline Parsons Miller (28th November 1927 Clarendon – 24th July 2020)

Marjorie Dawn Miller (30th April 1929 Clarendon – 17th May 2020)

Valma Jean Miller (8th November 1930 Edwardstown – 24th December 2014)

Leonard Kenneth Miller (21st October 1932 Blackwood – 19th April 2019)

Stanley Leslie Miller (12th November 1935 Queenstown - living)

To my mother and her siblings, her father Leonard Albert Miller (1890-1954) was a respectable man who was a strict Methodist, had a stern temper, was clever and a talented engineer and fitter who could make or fix anything. He also had problems with alcohol. Stella Rumbelow was a stay-at-home mother with twelve children and even more pregnancies (it was said that she gave birth to her last surviving child at home on her own, a twin, the other twin had died in-utero, but how she survived this is a mystery).

Leonard and Stella's first child, Dorothy Heslop Miller, was born in Norwood on the 5th October 1914. Dorothy would end up playing a parenting role for her younger brothers and sisters. Leonard and Stella Miller initially went to Melbourne to live for the first three years of their marriage. In 1915, Leonard and family lived at 31 Alice St, Coburg, with his father and sister Edith Elsie Miller. He was back at Phyllis Street, Maylands (where his in-laws lived) in February 1916, where he was living when he was hit by a car and thrown off his bike,[581] and the same month became a subscriber to the Minda Home.[582] His second child, Frank Albert Miller, was born in Coburg 25th November 1917. At the time Melbourne was very polluted and not good for Stella's asthma, and they soon came back to South Australia for good (initially living in Payneham where they purchased property).

Lenoard became a gardener at Payneham. My mum claimed that my great grandmother Ada Rumbelow (nee Heading) did not like her son-in-law Leonard, and I always wondered why. I was shocked to hear from mum that her father told her on her wedding day that he had got two women pregnant at the same time, an auntie and niece, and he had to make a choice of who to marry (he chose the niece, Stella)! My grandmother had aunties the same age as her, including Hilda Heading. Hilda and her much older sister Ada Heading both ended up marrying men in the Rumbelow family from Victor Harbour – a nephew and Uncle. There were also a number of Rumbelow aunties the same age as Stella.

Photo: Leonard Albert Miller (M. Miller) – with Hazlehurst/Bird origins (M.Miller)

Leonard was an advocate for better working conditions for workers and fairer treatment of returned soldiers. In 1917 he wrote to *The Daily Herald* in Adelaide advocating for gardeners, complaining to Mr Lundie (trade unionist) about gardeners working long working hours (60 hours per week) for low wages (7/ per day, or 42/ per week), highlighting that many of them were members of the Australian Workers Union, which Lundie headed.

The same year, Leonard wrote to the newspaper complaining about the misuse of funds allocated by the State War Council for returned soldiers to learn to drive motor cars, and suggested that these funds were being misused by government Ministers in cars being driven all over the state for leisure purposes (such as horse races), and Labor party promotion rather than official government work.

One thing Leonard tried to instill in his children was a sense of equality, saying to them that 'no one is better than anyone else, everyone is created equal' or words to that affect. It was a time when, mum remembered, people who went to university did not speak to the likes of their family.

In 1919, Leonard Miller passed his certificate to become an 'engine driver,' [583]the same year he was appointed 'poundkeeper' at Payneham council (local government official responsible for the feeding and care of stray livestock).

In June 1926 the family lived in a house at Arnold Street, Parkside which burnt down to the ground (but was insured, as were the contents). The newspaper reported that the parents and six children were out on a drive to Clarendon. An Engine Fitter, he had soon established his own motor and truck agency and engineering business (at Clarendon). In November 1926 his seventh child (of twelve children) was born at Clarendon.

Like many, Leonard became bankrupt in the lead up of The Great Depression. The business property at Clarendon was on a 10 year lease (1928-1938), but before the lease was up, they left. His eldest son Frank passed down a story of how he was forced to work all night in the business workshop at Clarendon, and he would get into trouble for falling asleep the next day at school.[584]

Leonard was no stranger to the law. Shortly after being awarded his 'engine license' in 1919, in 1920, 1925 and 1927 he was picked up for speeding or other offence, and in 1928 was fined for leaving his car standing in the street at Glenelg without his lights on. He was on the insolvency court list in 1927 and declared insolvent in 1928 (the judge 'awarded a second-class certificate, suspended for a month'), and it was said that he did not keep proper records or have good business acumen.

Another shock was the discovery that he had been charged when he was 36 years of age with attempted rape and committed to trial at Clarendon on the 20th March 1929[585] (a charge later dropped as the Crown filed a certificate of 'no information'[586]). This was just one month after his 9th child was born, and the year before my mother was born. The victim - Vera May Oakley (who had married Alfred Oakley) - was a young newly married woman who had just turned 21 years of age and was on her honeymoon. The couple were being transported around by Leonard who did this driving work as part of his motor and truck business (as was common at the time). Leonard was a member of the Methodist church at Kangarilla and Vera was a solo vocalist in the choir. It would have been difficult to prosecute for crimes of this nature at the time, as it still is today.

The family soon moved from Kangarilla. In the 1930 City Directory, Leonard Miller was listed as a motor mechanic at Clarendon., but by November of 1930, my mother was born at Edwardstown. The family then moved to Blackwood where Leonard junior was born in 1932, before finally settling in Queenstown, where son Stanley was born in 1933. The house at Queenstown was rented and not purchased until 1948. When leasing the house at Queenstown, Leonard said he was from Victoria, although when he owned and leased the previous properties, he listed his address as South Australia.

Leonard worked in his own business at Queenstown. It was said that he patented or fitted the conversion of motor vehicles from petrol to kerosene during WWII when there were fuel shortages, and with this conversion being in demand this enabled the purchase of the house at Queenstown. He was also an engineer/fitter at Islington Munitions Factory during World War II. As a skilled engineer, he would not have been permitted to serve overseas in the war. It was said of the factory that:

> *The Commonwealth factory for the manufacture of brass cartridge cases and fuses will be erected here for the Ministry of Munitions... A branch railway from the Port line near WOODVILLE is expected to be laid to the CHELTENHAM works, which will include foundries and rolling mills for melting and fabricating the brass.*
>
> *The Mail 3 Aug 1940*

I was surprised to find that Leonard owned or had mortgages on five pieces of land/and or houses prior to purchasing the Queenstown property: one at Payneham, three pieces of land at North Richmond (or North Plympton) and one at Clarendon in the 1920s.[587] Shortly after purchasing the properties at North Plympton, he transferred them to his wife's (or another person's) name (in 1924). There appear to be various mortgage holders in quick succession and part ownership of land. Many of the transactions appeared to involve Ernest Charles Saunders, a Real Estate Agent of Millswood, who had previously been sued (along with Edwin Ashy) by lawyer Howard Shierlaw[588] regarding a land transaction.[589]

Extraordinarily, land or mortgages on land were passed back and forth between the same group of people (including Real Estate agents) within a short period of time. For example, regarding a piece of land at North Richmond (title 1037/68) owned, it was:

- purchased by Leonard Miller on 5th January 1921
- sold from Leonard Miller to Joseph Brandwood on 11th February 1921.
- Another mortgage on the same land went from Leonard Miller to Joseph Brandwood on the 13th of March 1923.
- Another mortgage on the land was transferred from Leonard to his wife Stella on 6 May 1924. Another mortgage went from Stella to Ernest Charles Saunders (Real Estate Agent) (and Emily Constance Saunders) the same day, on the 6th May 1924.
- Another mortgage went from Stella Miller to Ernest Charles Saunders (Real Estate Agent) and his son Cyril Arthur Saunders on the 21st March 1925.
- A mortgage on the same land went from Stella Miller to Janet Agnes Parsons on the 10th March 1926.
- In September 1927 a mortgage on the land went from Janet Agnes Parsons to Ernest Charles Saunders and Cyril Arthur Saunders (Real Estate Agents).
- That mortgage was then discharged, and another mortgage on the land went from Janet Agnes Parsons to Ernest Charles Saunders and Cyril Arthur Saunders on 26 January 1928.

Real estate agents were also private lenders during this period, and may have held people's mortgage for a time so they did not lose their homes. Transferring ownership to one's spouse could also have occurred for tax minimisation purposes, or to save the property in the event of bankruptcy (and in the case of Leonard Miller, bankruptcy was pending).

The Queenstown house was a place generally well-remembered by my mother, and she recalled growing up in this house as a generally happy period, with strong camaraderie between her sisters – four of them shared a bed when they were young.

Photo above: the former Miller family home at 68 Victoria Street, Queenstown, with Stella and Stanley Miller out front (M. Miller). This was on 1600m2 of land and there are now nine properties on the site. Below, Alberton Primary School circa 1940 or 1941, with around 56 children in one class. Mum (Val Miller) is standing in the second row from top, fourth from left.

Above: Leonard Albert and Stella Lillian Miller at Queenstown, Below: Daphne, Val and Gwen after painting stools for sale (S. Miller)

Photo: The Miller girls outside of 68 Victoria Street, Queenstown, and the boys below (S. Miller, M. Miller)

Photo above: The youngest 7 Miller children. Back: Audrey, Gwen, Daphne and Marjorie. Front: Len, Stanley and Valma (S. Miller) Below: Audrey, Daphne, Gwen, Marjorie and Val. Front row seated: Leonard and Stanley, Source: S. Miller

Photo above: Uncle Frank Miller with one of the engineering business trucks (S. Miller) Below: Leonard (right) and a co-worker at Finsbury during WWII (Taken circa 1941-1945) (S. Miller)

Good memories passed down from mum included singalongs around the piano with the family (every Sunday night), going out with the sisters, helping in her father's business (painting stools), milking the cows and looking after the chickens, and the neighbourliness of the time. Mum loved reading books and would also stow away to a quiet area to read. One of her favourite books was Jane Eyre – with a strong, independent and morally principled female character who stands up for herself (my middle name is Jane after her).

Mum remembered her father as being authoritarian, telling her off at one stage for not peeling potatoes properly (when she was only around 9 years of age) – she apparently replied 'why don't you do it yourself' and walked out in a defiant manner, much to the shock of her sisters as 'you didn't' speak to your father like that.' However, he had trouble with alcohol and anger, and it appears his children were somewhat scared of him when he was in a temper. Mum recalled him calling out angrily when he could not find his 'drink', and the girls (my mother and her sisters) would hide from him at the bottom of the garden (the Queenstown property was on 1600 square metres). Stanley recalled picking him up from the pub when he was too drunk to drive. Stella endured her spouse, and as the working-class mother of twelve children (eight girls and four boys) during the Great Depression, there seemed to be limited options.

One sad incident was remembered from a child's perspective by mum as being when older sister Dorothy 'went to the toilet one night and never came back.' Poor Dorothy had fled the burden of looking after her younger siblings, and was married shortly after. She ended up living with her spouse and brother Uncle Frank and his second wife Margaret for a time (his first wife had sadly died giving birth to twins, and they were temporarily in the Kate Cocks Babies Home until Frank remarried).

Photo previous page: Daphne and Valma Miller at Semaphore circa 1945, (S. Battams),[590]and some of the Miller girls with their mother (and Cheryl) below: Audrey, Val, Gwen, Stella, Dorothy, Daphne, Marjorie (M. Miller)

The Miller Siblings

Throughout her life, my mother Val was very close to her siblings (especially sisters Marjorie, Daphne and Gwen), regularly meeting her sisters in Adelaide on a weekly or fortnightly basis when she lived near the city. She was also close to her younger brothers, Len and Stan, and at one stage my stepfather worked for my Uncle Frank at his farm in Willunga. For the women, it was a time when there was a strong social focus on 'getting women back to the home' post WWII, and they were all homemakers. My mother had gone to Alberton Primary School (when there were 50 children in a class at the time!) and then the Port Adelaide Girls Technical School which focused on subjects such as home economics, dressmaking and needlework and mum could cook, sew, knit and crochet, amongst other practical tasks. Subjects at her school included a general science and 'mothercraft instruction.'[591]

The Miller men were mainly small business owners in the farm machinery (Frank Miller) and motoring business (Len/Stan), and Uncle Len Miller set up an apprentice scheme, whilst Stan had a motor/spare parts business. Len Miller was an active member (Grand Master) of masonic lodges and was a life member of the Volkswagen Association, whilst Stan and his family were involved in managing the Speedway (Adelaide Motorsport Park). The Miller men all married strong women, with Joan Miller (Stan's wife) being the first woman in South Australia to have a motor racing license (she raced a pink mini!), whilst Margaret Miller (Frank's wife) played an important role in managing the farming business. I fondly member Len's wife (Auntie Lorraine) as an engaging person with a flamboyant fashion sense and an active interest in alternative therapies. Auntie Gwen Gilbert and Margaret Miller were particularly fond of (and had the means to) travel, travelling until their senior years. Margaret Miller engaged in family history research and contributed heavily to the research on the Miller/Thompson/Heslop families.

Top left: Dorothy Miller. Top right: Edith (Edie) Miller. Bottom: Frank with his 2nd wife Margaret and the twins

Top Photo: Gwen's wedding (to Reg Gilbert), with her father Leonard Albert Miller and sisters (from left) Daphne, Marjorie and Valma Miller as bridesmaids, 12th June 1948 Bottom Photo: Uncle Stan's wedding to Joan. My sister Cheryl is the flower girl second from right (S. Miller)

Photo: above: marriage of Audrey to Len Stewart, with Daphne as her bridesmaid (at right) Below: George Miller and his wife Ethel (S. Miller and M. Miller)

Photo above: Marriage of Daphne (nee Miller) and Glenn Last. Below: Len Miller junior's marriage to Lorraine Penley

Photo above: Majorie, Below left: Marjorie (nee Miller) and Frank Maidment,
Below right: Marjorie (our mother sewed the 'M' on her front pocket) (S.Miller)

Below: The Miller family with Ken Rumbelow (back). Back row: Dorothy, Frank, Ken, Edie, George, Joyce, Audrey, Daphne. Front: Gwen, Marjorie, Val, Len and Stanley (circa 2005) (S. Battams)

Part 5: Step-Father's Paternal Ancestry

1847: The Battams Family of Norwood, Payneham, Marden and Moorook, Riverland

Chapter 18: The Battams Family

Introduction

My step-father was Leonard (Len) Frank Battams, whose paternal Battams ancestors were a shoemaking family from Buckinghamshire, England. His direct forebear George Battams first settled in Payneham and worked as a market gardener. His Battams line then went to Moorook in the Riverland in South Australia after being granted soldier settlement land post WW1.

Len's mother's family was the Bormann family of Millendilla who were Prussians (from Meseritz, now Międzyrzecz in Poland) and came to South Australia as part of Kavel's people – in 1841. Len's forebear Johann Gottfried Bormann was naturalized in 1847, at the same time as Johann Gramp.[592] Len looked very much like his German side of the family, especially his grandmother Lydia Othelia (Ottilie) Hettner (a photo of her is on Ancestry).

I was surprised to find that both the Battams and Bormann family were shoemakers in their home countries – Len always insisted I wear good shoes!

A key theme from the Battams family was helping to plan or build communities in the city of Adelaide or town of Moorook, and of the 'brothers' supporting each other – in their adventure to Australia, through publican endeavours, through service in the World Wars, and in football teams. I was also surprised to find when researching this book that one of Len's relatives had married in 1904 someone who was born in India, during the time of the White Australia policy.

1st Generation to arrive in Australia

Len's great-great-great-great grandfather was William Battams (b.1791) who married Mary Ann Badrick on Christmas Eve, 24th December 1818 in Buckinghamshire, England. William died aged only 22 years old in about 1840. His widow Mary Ann then came to Adelaide, South Australia with her children on the ship *Phoebe*, arriving in Port Adelaide in 1847. Mary Ann remarried Edmund Taylor in Adelaide. The children of Mary Ann Battams (nee Badrick) and the late William Battams (1st) were:

George Battams (1819-1876)
Benjamin Battams (1824-1872)
Sarah Battams (1824-1864)
Daniel Jacob Battams (1829-1881)
Jacob Battams (1833)
Elisha Battams (1835-1870)
William Battams (1838-1870)

In the UK census of 1841, Mary Ann Battams[593] (40 years) was living in the east end of Weedon, Aylesbury district, Buckinghamshire with her five younger children: twins Sarah and Benjamin (both 15yrs), Daniel (10yrs), Elisha (5 years), and William (3 years). Her son George Battams, 20 years, was single and living nearby in Weedon, Hardwicke, Cottesloe.[594] The following year her son George married Sarah (b. 1820) nee Wesley (first husband Spargo)[595] on the 8th November 1842 in Hardwicke, Buckingham.

Mary's brother-in-law George Battams, shoemaker, wife Phoebe, twins Mary and Sarah (aged 10), and their grandfather Elisha Battams who is listed as a 'mealman' – someone who deals with grain are also listed in the 1841 census. In the 1851 English census there is another record of George and Phoebe Battams (now aged 56 and 53 respectively), and they are listed as a cordwainer/shoemaker and shoebinder respectively. Living with them is daughter 22 year old Sarah Battams (lacemaker), and father Elisha Battams who is 89 years old ('retired corn dealer'), as well as George Rolls, three years old, probably a grandson. This corresponds with the family history (passed down by Len Battams) that the family were shoemakers in England.

Arriving in South Australia on the 27th March, 1847 on the ship the 'Phoebe' were brothers Daniel (17 years), Jacob and **George Battams** jnr (with his wife Sarah and their child Harriet). Their mother (widow) Mary-Ann Battams (46 years)[596] and her two younger children Elisha, 11 years, and William, 9 years, also arrived on the same ship.

The previous year, on the 28th April 1846, George Simonds[597] and wife Sarah (21 years) (nee Battams –sisters to the above) arrived in South Australia, also on the *Phoebe* (the Simonds and George and Phoebe Battams, below, were living nearby in Buckinghamshire)[598]. Mary Ann's son Benjamin also emigrated to South Australia, where he married Mary Drage in 1857.

2nd Generation in Australia

The family eventually settled in Norwood, Payneham and Marden. In South Australia George Battams jnr was a farmer and involved in construction. George Battams's wife Sarah died in the colony 15 June 1856 at Lowe Farm, Payneham. Widower George Battams was left with a family of five children:

Harriet Battams (born c 1846 in England, married William Nicholas Spargo 6th Jan 1868)

Susan Battams (born 1st October 1847 in Adelaide and died 16th October 1872 in Marden)

William Alfred Battams (2nd) (born 1849, died 1902)

George Battams (born 11th January 1853 at River Torrens and died 19th April 1878 in Marden)

Ellen Battams (born 15th July 1854 at River Torrens and died 26th December 1855 in Payneham)

Less than four months after his wife Sarah died, George married Mary Ann Spargo (1833-1903) (his wife' sister in law) who had arrived in South Australia in 1848. The new marriage was announced in the *Register*:

> *11th October 1856*
>
> *On the 25th September at Trinity church, by the Rev Dean Farrell, Mr George Battams, farmer, Adelaide, to Miss Mary, only daughter of Mr Nicholas Spargo, late of Cornwall.*

George and Mary-Ann then had at least 11 children together, but four died in infancy.[599] The family lived in Payneham and Marden. There is still a Battams Road which crosses Marden and Royston Park, that is referred to early on in the Colony: on 29th June 1860 the *SA Adverstiser* reports the Payneham council minutes, stating that Councillor Green had engaged Mr. George Battams for forty yards of gravel, on Battams' Road, at 2s. 6d. per yard.

Chapter 19: Daniel Battams's Changing Fortunes

Daniel Jacob Battams (1829-1881)[600] was a well-known figure in Adelaide, mentioned many times in South Australian newspapers.[601] Arriving in the Colony with his family in 1847, the same year Daniel was appointed a Constable in the Mounted Police Force.[602] He captured two bushrangers at Rivoli Bay, who were robbing the outstations of a farmer at Mount Gambier.[603]

A few years later he found a considerable amount of gold (in 1852) in the Victorian goldfields, which he entrusted to his brother George in South Australia.[604]. The 91.5 ounces of gold he found would be worth around $367,914 today.

> *Battams, D consigned 3 oz of gold to Battams G which arrived by escort 2 on 50501852. Note: Delivered to Battams, George.*
>
> *Battams D consigned 57 oz 15 dwt[605] of gold which arrived by escort 2 on 5-5-1852. Note: Delivered to Battams D.*
>
> *[not recorded] consigned 30 oz of gold to Battams D which arrived by escort on 3 on 6-7-1852. Note Delivered to Battams Daniel.[606]*

Publican Brothers

Upon returning from Victoria, Daniel Battams married Ann Blight Potter, on the 30th August 1852,[607] and became a publican. In 1860 he was voted the Chair of the private company known as the 'Permanent Land and Building Association' in Adelaide,[608] the meetings of which were held in his hotels. Daniel became a money lender and worked at the Town Hall Loan Office.

His first child, Daniel Potter Battams, was born on the 3rd April 1854 at North Adelaide. In the early 1850s Daniel Battams leased the Fountain Inn, then the Thistle Inn, Weymouth Street, which in 1859 he transferred to W.H. Campbell.[609] This was where his daughter Clara Battams was born, on the 21st July 1857.[610] Another daughter was born in October 1859.[611]

Brother Benjamin was also a publican, and leased the Kangaroo Inn on South Road, whilst George Battams leased the Remarkable Inn at Melrose. On the 14th July 1860 it was reported in the *SA Advertiser* that Daniel Battams had purchased 8 parcels of land, at 5 pound 5 each, in the township of Willochra, Flinders Ranges (county not yet named), in the government land sale. This land was north of the famous Goyder line (known for its dryness and unsuitability as farming land). In December 1860, George Battams transferred the Remarkable Inn, Melrose, to Daniel Battams.

The Mount Remarkable Races livened up the quiet town.[612]

> *MOUNT REMARKABLE RACES*
>
> *The dull monotony of the township was greatly enlivened last week by the usual annual race meeting. On Tuesday, the 1st instant, the day fixed for the entry, stragglers might be seen coming in, making eager enquiries concerning the likelihoods of what sport &c., was expected, and who were to be the lucky winners. Diverse were the opinions as to the merits of the horses well know as about to be entered, more particularly between the rival champions of this place and Stirling (near Port Augusta). Everyone seemed, however, to have made up his mind to spend, if possible, a happy and agreeable day or two, and, as the result proved, did so to their heart's content, as on each day of the sports everything went on in the most orderly manner, and no occurrence took place to interfere with the bill of fare.*
>
> *Wednesday, the 2nd instant being the first day, from an early hour preparations were making for a start to the course, and a universal gathering might be seen at Host Battams' Hotel, waiting for their horses and conveyances to proceed. In fact the township looked quite alive with bustle. On reaching the ground, a large and commodious refreshment booth was visible, erected by the beforementioned Host, and in which all necessaries and comforts*

could be obtained. The day was delightfully agreeable, a refreshing south-easterly wind, and old Sol not interfering too much.

Daniel Battams had a bit of trouble and misfortune in Mt Remarkable. Firstly, in February 1861 it was reported in the *SA Advertiser* that someone had tried to steal a horse from him.

MELROSE, MOUNT REMARKABLE [from our Correspondent]

William Swift, aged 23, was charged with being on the premises of the Mount Remarkable Inn for some unlawful purpose. Daniel Battams, innkeeper, sworn, said – After shutting up his house about half-past 11 o'clock, he went round his stable and premises to see that all was right. Got to the end of the stable. Observed a man's head over his horse's shoulder. Saw a handkerchief round the horse's neck. Waited for a minute or two, then advanced towards the prisoner, and asked him what he wanted there, and with his handkerchief round his horse's neck? Prisoner snatched the handkerchief off the horse's neck and said that he wanted a place to sleep. Requested him to go to the police station. The prisoner refused, saying he hoped he would say nothing about it. Mr Battams took him to the Police station and gave him in charge to Police trooper Campbell. In answer to His Worship, the prisoner said he had nothing to say with respect to his character. His Worship asked Mr Battams if he wished to press the charge. He replied he did not, but hoped His Worship would deal summarily with him. His Worship admonished the prisoner, and told him in all probability in a few minutes more he would have been taken up for horse-stealing. As it was, it looked very suspicious; therefore, he should commit him to Redruth Gaol for two months with hard labour.

...The Committee for procuring a duly qualified medical man have nearly .8200 in hand and promised as soon as one comes to reside among us.

The lack of proper medical care may have contributed to the death of his elder son Daniel Potter Battams (1854-1861) shortly after:

> *25th May 1861   DIED*
>
> *Battams – on Wednesday May 15th at the Mount Remarkable Inn, Melrose, Daniel Potter, eldest son of Mr Daniel Battams, aged 7 years.*[613]

In June 1861 just after the death of his son, Daniel Battams transferred the lease of the Mt Remarkable Inn. On 10th September he took the lease at the Red Lion Inn, 13A Rundle Street, Adelaide. He was also an agent for tickets to travel to the Yorke Peninsula by boat. However, in the same year that his son died, his young daughter also died, this time from measles:

> *Battams DIED*
> *At the Red Lion Inn, Rundle Street, after 4 days illness, from measles, Annie, youngest and beloved daughter of Mr Daniel Battams aged 1 year and 11 months.*
>
> *The South Australian Advertiser, 16th September, 1861*

Another son was born at the Red Lion Inn on 6th September, 1862[614] and also named Daniel Potter Battams (2nd).[615]

Photo: Grave of Daniel Potter Battams 1st (7 years and 1 month), Annie Battams (1 year and 11 months), and Annie Battams nee Blight (42 years), West Terrace Cemetery, Road 3, Path 12, Plot E6. Photo above and below taken courtesy South Australian Police Historical Society, 2012, and Ms Kate Woodcock, Manager of the Society's Photographic Records Section

Photo: Grave of Annie Battams nee Blight and two of her children, West Terrace Cemetery. The size of the grave and plot also shows the one-time wealth of Daniel Battams senior (courtesy SA Police Historical Society)

Photo: Red Lion Inn at right of the photo. It was between King William Street ant James Place (now where Rundle Mall is).[616]

Daniel Battams was an active member of the Lodge, and in 1862 was involved in a celebration of the Loyal Newton Lodge, at the Glynde Hotel. The chair was the South Australian Attorney General, and a number of Members of Parliament in senior roles were also there. At this meeting:

> *Brother Battams gave "The Manchester Unity and the Board of Directors." The former had gained world-wide celebrity: but he was bound to state that he thought the District Officers had all been very remiss in absenting themselves on that occasion. It was indispensable for the purposes of conviviality that one or other of those officers should be present at such gatherings. The toast was drunk with Lodge honours.*

Daniel Battams was the Grand Master of the Friendly Societies Oddfellows Meeting (I.O.O.F. Lodge), King William Street, Adelaide, which amongst other things raised considerable money for the Widow and Orphan Fund.

Battams spoke about the fund at the 1862 meeting:

> *The widows had not ceased from their Order, and they made it a rule to alleviate distress where it existed. Brother Battams responded...The fund hat at the present time £215 to the good, and the other funds in connection were equally prosperous. The total sum in hand amounted to about £6104 13s 10d.*[617]

In 1863 Daniel Battams put in a mineral application with others for 'South of Mount Craig, Near Randell's Look-out, Northern District.' This was around 80 acres.[618]

In 1868 he purchased the Freemasons Tavern, Pirie Street, where Freemasons meetings were regularly held. Daniel Battams would later be publican of the Black Bull Hotel, Hindley Street, which currently still carries the same name.

Daniel Battams owned a considerable amount of land with Olivia Jane Galley, his business partner's (George Miller Galley's) wife. In 1866 they put forth their names on land in Norwood they wanted recognised as being owned by them under the 'Real Property Act.'

> *VILLAGE OF NORWOOD – Lots 48, 49, 50, 51, 52, 53, and 54 of Block 22 and 23 of Section 261, Hundred of Adelaide; Olivia Jane Galley and Daniel Battams; Residence, Adelaide.*
>
> *South Australian Weekly Chronicle, 10 March 1866*

Daniel Battams also had land at 'Hutt River Survey, Oakbank, and Port Adelaide. He held various land in trust.'[619] In 1866, he was executor for the will of Esther Rodda, wife of Stephen Rodda of Strathalbyn.

His business partner George Miller Galley was a publican, a money lender, land broker and Agent from the City Loan and Discount Company, shipowner and draper. He had also worked at Town Hall Chambers, Adelaide.[620] Daniel Battams was also a money lender and Chair of the Permanent Land and Building Association, whilst George was the Secretary.

In 1862, George advertises for shareholders of the Association to attend a meeting at Daniel Battams's hotel:

> *PERMANENT LAND AND BUILDING ASSOCIATION – The usual MONTHLY MEETING and SALE of SHARES will be held at the Red Lion Inn, Rundle-street, on Wednesday, the 9th instant at 8pm precisely. Members in arrears are referred to the 30th Rule. The Office will be Closed on Easter Monday, 21st April.*
>
> *GEORGE MILLER GALLEY, Secretary*[621]

Photo: Freemasons Tavern, Pirie Street, Adelaide, 1865 once owned or leased by Daniel Battams, B5099/4

George Miller Galley had founded the Apoinga Hotel, Apoinga, in the mid North of South Australia (1850-51). However, just four years later he (when described as a shipowner and draper), he was declared insolvent on 17th July 1855,[622] issued an Insolvency Notice and ordered to appear in court.[623] In 1860 Galley was charged with having assaulted a Director who went to his house out of hours and demanded information, or to know if a shareholder had been paid.[624] In 1874, Galley charged 'a little boy' for stealing 'kilndust'[625] and an Irish debtor who he states had the money to pay, with the debtor being imprisoned for three weeks.[626]

Daniel Battams and George Miller Galley were close, and in 1871 George appointed Daniel as his attorney during his temporary absence from the Colony.[627]

In 1986, the Department of Transport advertised that unless the Registrar is contacted by the owner, agent, or another person having knowledge of the whereabouts of a ship referred (or the ship's owner or agent), then the ship's registration would be closed. The ship Galley owned was the *'Harry,'* left abandoned at Port Adelaide.[628] It has been abandoned for many years.

Rubbing shoulders with Royalty and Governors

In 1866, Daniel Battams was invited to the opening of the Adelaide Town Hall, a highly ceremonious occasion with many dignitaries, a grand banquet, bands and singing. Tribute was given to the Queen and other members of the royal family, along with Sir Dominick Daly, Knight, Captain-General and Governor in Chief of South Australia.

> *The Gallery was filled with ladies, who gave grace and animation to the scene and one great delight of the evening seemed to be the appreciative manner in which the lords and the fairer part of the creation seemed to regard each other. Chapman's Band occupied the platform, and played throughout the evening with great spirit and effect. Mrs Wishart contributed not a little to the enjoyment of the evening by her singing.*[629]

In 1867, Daniel Battams was invited to a reception at Government House with the H.R.H Duke of Edinburgh, and of Saxe-Coburg and Gotha, Prince Alfred Ernest Albert (Queen Victoria's second son). The Prince would later marry (in 1874) in St Petersberg the Grand Duchess Maria Alexandrovna of Russia, the fifth child and only surviving daughter of Alexander II of Russia and Marie of Hesse and by Rhine.

The Prince was amused that he did not receive the reverence to which he was accustomed:

H.R.H seemed to be a little amused at the fact of a number of persons wo presented their cards and passed through without the least obeisance, or even glancing at the Duke. They evidently had not often been to a levee, and this little circumstance more than once induced a smile to suffuse the Prince's Face.[630]

The same year Battams was on the general committee, along with notables like Sir Henry Ayers, for the banquet to his Excellency the right Honorable Sir James Fergusson Bart, Governor in Chief, prior to his departure for England. This event was held at White's Rooms, or the Adelaide Assembly Room, King William Street, Adelaide (which was later known as the Bijou Theatre).

The Reform of Licensed Hotels

In 1872 Daniel was still at the Red Lion Hotel and looking for a cook for a seaside hotel, with 'liberal wages given.' In 1874, he was part of a deputation of six licensed victuallers meeting with the Attorney General to discuss resolutions determined the previous day at the Freemasons' Tavern.[631]

The publicans were concerned that *'persons of all classes obtain licenses irrespective of the character of the buildings,'* and were keen to keep the licensing system as it is, but desired the appointment of an Inspector of Public Houses, that the Inspector report to 20 Magistrates from a Licensing Bench. The publicans also wanted to ensure that *'colonial wines should be retailed by licensed victuallers only'* and that *'permits to carry on business after 11 o'clock be only granted on special occasions, the permits to be signed by Special Magistrates.'*

The publicans were concerned that they invested in high quality hotels with accommodation, and that run-down public houses could be set up in competition next door to them, without adequate buildings and amenities, and with undesirable customers (thieves and prostitutes). Adelaide is known as the City of Churches and Pubs, with a large number of public houses established in the Colony. The Attorney General said that

> *without pretending to be acquainted with or to know the 'ins and outs' of the trade, he thought if there were only half the number of public houses the public would be quite well served as now (Hear, hear). An enormous number of public houses in the colony were only fit for bar trade. There were comparatively very few public houses to which a man would like to take his family. ..From what he had seen here it would be difficult for an extensive hotelkeeper to thrive while there was a meaner building adjoining taking away his bar business (hear, hear.) He was of opinion that only restrictions that were absolutely necessary should be imposed on a publican. If the requisites for holding a license were suitable premises and good character, that would be a safe guide to adopt....Every class of the public required accommodation, and he did not see in what way they were to prevent persons in large town obtaining licenses for places resorted to by thieves and prostitutes. If some places were recognised as buildings where they might congregate they would go there in preference to others. This might be opposed to the moral doctrine put forward by some people but on the grounds of public convenience and public good he contended that it was better to let them assemble together in one or two places than to be distributed over the entire community. If they were excluded from the houses he mentioned, they would flock to other places, as they must go somewhere.*
>
> *Mr Bleechmore remarked that unfortunately the publicans were as a body looked upon from that standpoint. They were considered as being keepers of the lower class of houses such as that just described.*

The Attorney -General – Some then appear to think that publicans and sinners are synonymous terms (Laughter).

Mr Lithgow pointed out that the licensed victuallers were of opinion an Inspector of Public houses should be appointed; that, in fact, a man should be employed who was above taking a bribe, and who should report to the Bench of Magistrates upon the characters and conditions of the publicans and houses throughout the colony. It was well known that at the present time there were many houses which were dens of infamy and prostitution. Too many of this class of establishment were supported by the higher class of society. '[632]

The deputation also raised the issue of poor quality and dangerous Colonial wine being sold, and the Attorney General stated that

with respect to the ill effects of drinking colonial wine, that people would be astonished at the number of deaths that resulted annually from the practice. It was the new wine which was deleterious. The old wine was as wholesome as any other wine. He had been informed by the faculty that a new class of diseases was springing up, which were attributable to the habit of drinking colonial wine...He deprecated the practice which prevailed to a great extent throughout the country districts of hawkers disposing of colonial wine and colonial spirits. The Government would have to consider very carefully any proposed revision of the licensing systems, and any suggestions that were made by the licensed victuallers or others would be very carefully considered [633]

Celebration of the Telegraph Line from the Northern Territory to Adelaide

In 1872, there was The Telegraph Demonstration, a celebration of the completion of the Adelaide to London 'Trans Australian Telegraph', at which Daniel Battams spoke.

Mr D. Battams, on behalf of the executive officers of the Friendly Societies, read the following address:

To Charles Todd, Esq. Postmaster-General, and Superintendent of Telegraphs. Sir – We the Executive Officers of the various Friendly Societies in South Australia, representing in all over 16,000 members, beg to tender to you, your officers, and men, our hearty congratulations upon the completion of the Adelaide and London Telegraph, and beg to welcome you and party back to Adelaide after your arduous enterprise, and wish success to the great undertaking, Adelaide 15th November, 1872.

'Daniel Battams, G.M., M.U., John Stapleton, D. T., A.O.F, F.G. Hales, G.M., A.I.O.F., J.G. Osborne, P.P., U.A.O.D., Ephraim Gould, C.R., A.O.R., G.G. Newman, C.R, A.O.R., McCormack, D.V., S.A.R.S., Thomas Austin, P.G.M. of Ad. D., A.H. Beyer., G.C.S. of Ad. D.'

Mr Todd said – Gentlemen, I beg that you will accept the thanks of myself, officers, and men for the kind and flattering address that you have just presented to us. We shall take pride in preserving it, and handing it down to our children as a token of the appreciation in which our services in this great undertaking have been held. I can square with you that it has been a labour of love with us, and our chief and highest reward is in knowing that our labours are approved by our fellow-colonists. Sir, I thank you.

At the call of Mr Todd, three hearty cheers were given for His Excellency the Governor.[634]

Royal Exchange Hotel, Kadina

Daniel had already lost two children, but the 1870s would see a continued string of tragedies as his brother William died at Marden in 1870, aged just

32 years. Brother Elisha Battams[635] then died in Adelaide in 1870, aged just 35 years.

In 1874 Daniel became the proprietor of the Exchange Hotel, Graves Street, Kadina:

> *We are glad to say that fine hotelry, the Exchange Hotel, Kadina, has fallen into the hands of a man who thoroughly understands his business and who, we hope will not fail to make its conduct profitable to himself while he does not abate an effort to gratify his guests. Mr Daniel Battams, the new landlord, is a well-known and respected very old colonist, having formerly been a member of the mounted police, and for many, many years in the victualling line first at Mount Remarkable, and subsequently at Adelaide. At this city he was the host of the Freemasons' Tavern, then of the Red Lion, then of the Freemasons again, and then of the Red Lion again. In these various capacities Mr Battams made many friends, and he will probably not lose any of them when they come to the Exchange. Mr Battams is a considerable holder of mining property in this quarter, and those who know him in his private character, cannot fail to deem him an acquisition to the district. On Saturday night Mr Battams took formal possession, and a little champagne was made to flow on the occasion. Mr J. D. Cossins occupied the chair.*
>
> *The Wallaroo Times and Mining Journal, 16th September 1874*

The following year the hotel was named the 'Royal Exchange Hotel' and it was used for accommodation, meetings of state members of parliament (there was a debate as to whether the local Council or a Member of Parliament should foot the bill),[636] as a basis for expeditions,[637] a consultation room for people needing to see the local Doctor,[638] the site of coronial inquests,[639] and was a booking agent for Hill and Co's Mail Coaches, and advertised as 'the most commodious hotel in the Colony.'[640]

Photo: The Royal Exchange Hotel, Kadina, present day
(Photo by Roderick Eime)[641]

In 1876, Daniel's business partner and close friend George Miller Galley died whilst travelling:

> *GALLEY – On 24th July, on board ship Hesperus, in the tropics, G. M. Galley, Esq., late of Mowbray Lodge, Norwood, aged 61 years. Home papers please copy.*[642]

Less than a year later, in May 1877, Daniel's wife Annie Battams nee Blight also died, at the Royal Exchange Hotel, Kadina, aged just 42 years. Annie's death occurred in the same year that an inquest was held at the hotel to examine the death of a Mrs Lois Bails, who was found drowned in the tank at the back of her house.

Daniel briefly left the Colony and provided a notice upon his return:

> *Mr DANIEL BATTAMS EARNESTLY THANKS the MANY FRIENDS whose kindness and sympathy were so readily expressed during his sad bereavement and while absent from the colony. D. BATTAMS, Royal Exchange, Kadina, June 18, 1877*[643]

Daniel's daughter Clara became a key staff member working at the Royal Exchange Hotel, with her service providing dinner after a cricket match between Kadina and the Civil Service team being praised in the local media.[644]

Daniel Battams ceased to manage the Royal Exchange Hotel from 22nd December 1877 and moved back to Adelaide. He announced on the 1st January 1878 that he had appointed a debt collector (Mr Julius Ey) to collect all outstanding debts owed to him (from the Royal Exchange Hotel, Kadina) and to proceed against those who had unpaid accounts.[645] This advertisement appeared until the 6th March 1878.[646]

In 1878, Daniel's nephew George (aged 25) second son of George Battams, died at Lowe Farm, Payneham, after a few days' illness.

Daniel soon remarried in 1878 to Olivia Galley, his business partner's widow – by then her husband George Miller Galley had been deceased two years. Daniel had been Executor and Trustee of G. M. Galley's estate in October 1876, along with Olivia J. Galley and James F. Ogden (son-in-law of Olivia). The marriage was announced as follows, with Daniel referred to as 'Esquire':

> *BATTAMS-GALLEY – On the 12th inst., at St Peter's Church, Melbourne, by the Rev. H. H. P. Handsfeld, Daniel Battams Esq., of Adelaide, to Olivia Jane, relict of G. M. Galley, Esq., Norwood, South Australia.*
>
> *The Argus, 16th January, 1878*

At the time of her marriage, Daniel Battams Esq. was living at Mowbray Lodge, Clarke Street[647], Norwood,[648] near the Britannia Hotel. This residence is still standing – it had been the home of his friend G. M. Galley and where he and his new wife lived. It appeared to be a large house, as at various times there was advertising for servants.[649]

Connection with a famous abolitionist British family

Daniel Battams's only surviving daughter Clara Battams married Frederick Wilberforce Stephen at St John's, Camberwell, Victoria on 18th December 1879.[650] Frederick was the Engineer in Chief at the South Australian Railways.[651] Although married in Melbourne, their first child was born back in Kadina, and the couple lived around the state due to Frederick's railway engineering work. Frederick came from a well-to-do family in England, who were famous abolitionists. Frederick changed his middle name to 'Wilber.' The name Wilberforce was passed down from William Wilberforce's family (the leader of the movement to abolish the slave trade). The couple last lived at Glenelg.

Photo: Clara Battams, daughter of Daniel Battams[652]

Frederick's father was William Ravenscroft Stephen (1826-1899), grandfather was Sir George Stephen (1794-1879) and great grandfather James Stephen (1758-1832). William was educated at St John's College, Cambridge University, and came to Port Melbourne in 1852, marrying Mary Anne Walkden whom he met on the boat from Liverpool. He became a civil servant in the Treasury Department of Colonial Victoria. Sir George Stephen (QC) was an English lawyer, author and key advocate in the anti-slavery movement. He was born at St Kitts in the West Indies, knighted by Queen Victoria in 1838, travelled to Victoria in 1855 on the 'Oliver Lang,' and later worked as a barrister in Victoria. His father James Stephen was said to be the principal lawyer associated with the abolitionist movement, and the main architect of the *Slave Trade Act* 1807. James Stephen's second wife was Sarah Wilberforce, the sister of William Wilberforce.[653]

Liquidation, Death in Custody and a Tragic End

The Permanent Land and Building Association became officially insolvent on the 19th July 1878, but had been trading insolvent for some time and engaging in unethical business practices.[654] The Melbourne *Argus* reported on these events from their correspondent in South Australia:

> *We are becoming alarmed about the safety of building societies. A special audit has been made into the affairs of the Permanent Land and Building Association, and it appears that there is a deficiency of about £5000. The society, it seems, has been insolvent for some years past, and the balance sheets have not represented the true position of the accounts. Great distress has been occasioned at Moonta among a number of widows whose husbands had invested their money in the society, and who imagined that they had to that extent provided for their families. The question has been raised whether this association is singular in its unfortunate position, and not a little anxiety has been occasioned in consequence of the inquiry. It is known that there is a good deal of laxity in reference to the management of building societies, and the press is very properly crying out for better audits and more care on the part of shareholders in the appointment of directors and other officers.*
>
> *The Argus, 25th July 1878*

In February 1880 the Permanent Land and Building Association finally went into liquidation,[655] 'in order to ascertain the state of affairs.'[656] These events would have greatly impacted Daniel Battams.

In September 1800, the human remains of an Aboriginal man were found on the banks of the Rocky River at Laura (Nukunu country), and Daniel Battams reported that this man, Warria (also known as Mambery or Mumbery Bill), died in his custody (in 1849) when he was a Mounted Policeman.

> *DISCOVERY OF HUMAN BONES – A correspondent wrote to us a few days ago stating that some human bones, which evidently were those of an Aboriginal [person], had been disinterred in making an excavation on the banks of the Rocky River, Laura. We have been favoured by Mr. Daniel Battams, of this city, with an explanation, which in all probability accounts for the presence of these remains. It appears that in 1849 Mr Battams, who was then a member of the Mounted Police Force, was engaged in bringing down from the Far North to Adelaide an Aboriginal [man] named Mambery Bill, whom he had captured for having been guilty of the double murder of a Chinaman [Chinese man] at Nelshaby and also the son of Mr Jacob Hart,*[657] *of Baroota. When the trooper and his prisoner were about crossing the Rocky River, the horse which the [Aboriginal man] was riding threw him, and he was killed on the spot. Mr Battams buried him at the place referred to by our correspondent, so that there is little doubt of the identity of the remains.*[658]

It appears that, at the time, Aboriginal people in custody were expected to walk (in this instance from Burra to Adelaide!), but as Warria became tired after five miles (8 kilometres), Battams went to fetch a horse for him from the nearest station, which then threw him causing his death, according to the story. Battams's police partner Constable Whish stayed with the deceased whilst Battams went to inform the Magistrate/Justice of the Peace Gleeson, who resided at Clare. Warria's wife was also present and a witness.[659] Surgeon Charles Webb from Clare medically examined the body of the deceased and stated that in his opinion the death was caused by falling from a horse and several kicks from the horse.[660] Gleeson instructed Battams to bury Warria after the examination. The Commissioner of Police, Alex Tolmer, then reported the death to the Colonial Secretary and Lieutenant Governor Robe.[661]

In May 1881, Daniel Battams, then described then as a 'gentleman,' participated in the 'levee' for the Queen's Birthday Celebration at Government House, hosted by the Governor, His Excellency Sir W.F. D. Jervois. It was a large affair with all senior political, government, judicial, military and community personnel attending, with one of the largest attendances at such event.[662] A guard of honour and military band were in attendance, with an aide de camp announcing visitors names.

In contrast to this grand event, in June 1881 Battams sued 'Hayter' for £10, money that was due on a promissory note, but *'Mr. Wadey, for the defendant, produced a deed of assignment executed subsequently to the date of the note. Nonsuit.'*[663] Mr Hayter was having some difficulty selling shares in the Barossa Flax Milling Company.[664] There was another case involving Daniel Battams due in court in June 1881, with Oswald being the defendant, which never eventuated. Mr E. Oswald was the chair of the Flinders District Local Road Board.

On the 20th July 1881, Daniel Battams, aged 52 years, was found in a cellar at Norwood with his throat cut, a supposed suicide.[665] The report on his death stated that he was a well-known money-lender and formerly landlord of the Red Lion Hotel, Rundle Street.[666] As well as being haunted by his past, Daniel Battams had been through a lot of grief with the loss of his spouse, children, close friend and other family members, but he was also in financial difficulty.

> *Early this morning the residents of Clark-street, Norwood, and neighbourhood were alarmed to hear that Mr Daniel Battams, agent, of Norwood, had committed suicide during the previous night. It appears that the deceased came home to his dinner in his*

usual spirits on Wednesday about 1 o'clock, after which he went out and dug in the garden for about a couple of hours. He was first missed at tea-time, but nothing serious was suspected till later in the evening, when the family, finding he did not return, began to feel anxious about him. They accordingly informed their next-door neighbours and sent to the Adelaide Police Station. Police-constable Cunnningham came out, and assisted Mr W. Shire, a neighbour, to search for deceased: but it was not until 1 o'clock on Thursday morning that they discovered him lying in the cellar of an unoccupied house in the same street with his throat cut, and quite dead....Mr Battams was a very temperate and steady man, and it is difficult at present to account for his having committed such a rash deed. He leaves a wife and grown-up family of seven. An inquest will be held at the Old Colonist this afternoon.

Evening Journal, 21st July 1881

The deceased was seen in his garden pruning trees at 4 o'clock that afternoon, and was missed shortly afterwards. His absence at first excited no surprise, but subsequently as he did not make his appearance his friends became anxious, and reported the matter to the police. Constable Cunningham was immediately dispatched to the house, and after a brief search discovered the unfortunate man lying in the empty cellar of an adjacent vacant house.

The Wallaroo Times and mining Journal, 23rd July 1881

The jury at the inquest of Daniel Battams's death 'returned a verdict of suicide while in an unsound mind.'[667] A report provided more information, and whilst reference was made to recently dishonoured bills to the value of £140, there was no mention of the collapsed Permanent Land and Building Association, of which Battams was once chair in Adelaide. Reference was also made to his 'usual good spirits.'

The City Coroner (Mr T. Ward) held an inquest on Thursday afternoon at the Old Colonist Inn, Norwood, on the body of Daniel Battams, who was found dead...on Wednesday evening, July 20. Mr Thomas Veitch was chosen Foreman of the Jury.

James Henry Battams, son of the deceased, stated that his father formerly kept the Red Lion Inn, and was fifty-one or fifty-two years old. Last saw him alive about 2 o'clock on Wednesday, when he seemed in his usual good spirits. Heard him mention some monetary losses a fortnight or three weeks ago, and believed that he had lost more than £140 lately by dishonoured bills. Never heard him make any allusion to being tired of life. Deceased had a brother who was formerly in a lunatic asylum. Knew of no one who had an ill-feeling towards deceased. Believed his father was in good circumstances.

Dr F. W. Baily stated that...deceased had two running sores on his legs which would be a cause of great pain, and consequently of despondency.

Emily Bertha Galley, stepdaughter of deceased, gave corroborative evidence as to deceased being in his usual good spirits on Wednesday. There had been no quarrel between deceased and any members of his family.

William Arthur Weir, warehouseman, of Stepney, stated that he had known deceased intimately for some years past. Saw him last on Tuesday night, when he was in very good spirits. Was at deceased's house on Wednesday evening to tea. Rang the bell twice for tea, and as deceased did not appear searched for him about the house without success. Then went to the Norwood Police Station and enquired of the neighbours, and as this was unsuccessful drove to the Hospital. Heard nothing of deceased there, and afterwards went to the Adelaide Police Station and brought out a detective.

> When the Constable searched his office he *'found two notices from the Bank of South Australia re dishonoured acceptances, due July 20, to the amount of £140 10s which deceased was required to meet.'* *South Australian Register, 22nd July 1881*

Given the day of his death was the day that his bills were due, it appears that his death was linked to not being able to pay these bills, and a great shame (in the context of him socialising with the highest and riches echelons of society). A year later, one of Daniel Battams's colleagues in the Town Hall Loan Office also died by suicide:

> *A correspondent at Blumberg [Birdwood] sent us the following: "Old Mr. Saunders, who was with Daniel Battams in the Town Hall Loan Office, drowned himself on June 28 in a very small waterhole in this neighbourhood.*
>
> *South Australian Weekly Chronicle, 1st July 1882*

A strange postscript

In 1912 there were mysterious statements made in the Miscellaneous sections of the *Observer* and *Register* newspapers that said the same thing, but had incorrect information about Daniel Battams's place of death and proprietorship of the 'White Lion' Hotel at Kadina:

> *'Wager' (Turretfield) – (1) Mr Daniel Battams kept the Red Lion between 30 and 40 years ago: (2) He also kept the Black Bull in Adelaide, and the White Lion at Kadina: (3) He died in Kadina a number of years ago: (4) It would be legal to advertise for a man's address irrespective of his wish to the contrary.*
>
> *The Register, 4th March 1912 and Observer 9th March 1912*

It is unknown what the above is referring to, or why Daniel Battams would suddenly be mentioned by 'Wager' so long after his death. Being centrally involved in the Permanent Land and Building Association (which was liquidated), a money lender (with bad deals or debts he brought to the police), a publican, and general public figure through the Odd Fellows and other societies, was Daniel Battams the victim of foul play?

Chapter 20: Third and Fourth Generation in Australia: the Battams Brothers go to War

3rd Generation in Australia

William Alfred Battams snr (2nd) was the eldest son from George Battams's first marriage to Sarah nee Wesley (formerly Spargo). William Alfred Battams snr married Caroline Neale[668] on the 12th Feb 1872 Adelaide and they had 12 children together:

William Alfred Battams jnr (1873-1947) (3rd) (served WW1) (Sand Carter) (married Hannah Gilbey)

Annie (Laura) Battams (born 1875, married Abbot)

George Albert (or Albert George) Battams (born 1877 – died 1953, His son Leslie George served in WW1. His eldest daughter was the extraordinary Mary Jane Battams 1897 -1974, see below)

Frederick John Battams (1879-1940)

Archibald Frank Battams (1881- 1920) (died age 38, buried Payneham cemetery)

Thomas James Battams (1883-1942)

Matilda (Till) May Battams (1886-1964) (married William Simpson Addison in 1908)

Winifred (Winnie) Caroline Battams (1888-1954) (married William Johnson)

Ellen Maria Battams (1890-1962)

Frank Norman Battams (1893-1959) married Ivy Florence Williams

Henry (Harry) Gordon Battams (1894-1961) (served WW1) (Carpenter) married Cora Bertha Mangelsdorf (1907-2003)

Joseph Wesley Battams (1896 -1918, died aged 21 during WW1) (Carpenter)

The family lived at River Street, West Marden, Beulah Park and Payneham.

Brothers in Arms - Impact of the First World War

The Battams family were heavily influenced by the First World War. Altogether there were 7 Battams men in close family relationship who went to WW1. These included brothers William Alfred Battams (jnr), Henry Gordon Battams and Joseph Wesley Battams.

Two of Len's relatives remained behind in Europe, buried in France and Belgium: Great Uncle **Joseph Wesley Battams** and **Frederick Stanley Battams** (son of Daniel Potter Battams). They were both in the 50th Battalion, Australian Infantry (the same Battalion as Fred Bignall from Minnipa). It is likely that these two knew each other well and enrolled together as they were the same age, in the same battalion and had service numbers only one number different from each other. Frederick Battams died aged 23 on the 18th July 1917, and was buried in Belgium (70 Ploegsteert Wood Military Cemetery, Warneton). Less than a year later, Joseph Battams died at the same age, on the 5th April 1918, and was buried in France (196 Ribemont Communal Cemetery Extension). All that returned from the cousins were, from Joseph, a black cat and kangaroo charm and, from Fredrick, a small German calendar and military rejection certificate, as he had also once been declared unfit for service. When Joseph died his effects went to older brother W.A. Battams (Len's grandfather), despite Joseph having bequeathed his assets to his sister Matilda May Addison, Henry Street, Payneham.[669] Sadly, shortly after the war ended, Archibald Frank Battams died 14th September, 1920, aged 38 years.

Many of the sons of these Battams men also enrolled in WWI, for example Frederick Alfred Roy Battams and his brother William Henry (Bill Battams). Bill was underage when he joined WWI on 5th July, 1915 - he stated that he was 18 years and 10 months of age, however he was only **16 years old** at the time (born 5th September 1898).

Photo: Frederick Alfred Roy Battams, who served in both World Wars, Source: Virtual War Memorial Australia https://vwma.org.au/explore/people/555904

4th Generation in Australia

William Alfred Battams jnr (3rd)

William Alfred Battams jnr was born 17th Aug 1873, Marden, South Australia and died 13th October 1947, Moorook, South Australia. William married Hannah ('Annie') Mary Gilbey on the 1st March 1897 in Adelaide. Hannah, known as 'Annie,' was born in 1860 in Bishop Stortford, Essex, England and died at Moorook, South Australia on the 27th September 1937.

William Alfred jnr initially lived at George Street, Payneham. Before the war he was a 'sand carter' – there was the 'Royston Sand Washing Plant' at Battams Road, Payneham. In 1913, he went to court for possession of land – George Brook had leased him land which he was gardening on, without the landowners consent.[670]

William was in his 40s when he enrolled for WW1 and discharged from the war with 'synovitis' in the left knee, a kind of swelling related to arthritis.

William Alfred Battams jnr and 'Annie' Gilbey had 11 children (7 boys and 4 girls). All of the men (including William jnr) served in WWI or WWII, or both. Their children included:

Frederick Alfred Roy Battams (1896-1966, married Elsie Myra McKinnon, Fruit grower at Moorook, served in WW1 & WW11)

William Henry (Bill) Battams (1898-1980, Labourer, served WW1, married Eva Minnie Quinton)

Ruby Florence Maude Battams (1900-1968, married Patty Booth)

Leonard George Battams (1905-1998, married Meta Bormann, served at Loveday in WWII - my step-father's Dad, gardener)

Gladys Irene (Rene) Battams (1906-2002, married George Dingwell and Alfred Hugo Schulz)

Sydney Clement Battams (1909-1992, married Merle Hamilton, served WW11)

Frank Edward Battams (1911-2001, married Marjory (Molly) Munn at Moorook, served WW11)

Hazel Evelyn Battams (1913-2010, married Kennith William Blight) (twin)

Ellen May (Nell) (1913-1997, married Herbert Thomas Loxton) (twin)

Archibald John (Jack) Battams (1914-2003, married Isabel Hodgson, served WW11)

Henry Bernard (Harry) Battams (1917-1999, married Freda Gladys Pope, served WW11)

***

Prior to and up until WWII, there were dramas involving Annie Battams's sister Florence Maud Gilbey which Annie and her other sisters were drawn into. Florence, or Florrie, was an attractive and hardworking young woman, a needleworker/ sewing machinist who worked for an Indian clothing manufacturer in the West End of Adelaide, whom she fell in love with (and 'made wealthy').[671] She married Bhagat Singh [672] (born 1874, Bombay, India) on the 5th December, 1906.[673] Whilst Baghat was likely a British citizen (from 'British India'), due to the White Australia policy he could not be an Australian citizen.[674] Bhagat's father Khem Singh had served in the (British) East India Company[675] and the Indian Army.[676]

Three years prior to the marriage, Baghat Singh had a robbery with violence charge brought against him in Adelaide.[677] In 1907, he was involved in a perjury trial brought against his brother Sant Singh (represented by Sir John Downer).[678,679] At the time, Bhagat and Florence Maud Singh lived on Currie Street, west of Light Square. They had a child in 1910 that took on the surname Gilby. Their marriage lasted until 1913, when Bhagat left Australia and went back to India.

In 1915, Florence started a new relationship with another Indian (Punjabi) man, Natto (or Nattoo) Khan who it appeared she also worked for. He was a travelling hawker,[680] and a jealous and violent man who eventually shot her because she would not marry him[681] and was friendly with another man who was going to WWI.[682] At least one paper reported that she was murdered. Natto Khan was initially held in remand for the attempted murder of Florence, until she got out of hospital, when he would be tried. Natto Khan was imprisoned for five years, and he tried unsuccessfully to appeal his sentence.[683] He died in jail whilst serving his sentence.[684]

Florence remarried, to Phillip Sydney Wilson (a Labourer from Sydney), on 10th October 1916. When she remarried, she gave her name as 'Florence Maud Bagot' and stated that she was a widow. The witnesses to her wedding were William and Annie Battams.[685]

It was unlikely that Baghat Singh had died. In 1929, a Baghat Singh (described as a native of the Punjab) was arrested in the Indian Legislative Assembly in Delhi after bombs were hurled from the gallery, causing injuries to five members[686], and was also wanted in connection with the murder of an Indian policeman, who was shot on his motorcycle when riding through the streets of Lahore. A communist pamphlet was also thrown into the Chamber at the same time.[687]

Florence died aged 69 in 1949 from a death which puzzled doctors. She was admitted to hospital suffering severe headaches. Her death was deemed caused by a broken blood vessel in her head. On postmortem examination, the doctors found a bullet in her lung, which had been there since 1915, and considered too dangerous to remove at the time.[688]

***

After WWI, William Alfred Battams snr and son William Henry (Bill) Battams jnr (and their families) went to Pompoota Station, the first training farm for soldier settlers, before settling at Moorook. Both W.A. Battams and his son W.H. Battams were allotted soldier settlement blocks of land at Moorook by the government, with the son having one of the first allocations (Blocks 110-100A) and father receiving a later and larger allotment for his family (132-194).

Picture postcard: Harry, Gladys and baby. Postcard from Harry's family to his brother Syd, WWII

On the back reads: *To Syd. Wishing you all the best of luck. Harry, Glad and family* (S.Battams)

The Battams family became pioneers of Moorook, which means 'bend in the river.' The place was part of the lands of the Erawirung (Yirawirung)

people, who came under the broader Meru peoples. Soldier settlers were issued with two tents per family (one to cook in, the other to sleep in).

> *Moorook really started to grow with the arrival of 20 repatriated soldier settlers and their families. They arrived on the P.S. Gem in 1917, carrying all their worldly possessions, from the Poompoota Training Centre. The Moorook school children, guided by teacher J.B. Ruediger, formed a guard of honour on the river bank to welcome them.*
>
> *The settlers – soon to be known as 'blockers' – were issued with two tents per family (one to cook in, the other to sleep in). Storekeeper Roberts, a champion of the soldier settlers, and whose brother-in-law had been killed in action, gave to each family a box of provisions.*
>
> *T.B.A. Wachtel drove each family in turn to their allotted block in his horse-drawn buggy. The second batch of 19 returned soldiers arrived later in 1918 on the P.S. Ellen, and they were also accorded the same welcome...*
>
> *Block numbers were drawn from a hat to decide whose homes would be built first...Discharged Soldier Settler lands in the Hundred of Moorook and Pyap on the River Murray, under the Irrigation and Reclaimed Lands Act, were gazetted on 7 September 1922...In the Murray Pioneer, 21 March 1919:*
>
> *"Government Surveyors are pegging out quarter acre blocks as business sites on the flat between the river and the road in front of the older blocks. The beginning of the Moorook Township'"*
>
> *Wachtel, p 65-67*

Photo: Families arriving at Pompoota Station, 1917, Source: Wachtel, 1982

W. Battams (unsure if father or son) was one of the first Presidents of the Returned Soldiers and Settlers Association (RSA) in Moorook. The following issues were documented at this association in 1919

> *The State Executive of the R.S.A. arranged for the sub-branch of Moorook (in 1919) to send a deputation to meet Mr Grace, Minister for Irrigation, in Adelaide. Mr A.E. Betts put forward the case of cows and lucerne; Mr M.J. Herbert –vines and plantings, and Mr W.Battams – subsist. Results revealed that there were not enough rooted Doradillo vine cuttings to go around; the cows could not be taken back by the government as they already had 700 cattle under their care being hand fed, and subsist was to be forthcoming.*
>
> *Wachtel, p. 108*

Many of the sons of William Alfred Battams were active sportspeople, with both Leonard George and William H. Battams being mentioned as prominent names in the Moorook Swimming Club[689], with anecdotal stories that Leonard was an excellent swimmer. Syd and Frank Battams were also mentioned in the Juniors and Schoolboys teams respectively. Fred was also President of the RSL, and his wife Elsie was a stalwart of the Moorook Welfare Club. Frank, Syd and Len Battams were also in the Moorook-Kingston Football Club[690]. They were all still listed as playing in the club in 1932 and played in its premiership sides in 1926 and 1932.

The lives of this family would have been deeply affected by the outbreak of WWII in 1939, as Fred, Syd, Frank, Jack and Harry all went overseas with the Australian Army, whilst Len served at Loveday. Their father William Alfred Battams was still alive at this time (he died 1947), but their mother 'Annie' died just before the war, in 1937.

Below: 1927 Footballers – **Back Row:** M. Royal, A. Todd, N. Huddy, Frank Battams, Dick Knapp, Doug McCallum, Charlie Farley, Joe Summers. **Centre:** Art Miller, Syd Battams, Wilbur and Ray Swanbury. **Front Row:** Len Battams, S. Burford, Ray Farley, Harold Gogel, ... Clark. (M.J. Droge-muller)

Above: Bottom Left of photo: Leonard George Battams, with two of his brothers in the same team (Frank and Syd)[691]

When matriarch Hannah 'Annie' Mary Battams died in 1937, her obituary read:

> *Mrs Hannah Mary Battams, who died on September 27 at Moorook [1937] after a long illness, was one of the early river pioneers. She*

was born at sea in 1877 while her parents, Mr and Mrs. R Gilbey, were on route to Australia. They settled in Adelaide, and at the age of 18 Hannah Mary married William Albert Battams, a member of the family whose history is so closely associated with that of Payneham. Shortly after, the family moved to the settlement of Moorook, and took up a holding near the river. Here they raised a large family. Her husband and three sons served with the A.I.F. in France. She is survived by her husband and 11 children. Mesdames E. Booth, G. Dingwall, H. Loxton, Miss H. Battams, and Messrs. W., S. (Glossop), F.A.R, L.G., H. C., F. E., A. J. and H. B. Battams. There are 31 grandchildren.

The Chronicle, 14th October 1937

Chapter 21: Miss Mary Jane Battams's extraordinary life

One of the most extraordinary people in Len's family was the daughter of his great Uncle George Albert Battams. Her name was Miss Mary Jane (May)[692] Battams (1897 – 1974). May became blind at the age of 9 years old following a brain operation, but did not let her disability get in the way of leading a full life.

May was the eldest child of five children (one boy and four girls). In 1909, when May was 12 years old she was enrolled in the Blind, Deaf and Dumb Institution, known in 1946 as the Townsend House Schools for Deaf and Blind Children, and later Townsend House, Brighton.[693] She also lived there, and was a keen and bright student. In 1910, she received a prize for her work, presented by Lady Bosanquet (wife of His Excellency the Governor of South Australia) who was visiting the school.[694] In 1911, she also received a prize in the Third form (First Division), along with a prize for 'sewing' and 'best girl worker and good conduct.'[695]

May also went to the Royal Institute for the Blind in North Adelaide (formerly the Industrial School for the Blind). At the time, the situation for blind people in South Australia was somewhat progressive due to the 'vision' of Mr. Andrew Whyte Hendry (1859-1918). He was blind himself and became Manager of the Institute for the Blind, working with Sir Charles Goode (President of the Industrial School's committee), to establish a school for training blind workers. Classes at the Royal Institute for the Blind included brush making, basket and mat making, hair-curling and drafting, chair caning and halter making, broom making and mat weaving.[696] Goods were sold to the general public to raise funds for the Institute, including through an 'Australia fair' in 1893 which raised funds for a new building. May learnt chair caning, and she was the first blind woman in Australia to learn weaving.

The new Royal Institute for the Blind building (foundation stone laid 1915) was used as a hospital for soldiers during WWI.[697] At this time, May was still living at Brighton. In 1914, May donated to the Red Cross Society for the War effort,[698] and in 1915, May organised a successful concert (in which she performed, among others) in St Martin's Hall (St Martin's Church, Campbelltown), with the proceeds going to the Wounded Soldier's Fund.[699]

May's much-loved mother (Elizabeth 'Lizzie' Hann) died 2nd July 1916 at Hectorville, when May (the eldest child) was 19 years old. A memorial notice was placed in the newspaper in 1917, which read:

> *When days are dark and friends are few,*
>
> *Darling mother, how we mourn for you.*
>
> *Your memory is as dear today*
>
> *As in the hour you passed away*
>
> *-Inserted by her loving husband and children.*[700]

May's father remarried two years later (her siblings were 19, 17, 14 and 10 at the time) and the family was said to be 'split up' at this time.[701]

May was a devout Christian and in 1918 (when she lived at 'Wellington Square,' North Adelaide) participated in the South Australian Sunday School Union Awards, and received a prize in Adult Section A.[702] In 1926, the Walkerville Methodist Church expressed that it owed much to 'The several well-memorised and perfectly expressed, well-chosen Scripture recitals of Miss May Battams, the blind girl.'[703]

In 1932, when she was 35 years of age, May travelled around Australia with the famous and controversial missionary Annie Lock (who hailed from Rhynie), travelling on one six week journey over 650 kilometers across the Nullarbor by pony and buggy, and traversing sandhills and the desert of the Nullarbor Plain at Ooldea Soak.[704] When Miss Annie Lock left Adelaide on a second occasion to travel to Ooldea to take up mission work, it was said that:

> *An interesting item was given by Miss Battams who had gone with Miss Lock to see the possibilities of Ooldea as a mission stie. The two ladies had set out on a five mile walk from Ooldea station to the Soak, and on the way missed the track. After much wandering about they eventually returned to the station but not before the townspeople had become so alarmed that an engine in the station was used to send out a whistling warning to the lost ones. Miss Battams put the experience into a poem of many verses, which she recited at Miss Lock's farewell meeting, to the amusement of all present.*[705]

Photo: Institution, Brighton, later known as 'Townsend House,' B11623, State Library of South Australia

Photo: Institution, Brighton, Later known as 'Townsend House,' B3102, State Library of South Australia

Photo: Back of the Industrial School for the Blind (1884-1917), 92 Brougham Place, North Adelaide, PRG 631/2/323, State Library of South Australia. This building is still standing (heritage listed).

Image: Royal Institute for the Blind Building, King William Street (near the corner of Brougham Place, opposite the Women and Children's Hospital), North Adelaide (1915-1974) Artwork scanned from 'Chronicle of a Century (1881-1984) - Royal Society for the Blind of South Australia Inc[706] This building was demolished.

Foundation stone being laid (1915, Royal Institute for the Blind, North Adelaide (near the cnr Brougham Place and King William Road). State Library of South Australia, PRG 280/1/10/19. This building was demolished.

May Battams's many activities included 'weaving, typewriting, sewing, memorising Scripture, hiking, composing poetry, making raffia work, and playing the piano, organ and violin.'[707] She identified bird song as well as plants by the smell of their crushed leaves.[708]She made her own clothes, regularly walked along West Beach on her own (counting her steps), and had a shack at Glenelg North/West Beach (see photo below), and would swim on her own with the assistance of a piece of rope tied to a hutt.[709] She lived on Argyle Street, Prospect in 1932 (a street I once lived on when a student!), then around Norwood/Magill, and later lived on land and a house at Croydon Park which backed on to the Church of the Nazarene, and donated the land and house to the Church when she died. Initially there were two small cottages on the property, with one used for families engaged in caring for May.[710]

May Battams had memorised 200 chapters of the Bible, 100 hymns and 60 other pieces of music. She had hundreds of books in Braille and played and adapted a number of games (including drafts, solitaire, dominoes and snakes and ladders) for people who were blind. She translated children's stories and educational resources into Braille for the Institution for the Blind and the Deaf and Dumb Incorporated (now Townsend House).[711] Her inventions included 'a wool winder, a board to teach blind children Braille, a money counter, a measure to stop tea overflowing and other gadgets to make her life easier.'[712] The *Sydney Morning Herald* reported, from an exhibition of handicrafts for the blind, that her inventions were used in England, America and Egypt.[713] May Battams said that:

> *the secret to happiness is in being busy in the service of others and in always looking on the bright side of things.*[714]

May died on the 5th June 1974, and is buried at Centennial Park. She was placed on the Memorial Roll of the Nazarene World Missionary Society (Nazarene Missions International) in 1975.

MISS MARY JANE BATTAMS, blind since she was nine, lives in a shack at West Beach and finds her way round the district by counting the number of steps she takes. Today she was walking along the beach.

Photo: Miss Mary Battams walking along West Beach: *The News, 13th June 1949.*

Photo: Miss Mary Jane Battams, Pix Magazine 4th Marh 1950, Photographer Bob Donaldson, cited in Bishop (2021). Below: Miss Mary Battams reading a book in Braille, Source: Marilyn Rodda

Chapter 22: The Battams Family in the fifth and sixth generations

5th Generation in Australia

Leonard George Battams

Leonard George Battams (1905-1998), my stepdad's father, married Meta Otillie Bormann in 1924. Her Christian name was tattooed on his upper arm. Leonard and Meta had 9 children together, 7 girls and 2 boys. These included:

Ivy Florence Battams (1924-1989, married Richards)
Rita Jean Battams (1926 at Kingston d. 2001, married Stokes)
Doris Eileen (known as Eileen) Battams (1927-1997, married Walter Amos McDonald, went to Victoria)
Ruby Loraine Battams (1928-2005**,** married Ralph Reginald Stainer)
Hazel Evelyn Battams (1930-1999, married John Bottom)
Leonard Frank Battams (9th September 1933-6th September 2000)
Janet Battams (went to Victoria)
Viola/Violet Rose Battams (1935-1992, married Mathew Storey, went to Victoria - Len was close to)
Stanley James Battams (1940-1957)

Boormann and Hettner Families: 1841 and 1849

Like the Schulz family, the Bormann family was part of the Prussian group of emigrants to South Australia. The Boormann family was from Meseritz in Germany (now Międzyrzecz in Poland) and settled in Greenock, Mannum and Milendella in the Riverland of South Australia. Johann Gottfried Bormann (and family) left Altona on the *Skjold* on the 3rd July 1841 and arrived at Port Adelaide 5th November, 1841, travelling with Pastor Fritzsche (there were many deaths on this ship due to the poor conditions and facilities). Boormann was the elder or 'representative' of the group from

Posen, Prussia, and a shoemaker – just like the Battams family in the UK. They arrived in South Australia six years before the Battams family. However, Meta's parents, the first generation born in Australia, did not speak English at home and Meta grew up with her parents only speaking German at home.

The Hettner family (Meta's maternal ancestors) were from Panten, Germany. They departed Hamburg on the 21st October 1848 on the *H.G. Wappäus* (Georg Heinrich Wappäus) and arrived in Port Adelaide 31st March 1849, with Johannes Gottfried Hettner settling at Lobethal[715]

Loveday Internment Camp

Whilst his brothers served in the Australian army overseas in World War II, Leonard served in Australia at the due to his large family. Leonard quickly moved from Private to Corporal to Sergeant in the army, first enlisting in October 1941 at Wayville and immediately working at the Prisoner of War camp at Loveday Internment Camp, part of the 25th/33rd Garrison Battalion. He was a Transport Driver upon enlistment but came from a family of gardeners and became a Gardener and Guard at Loveday, where Lieutenant Colonel Deam was Group Commandant.

> *In 1941, the P.O.W. Group was formed at Loveday under Lt. Colonel Dean. By 1943, 1,374 armed personnel and 5,382 prisoners (Italian and Japanese) were in residence. The war had produced a shortage in labour. Subsidiary camps were developed in wooded areas at Moorook West, Katarapko and Woolenook Bend, where prisoners-of-war were set to work to cut wood for the irrigation pumps. These three camps resulted in 56,372 tons of firewood being cut in a little over two years.*
>
> *Two hundred and one Italian prisoners-of-war were moved to a virgin Moorook West property on 21 February 1943. They built a guard fence and facilities, and they were moved away via Yinkanie*

Railway. 138 Japanese internees were sent to Moorook West on 1 March 1943. The prisoners-of-war received 13 cents per day, and the internees 9 cents per day. When transported from camp to camp, the internees clad in brightly coloured clothes waved cheerily to children from the back of trucks. This camp closed on 28 January 1944, and the Japanese internees were moved to Woolenook Bend (A.E. Whitmore, Barmera).[716]

Loveday was significant as one of the largest camps in Australia which covered 440 acres of cultivated land, feeding the nation and developing poppies for raw opium and morphine for use in the Australian Military Force. Products of the camp included 46,000 pounds of seed (tomatoes, beans, beetroot, lettuce and cabbage), 130 tons of tomatoes (during 1944/45), 11,500 tomato plants, over 85,000 tons of felled wood, between 30 to 35 tons of poppies, 10 tons of pyrethrum flower heads (for insecticide), a piggery (760 pigs in 1943 and 1200 were sold in total), poultry farm (30,000 eggs and 2,800 chickens for the army and army hospital use), and more that 110,000 pounds of soap (from surplus animal fat).[717]

Only one internee escaped through the perimeter fence, nine escaped from working parties outside the compounds, and a tunnel was built by the Germans and discovered before it was completed. Jimmy James, the first, the famous black tracker was used to recover escapees.

Official Visitors and International Red Cross frequently visited the camps to inspect the conditions and attend to requests and complaints by the Internees. Family and friends could apply for visitors passes at the Keswick Headquarters.

Playing grounds for tennis, football, baseball and bowls were provided in all compounds. The Japanese arranged inter compound

> *matches, the Italians played soccer and bowls, the Germans played tennis and golf.*
>
> *The Italians loved to hold concerts and formed an orchestra which was led by a famous conductor. All nationalities made artefacts, using mallee stumps for carving, and tins for a range of metal trinkets. The Germans conducted 33 different classes to fill in their days and ease the boredom.*[718]

Leonard only received 4 days' weekend leave every couple of months, so his wife Meta was largely left on her own to raise the 9 children during the war years, although she would have received help from her family. There would have been tension in the family at the time, as Meta's parents only spoke German at home, even though the Bormann family in Australia were naturalised almost 100 years before WWII. Their name may have been cause for suspicion during WWII as Martin Bormann (in Germany) was a nazi war criminal and deputy to Hitler.

Leonard also had some land and his son Len junior described doing hard labour on the farm and pulling a plough when he was just 9 years old – about the time that his father started in the POW camp at Loveday. He also described holes in shoes being filled with cardboard, using newspaper as toilet paper, and 'bread and dripping' lunches.

There were three subsidiary camps of Loveday, including at Moorook West where wood was cut for irrigation pumps, where Leonard may have been located at one stage. Leonard had a shoe/clothes brush in a wooden casing carved into a dog – with the tongue being the handle of the brush which had been given to him by a Japanese prisoner of war at Loveday. Hearing that Leonard could be violent, I wondered if this gesture was 'a curse or just a carving.' It was something that he treasured, the gift in the harsh context that seemed to be meaningful. When Leonard George was living with my parents, he gave me the shoe brush. It featured in an *Advertiser* article when historian Professor Peter Monteith launched his book on internment camps, *Captured Lives* (2018).

Photo: Wood carving of a dog with the handle being a shoe/clothes brush, carved by a Japanese POW (S. Battams)

of internment during the wars in the State saw many injustices committed, including putting those in prison for simply having the wrong surname.

"Lots of those interned would have considered why they were there," he says. "You wonder about the motives of those that voiced suspicions of others.

"It could have been they had a personal vendetta against someone or be a business rival and this was an opportunity on very little evidence to see them suffer."

Other reasons for why someone was interned were more straightforward.

"If you were a young man and a

A customs vessel came out of Port Adelaide and gave Captain August Strycker the news the two countries were at war. He was told that he, his crew, his vessel and his cargo were now under Australian control. The German crew members were put on parole and moved into a house in Port Adelaide.

Within days Australian authorities were told to arrest and detain Germans who had military training and might be called up to serve.

Soon, as war escalated, SA authorities – free to interpret which enemy subjects showed "suspicious or unsatisfactory" conduct – took firmer action.

While few Australian-born Germans would be interned, there were

search of timber to help make their improvised eight-man tents more liveable.

A new commandant of the Torrens Island camp, Captain George E. Hawkes, a 37-year-old bank teller from Glenelg, instituted brutal treatment of the internees.

It reached a crisis when he ordered the cat o' nine tails flogging of two escapees.

A military inquiry followed, where Captain Hawkes was exonerated. However, an independent investigation by the US consul-general uncovered a litany of cruel treatments at the camp, documented by Dubotzki's photographs.

Prof Monteath says there were shameful acts committed in SA internment camps, with the worst violations happening under the regime of Hawkes at Torrens Island.

"On his watch, guards used bayonets on prisoners and a prisoner was shot and injured but it happened out of the public eye," he says.

"At the time, there were secret facilities people were not supposed to know anything about. No one had much of an interest shining a light on things then – or since.

"There are connections with what happened at the time of wars with what happened in Australia before then and even in the present day because we're still putting away people on islands."

In World War II, an entirely new concentration camp was created in

Curse or just a carving

PROFESSOR Peter Monteath's colleague at Flinders University, Associate Professor Samatha Battams, has a personal connection to the Loveday camp as her step-father's father, Leonard Battams, a sergeant from the 25th/33rd Garrison Battalion, worked there.

"Grandpop worked at Loveday internment camp as a gardener and guard from 1941 when it opened until 1945," Ms Battams said.

"He was English but married someone of German descent (Meta Bormann) and it would have been a conflicting time as her parents still spoke German at home.

"I've seen in records that he got

Peter Monteath and Samantha Battams with the carving. Picture: TRICIA WATKINSO

Image: From *The Advertiser*, to promote Prof Peter Monteith's and colleagues (Mandy Paul & Rebecca Martin) book on internment: *Captured Lives* (2018)

In 1943, eight months after becoming a Sergeant, Leonard was charged with neglecting to obey Loveday orders – although his army record does not detail what orders were disobeyed. The gardening work must have been very hard physical labour, and he suffered from hernias on a few occasions and had to go to the Army General Hospital at the camp. Leonard would likely have known some of the POW interns of German descent via his wife's family, and it would have been a very conflicting time for those in the SA regions where German communities had been integrated with other European settlers.

Photo: Leonard George Battams upon enlistment in WWI (Source: NAA)

... repatriation.

CORRESPONDENCE.

Four copies of 'The Awakening', the newspaper for Italians in Australia, arrived this week for the following PW:-
59065 LANZERA V., 45851 CORRADINI A., 59694 COLONNO G., and 69124 PAPPANO A.

A short article entitled "The Deadly Sin of Racial Intolerance" charges Australians with "consciously or unconsciously subscribing to racial intolerance because their outlook is not international". The article contends that an international outlook is vital to Australia if she is to expand and become a truly great democracy. It adds that the average Australian knows little or nothing about the Italians who are domiciled in Australia and less about Italians overseas. There is little or no opportunity for co-operation or getting together. It criticises the government for having no scheme whereby Italians already settled in this country can learn to speak and read English or whereby an exchange of cultural and social activities can be made.

In conclusion the writer describes racial prejudice as a vicious example of Fascism and pledges himself to work for its overthrow.

Image: Intelligence report from Loveday internment camp Source: NAA

All correspondence to and from the Loveday camp was monitored. There was an interesting intelligence report from Loveday which reports on an Italian newspaper with an article *titled 'The Deadly Sin of Racial Intolerance.'* The article discusses the lack of international outlook of Australians, causing them to 'consciously or unconsciously' subscribe to 'racial intolerance' and it describes 'racial prejudice as a vicious example of Fascism.'

Photo: Loveday internment camp. Leonard George Battams is on the left (Source: S. Battams)

In May 1945, Leonard applied for discharge and was subsequently discharged from the army. He later worked as a gardener and groundskeeper at St Peters School, when author Colin Thiele was Headmaster – Colin Thiele gave him a book with a signed dedication to him when he left employment there.

In 1957, a tragedy occurred which was harshly felt. Leonard and Meta's youngest child Stanley died in a motorcycle accident on the corner of King William Street and North Terrace, when he was just 16 years of age (a few weeks before his 17th birthday). He was a trainee firefighter with the South

Australian Railways and lived at Unley at the time. There was an inquest into his death. My step-Dad Len always kept a picture of his parents with his younger brother Stanley in a prominent position (see below).

Photo: Meta, Stanley and Leonard George Battams (circa 1945). Stanley died in a motorcycle accident when he was 17 years of age at the corner of King William Road and North Terrace in Adelaide (in 1957). Len junior always kept this photo in a central place on display at home (Source: S. Battams).

Meta died in 1979 but her husband Leonard lived until the age of 93, dying in 1998. Leonard had mellowed in his later years, and son Len saw him regularly when he was older, and was at his side when he died.

Many times I have been asked if the Battams Rd somewhere in South Australia was named after the Battams family, and yes, Battams Rd Marden, Stepney, Royston Park, Glossop and Moorook are all named after the Battams family!

6th Generation in Australia

My mother Val remarried, to Leonard Frank Battams in 1979, and they moved to Aldinga Beach where I spent the rest of my childhood and most of my adolescence (they lived there for 8 years). My parents later moved to Elizabeth Park (5 years) before they retired to Morgan in the Riverland (9 years), where my step-father died in 2000, and following this Val moved back to the city.

Leonard Frank Battams

My stepfather Len Battams was born in Waikerie on the 9th September 1933. He came from a large family of nine children, with his father being Leonard George Battams and mother Meta Otillie (nee Bormann). Len was fond of his mother Meta and his German grandparents. His mother was close to her German family and spoke in German with them, and Len had also spoken German when younger. According to the a Moorook community history, there was a great deal of tension between people of German and English descent in the Riverland region during WWII. This would not have helped in the Battams family with Len's dad working at the Loveday Internment Camp.

Len life had not always been easy, as his family was quite poor and he worked on the farm in the Riverland (pulling a plough) when he was just 9 years of age. Len grew up to be a hard worker and practical man who was outgoing, irreverent and had a good sense of fun and humour but valued being of practical service to others. He had been in the airforce and a Labourer, truck driver, earth-remover and involved in building houses in new subdivisions.

He loved 'going bush,' the outdoors, fishing, the Riverland and country in general, country and western music, gardening and having a joke. He would tell me *'you need to get outside girl!' 'breathe the fresh country air.'* When Len was 18 years old, he spent one year in the air force where he got the opportunity to do some traveling around Australia (he quit the airforce as he was frustrated by not having qualifications and being able to progress). Something that would have greatly affected Len during his 20's would have been the death of his only brother Stanley who had died aged 17 years from a motorcycle accident.

Later Len would be a transport driver and spend some time regularly traveling interstate and to the northern Flinders Ranges (there is a picture of him at Wooltana, below). He later worked as an Earthremover/Construction worker on subdivisions around the southern suburbs of Adelaide (for Matulick company) and on Uncle Frank Miller's (my mother's brother) small farm at Willunga when our family lived at Aldinga Beach, until he was injured in a work accident (and later doing gardening when he retired).

He loved going to the Riverland where he had grown up and to where he retired with mum. He was a proud Australian, with a colourful language, full of jokes, ditties and songs, and he loved telling stories. He was a happy character and liked to have a laugh and amuse others. He was a perfectionist (hard on himself) and a hard and reliable worker. He was also an extremely practical person, someone who could make or fix anything.

Identifying as been working-class, Len would have been amazed to discover that a relative (Daniel Battams) had been introduced to Royalty (HRH Prince Albert) (and his daughter Clara married into the upper echelons of society), been a key part of the early publican trade (along with his own direct ancestor), head of the friendly societies and spoken at public events, although he was not reverent towards royalty; he would sing 'God save our gracious cat, feed it on bread and fat. God save our cat,' to the national anthem!

Photo above: Meta Battams with children Len, Stanley, Violet (S. Battams) Below: Len holding Janet with other sisters (S. Battams)

Photo above: Len junior in the middle with a donkey (S.Battams) Photo below: Len jnr, Len snr, child Janet, wife Meta, unknown (S. Battams)

Photo above: Len fishing (S.Battams)

Photo above: Len on right during his time in the airforce (S. Battams)

Photo: Len (18-19 years old) with his sister Vi (who he was close to) and her daughter (S. Battams)

Photo: Len at the AWM, Canberra aged around 18 years of age (S. Battams)

Photo: Len at Wooltana Station (Paralana Hot Springs), Flinders Ranges, in Humphrey Bogart style (near Arkaroola) (S. Battams)

Although his family were strongly tied to the Wesleyan faith (with one ancestor Sarah Wesley said to be ‘from the wrong side of the bed’ of the original Wesley family who created the faith), Len was an atheist and expressed Marxist sentiment when it came to religion, saying something along the lines of ‘religion is the opium of the people.’ Marx saw religion as a balm for suffering in the universe and society.

I wondered how much of Len's world view was shaped by the suffering experienced by his family, many of which went to both World Wars, and him being born at the time of the Great Depression. Len remembered having bread and fat for lunch, using newspaper as toilet paper, putting cardboard in shoes, and having a father who could be drunk and violent, and protecting his mother against him – he remembered raising his fists to his Dad once when he was treating his mother poorly. Leonard George used to be a part of the Freemasons and Len remembered him coming back from meetings drunk.

Having a strong sense of duty, Len cared for his Dad in older age (at one time he lived in the granny flat in the back of our house at Aldinga Beach) and regularly visited him when he was in a residential aged care home.

Len had been married twice before he married my mother (and had five children with his first wife), although he raised me from when I was 8 years of age, as his own child. He regularly took me and my friends around the southern vales region for netball, tennis or blue light discos. He was married to my mother Val for 21 years (an anniversary that he was proud of and occurred just before his death). They lived in Aldinga Beach, Elizabeth Park and Morgan together before Len died on the 6th September 2000, just three days before his 67th Birthday (the funeral was the week of Les and Lyndi Parsons's wedding, and I was MC for their wedding and Dad's funeral the same week). He is sadly missed and fondly remembered.

Photo above: Val and Len's wedding, 1979 with the reception at Auntie Gwen's house (Mum's sister Daphne, Len, Val, mum's sister Gwen) Below: Len and Sam at Raelene's house, Vista, 1998 (S. Battams)

Chapter 23: Conclusion

What is a family? The secrets that have been revealed

This family history is a bit complicated due to adoption and step-parenthood, and family secrets, and has made me reflect on the nature of families and the burden of secrets that women have carried. Generations have come and gone believing that our biological family on our grandfather's paternal side was the Miller and Heslop families – when in fact it is the Hazlehurst and Bird families! This has added some interesting new stories to the family history. One rumour that we can definitely dispel (based on DNA testing) is that we have Maori blood (we do not!).

In the early days of the Colony and for many years after, women's fates were largely determined by the family they were born into and the men in their lives and not having a good, stable and healthy man to rely upon could have drastic consequences. The plight of some of the women in the Lomman family was tragic, with babies born in the Destitute Asylum and at least one woman resorting to prostitution as there were no other means of survival.

The early days of South Australia were quite wild, with struggles with alcohol common among men (including for the Lomman and Schulz families), giving rise to the Temperence movement, from which the Women's Suffrage movement arose. It was inspiring to see family members, both men and women, having signed the Women's Suffrage Petition.

There were a number of so-called 'illegitimate' children in the family, and it was interesting how they were all treated differently: the Church of England Lomman family kept their children; the Catholic Fahy family adopted out our father who was somewhat a secret in his birth family; the White family brought up Alec White as if he were the youngest in the family and the fact that he was Sadie's son was kept a secret; Edith Thompson kept the secret of having a child to a man that was not her husband; and the Rumbelow family raised Dulcie Rumbelow in the family, whose 'illegitimacy' was not a secret. Perhaps the latter was enabled because it occurred in a rural area, however usually smaller communities are more concerned about social mores.

It is difficult to know the full circumstances around how some of the women became pregnant - some may have been the result of women being taken advantage of, or abuse or were at least unwanted pregnancies. In some cases where a woman did want to partner with a man, the men simply disappeared once a woman became pregnant, often without consequences for them. A prospective partner may have been considered undesirable due to the ‘wrong’ religion, cultural background or family of origin.

I feel for Iris Fahy and other women in the family who have had childbirth associated with shame, and a secret carried throughout their lives, or where the women raised their children from teenagerhood and had to resort to religious or public welfare which was likely to be shaming. It was interesting that the late Pat Nash said that she remembered Iris as always being a ‘fun’ person, and perhaps she really made an effort around children in the Fahy family, since she never had any further children of her own.

Changing Times

The status of women has come a long way through progress in public welfare, childcare, increased access to education and women’s participation in the workforce. Increasing numbers of women are now well educated, have careers and are able to financially support themselves, and work in a range of professional roles, including beyond female dominated industries such as nursing and teaching. However, despite South Australia’s leadership in women’s suffrage, and SA having the first female local government Councillor, it is the only state of Australia to not have had a female head of government.

Changes in our family have reflected changes in social conditions over time. Defacto relationships, divorce, remarriage, stepfamilies and single parenthood became more common, and adoption less common. Religion, especially Wesleyan-Methodist Congregationalism (which became the Uniting Church), Catholicism, Lutheranism and the 'Free Christian Church,' was once such an integral part of the lives of our ancestors. It was part of the motive for the Lutheran Schulz ancestors to arrive in Australia or for 'Jack Fahy' to become adopted by his unmarried Catholic mother! Consistent with the increasingly secular Australian culture, religion is not currently a strong part of my family.

Family members have become more dispersed and ours is (or was) no exception, as members of the 6th and 7th generation have lived interstate and overseas, although most have returned to Adelaide to live.

Whilst some of the forebears came out as agricultural labourers, they later became skilled tradespeople, business owners, civil servants, employees of service industries and even academics (!). Many of us in the sixth-generation work in government or the health and community services sector (which I have also done, as well as teaching/research in a university). In the Miller family there appears to have been a strong focus on service professions (health, education) – as well as motoring/engineering related professions.

For our family, tertiary education has occurred for the first time in the sixth generation; we have come a long way from the illiterate ancestors! I was a first-generation university student, but have a Doctor of Philosophy (PhD), although my parents did not complete high school. In my immediate family, Lyn, Raelene and Cheryl all completed tertiary qualifications - in nursing, social sciences and teaching respectively.

Women's progress is not always linear, and Marsden's (2004) research and commentary on women's role in famous winemaking families showed how women's role diminished across time in the Gramp family.

Photo: Pierre-Alain Wusler (ex-husband), Sam, Lyn, Val at Sam's PhD graduation, Dec 2008 (S. Battams)

Photo: Tessa St Clair on tour whilst on a study semester in Malaysia (S.Battams)

Surfing the world wide web and communicating via email and social media has become a part of daily work and leisure practices, including for the development of this family history. There are many more choices available to 'Generation Xers' and younger generations, especially because of higher education, and more challenges (in terms of discerning 'truth' in an age or artificial intelligence). One of the more negative aspects of our current society (or at least our family) is not having access to the close-knit communities that were associated with coming from a certain cultural background (i.e. Irish or German), religion or geographical region, and families being dispersed across geographical areas (as ours has been) can contribute to this.

Interactions with First Nations Peoples

There were several examples where my ancestors (whether biological, adoptive or in my step-father's family) had interactions with Aboriginal people, especially the Germans who had close interactions through the establishment of the missions (which it has been acknowledged played a role in children being removed from families). I had previously not known of any strong connections with Aboriginal communities prior to discovering the German ancestral links, but there were detailed reports on populations and descriptions of the missions and individuals who lived there in contemporary reports.

It was interesting to see Fred Glassenbury's story where he describes both tension in the mid-north in his father's time and his father distributing provisions to Aboriginal communities, and Fred being rescued by Aboriginal people, or receiving relief from traditional medicines as advised by a well-known Aboriginal man (Pantonie) in the Goolwa community. I was shocked to discover Daniel Battams's link to the death in custody of Warria at Stoney Creek. I feel saddened by this along with the displacement and dispossession of communities and deaths that have occurred through colonisation.

I was also surprised to discover a 'new' line of ancestors in the Hazlehurst family. Coincidentally, on the last trip to Auckland in 2025 I bought and read the wonderful historical fiction book *The Space Between* by Lauren Keenan, which is set around the time of the first Taranaki War, 1860,[719] and then was only later to find a connection to the story through the Hazlehurst family, with William Hazlehurst travelling to Aotearoa New Zealand as a Farrier in the Auckland Militia, which fought in the second Taranaki war.

I believe that we still have much progress to make for reconciliation, acknowledging and addressing the effects of European colonisation, and the social determinants of Aboriginal health. The current Aboriginal health and regressive incarcerations rates (and deaths in custody), both nationally and in South Australia, speak to this issue.

The Ancestral Continuum

I enjoyed reading the book *The Ancestral Continuum*[720] in 2020 and have reflected upon 'ancestral memory' and how family patterns can repeat, or how family trauma can be 'inherited.' There were a number of synchronicities in the family, for example repeated birthdays – even where a child or descendant was not biologically from the same family.

My mother could not have known about the secret baby of Freda Rumbelow (Mora Dawn) who was born in 1927. But when she had her first baby in 1951 she named it 'Jennifer Dawn.' Sadly, this child was stillborn and died at Woodville, where Freda's baby also died. Jennifer Dawn was born on 26th May 1951 around 6pm, whilst I was born at the same time and same place nearly exactly twenty years later.

There were many seafarers and mariners in the family, including in the Rumbelow and Miller families - and by DNA discovery the Bird family. There were many drownings at sea in the Rumbelow family and it was interesting to see this also on our mother's paternal side through the now famous 'Hoylake Boatmen.'

There were also many stories of financial bankruptcy in the 1890s and the Great Depression, including for the White, Fahy and Miller families, and examples of family members travelling to Victoria during the 1890s (White,

Miller-Abbott and Rumbelow families) and the earlier Goldrush period (Battams, Rumbelow, Glassenbury).

Discovering the story of Henry Lomman was surprising, given he was one of the first residents of the Parkside Asylum (Glenside). I had been told by my mother that there was no known history of such illness in the family - the story of her great-great grandfather Henry Lomman had well and truly been buried in the passage of time (just like the character in Jane Eyre who is locked away in the attic).[721] Some of his descendants have ended up in the same institution, whilst others in the wider family have worked there as employees. My sister Margret had chronic schizophrenia from a young age (before I was born), and died on the 1st October 2002, aged just 48, at the Royal Adelaide Hospital, with finalisation of even the inquest taking two and a half years, and the Coroner calling out the senior police officer involved for a lack of prioritisation and timely response on what should have been a routine investigation. My sister Cheryl, who was well educated and well-travelled and lived a full life prior to developing schizophrenia in her early 30s, also died relatively young, aged 57. Both died from conditions related to smoking. Lack of adequate and timely support had a profound impact on our family, and adequate mental health, general health and related housing services has been a cause that I have advocated for (and was the subject of my PhD research) in South Australia and nationally. Many people with intellectual and psychiatric disabilities and the most chronic mental health conditions, the sickest people in our society with the shortest life spans, will not seek out and regularly attend GPs or benefit from mass media health promotion campaigns. The fact that my great-great-great grandfather Henry Lomman, the first generation of Europeans to arrive in the Colony lived until 87 whilst his 3x great grandchildren (probably with the same mental health condition) died in their 40s and 50s speaks volumes.

Impact of Both World Wars and Soldier Settlement

My family history has highlighted the significant impact of both World Wars - for those who went to active service in the war (some of whom paid with their lives), for those that served at home (e.g. at Loveday), for those who were ostracised such as some of the German community (even though many arrived in the state of South Australia before the British), and for the parents, widows, siblings and children left at home. The failed Soldier Settlement Schemes in WWI quickly followed by the Great Depression also had an immense impact, in this case on the White and Battams families who served and returned to Australia.

Travelling back to the lands of the forebears

In the sixth generation, long distance air travel has become more common along with interstate travel for work and leisure, whilst overseas travel for leisure occurred for the first time in the fifth generation. An overseas (especially European) trip at the end of high school or university is seen as a 'right of passage,' for those who can afford it! I have always been drawn to continental Europe and aside from travelling in Europe, I have lived in Geneva, Switzerland for 3 years. As I write (December 2025), this holiday period some of the eighth generation great nieces and nephews will be overseas for Christmas or the holiday period. Throughout my life I have been very fortunate to be able to travel and return to some of the places that the ancestors were from, some of which have been described throughout this book.

So who was the biological grandfather?

The main question I wanted to answer through researching this family history was 'who were my biological grandparents?' After all of the years of research, I still have not been able to identify my biological grandfather.

In 2021, I sought the help of a genetic genealogist (Cate Pearce) and a 'DNA angel' (Merrie Bott) to try to ascertain who our paternal biological grandfather was. From our DNA matches on Ancestry, MyHeritage and FamilyTreeDNA it may be one of the 'German Cousins.' However, there was a lot of endogamy among the early Prussian community in South Australia, so it is difficult to confirm exactly who our biological grandfather was (or even if he was a German cousin).

DNA results seem to be constantly changing, but in 2025 according to Ancestry I am mainly Celtic and Gaelic from **Northern Wales and North West England** (25%), **Irish** from Munster (14%), Leinster (11%) and Connacht (2%), followed by **North Central European** (16%), **English** from North East England (12%), Cornwall (2%) and Southeast England and Northwestern European (2%), and then Nordic (Danish 8%), and Dutch (8%).

MyHeritage DNA results (2026) are largely consistent with this, and include: **Scottish and Welsh** (27.4%), **Irish** (18.1%), **English** (17.3%), **German** (15.6%), Eastern European (7%), (Danish 3.9%), Breton (3.7%), Dutch (2.5%), French (2.4%) and Baltic (2.1%) heritage.

Perhaps in the future with more people undertaking DNA tests and refinement in DNA technology we will be able to discover who our paternal biological grandfather was, and who our maternal biological great grandfather was.

Future generations

The sixth generation of the White family all has various surnames due to some taking a different name in marriage (and remarriage of Val), and the White surname has not carried on into the seventh generation. There were ten children born into the seventh generation across three families (carrying the names Parsons, Harris, Linden). Lyn and Robert Parsons had four boys, and one girl, Margret and Ken Harris had two children, Raelene Linden had three children, and Cheryl and I had no children. So far there have been 15 children born into the eighth generation (carrying the name Parsons, de

Heus, Carr, St Clair and Linden). A positive legacy from the Miller, Rumbelow and Schulz families appears to have been twins which have continued through the Miller (6th generation), Parsons (7th generation) and De Heus (8th generation) lines. I close this family history with some photos from the 5th, 6th and 7th generations in my family tree.

Above: Samantha, Raelene, Cheryl, Margret and Lyn at Aldinga Beach (circa 1986) (S. Battams); Middle: Raelene, Lyn, Cheryl at a family reunion (2017); Below: Raelene, Samantha, Lyn at Sam's 50th, Adelaide (2021) (S. Battams)

Photo above: 7th Generation at Sam's wedding, Waterfall Gully Adelaide 2007 (from left to right Jeremy, Leslie, Calli, and twins Adam and James) (S.Battams)

Below: 8th generation of Parsons, Back: Jesse Parsons, Jacob Parsons, Oliver Parsons. Front: Jade de Heus, Charlotte Parsons, Annabel Parsons, Lachlan Parsons, Tahlia Parsons, Amber de Heus (Sam's house, Xmas 2015) (S. Battams)

Photo above: Raelene's family, Hobart, Xmas 2008 (back, Jessica and Scott Carr with Michael Linden. Front: Steven St Clair (Tessa's ex-husband) and Tessa St Clair with Brock and Isabelle (R. Linden) Photo below: Scott, Jessica and Abigail Carr, at Michael and Natalie Linden's wedding, 2025 (R. Linden)

Photo above: Jessica, Raelene, Abbey, Isabelle and Tessa after one of Abbey's musical theatre performances, 2025 (S. Battams)

Acknowledgements

There are many people to thank for research, photos, information and assistance across the 30 years that this book has been written. If I have missed anyone out, I apologise as it has been done inadvertently, and I request that you contact me to rectify this.

Family and professional historians and other

Thanks to my late mother Val Battams for passing down family stories and 'keeping Dad's memory alive' as she promised. Also, thanks to her brothers, the late Uncle Len Miller and Uncle Stan Miller for the discussions about the Miller family. Also, thanks to Raelene Linden and Jessica Carr for collecting stories from Minnipa with me on our trip in 2000 and to Raelene for being interested and involved in the search, collecting information and photos about the Schulz family, listening to endless family tidbits and discoveries, and for proofreading.

I wish to acknowledge all of the work of the other family historians. On our mother's maternal side, the story of the Rumbelow family has largely been told in *The Rumbelows of Encounter Bay: 150 years of the family in South Australia (2005)*, and the Rumbelow and Descendants website. Thanks to the researchers and authors (Peter Rumbelow, Lesley Avery, Mary George, Matthew Rumbelow), and Matt Rumbelow who maintains the Rumbelow Descendants family website from where some photos were obtained.

Thanks to the late Margaret Miller who first researched the Miller and Heslop / Thompson lines in New Zealand and produced the unpublished family history books: *The Miller Family by Margaret Miller, available from SAGHS 2005*, *This history of Heslop, Miller, Thomson Families is compiled and submitted by Margaret Miller (2010) and The Heading Family History (2000).*

From the limited information I know about the Schulz family, much of it comes from the late distant biological relative Earle Wilson (in 1999). If not for the research of Earle Wilson and his contribution to the *Biographical Index of South Australians*, obtaining information on the Schulz family would have very difficult.

Thanks also to another family historian John Schulze (SA) for providing information on the life of Johann Gramp based on his own research and giving me many other resources on the Gramp family. Also thank you to Heather Webb for information on the Lomman/Nitschke family (2023).

Thank you to Leandra Ford and Di Booker (2019) (SA) who provided information on the Lomman family, and to Lynette Crundwell (2024) who provided information about Edward Garrett and John Lomman.

Also thank you to Valerie Smart (2007) (UK), Marilyn Carpenter (2008) (Vic) and Diane Barnes (SA) who provided information on the White family.

I also thank Judith Long (Vic) (2020/2021) who provided information on White's soldier settlement at Minnipa – Judith is currently researching and writing a book on soldier settlement in the Eyre Peninsula region and I look forward to reading this.

Thank you to Rick Elefsen and the late Doug Elefsen (former owners of the Minnipa Hotel) for providing information and contacts on the White family around the Minnipa region.

Also thank you to Helen Lewis (SA) who provided information on the Fahy family, and Marea (Ree) O'Brien (SA) and Anne Whitehead (NZ) who provided information on the Graney family (in 2021). Also thank you to Colleen Rohan Curro (US) who provided information on the Rohan family.

Also thank you to Diana (RoseDM) (NZ) and Donald Porter (US) for information on the Heslop family (2019). Thank you to Harriet Taylor (UK) (2022) who provided information on the Abbott family. Also to Heather Hobbis (SA) from Genealogy.com for research (Battams family 2007).

Also thank you to historian Catherine Bishop for telling me about Miss Mary Jane (Mae) Battams and her work with missionary Annie Lock, which is described in her book '*Too Much Cabbage and Jesus Christ*' (Wakefield Press, 2021).

Thank you to Catherine Bishop, Moira Were, Helen Lockwood and Angela Schilling (Lutheran Archives) for making suggestions about contacts for advice on Aboriginal cultural sensitivity. I greatly thank Dr Skye Krichauff (Adelaide University) for reviewing some sections, providing advice and making connections with Aboriginal people for advice. Thank you to Angie Faye Martin for providing cultural consultation.

Genealogists

I also wish to acknowledge genealogist Cate Pearce (2022) for her DNA report and advice. I would also likely to greatly thank Merrie Bott from Facebook site DNA Angels for her DNA related and family tree searching (in 2021, 2023 and 2025). This work has been invaluable for research on our paternal grandfather and previously unknown links in mum's side of the family.

Volunteers, Libraries and National Resources

The primary sources used were document research, however some history has been included from personal communication and written correspondence. I especially wish to thank all of those who work on the National Archive of Australia's resource Trove, and Papers Past, New Zealand, which have both been used extensively throughout this family history.

Sources included South Australian Genealogy and Heraldry Society (now Genealogy SA) publications or library resources (including in the old days cards and microfiche records!) and online databases. I also greatly thank the volunteers at Genealogy SA for their assistance, particularly in the first iterations of this family history (2006 and 2009) when searching was done manually. Also thank you to Carmel Dundon for advice, from the Genealogy and DNA course (2026).

Also thank you to David Buob, President of the Glenside Historical Society, for conducting research and providing information used in the Henry Lomman story.

Books such as that on the early German/Prussian families by Iwan's *Kavel's People* and *Because of their Beliefs* were invaluable, along with the Biographical Index of South Australians. Community histories such as *Moorak: Bend in the River* and library collections were also very helpful.

Photographs

I also wish to acknowledge the late Cliff (Clive) (1925-2001) and Mavis Schulz (1930-2014) and my sister Raelene Linden. Clive Schulz kindly passed on photographs of the Schulz family to my sister Raelene Linden when she visited him in 2000, along with family stories. Thank you to Raelene for obtaining these original photographs and obtaining stories about this family.

After contacting Mrs Pat Nash in 2005, I received the first photos of my grandmother Iris Fahy and her family. I wish to acknowledge the late Pat Nash who provided these photos along with information on the Fahy family.

Also, thanks go to the librarians at the Mount Gambier library for assisting with information and photos on the Fahy family (in 2020).

Also thank you to Stan Miller, the late Margaret Miller and Carolyn Wesley for photographs and documents on the Miller, Abbott and Heslop families, and to the late Margaret Miller for the extensive research that she undertook.

Thank you to Jean Kammerman (nee Kwaterski) who was able to provide us photos (and enabled them to be copied) and stories of our late father Stephen Raymond White, who grew up at Minnipa with Jean. I also wish to again gratefully acknowledge the former proprietors of the Minnipa Hotel, Rick

Elefsen and his father the late Doug Elefsen, who put us in touch with Jean Kammerman, and for their hospitality when staying at Minnipa.

Thank you to Christine Tovey for permission to use the two photos of the White family. Thank you to Donald Porter for permission to use the photo of Mowbray Heslop. Thank you to Roderick Eime for permission to use his photo of the Royal Exchange Hotel, Kadina. Thank you to Marilyn Rodda for permission to use the portrait photo of Miss Mary Battams.

I also acknowledge the South Australian Police Historical Society, Kym Hardwick and Ms Kate Woodcock, Manager of the Society's Photographic Records Section, for the photos of the grave of Daniel Battams's wife and children.

Thank you to James 'Jimmy' Keane, formerly Public Relations and Promotions Manager, Pernod-Ricard, for information on the Gramp family (2019-20). Thank you to Vinarchy for providing permission to use two photos, one of Johann Gramp and of the Gramp family which both appeared in Baker, T. (1987). *The Orlando Way. A Celebration of 150 Years 1837-1987*. G. Gramp and Sons 1987.

Endnotes

[1] There are two unpublished earlier versions at the South Australian Genealogy and Heraldry Society (2006 and 2009).
[2] City of Campbelltown, Indigenous History, https://www.campbelltown.sa.gov.au/__data/assets/pdf_file/0018/234504/Indigenous-History.pdf
[3] Mentioned pg. 51 in Rumbelow, P et al. (2015) *'The Rumbelows of Encounter Bay: 150 years of the family in Australia.*
[4] Tony Baker, *The Orlando Way: A Celebration of 150 Years 1837-1987*. Gramp and Sons, Adelaide.
[5] Mrs Mahalia Philps, SA History Hub https://sahistoryhub.history.sa.gov.au/people/mrs-mahalia-philps/
[6] Stephen White's son Edward White is listed in *the Biographical Index of South Australians* as a Labour and his residence is Hanson. He married 18th Dec 1866 Susann Elizabeth Barden at Gawler Plains and had 10 children: Joseph, Edward, John George (1872-1941), Martin, Frank, Ernest (1876-), May, Lucy, Lill and Rose. Edward White entered the Royal Adelaide Hospital for 'neuralgia' on 25th October 1876, aged 30. His address in the colony at this time was: Farell's Flat (Clare), and he is discharged the following day. He also enters the hospital for 'debility' on the 3rd February 1899, and is discharged 8th February 1899, and at this time is living at Glanville Blocks, where his brother's family lived.
[7] Shipping record, SAGHS (Genealogy SA)
[8] In the IGI and Ancestry, someone has listed her name as Lucy Edney, however one correspondent from Genes Reunited in UK claims that this should be Lucy Muggridge.
[9] https://en.wikipedia.org/wiki/Rodmell
[10] Fishbourne Roman Palace (Villa Regis Cogidubni), Roman Britain https://www.roman-britain.co.uk/places/fishbourne-roman-palace/
[11] http://www.sussexpast.co.uk and http://www.travelpublishing.co.uk and http://www.great-britain.co.uk).
[12] Free BMD Vol 7, pg. 489 http://freebmd.rootsweb.comcgi/districts
[13] Charlotte Smith, 25 and children Hariet Ayling, 10 years old, and Alfred Hoomwood, 7 years old. *UK Census 1841*, Ancestry
[14] East Sussex, England, Church of England Births and Baptisms, 1813-1920, East Sussex, England, Church of England Deaths and Burials, 1813-1995
[15] Stephen White's younger brother Henry White (b. 1824) also migrated to Australia, married in Melbourne (to Elizabeth Raney) and remained in Victoria (died 1852). Stephen White's younger brother Joseph White (Agricultural Labourer) stayed in England.
[16] This corresponds with the birthplace of the couple's daughter Mary Hannah White (1850), and the death of his son Stephen White (1868).
[17] Ancestry.com. Australia, Death Index, 1787-1985 [database on-line]. Lehi, UT, USA: Ancestry.com Operations, Inc., 2010.
[18] Andrew & Sandra Twining. (1992) *SA Military Volunteers for 1855*. Mr. A. Twining.
[19] *SA Government Gazette* 1858
[20] Newspaper beta website: http://ndpbeta.nla.gov.au/ndp/del/home
[21] Information about lodge or benefit societies found in articles by Dr Bob James (1999) at: http://www.takver.com/history/tragedy.htm and

http://www.takver.com/history/secsoc02.htm accessed 27th March 2006 and also in Weinbren, Dan and Bob James, 'Getting a Grip : the Roles of Friendly Societies in Australia and Britain Reappraised.' *Labour History* 88 (2005): 60 pars. 28 Mar. 2006 http://www.historycooperative.org/journals/lab/88/weinbren.html and http://www.fraternalsecrets.org/index.php accessed 27th March 2006

[22] Noting there were a few people named Stephen White in the city at the time.

[23] *South Australian Chronicle and Weekly Mail*, 1 May 1869

[24] Now Symonds place

[25] *South Australian Chronicle and Weekly Mail*, 1 May 1869

[26] *South Australian Chronicle and Weekly Mail*, 24 April 1869

[27] *Adelaide Observer*, 24 April 1869

[28] Sir John George Shaw Lefevre, SA History Hub https://sahistoryhub.history.sa.gov.au/people/sir-john-george-shaw-lefevre/

[29] *South Australian Chronicle*, 12 Nov 1892, The Junction Mine, p 16

[30] Died 7th November 1878, at Port Adelaide (No 158)

[31] *South Australian Government Gazette*, 18th October 1883

[32] There was a Samuel White (1870-1954) living at Fulham, Reedbeds, South Australia who was likely the son of the famous ornithologist, Samuel White (1835-1880), who settled at Reedbeds – his father John and Uncle George had come over to South Australia on the *Tam O' Shanter* in 1836. Given that my relative Stephen White had stayed at Reedbeds when he was ill in 1886, the two families may have been related.

[33] Record dist. Ade sym H b 227, p 374

[34] SAGHS Marriage Registrations, Dist Ade, b 47, p 229, 1861

[35] *Government Gazette* April 1864.

[36] Dist Ade b20, p 332

[37] Mt Serle, b 36, p 463

[38] Prospect, b 33, p 615

[39] She was named after Mary Hannah White as well as mother Sarah Mary Hannah Sarah White also interchangeably called herself Hannah and Anna like her mother source: M. Carpenter, descendant, personal communication.

[40] Died 6 Feb 1870 aged 12 months at North Adelaide, rel Stephen White (F), Dist. Adel, sym S b 29, p 261. Certificate 1859 of 1870, son of Stephen White (deceased) Fisherman, usual residence, Glenelg. Signed by Phillip Le Cornu of North Adelaide.

[41] At the time it was also known as Angepena, which was a station leased by Snell south-west of Mt Serle

[42] Native Troubles in the Far North, *South Australian Register*, 11 Aug 1865

[43] Cattle killing on Stuckey's station , March 1860, Interactive Map. The South Australian Frontier and its Legacies. The University of Adelaide 2024.

[44] The shooting of Pompey, 8 January 1864, Interactive Map. The South Australian Frontier and its Legacies. The University of Adelaide 2024.

[45] Native Troubles in the Far North, *South Australian Register*, 11 Aug 1865

[46] Paralana, North East of Mount Serle, *Adelaide Observer*, 29 April 1865, page 3

[47] https://collections.slsa.sa.gov.au/resource/B+46450

[48] 'Killing of shepherd John Walter Jerrold near Mount Fytton, 13th April 1865, Interactive Map. The South Australian Frontier and its Legacies. The University of Adelaide 2024.

[49] SA Police Historical Society

[50] *SA Government Gazette*, 3 May 1866

[51] SA memory website. www.samemory.sa.gov.au

[52] *Adelaide Observer*, 7 May 1864
[53] Ibid.
[54] A Noted Blackfellow. Big Bobbie and the Whites, *The Register*, 4 June 1924.
[55] Mount Serle, Wikipedia. https://en.wikipedia.org/wiki/Mount_Serle
[56]*Pastoral Pioneers of South Australia*. There is a possibility that landowner R B James was related to Sarah James, although her father is listed as William James on her marriage registration.
[57] He would later become Mayor of Adelaide and Member of the Legislative Council of SA Parliament
[58] *Pastoral Pioneers of South Australia*, p. 67
[59] *Pastoral Pioneers of South Australia*, p. 139
https://history.cass.anu.edu.au/files/ncb/documents/PASTORAL%20PIONEERS%20OF%20SOUTH%20AUSTRALIA%20VOL.1.pdf
[60] *SA Government Gazette*, 11 June 1868
[61] Dist Ade b 29, p 123, Certificate no 730 of 1868, signed by Phillip Le Cornu on the 2nd Nov 1868
[62] Dist Ade, certificate 730 of 1868
[63] *Register Personal Notices* Volume 3 1866-1870, Compiled by Reg Butler & Alan Phillips (1991), Gould Books, Ridgehaven
[64] *The Express and Telegraph*, 2 October 1868
[65] His father was Hugh Graham.
[66] The replacement Methodist Parsonage built in 1881 is still standing on the corner of Tynte Street and Wellington Square, and is more recently known as the former channel 9 studios.
[67] Ibid.
[68] *Southern Argus*, 5th February 1870
[69] *Adelaide Observer*, 23rd September 1871
[70] She was listed as 18 on her marriage certificate in 1861.
[71] Dist. Ade, sym S b 31 p 463, 1864
[72] Spelt Linda, Linder and Lynda on different documents
[73] Dist Ade b 128, p 10, 1881
[74] Dist Ade, b 27, p 52, 1863
[75] She may have had another sister Linda who died before she was born (born May 1861 and died in January 1862, five weeks before her parents were married in 1862)
[76] SAGHS (Genealogy SA)
[77] *SA Coronial Inquests*, Ancestry
[78] CD on SA Births, via Carpenter 5/12/2005
[79] Dist Pt A 276/35, 1882
[80] Dist Pt A 314/367, 1883
[81] Dist Pt A 369/473, 1886
[82] Victoria Registration No 32089, 1890
[83] Victoria Registration No 9242 Possibility only – father of this child is David, mother not recorded.
[84] Victoria Registration No 14459
[85] Australia, Birth Index 1788-1922, Ancestry.com, Ancestry.com Operations, Inc, 2010, Provo, UT USA
[86] Had at least 1 child out of wedlock, John Alexander Stephen 'Alec/Alex' born 1908, when she was around 20 years. Also possibly Charles Roy Tucker b 1914 Glanville
[87] Glanville District Pt A 648/158, 1899

[88] Williamstown Pt A 689/177, 1902. Died aged 15 months: source V. Battams 2005, and Australia Death Index, Ancestry (Vol 293, pg. 371).
[89] Dist Pt A 751/142, 1905
[90] Dist, Pt A 751/142, 1905
[91] News, 23 July 1945
[92] SA Certificate of Title, Vol CCCV, Folio 245
[93] *The Register*, 27th Feb 1927, Alleged Poisonous Food
[94] *The Advertiser*, 8th April 1927
[95] Sandwell – old name for Birkenhead or Peterhead.
[96] NAA WW1 records (Record Search)
[97] South Australia, Australia, Adelaide Hospital Admission Registers, 1841-1952, 1945 Jan-1946 Dec, Ancestry
[98] SAGHS SA Births Registrations 1842-1906, vol 11 w-z
[99] *The Register*, 3rd March 1913
[100] Sandwell was formed into Birkenhead and Peterhead
[101] Linda White was variously listed as Linder (birth record Ade, 27/52), Linda (marriage record Ade 121/10) and Lynda or Lydia (Stephen White's army record, National Archives of Australia), original microfiche records accessed at the South Australian Genealogy and Heraldry Society through the SAGHS, *South Australians 1836-1885 Book Two,* SAGHS *South Australian Births - Index of Registrations 1842-1906* and SAGHS *SA Marriages Index of Registrations 1917-1937*
[102] Adam-Smith, P, *The Anzacs*, Penguin Books, Australia, pg. 476
[103] Recruitment Poster *'Whose son are you?'*, From www.anzacday.org.au accessed 27th March 2006
[104] Victoria State Recruiting Committee Poster, Hoover Institute Library and Archives, Standford University https://digitalcollections.hoover.org/objects/9797/whose-son-are-you--enlist-today-i-didnt-raise-my-son-to
[105] *Honor Roll 18th Battery 6th Field Artillery Brigade, WW1*, private collection, S Battams
[106] Adam-Smith, P, *The Anzacs*, pg. 216
[107] Adam-Smith, P, *The Anzacs*, pg. 155
[108] Dyer, J, *The Story of the 18th Battery 6th Brigade, Field Artillery, 1st AIF, 1915-1919*, 1965, unpublished document, page 2, private collection, S Battams
[109] Adam-Smith, P, *The Anzacs*, pg. 208-209
[110] Dyer, J, *The Story of the 18th Battery*, pg. 2
[111] Dyer, *The Story of the 18th Battery, pg. 1*
[112] Australian War Memorial, Private record 3DRL/7566A, Diary of Private C.P Melville, 18th Battery, 6th Brigade, Field Artillery, Australian Division (pages unmarked)
[113] Dyer, J, *The Story of the 18th Battery, pg. 11*
[114] Ibid.
[115] Australian War Memorial Private Record PR00314. Diary of Colin C Twist, 18th Battery, 6th Brigade, Field Artillery, 2nd Australian Division, pg. 22
[116] Read Longeval - Should read Longaeval
[117] Australian War Memorial Private Record PR00314. Diary of Colin C Twist, 18th Battery, 6th Brigade, Field Artillery, 2nd Australian Division, page 27
[118] For anyone interested, there are two diaries which I have as photocopies from the Australian War Memorial written by soldiers who were part of the 18th Battery and same section as Stephen William White; these are Bombardier C. Twist (57 pages) and Bombardier C.P. Melville (154 pages).

[119] A Taube was a stealth-plane see http://www.ctie.monash.edu.au/hargrave/etrich_taube.htm, accessed 27th March 2006
[120] Australian War Memorial Private Record PR00314. Diary of Colin C Twist, 18th Battery, 6th Brigade, Field Artillery, 2nd Australian Division, pg. 29
[121] DAC – Divisional Ammunition Column, 1st AIF http://www.awm.gov.au/glossary/result.asp?browse=1
[122] Australian War Memorial, Private record 3DRL/7566A, Diary of Private C.P Melville
[123] From http://www.bbc.co.uk/history/war/wwone/australia_05.shtml accessed 27th March 2006
[124] A lark is a noisy bird that gave rise to the expressions 'happy as a lark' and in French is known as the 'alouette' the subject of the song sometimes known in English 'Alouette, gentille alouette' about plucking the bird in preparation for cooking.
[125] CCS – Casualty Clearing Station. Later in the diary he reports he was at Poperinghe CCS on the 24th September 1917.
[126] Australian War Memorial, Private record 3DRL/7566A, Diary of Private C.P Melville
[127] AIF project, Australian Defence Force Academy http://www.aif.adfa.edu.au:8080/index.html
[128] *The Express and Telegraph*, 22nd November 1917
[129] Battams, V, personal communication
[130] National Archives of Australia, NAA: D2994, WHITE S W. Series No. D2994.
[131] Dyer, *The Story of the 18th Battery*, pg. 22
[132] Dyer, *The Story of the 18th Battery*, pg. 22
[133] Honor Roll of the 18th Battery, 6th Field Artillery
[134] Dyer, *The Story of the 18th Battery* pg. 22
[135] National Archives of Australia record 1850441 http://www.naa.gov.au/the_collection/defence/conflicts/ww1/ww1.html
[136] Dyer, *The Story of the 18th Battery*, pg. 22
[137] National Archives of Australia World War 1 record 1850441 http://www.naa.gov.au/the_collection/defence/conflicts/ww1/ww1.html
[138] Dyer, *The Story of the 18th Battery*, pg. 25
[139] Ibid
[140] Dyer, *The Story of the 18th Battery*, pg. 41
[141] Dyer, *The Story of the 18th Battery*, pg. 25
[142] National Archives of Australia record 1850441
[143] National Archives of Australia, NAA: D2994, WHITE S W. Series No. D2994.
[144] National Archives record 1850441
[145] *The Chronicle*, 27th April 1918
[146] Source: V Battams
[147] *Lonely Planet* (2005) France, 6th edition, Lonely Planet Books
[148] Dyer, J, *The Story of the 18th Battery, pg. 42*
[149] Ibid
[150] See the English website http://www.westernfront.co.uk/aboutus/membership.php for more information on the Western Front.
[151] *Lonely Planet* (2005) France, 6th edition, Lonely Planet Books
[152] Information from http://www.firstworldwar.com/today/thiepval.htm accessed 27th March 2006
[153] Dyer, J, *The Story of the 18th Battery, pg. 23*

[154] The Long Long Trail: The Story of the British Army in the First World War http://www.1914-1918.net/sacredground/ypres/ieper.htm accessed 6th November 2005
[155] Battams, V, personal communication
[156] Department of Family and Community Services, Adoption and Family Information Service, letter and other material from adoption records dated 30th January 1998, via mail Ref: APP:R5808/2881
[157] Scarfe, W. (2014). *Hunger Town*, Wakefield Press
[158] Information courtesy Judith Long (nee Darby) who originated from Wudinna.
[159] According to the former Minnipa Hotel proprietor, Dough Elefsen
[160] *Port Lincoln Times*, 4th December 1936
[161] Information courtesy research undertaken by Judith Long and emailed to S. Battams
[162] *Commonwealth of Australia Gazette*, 21st May 2936
[163] His son would recall his mother visiting Port Lincoln with him when he was young and meeting up with another man, and his father coming to claim them according to V. Battams in her later years.
[164] *Police Gazette*, 12 August 1936, via Ancestry
[165] See Adam-Smith, P, *The Anzacs*, for an account of the Discharged Soldier Settlement Acts, pgs. 465-466
[166] Personal communication, 2020.
[167] According to V. Battams, personal communication.
[168] *The Advertiser*, 14 May 1946
[169] www.wool.net.au
[170] Adam-Smith, P, *The Anzacs*, pg. 14
[171] White, C, personal communication
[172] Dennis, C. J *Digger Smith*, Trench Series, Angus & Robertson Ltd, 1918, A Square Deal, pg102, 104
[173] announced in *The Advertiser* 27 November 1940
[174] NAA Service Record, William Surman, Series B884, S33321, Item ID 6330276, and B883, SX11977
[175] Dist. Pt Ade, b 281, p 626, her parents were Elijah Holman and Annie Louise Vierk.
[176] S. Battams Diary, personal collection
[177] *The Adoption of Children Act 1925 (Act No. 1692/1925)* commenced on 17 December 1925
[178] https://www.csmc.org.au/2023/05/29/single-mother-wins-then-and-now/ and https://www.findandconnect.gov.au/entity/supporting-mothers-benefit/
[179] Find and Connect website, Commonwealth of Australia, 2011, accessed 18 October 2025 https://www.findandconnect.gov.au/entity/adoption-in-south-australia/
[180] Battams, V, personal communication
[181] New South Wales Government Gazette, 1 Sept 1871, Trove
[182] *The Advertiser* article on the accident from 19th November 1935
[183] Fay Bignell was first cousin to my sister Lyn Parsons's father-in-law Allan Parsons. Jessie Poole married Fred Bignell and Fred's sister Eva Bignell married Richard Poole. Emily Poole another sister married a Parsons (my brother-in-law Robert's grandpa). Fred Bignell was born in Minlaton, as were the Parsons.
[184] Source: V Battams
[185] *Australia's mothers and babies*, web report, 27 Feb 2026, Australian Institute of Health and Welfare. https://www.aihw.gov.au/reports/mothers-babies/australias-

mothers-babies/contents/stillbirths-neonatal-deaths/stillbirths-and-neonatal-deaths-in-australia and ABS Mortality, Life Expectancy and Causes of Death https://www.abs.gov.au/ausstats/abs@.nsf/Lookup/by%20Subject/1301.0~2012~Main%20Features~Mortality,%20life%20expectancy%20and%20causes%20of%20death~231

[186] Gibb & Miller Engineers at Port Adelaide build regard for contributing to South Australia WWII big industrial efforts, AdelaideAZ website, https://adelaideaz.com/articles/gibb-and-miller-engineers-at-port-adelaide-build-regard-for-contributing-to-world-war-industrial-efforts

[187] 'American Machine Tools,' *The West Australian*, 22 Feb 1946

[188] 'Unusual Task for SA Firm,' *The Advertiser*, 27 September 1954

[189] 'Big New Industry Opened at Whyalla,' *The Chronicle*, 30th September 1954

[190] Ibid

[191] 'Defence Production,' *The Cairns Post*, 10th February 1953

[192] 'Prices up 50 pc; Wages 134 pc', *The Courier-Mail*, 12 Nov 1952

[193] 'Margins Dispute for Labor Council,' *The Advertiser*, 30th April 1954

[194] 'SA unity: Metal Men stop on Wages,' *Tribune*, 29th January 1958

[195] Ibid

[196] *Adam Gwinnett keeps ROH Wheels rolling faster from family links to British factory set up 1946 in South Australia*, AdelaideAZ website, https://adelaideaz.com/articles/adam-gwinnett-keeps-roh-wheels-rolling-faster-from-family-links-to-british-factory-set-up-in-south-australia-in-1946?fbclid=IwY2xjawQsyVZleHRuA2FlbQIxMABicmlkETFHclliSDFqMFlhRmF1OGM3c3J0YwZhcHBfaWQQMjIyMDM5MTc4ODIwMDg5MgABHnrn-OkTkONyqs2XiSsnPPGWHLF2epYAAQRfVfAEBVLyGqlOHd1QFa9JY9fR_aem_iF81Gaog6DDLQDaXfz5IlQ

[197] Ibid

[198] 'SA Engineering Co.'s Expansion, *The Age*, 22nd April 1950

[199] Robert Parsons, husband of Lyn Parsons nee White

[200] Fred Bignell was allocated land adjacent to Stephen White - S22 in Oct 1922 - but before that it was allocated to Allan Campbell in who gave a Yaninee Address when he enlisted in WWI – it appears that Campbell left the block in 1922 - information from Judith Long.

[201] http://scripts.ireland.com/ancesto

[202] The NSW death certificate of Michael Fahy, who could be Edmund's brother (according to DNA links) states that his parents were Patrick Fahy and Mary Linnane. There are also DNA links where a couple is Patrick Fahy (born 1807, Cahernagarry Bullaun, Athenry, Loughrea, County Galway, died 1886) and Mary Mannion/Manion (born around 1817 Galway, Ireland, died 6 Aug Caherakillen, Galway, Ireland). The latter did have a child named Honor Fahy. There are also strong DNA links to the Rohan family from the US.

[203] Marea O'Brien, personal communication – states they were from Loughrea, Galway.

[204] Clare Library

[205] In the shipping list their name is spelt "Fahey"

[206] https://www.immigrantships.net/v12/1800v12/ladyann18591001.html

[207] Lady Ann shipping list, SA Archives https://www.archives.sa.gov.au/__data/assets/pdf_file/0006/831660/GRG35_48_1_57-11_Lady-Ann.pdf

[208] Shipping Record, SAGHS (Genealogy SA)

[209] Information from Doreen McDonald passed down to Anne Whitehead, sent to Samantha Battams on the 19th February 2021. Also information from Marea O'Brien.
[210] As identified by Cate Pearce
[211] Roots Ireland, as identified by Cate Pearce
[212] Ireland, Griffith's Valuation, 1847-1864 for Edmund Fahy, Ancestry, Parish of Kilthomas, Doonally East, Loughrea, Galway
[213] Ireland, Valuation Records, 1824-1856 for Edmund Fahy, House books, Galway, Loughrea
[214] Ireland, Griffith's Valuation, 1847-1864 for Patrick Fahy, Parish of Loughrea, Loughrea, Galway
[215] Petty Session Court Registers, 7 Feb 1860, Court name: Athenry, Galway Ireland. Residence Place: Loughrea. Ancestry
[216] Arthure, S, 'Kapunda's Irish Connections,' chapter in Arthure, S, Breen, F, James, S, Lonergan, D (eds) (2019), *Irish South Australia: New histories and insights.* Wakefield Press, Adelaide.
[217] Ibid.
[218] Ibid
[219] http://freepages.genealogy.rootsweb.com/~dicummings/EmigrationIrish.htm accessed June 2005 and http://www.clarelibrary.ie/eolas/coclare/history/emigrate.htm
[220] White, Rev. P *History of Clare* (SAGHS library)
[221] Clare Library
[222] *Biographical Index of South Australians* 1836-1885, vol 11, SAGHS.
[223] Dis. Adel (Marriage Index book 41, page 194). Certificate 1228 of 1860
[224] Shipping List, Octavia
[225] *The Irish Harp and Farmers' Herald*, 16 Apr 1870
[226] Dis. Adelaide reference b18 p268
[227] Also referred to in the records as Edward John Fahey.
[228] Edward John Fahy married Edith Delbridge and had at least six children: Sidney John Fahy (married Sylvia Camp), Alice Edith, Edmund Delbridge (married Ruby Collins), Florence Margaret, Irene and Gladys Veronica. They lived at Mile End in 1917 when Alice Edith married John Augustus Anderso]. Edward John Fahy died 9th May 1921, aged 53 years. Sidney John Fahy was living in Torrensville in 1925, his wife gave birth to a child (Frederick Edward Fahy) on 2nd June 1926.
[229] Gawler Baptisms no 952
[230] *Biographical Index of South Australians 1836-1885*
[231] *Kapunda Herald*, 27 June 1890
[232] FamilySearch - Probate and Administration Records: Probate Registry 1890-1891
[233] Stratton and *The News*, 4 Sept 1933
[234] *The Chronicle*, 24th November, 1906
[235] *The Chronicle*, 16th July, 1910
[236] *The Advertiser*, 13th January 1910.
[237] *SA Government Gazette*, 10 May 1888. Government Gazettes 1841-1889
[238] Adelaide Hospital Admission Registers, 1841-1952
[239] *Southern Cross*, 10th December 1909
[240] https://www.healthmuseumsa.org.au/menu/1991-tuberculosis-control-in-south-australia/

[241] According to the *Irish Independent*, prog can mean gain or profit in a bargain. https://www.independent.ie/life/prog-has-many-definitions-but-it-means-lucky-to-me/38455317.html
[242] The command 'sool-em' was the verbal signal to initiate the coursing chase, when the slipper would release two greyhounds going after a hare. Sool means to set a dog on, or urge to chase or attack and was used in coursing/hunting.
[243] *Kapuna Herald*, 25 December 1891
[244] *South Australian Chronicle,* 2 July 1892, Kapunda Coursing Meeting
[245] Ibid
[246] *Kapunda Herald*, 28th April 1893, Football Notes
[247] South Australian Births – Index of Registrations 1842-1906, b 593, pg270
[248] This could have been Bridget Agnes Geier who was born in Kapunda in 1874 (whose mother was also Bridget and born in County Clare, Ireland). She later married Arthur Staples and adopted a child in 1900.
[249] *SA Police Gazette*, 14 Sept 1921
[250] Australia, Death Index, 1787-1985, Registration no 880
[251] The Aboriginal people at Moorooroo referred to Jacob's Creek as 'Cowieaurita,' which meant 'yellow-brown water.' Young, G., Harmstorf, I., Langmead, D. *Barossa Survey* (1977), SA Institute of Technology and Adelaide College of Advanced Education for the Australian Heritage Commission https://data.environment.sa.gov.au/Content/heritage-surveys/3-Barossa-Survey-Vol-3-1977.pdf
[252] There is a record of a Fahy and Schulz travelling on the Pilbarra, arriving 4 August 1900 at Fremantle. National Archives of Australia passenger records.
[253] According to Pat Nash, daughter in law of Dorothy Nash nee Fahy.
[254] Source: Pat Nash
[255] Could be Edmund W. Fahy
[256] Source: Pat Nash
[257] Wratten, 'The unexpected Irishmen: How David Power and Anthony Sutton established an Irish colonial presence in the South East of South Australia, chapter in Arthure, S, Breen, F, James, S, Lonergan, D (eds) (2019), *Irish South Australia: New histories and insights.* Wakefield Press, Adelaide.
[258] *The News*, 6th September 1937
[259] *Recorder*, 5th September 1928
[260] *The News*, 28th May 1947
[261] *The News*, 12th February 1949
[262] *The News*, 17th December 1953
[263] *Border Watch*, 20th June 1919
[264] *The Border Watch* (Mount Gambier), 11 Apr 1919, Page 3, MOORAK AGRICULTURAL BUREAU
[265] *The Border Watch* (Mount Gambier), 1 Mar 1921, Page 4, Moorak C. and B. Coy.
[266] *The Border Watch* (Mount Gambier), 22 Mar 1949, Page 1, Death Of Mr. J. W. Barry
[267] Sands & Mac Dir no 192, pg. 1010
[268] *The News*, 'Fahy, of Torrens, Impresses,' 18th Aug 1927
[269] *Southern Cross*, 'Personal' section, 5th June 1936, Trove, 'Hobbies of Adelaide's Heavyweight Policemen,' The Mail, 14th December 1935
[270] 'Farewell to Court Reporter' *News* article posted on Ancestry by H. Lewis https://www.ancestry.com.au/mediaui-

viewer/collection/1030/tree/105055001/person/432201642802/media/2e3d3039-1901-4729-9c84-827ef0009002?galleryindex=5&sort=-created

[271] *The Advertiser*, 8th November 1927

[272] Sands and MacDougall Directories

[273] Death Index, vol 560, pg. 2919, dist. 1, Adelaide

[274] Sands & Macdougall Directories

[275] *Leader* (Angaston), 7th January 1937

[276] According to Mrs P. Nash

[277] *Border Watch*, 11th November 1916, Moorak Picnic

[278] *Border Watch*, 16th November 1917, Moorak Picnic

[279] *Border Watch*, 7th November 1919, Moorak Picnic

[280] *Border Watch*, 27th January 1920

[281] *Border Watch*, 8th April 1921

[282] *Border Watch*, 2nd July 1918

[283] *The Advertiser*, 15th July 1935

[284] National Archive of Australia records

[285] *The News*, 2nd November 1939

[286] *The News*, 2nd November 1939, pg. 5

[287] ALP Expels Four; Disciplines Three, *The Advertiser*, 30 July 1954.

[288] Pat Nash, personal communication with S. Battams circa 2005

[289] *The News*, 24th October 1950

[290] Personal communication with Pat Nash, circa 2005

[291] Hart JE, Laden F, Eisen EA, Smith TJ, Garshick E. Chronic obstructive pulmonary disease mortality in railroad workers. *Occup Environ Med.* 2009 Apr;66(4):221-6. doi: 10.1136/oem.2008.040493. Epub 2008 Nov 27

[292] Donohue, J. Anam Cara. *Spiritual Wisdom from the Celtic World*, Penguin Books. Updated 2023.

[293] One who prunes and cultivates wine. Referred to in the bible as meaning 'keeper of the vineyard.'

[294] Two-month-old Barbara died in February and both Johann Erhardt, 5 years and Kunigunda, 3 years, died in May. Source: John Schulze.

[295] Sometimes referred to as Eichig, not to be confused with the current town of the same name (Eichig, Ahorn Valley). Both Eichig and Aichig are 22km from Kulmbach

[296] Wikipedia, Aichig, K

[297] Photo from Baker, T. (1987). *The Orlando Way. A Celebration of 150 Years*. G. Gramp and Sons 1987. Used with permission from Vinarchy.

[298] https://baturina-homewear.com

[299] Dropsy is now known as oedema and can be a symptom of congestive heart failure.

[300] The German Americans: An Ethnic Experience. https://library.indianapolis.iu.edu/static/collections/kade/adams/toc.html

[301] United Status, Census, 1840, Ancestry. The other Gramps may be family members.

[302] Kingdom of Bavaria, https://en.wikipedia.org/wiki/Kingdom_of_Bavaria

[303] Lola Montez, Dancer and King's Mistress, The Goethe Institut, https://www.goethe.de/ins/ie/en/kul/sup/deutsche-spuren-in-irland/25702166.html

[304] Lola Montez, https://en.wikipedia.org/wiki/Lola_Montez#:~:text=For%20more%20than%20a%20year%2C%20Montez%20exercised,at%20Montez's%20insistence%2C%20to%20close%20the%20university.

[305] Baker, T. (1987), op cit.
[306] *Bunyip*, 29th October 1937
[307] Encyclopaedia Britannia. Germany 1871 to 1918.
https://www.britannica.com/place/Germany/Germany-from-1871-to-1918
[308] Ibid.
[309] SLSA South Australian Company
http://www.samemory.sa.gov.au/site/page.cfm?u=1483
[310] *Bunyip*, 1937, op cit.
[311] Australian Dictionary of Biography, Frederick Hansborough Dutton (1812-1890) by Geoffrey Dutton Biography - Frederick Hansborough Dutton - Australian Dictionary of Biography
[312] *Bunyip*, 1937, op cit.
[313] Tour Kangaroo Island website
https://www.tourkangarooisland.com.au/experiences/old-mulberry-tree
[314] Personal communication, Kym Scholz, Hope Cottage Museum, 2023.
[315] Baker, op cit, pg 11
[316] Late Johann Gramp, Pioneer Winemaker of 100 Years Ago, *The Leader*, Angaston, SA, p. 1
[317] Information from John Schulze, descendant.
[318] 'Lyndoch,' *The Register*, 16th April 1927
[319] Late Johann Gramp, Pioneer Winemaker of 100 Years Ago, *The Leader*, Angaston, SA, p. 1
[320] Ibid.
[321] 'John and William Jacob,' *Pastoral Pioneers of South Australia*,' p. 138
[322] Source: Iwan, (1995). *'Because of Their Beliefs: emigration from Prussia to Australia'* W. Iwan / translated and edited with additional material by David Schubert, H. Schubert, Highgate, South Australia
[323] Schulze, J. (n.d.). Timeline of known facts about Johann Gramp. Unpublished timeline.
[324] 'Diamond Wedding. Interesting Reminiscences' *Daily Herald,* 1st Jun 1912
[325] Late Johann Gramp, Pioneer Winemaker of 100 Years Ago, *The Leader*, Angaston, SA, p. 1
[326] Ibid.
[327] *Bunyip*, 1937, op cit
[328] 'Diamond Wedding. Interesting Reminiscences' *Daily Herald,* 1st Jun 1912
[329] Evolved into Nitschke
[330] Ibid
[331] Schulze, op cit.
[332] whose first husband was John Lomman, my great-great-great grandfather Henry Lomman's brother (from mum's side of the family)
[333] Lynette Crundwell, by email, 12th February 2024
[334] Baker, T. (1987). *The Orlando Way. A Celebration of 150 Years*. G. Gramp and Sons 1987
[335] Ibid.
[336] Iwan, op cit.
[337] The Barossa Valley is on Ngadjuri and Kaurna Country. It was previously understood to be Peramangk Country.
[338] *Barossa Valley Heritage Study*, May 1981. ISBN 0959 92300
[339] *The Wakefield Companion to South Australian History*, Wakefield Press.2024 (Prest W, editor)
[340] State Records of South Australia, Land Tax Return of 1885

[341] PIRSA (2018), *Pioneer Vignerons, Johann Gramp*. Prepared by Kevin Gogler and Barry Philphttps://pir.sa.gov.au/__data/assets/pdf_file/0006/347343/Pioneer_Vigneron_-_Johann_Gramp.pdf
[342] *South Australian Register,* Coroner's Inquest, The Tragedy at Angaston, 30th August 1890
[343] I had not heard of this ancestral story when I wrote *'The Secret Art of Poisoning'* which is set in the same era, place and had similar themes.
[344] Probate and Administration Books - Probate Registry, Supreme Court of South Australia, Volume GRS_11585_1_61_61, Family Search
[345] *The Chronicle*, 18 May 1939, Obituary
[346] *The Mail*, 26th August 1939
[347] https://www.wikitree.com/wiki/Gramp-9
[348] *The Journal*, 6th December 1918 https://trove.nla.gov.au/newspaper/article/213251267?searchTerm=Yalata%20%2B%20Gramp
[349] *The Leader* (Angaston), 28 October 1937
[350] 'A teetotaller toasts Orlando as the name 'known favourably all around the world,' chapter 4 in Tony Baker (1997) *'A Heritage of Innovation,' Orlando Wines, 1847-1997,* Anvil Press, Adelaide
[351] Baker, T. (1987). *The Orlando Way. A Celebration of 150 Years. G. Gramp and Sons 1987*
[352] https://sahistoryhub.history.sa.gov.au/organisations/orlando-wines/
[353] Orlando Wines https://sahistoryhub.history.sa.gov.au/organisations/orlando-wines/
[354] https://www.mi-3.com.au/18-07-2024/pernod-ricard-sell-jacobs-creek-orlando-st-hugo-brands-accolade-wines-owner
[355] Global Brand Director on building Jacob's Creek's reputation amid Vinarchy transition, Cody Profaca, Aug. 5, 2025, 'Drinks Trade' website: https://www.drinkstrade.com.au/news/global-brand-director-on-building-jacobs-creeks-reputation-amid-vinarchy-transition/
[356] Tolley, J. (2004). *A social and cultural investigation of women in the wine industry of South Australia*. Project Number TOL 01/01.
[357] *The Australian Lutheran*, 23rd June, 1965, pg 199
[358] Baker (1987), op cit, Photo used with permission from Vinarchy.
[359] The Synod linked to Kavel's group.
[360] Likely referring to Gustav Gramp
[361] Lutheran Mission, *The Observer*, 18 March 1911
[362] Koonibba Mission Station, *West Coast Sentinel*, 28 Aug 1914, p.5
[363] Koonibba Mission Station, *West Coast Sentinel*, 28 Aug 1914, p 5
[364] Wirangu, Kokatha and Mirning Peoples.
[365] *The Chronicle*, 5 September 1914
[366] Koonibba Mission Station, *West Coast Sentinel*, 28 Aug 1914, p 5
[367] Ibid
[368] Find and Connect, Australian Government. https://www.findandconnect.gov.au/entity/koonibba-childrens-home/
[369] Iwan, (1995). *Op cit.*
[370] George Friedrich Schulz is named 'Friedrich Schulz' on the shipping record. He appears to have retained the 'Schultz' spelling, along with his other ancestors. There are strong DNA connections to his other descendants on Ancestry.

[371] Iwan, W, (1995). *Because of their Beliefs: Emigration from Prussia to Australia* (edited by David Schubert), Openbook Publishers.
[372] Schubert, D. (1997) *Kavel's People*, 2nd Edn. H. Schubert, Highgate.
[373] Ibid.
[374] 'German Geographic Origins' pamphlet 2003, Migration Museum, Adelaide
[375] Schubert, D. *op cit.*
[376] Johann Gottfried Schulz is listed as a Farmer at Light's Pass in the *SA Government Gazette* 1872 p1146
[377] Original source: the late Earle Wilson
[378] *South Australians 1836-1885*, Book 2 (SAGHS)
[379] https://www.churchhistories.net.au/church-catalog/rowland-flat-sa-trinity-lutheran
[380] *South Australians 1836-1885 Book 2*, with additional information from Earle E Wilson, May 1999
[381] Son Glenn Schulz was buried in Lae, PNG 1944
[382] According to Earle Wilson, went by the name Heine Seidel (Clive Schulz claimed he had a fallout with family)
[383] Cliff and Mavis Schulz, Tanunda, via Raelene Linden
[384] Source: Supreme Court documents, see below
[385] Stratton
[386] Stratton
[387] E.E. Wilson. Also accessed at: Probate and Administration Books: South Australia. Probate Records 1903, FamilySearch
[388] *The Advertiser*, 18 October 1932
[389] Supplement to the Australian Lutheran, 9th December 1932, page 100, Ancestry
[390] Mr R. Guerin, Head Teacher at the Tanunda School
[391] What's in a name? https://names.gukutils.org.uk/Rumbelow.shtml
[392] Rumbelow and Descendants Family Website: https://www.rumbelow.net/name
[393] Baptisms, 1812, Mildenhall, Suffolk, Ancestry
[394] The Rumbelow Family History complied by Margaret Miller (nee Croxton)
[395] Sir Charles Forbes, Diane Cummings 2010-2017 https://bound-for-south-australia.collections.slsa.sa.gov.au/1839SirCharlesForbes-Memories.htm
[396] Ibid
[397] Story told to Margaret Miller by 'Mrs Honeyman.'
[398] Mrs Mahalia Philps, SA History Hub https://sahistoryhub.history.sa.gov.au/people/mrs-mahalia-philps/
[399] Ibid
[400] Preface to Rumbelow History, by Margaret Miller
[401] Libraries Tasmania, Name Indexes: 1066441
[402] or Mary Ann Geary or Ann Geary on her marriage in Victoria in 1842. Registration of Marriage number 606. There is a Mary Anne Geary who was a convict in Tasmania, who came over on the Sea Queen, but she married a John Davis in 1847, so this appears to be a different person (Libraries Tasmania).
[403] Libraries Tasmania
[404] Registration number 544, Australian Birth Index 1788-1922
[405] Registration number 14208, Australian Birth Index 1788-1922
[406] Port Phillip Gazette, 29 September 1841, pg. 3
[407] Austral-Asiatic Review, *Tasmanian and Australian Advertiser*, Hobart Town, 1837-1844, Launceston Examiner, Advertising, 1842-1843
[408] *Port Phillip Gazette*, 29th September 1841
[409] Arrival 23rd March 1845, https://passengers.history.sa.gov.au/node/575631

[410] *Colonial Times*, 4th December 1849
[411] Tasmania, Passenger and Crew Lists, 1834-1837, 1841-1887, Ancestry
[412] Rumbelow and Descendants website, https://www.rumbelow.net/tragedyandvalor/edward1845
[413] Passengers in History https://passengers.history.sa.gov.au/node/575633
[414] A brig of 130 tons, reported throughout 1860s newspapers in Trove
[415] 'New Zealand,' *The South Australian Advertiser*, 10 July 1865
[416] 'Shipping News,' *The South Australian Advertiser*, 5 July 1867
[417] On 9th April 1850 the boat of a Captain Bolger was cleared out for the 'south seas.' This may be Captain E Bolger - in September 1851 Captain Bolger arrives in Sydney with Mrs Bolger and two sons, from the South Seas Fisheries and Bay of Islands.
[418] New South Wales, Australia, Unassisted Immigrant Passenger Lists, 1826-1922, Ancestry, for Robert Bolger, Series 1291: Reports of vessels arrived (or Shipping reports) Reel 1277: 1850 Jan 01-1850 Dec 29
[419] per North Esk 13 Oct 1850, Biographical Index of Australians
[420] 'Law Report,' *The Argus*, 2 December 1857
[421] https://www.legislation.sa.gov.au/home/historical-numbered-as-made-acts/1871/0004-Deceased-Wifes-Sisters-Marriage-Act-No-4-of-33-and-34-Vic.-1870-1.pdf
[422] The Rumbelows of Encounter Bay, 2005, op cit
[423] where my sister Lyn Parsons lives
[424] *Victor Harbor Times*, 27 July 1977
[425] Old Colonists of South Australia https://oldcolonists.weebly.com/-1840-fairlie.html
[426] Obituary of son William Glassenbury, who settled in Wangaratta.
[427] Ann McDonald married George William Bignell. She was also known as Mary Ann.
[428] 'The Wonder of the World', *The Advertiser*, 7th July 1909
[429] Ibid
[430] Ibid
[431] Simpson (Sim) Newland 1835-1925 https://adb.anu.edu.au/biography/newland-simpson-sim-7828
[432] Ibid.
[433] *The Advertiser*, The Wonder of the World, 7 July 1909
[434] *The Observer*, 19 Jan 1918, Well known Aboriginal Identity. The Register, 10 Jan 1918 and The Observer, 12 Jan 1918. 'Memories of Pantonie', The Register, 21 Jan 1918.
[435] *The Register*, 21 Jan 1918
[436] The Redlegs Museum www.redlegsmuseum.com.au accessed 28th August 2025
[437] 'Arrived in State 100 Years Ago' *Victor Harbour Times*, 10 Dec 1954.
[438] 'The Rumbelows of Encounter Bay' *Victor Harbour Times*, 27 July 1977
[439] *The Mail*, 10 August 1940
[440] *The Observer*, 24th April 1920
[441] Ibid
[442] Photo restoration Claude Gervais
[443] *The Mail*, 4th December 1926, Heroine of 'Paving the Way' Hale and Hearty
[444] Notes from Margaret Miller
[445] Rumbelow and Descendants website: https://www.rumbelow.net/encounterbay/pavingtheway

[446] Newland, S. *Paving the Way: A Romance of the Australian Bush*, Centenary Edition, Adelaide: F. W. Preece & Sons, 1936
[447] Rumbelow and Descendants website, Ibid
[448] Australian Dictionary of Biography, Simpson (Sim) Newland (1835-1925), by. G. K. Jenkin. https://adb.anu.edu.au/biography/newland-simpson-sim-7828
[449] Boisvert, Eugene (2023). Indigenous project to 'tell the whole story' of 1840 Maria shipwreck killings near Kingston SE, ABC https://www.abc.net.au/news/2023-11-27/indigenous-telling-whole-story-project-maria-shipwreck/102726758
[450] Ibid.
[451] Ibid.
[452] Australian Dictionary of Biography, Simpson (Sim) Newland (1835-1925), ibid
[453] News, 3 April 1954
[454] Referring to the folklore surrounding Richard Whittington, who rose from a poverty-stricken childhood to become a wealthy merchant and later Lord Mayor of London.
[455] As above
[456] Estcourt House, SA History Hub https://sahistoryhub.history.sa.gov.au/places/estcourt-house/
[457] *The Advertiser*, 16 October 1954
[458] Rumbelow, P, et al. (2005). *The Rumbelows of Encounter Bay*: 150 yeas of the Family in Australia, Page 126
[459] *The Advertiser* 15 September 1954
[460] *The Advertiser*, 24 Sept 1954
[461] *The Advertiser*, 28 October 1954
[462] https://sahistoryhub.history.sa.gov.au/people/mrs-mahalia-philps/
[463] Recorder, 20 May 1942
[464] *The Advertiser*, 20 June 1945
[465] *The Advertiser*, 27 October 1954
[466] *The Advertiser*, 15 October 1954
[467] *The Advertiser*, 6 October 1954
[468] *The Advertiser*, 14 September 1954
[469] *The Advertiser*, 5 November 1954
[470] *The Advertiser*, 13 November 1954
[471] *The Advertiser*, 28 September 1954 - reported that Miss Sally Butler's job was 'legislative research director of the General Federation of Women's Clubs in America.'
[472] *The Advertiser*, 5 October 1954.
[473] *Daily Mirror* (Sydney), 30 Sep 1954, Page 33, AGE NO HANDICAP TO U.S. BUSINESS WOMAN
[474] *The Advertiser*, 24 August 1954
[475] https://en.wikipedia.org/wiki/Grace_Benny
[476] Rumbelow, P et al (2005) *The Rumbelows of Encounter Bay.150 years of the family in Australia.*
[477] Genealogy SA online database, Births
[478] Likely at the Mareeba babies home for sick babies.
[479] To Be Married, *The News*, 12th June 1947
[480] It is noted that the Kate Cocks babies home was at Parkside
[481] Rumbelow, P. et al., op cit
[482] https://www.rumbelow.net/lakeside

[483] Di Booker, Making Connections through Oral History, *Word of Mouth*, August 2018.
[484] A seventh child died in childhood - Leandra Ford, email communication, 2020
[485] Diary of Elizabeth Archer, The John, held in the Mitchell Library
[486] The Illustrated London News, 19th May, 1855
[487] Supplement to the 'Royal Cornwall Gazette' Newspaper, Truro, Friday May 11th, 1855 'Wreck of an Emigrant Ship on the Manacles'
[488] SAGHS Online Database - Baptisms
[489] Ibid
[490] 'Local Intelligence,' *Adelaide Observer*, 15 December 1849
[491] 'Government Land Sale,' *South Australian*, 14th October 1850, and 'Land Sales and Contracts', *South Australian gazette and Mining Journal*, 12th October 1850
[492] 'Sale of Crown Lands. Last Thursday's Land Sale', *Adelaide Observer*, 25th February 1854
[493] 'Church News: Athelstone Gorge,' *Australian Christian Commonwealth*, 29 Jan 1915
[494] Ibid
[495] Obituary, *The Advertiser and The Register*, 10 Aug 1927
[496] 'Criminal Sittings of the Supreme Court,' *The South Australian Advertiser*, 8 February 1861
[497] At this time their surname in the newspapers seemed to change from 'Lomman' to 'Loman'. In the UK, the surname had also been 'Lowman.'
[498] Leandra Ford, email communication 18 June 2020
[499] SAGHS Death Registrations, Book 9/Page 336
[500] 'Government Advertisements: Real Property Act Notices,' *South Australian Register*, 18th December 1862
[501] Pike, D. Introduction of the real property act in South Australia. *Adelaide Law Review*, 1961. https://www5.austlii.edu.au/au/journals/AdelLawRw/1961/4.pdf
[502] 'Government Advertisements,' *The South Australian Advertiser*, 23rd January 1865
[503] Around this time, there were only 3 diagnoses, mania, dementia and melancholia: https://www.ncbi.nlm.nih.gov/pmc/articles/PMC539549 /
[504] As advised by David Buob, Glenside Historical Society: It was probably a psychotic condition, not amenable to drugs at the time & likely compounded by institutionalisation. At the time of his admission to Parkside, the Adelaide Asylum was the acute facility for those expected to improve within 6-12 months and Parkside was the asylum for chronic cases with less optimism with regard to recovery, so it is not surprising that he was hospitalised for the rest of his life after 1866. It is unusual that he was sent back to the Adelaide after his stroke as most would have died at Parkside, perhaps they wanted him close to the RAH for medical treatment or review.
[505] South Australia, Australia, Prison Registers, 1838-1912, Ancestry
[506] Ancestry, Destitute Asylum Ledgers and Admissions to Industrial and Reformatory Schools 1849-1913, Register of Admissions to the Destitute Asylum, 1881
[507] Information from Di Booker, emailed 27 June 2019, based on research on the 1882 application (Lunacy petition 48A/1882) for Martha and Thomas Henry to take over Henry's affairs
[508] *The Advertiser*, 26th August 1897
[509] South Australia, Australia, Supreme Court Criminal Records, 1837-1918; Reports to the Police Coroner, 1842-1961 for Joseph Lomman, Ancestry

[510] Spelt Loman on the petition
[511] Also referred to as Mary Ann and Ann
[512] As reported in *The Express and Telegraph* daily newspapers.
[513] https://adb.anu.edu.au/biography/heading-sir-james-alfred-jim-10467
[514] 70 Gore Street, Sir James Heading Memorial Park, Murgon
[515] The Maid of the Mill, *Press*, Volume XII Issue 1529, 2 October 1867
[516] *Press*, 23 October 1867; New Zealand Herald, 23 November 1875. In Auckland, George William Heslop (possibly another relative) was also having difficulties in his mechanical engineering business and filed for bankruptcy in 1875 in the Supreme Court of New Zealand. However, in 1885 he applied for a patent for an invention which gave alarm in the case of rising or falling temperature, to be known as a 'thermo-electric heat or cold attachment.' A George Heslop was in the New Zealand Force and received the New Zealand Medal, but it is uncertain if this is George William or his son George William Heslop.
[517] https://canterburyphotography.blogspot.com/2008/08/blog-post_29.html?fbclid=IwAR0WprGIpfuQAxY8BUJykLHf5NRYKyHyBpHtBWzekrnRSd09hnahZjmk7Zg
[518] Information from Donald Porter, Ancestry
[519] According to his marriages in 1864 and 1866 Charles Miller was born in 1838. It is difficult to trace the birth of Charles Miller in Scotland or England as there are so many. There is a Charles Miller who was born in 1836 in Dundee, Scotland, who obtained his Master Mariner certificate.
[520] Personal communication, Len Miller.
[521] When Amelia Emma Magdalene grew up, she married someone by the name of King, 20 years her senior, which may have been her cousin.
[522] 21st August is the same birthdate as his great granddaughter
[523] According to the NZ electoral rolls, listed on Ancestry.
[524] His wife gave birth to a daughter at St Albans, on 10 April 1874.
[525] New Zealand, City & Area Directories, 1866-1954, 1876, Ancestry.
[526] Bishop, C. (2019). *Women mean business. Colonial businesswomen in New Zealand.* Otago University Press, New Zealand.
[527] *Evening Post*, Napier, Volume XIII, Issue 147, 23 June 1876, pg. 2.
[528] Personal communication, Harriet Taylor, descendent of Harriet's older brother Thomas George Abbott, October 2022. Also included in am email from Harriet Taylor to Margaret Miller on the 5th May 2010
[529] Harriet Taylor claims that Albert was studying botany.
[530] Can not find a record for her birth, however her death certificate indicates she was born 1885
[531] *Lyttleton Times*, 16 April 1888
[532] *Lyttleton Times*, 6 September 1888
[533] The Project Gutenberg eBook of Crimes of Preachers in the United States and Canada.
[534] Marching to Zion, Christian History Institute https://christianhistoryinstitute.org/magazine/article/marching-to-zion-ch-142
[535] https://my.christchurchcitylibraries.com/addington-cemetery/
[536] *Lyttelton Times*, Volume LXX, Issue 8651, 28 November 1888, Page 3
[537] Harriet Taylor, New Zealand
[538] He commenced 1890, according to communication from Harriet Taylor
[539] *The Weekly Times*, 21 March 1891
[540] *The Argus* 28 December 1893
[541] Ibid

[542] *The Truth*, 18 March 1916
[543] *The Daily Telegraph*, 8 April 1938
[544] *The Daily Telegraph*, 22 May 1923
[545] *The Daily Telegraph*, 16 October 1928
[546] Ibid
[547] Born between 12th August 1840 and end September 1840. According to the 1851 census she was 10 years old in 1851, according to the shipping record departing 11th August 1859 she was 19 years old. There is a record of a baptism for Jul-Aug-Sept 1840 for Elizabeth Heslop of Sunderland.
[548] Personal communication, Harriet Taylor, descendent of Harriet's older brother Thomas George Abbott, October 2022
[549] Extract from letter from Robert Norman Hughes to Margaret Miller.
[550] *Evening Star*, 22 April 1892 'The Though Trains – Passenger This Day.
[551] Passengers per Southern Express, *Press*, volume L, issue 8523, 30 June 1893, *Lyttelton Times* 30th June 1893, *Evening Star*, 29th June 1893, *Evening Star*
[552] *Evening Star*, 12th January 1895, *Otago Daily Times*, 14th January 1895
[553] *North Otago Times*, 20th November 1895
[554] Lincoln shipping list:
https://www.yesteryears.co.nz/shipping/passlists/lincoln.html
[555] A Spanish name featured in an opera, a Portuguese love song, also the name of a famous yacht that sailed to Iceland in 1858.
[556] Canterbury Passenger Lists 15 Feb 1867-19 June 1867. FamilySearch.
[557] *South Canterbury Times*, Issue 3185, 18 June 1883, Page 2
[558] *South Canterbury Times*, Issue 3339, 14 December 1883, Page 3
[559] Photos of Joan Williams
[560] His son was just 15 at the time, and Edith was 20 years old
[561] Notably, a William Heslop also worked as a Blacksmith in Prebbleton (born around 1840). This is according to the death certificate of this son George Heslop (1864- died 1922)
[562] *Lyttelton Times*, Volume XXII, Issue 1258, 2 July 1864, Page 1
[563] *Press*, Volume XVI, Issue 2167, 29 March 1870, Page 1
[564] *Press*, Volume XXII, Issue 2916, December 1874, Papers Past
[565] *Press*, Volume XXVIII, Issue 3854, 28 November 1877, Press, Volume XXVIII, Issue 3859, 4 December 1877, Page 3, Papers Past
[566] *Press*, Volume XIX, Issue 2853, 24 June 1872, Page 1
[567] Obituary, *Press*, Volume LXVI, issue 13727, 7 May 1910, p. 9
[568] *Lyttelton Times*, Volume LXXVIII, Issue 9806, 17 August 1892, Page 3
[569] *Lyttelton Times*, Volume LVII, Issue 6645, 15th June 1882, page 6
[570] *Lyttelton Times*, Volume XXIX, Issue 2288, 23 April 1868, Page 4
[571] *Star* (Christchurch), 17 September 1881
[572] *Lyttelton Times*, Volume CXXI, Issue 15296, 4 May 1910, Page 1
[573] 23rd Company, 8th Battalion https://www.angloboerwar.com/name-search
[574] Robert Stewart Brown, 1911, *The History of the Manor of Allerton in the Country of Lancaster.'*
[575] Hannah West, profile of Grace Roscoe, Wikitree, and Ancestry source 'Grace ran off with the Coachman,' and 'Runaway Marriage Romance', Million and a Half in Court,' *Glasgow Weekly Mail*, 1889.
[576] My 5th great-grandfather.
[577] Extract from original newspaper article located on Ancestry, accessed 27 October 2025.

[578] *Liverpool Echo,* 23 Dec 2013, https://www.liverpoolecho.co.uk/news/liverpool-news/forgotten-wirral-lifeboat-rescue-hero-6440532
[579] Statue unveiled to commemorate 1810 Hoylake lifeboat tragedy, *Wirral Globe* (Craig Manning), 22nd December 2010.
[580] Hoylake lifeboat disaster remembered through descendant's musical drama, Lifeboats news release 8 April 2019.
[581] *Daily Herald*, 9th February 1916, page 3
[582] *The Chronicle*, 5th February 1916, page 45, Subscriptions in aid of Minda, The home for weak-minded children
[583] *The Advertiser*, 7 Nov 1919, Page 8, ENGINEDRIVERS.
[584] Personal communication Carolyn Wesley, December 2025
[585] *SA Police Gazette*, 3rd April 1929
[586] *SA Police Gazette*, pg. 149, 287.
[587] Information from an Historical Name Index Search, Land Titles Office
[588] He had worked on the Rhynie Poisoning Case which is a subject of one of my books
[589] *The Advertiser*, 3 May 1922
[590] Restoration courtesy Stephen McCauley, Free Photo Restoration, Repair & Photoshop, Facebook group
[591] *The News*, 8 Dec 1945, Display at Port Girls' Technical School, p. 6
[592] Frederick Robe, Lieutenant-Governor. Passed by the Legislative Council 12 March 1847
[593] spelt Batams
[594] with a Sarah Bumpas, 25yrs and Susannah Houslow, 15yrs
[595] She was christened 3 August 1823
[596] who had been married to William Battams
[597] Also listed as Simmons
[598] In 1851 next door to the Battams family is the Rolls family, where one Mary Battams is the sister and house servant. The Rolls family are grocers. Next to the Rolls family are the Simonds, who are Agricultural Labourers.
[599] Charles Battams born 2nd July 1857 in Payneham death date not recorded
Caleb Battams born 28th March 1859 in Payneham and died 14th May 1859 in Payneham
Josiah Battams born 12th June 1860 in Payneham
Caroline Battams born 25th July 1861 in Payneham and died 24th August 1861
May Ann Scott Battams born 15th August 1863 in Marden South Aust.
Jacob Battams born 16th December 1865 in Payneham and died 4th January 1866 in Payneham
Grace Battams born 6th January 1867 in Payneham death date not recorded
Alfred Battams born 9th May 1868 in Payneham
Nicholas James Battams born 10th November 1869, died 4th December 1938 (married Helen McArthur, 9th October 1902, Kalgoorlie)
Ernest Battams born 6th January 1871 in Marden South Australia and died 22nd January 1871
Albert Battams born 26th May 1873 in Marden, died 1933 in Queensland
[600] Married Ann Blight Potter (1834-1877)
[601] Newsbeta website
[602] *Adelaide Observer*, 5 June 1847
[603] *Adelaide Observer*, 31st May 1851

[604]There is a database of those who deposited gold at the SA gold assay officer, and consignors and consignees associated with the first three mounted police escorts. Maureen M Leadbeater, Family History South Australia website.
[605] A pennyweight, equivalent to 24 grains or 1.55 grams. https://www.lbma.org.uk accessed 31st October 2025
[606] State Records of SA (GRG 45/43 and 5/30) record
[607] SAGHS Marriage Registrations, 5/189
[608] *South Australian Weekly Chronicle*, 17th November 1860
[609] *SA Advertiser*, 1859.
[610] *South Australian Register*, 22nd July 1857
[611] *SA Register*, 10th October 1859
[612] *SA Advertiser*, January 1861
[613] Daniel Battams had another son he named Daniel Potter (NAA WW1 records – Daniel Potter's son served in WW1)
[614] *South Australian Weekly Chronicle*, 13th September 1862
[615] Daniel Potter Battams (1862-1947) married Annie Florence McKinnon. In 1885, he was the first caretaker of the Naracoorte Caves.
[616] Lost Pubs of Adelaide, Adelaide Economic Development Agency 2025.
[617] *South Australian Register* 19th April 1862
[618] *South Australian Government Gazette*, 14th January 1864
[619] From Reg Butler's unpublished computer working files, 2014.
[620] *South Australian Register*, 14th October, 1876
[621] *South Australian Register*, 9th April 1862
[622] *Adelaide Observer*, 1855
[623] *South Australian Register*, 3rd August 1855
[624] *South Australian Weekly Chronicle*, 26th May 1860
[625] *South Australian Chronicle and Weekly Mail*, 19th September 1874
[626] *The Express and Telegraph*, 11th November 1874
[627] *The South Australian Advertiser*, 8th March 1871
[628] *Commonwealth of Australia Gazette*, 14th March 1986
[629] *The SA Advertiser*, 21 June 1866
[630] *The Express and Telegraph*, 2 November 1867, Visit of H.R.H. The Duke of Edinburgh
[631] *Evening Journal*, 12th June 1869
[632] Ibid
[633] Ibid
[634] *The SA Advertiser,* The Telegraph Demonstration, 16 November 1872
[635] Elisha (1835-1870) had married Susannah Guley in Mt Gambier
[636] *The Wallaroo Times and Mining Journal*, 30th December 1876
[637] *The Wallaroo Times and Mining Journal*, Visit to Barunga Gap, 29th April 1876
[638] *The Wallaroo Times and Mining Journal*, 30th December 1874
[639] *The Wallaroo Times and Mining Journal*, Inquest at Kadina, 1 May 1875
[640] *The Wallaroo Times and Mining Journal*, 14th October 1876
[641] Photo by Roderick Eime, used with permission. Located at: https://www.gdaypubs.com.au/SA/kadina/51493/royal-exchange-hotel.html
[642] *The Express and Telegraph*, 20th September 1876
[643] *The Wallaroo Times and Mining Journal*, 20th June 1877
[644] *The Wallaroo Times and Mining Journal*, 28th November 1877
[645] *The Wallaroo Times and Mining Journal*, 20th February 1878
[646] Ibid, 6th March 1878
[647] Formerly Clark Street, Norwood

[648] *The South Australian Advertiser*, 30th December 1879
[649] *The Express and Telegraph*, 13th April 1874
[650] *The South Australian Advertiser*, 30th December 1879
[651] *The Times and Northern Advertiser* (Peterborough), Death of Mr F. W. Stephen, 3rd Feb 1939
[652] Ancestry
[653] WikiTree: William Ravenscroft Stephen (1826-1899) and Sir George Stephen QC (1794-1879) and James Stephen (1758-1832)
[654] *The Pastoral Times*, 27th July 1878
[655] *Yorke's Peninsula Advertiser*, 9 April 1880
[656] *South Australian Register*, 9th February 1881
[657] Referring to William Hart
[658] South Australian Register, 25th September 1880 and *Adelaide Observer*, 2nd October 1880
[659] Gleeson to Colonial Secretary, 22 December 1849, GRG 24/6/1849/2331
[660] Daniel Battams (misspelt Batham in the original), deposition taken before EB Gleeson, 18 December 1849, GRG 24/6/1849/2331, SRSA, EB Gleeson to Colonial Secretary, 22 December 1849, GRG 24/6/1849/2331, SRSA, all cited on SLSA The South Australian Frontier and its Legacies Interactive Map https://experience.arcgis.com/experience/4755c59ae93447a9b0acf9b2b0b265f6/page/Interactive-Map
[661] Commissioner of Police to Colonial Secretary, 22 December 1849, GRG 24/6/1848/2317
[662] *The South Australian Advertiser*, 25th May 1881, The Queen's Birthday, page 5
[663] *The Express and Telegraph*, 9th June 1881
[664] *The Express and Telegraph*, 16th June 1881
[665] *Bendigo Advertiser*, 22 July 1881
[666] *The Age*, 22nd July 1881
[667] *The Sydney Daily Telegraph*, 23rd July 1881
[668] The Neale family were one of the early pioneers of South Australia who arrived in 1836: *SA Register*, The Pioneers of South Australia, 6 November 1877
[669] National Archives of Australia, WWI record, Joseph Wesley Battams
[670] *The Advertiser*, 20th March 1913
[671] *Truth*, 13th February 1915
[672] Also spelt Bhagot (in marriage index), Bazhat and Bhagwan (The Express and Telegraph, 15th October 1907)
[673] Australian Marriage Index, Ancestry (page 1037, vol 229)
[674] https://sahistoryhub.history.sa.gov.au/subjects/indians-in-south-australia/
[675] UK, Registers of Employees of the East India Company and the India Office, 1746-1939 for Khem Singh, Ancestry
[676] Indian Army Quarterly List for 1 January 1912, Ancestry
[677] *The Advertiser*, 6th August 1903
[678] *The Express and Telegraph*, 15th October 1907
[679] Ibid
[680] *The Advertiser*, 22nd January 1915
[681] *The News*, 9th June 1949, Bullet in SA Woman's Lung 34 years
[682] *Truth*, 13th February 1915
[683] *The Journal*, 12th April 1915, Natto Khan Case.
[684] *The Advertiser*, 10th June 1949
[685] Genealogy SA, South Australian District Marriage Certificate Transcript
[686] *Daily Advertiser*, 12th April 1929

[687] *Evening News*, 9th April 1929
[688] *The Advocate*, 10th June 1949. Bullet in Lung since 1915
[689] Wachtel, J.A. (1982) *Moorook, Bend in the River*, Investigator Press, Adelaide.
[690] Sometimes the team was combined as the Moorook-Kingston Football club. In 1926 and 1932 it was a combined team.
[691] Wachtel, J.A. (1982) *op cit.*
[692] Sometimes spelt 'Mae'
[693] Rodda, M. *Miss Mary Jane (Mae) Battams 18 July 1897 – 5 June 1974. A Little Women with a Big Heart-And Gave So Much.*
[694] *Daily Herald*, 12th Dec 1910
[695] *The Express and Telegraph*, 11th December, 1911, Blind Deaf and Dumb.
[696] *The Advertiser*, 10th March 1894
[697] South Australian Heritage Council application, 2021, 92 Brougham Place, North Adelaide
[698] *The Mail*, 28th September 1914, Red Cross Society
[699] *The Express and Telegraph*, 14th September 1915
[700] *The Express and Telegraph*, 2nd July 1917
[701] Rodda, M. *Miss Mary Jane (Mae) Battams 18 July 1897 – 5 June 1974. A Little Women with a Big Heart-And Gave So Much.*
[702] *The Register*, 5th September 1918
[703] *Australian Christian Commonwealth*, 9th July 1926, Walkerville Methodist Church
[704] See Bishop, C. (2021). '*Too Much Cabbage and Jesus Christ*,' Wakefield Press
[705] *The United Aborigines Messenger*, Vol 4, no 10, 1 July 1933
[706] Rob Nankivell, Old Adelaide & South Australia Album, FB group
[707] *The Mail*, 6th August 1932
[708] Bishop (2021), op cit, p. 210
[709] *The News*, 13th June, 1949
[710] Marilyn Ann Rodda, care of Croydon, Dudley, Devon & Renown Parks (South Australia) Local History (Facebook Group)
[711] Marilyn Ann Rodda, care of Croydon, Dudley, Devon & Renown Parks (South Australia) Local History (Facebook Group)
[712] Bishop, C. (2021), op cit, Figure 35
[713] *The Sydney Morning Herald*, Blind Hold Exhibition of Crafts, 30th April 1953
[714] *The News*, 13th June 1949, op cit.
[715] https://www.lostkatanning.com/hettner-family/
[716] *Moorook, Bend in the River*, Joan Watchell, 1982, p. 107
[717] *Loveday Internment Camps*, Loveday, South Australia, 1941-46, pamphlet
[718] Ibid.
[719] Keenan, L (2024). *The Space Between*, Penguin Books Australia
[720] O'Sullivan and Graydon, *The Ancestral Continuum* (2013).
[721] There were also some by the name of Schulz who suffered a mental illness around the time of WW2.

References

The White Family

Books and other documents

Adam Smith, Patsy, (2002) *The Anzacs,* Penguin Books

Australian War Memorial Research Centre (photocopies of Twist and Melville diaries from World War 1, see endnotes below)

Battams, Val, oral communication

Butler, R & Phillips, A (1991) *Register Personal Notices* Volume 3 1866-1870, Gould Books, Ridgehaven

Cockburn, Rodney (1925) *Pastoral Pioneers of South Australia* (State Library of South Australia, Mortlock collection, accessed 28th May 2005) (section on Abraham Scott, Henry Scott, William L Beare, Edward Stirling).

Dennis, C. J (1918) *Digger Smith*, Trench Series, Angus & Robertson Ltd, A Square Deal

Department of Family and Community Services, Adoption and Family Information Service, letter dated 30th January 1998, via mail (information obtained on the adoption of Stephen Raymond White) Ref: APP:R5808/2881

Dyer, J (1965) *The Story of the 18th Battery 6th Brigade, Field Artillery, 1st AIF, 1915-1919*, unpublished document, page 2, private collection, S Battams

East Sussex, England, Church of England Births and Baptisms, 1813-1920, East Sussex, England, Church of England Deaths and Burials, 1813-1995

Eyre, E.J (1997) *Journals of Expeditions of Discovery into Central Australia and Overland from Adelaide to King George's Sound in the Years 1840-41*, Vol 1, published 1997 by the Friends of the State Library of South Australia.

Honor Roll 18th Battery 6th Field Artillery Brigade, WW1, private collection, S Battams

Lonely Planet, (2005) France, 6th edition, Lonely Planet books

National Archives of Australia World War 1 record Stephen William White, 1850441, digital copy accessed http://www.naa.gov.au/the_collection/defence/conflicts/ww1/ww1.html

National Archives of Australia World War II Service Record, William Surman, Series B884, S33321, Item ID 6330276, and B883, SX11977 (note 2 records online) View digital copy

SAGHS, copies of *The Advertiser*

SAGHS, *Sands and MacDougall Directories*

SAGHS South Australians 1836-1885 Book Two (information on White family accessed May 2005).

SAGHS (1997) South Australian Births - Index of Registrations 1842-1906, (listing of Harold Edward Fahy, Margaret Holman & siblings, Stephen William White, Linda Cox)

SAGHS Royal Adelaide Hospital records (information on White, accessed April 2005)

SAGHS SA Births Registrations 1842-1906, vol 11 w-z

- Dist Ade, b 27, p 52, 1863
- Dist Ade, sym S b 31 p 463, 1864
- District Pt A 648/158, 1899
- Dist Pt A 689/177, 1902
- Dist Pt A 751/142, 1905
- Dist Pt A 276/35, 1882
- Dist Pt A 314/367, 1883
- Dist Pt A 369/473, 1886
- Victoria Registration No 32089, 1890
- Victoria Registration No 9242, 1892
- Victoria Registration No 14459

SAGHS Death registrations

- Dist Ade sym H b 227, p 374, ,1895
- Dist Ade b 29, p 123, Certificate no 730 of 1868, signed by Phillip Le Cornu on the 2nd Nov 1868
- Dist Adel, sym S b 29, p 261. Certificate 1859 of 1870

SAGHS SA Marriages Index of Registrations 1842-1916, Vol 5 (information on marriages of Stephen Jnr White and David Edward White, accessed May 2005)

SAGHS SA Marriages Index of Registrations 1917-1937 (marriage of Margaret Holman and Stephen William White)

SAGHS Marriage registrations

- Dist Ade, b 47, p 229, 1861
- Dist Ade b 128, p 10, 1881

SAGHS Biographical Index of South Australians 1836-1885, Vol 11

SAGHS South Australians 1836-1885 Book Two (information on White family accessed May 2005)

SAGHS Shipping Index - White Family (Marion 49/4) accessed 22nd May 2005)

SA Government Gazette April 1864

SA Government Gazette, 3 May 1866

SA Government Gazette, 11 June 1868

Scarfe, W. (2014). *Hunger Town*, Wakefield Press

State Library of South Australia – Australiana database (photographs-see below), copies of government gazettes, newspapers on microfiche

Stratton: *Coronial Inquests,* State Library of South Australia

Stratton: *Burial Orders*, State Library of South Australia

Tusmore, J. Dyer, (1965), *The Story of the 18th Battery 6th Brigade Field Artillery*, 1st AIF, 1915-1919

Twining, A & S, *SA Military Volunteers for 1855* (State Library of South Australia)

West Terrace Cemetery, Historical Data Maintenance 2nd Feb 1998

Newspapers

Adelaide Observer, 7 May 1864

Adelaide Observer, 24 April 1869

South Australian Chronicle and Weekly Mail, 1 May 1869

South Australian Chronicle and Weekly Mail, 24 April 1869

Native Troubles in the Far North, *South Australian Register*, 11 Aug 1865

Parallana, North East of Mount Serle, *Adelaide Observer*, 29 April 1865, page 3

A Noted Blackfellow. Big Bobbie and the Whites, *The Register*, 4 June 1924

South Australian Register, 11 Aug 1865

The Express and Telegraph, 2 October 1868

Adelaide Observer, 7 May 1864

Evening Journal, 7 November 1904

The Register, 8 Nov 1904

News, 23 July 1945

Parallana, North East of Mount Serle, *Adelaide Observer*, 29 April 1865, page 3

West Coast Sentinel, 6 Dec, 1924. Trove

West Coast Sentinel, July 1939. Trove

Web resources

Ancestry

- Ancestry.com. Australia, Death Index, 1787-1985 [database on-line]. Lehi, UT, USA: Ancestry.com Operations, Inc., 2010.
- UK Census 1841, Ancestry.com
- Government Gazette 1858
- Australia Death Index, Ancestry (Vol 293, pg 371)
- Australia, Birth Index 1788-1922, Ancestry.com, Ancestry.com Operations, Inc, 2010, Provo, UT USA

Australian Newspapers beta: http://ndpbeta.nla.gov.au/ndp/del/home

Australian War Memorial Research Centre

- Private record 3DRL/7566A, Diary of Private C.P Melville, 18th Battery, 6th Brigade, Field Artillery, 2nd Australian Division (154 pages).
- Private Record PR00314. Diary of Colin C Twist, 18th Battery, 6th Brigade, Field Artillery, 2nd Australian Division, (57 pages).

Family Search Ancestral File v4.19, www.familysearch.org, accessed January 2005 (IGI accessed numerous times)

Family History Online: (UK resources, BDMs) http://www.familyhistoryonline.net/

Free BMD site: http://freebmd.rootsweb.comcgi/districts (UK births, deaths and marriages)

Genes Reunited: www.genesreunited.com.au (family histories-UK and Australia)

Gen Forum: http:://genforum.genealogy.com (Heather Hobbs)

Genes Reunited

International Genealogical Index (IGI) – Family Search

Victoria State Recruiting Committee Poster, Hoover Institute Library and Archives, Standford University https://digitalcollections.hoover.org/objects/9797/whose-son-are-you--enlist-today-i-didnt-raise-my-son-to

Family Histories and Information

- Barnes, Diane (Information obtained on the White family through Genes Reunited website)
- Carpenter, M, 2005, NSW (Information obtained through Genes Reunited website and follow-up email communication on the 2nd and 4th generation White family, first accessed 29th April 2005)
- Smart, Valerie (Information obtained on the White family in England, initially through Genes Reunited website and by email)

Websites

Information on Sussex:

http://www.sussexpast.co.uk

http://www.travelpublishing.co.uk

http://www.great-britain.co.uk

https://en.wikipedia.org/wiki/Rodmell

Lewes Castle:

http://www.castlexplorer.co.uk/england/lewes/lewes.php

https://www.visitsoutheastengland.com/things-to-do/lewes-castle-and-museum-p44473

www.tinstaafl.co.uk

SA memory: www.samemory.sa.gov.au

SA Police Historical Society – information about Mt Serle police station

Mount Serle, Wikipedia. https://en.wikipedia.org/wiki/Mount_Serle

Trove newspapers online, NLA

Ships Lists:

Convictions Australian Shipping: http://www.blaxland.com/ozships/

SA Family History SA Passenger Lists (incomplete):
http://www.familyhistorysa.info/shipping/passengerlists.html

The Ships List: Immigrants to South Australia:
http://www.theshipslist.com/ships/australia/SAassistedindex.htm

World War 1 Information:

AIF project, Australian Defence Force Academy
http://www.aif.adfa.edu.au:8080/index.html

Anzac Day: www.anzacday.org.au

Australian War Memorial site collections database
http://www.awm.gov.au/database/collection.asp and glossary:
http://www.awm.gov.au/glossary/result.asp?browse=1

BBC war history: http://www.bbc.co.uk/history/war/wwone/australia_05.shtml
accessed 27th March 2006

Digger History website: www.diggerhistory.info accessed 25th and 29th April 2005

First World War website: http://www.firstworldwar.com/atoz/trenchfoot.htm
accessed 18th January 2005 and http://www.firstworldwar.com/today/thiepval.htm
accessed 27th March 2006

National Archives of Australia, item 1850441, first accessed 5th May 2004 and then
full item available January 2005.
http://www.naa.gov.au/the_collection/defence/conflicts/ww1/ww1.html (several
items subsequently accessed)

The Long Long Trail: The Story of the British Army in the First World War
http://www.1914-1918.net/sacredground/ypres/ieper.htm accessed 6th November
2005

Taube information: http://www.ctie.monash.edu.au/hargrave/etrich_taube.htm

South Australiana:

Government of South Australia, Regional Profiles: Mid North,
http://www.planning.sa.gov.au/regional_profiles/publications/mid_north.pdf
accessed 1st June 2005

Mt Serle station information: http://www.yaldawi.com/album.html

SAGHS website: http://www.saghs.org.au/ (death and burial records database)

South Australian Family History: http://www.familyhistorysa.info/

South Australiana Database (Mortlock Library – pictures):
http://www.catalog.slsa.sa.gov.au:1084/search/

Spence, Catherine Helen, An Autobiography,
http://setis.library.usyd.edu.au/ozlit/pdf/p00014.pdf Accessed 1st June 2005

State Records of South Australia: Archives Search:
http://143.216.32.39/archivessrsa/t1tbmain.asp (information on Military Records)

Women & Children's Hospital Website: WCH History
http://www.wch.sa.gov.au/ceo/history/html accessed 30th Oct 2003

UK

General Register Office www.gro.gov.uk (marriage certificate – Stephen White & Hannah Luxford)

Sussex information:

http://www.answers.com/topic/kingdom-of-sussex

http://www.sussexpast.co.uk

http://www.travelpublishing.co.uk

http://www.great-britain.co.uk

http://www.sfhg.org.uk/newmap_of_parishes.html

Photos:

Wesley Church and School, Norwood, c1900, State Library of South Australia [B 17555]

Mount Serle station: http://www.yaldawi.com/album.html

Glanville Methodist Mission, Carlisle Street, Glanville, Australian Christian Commonwealth, 24 Dec 1937, Trove

52 King Street Alberton, source: www.realestate.com

'Whose son are you?' Propaganda poster, WW1, available at: www.digitalcollections.hoover.org

Australian Troops in Egypt negotiating a price for the hire of donkeys near the pyramids at Giza, c1915, State Library of South Australia [PRG 280/1/27/48]

Somme, Winter 1916, Source: AWM E0092

'Australian wounded on the Menin Road, near Birr Cross Road, on September 20th, 1917. Taken by Frank Hurley. Source: National Library of Australia

Hospital Tents, Australian war memorial P00156.047

Returned soldiers marching along King William Street, Adelaide after WW1, 1918, State Library of SA [PRG 280/1/15/506]

War memorial unveiling at Glanville by Sir Henry Galway (Governor), 1918, State Library of South Australia [PRG 280/1/15/289]

Post office and general store at Minnipa, circa 1923, State Library of South Australia [PRG 280/1/41/249]

Port Adelaide police court, circa early 1870s, now the Tourist Information Centre Source: SLSA

[B1874]

School photos, Minnipa: Jean Kammerman nee Kwaterski

The Fahy Family

Australia, Death Index, 1787-1985, Registration no 880

Adelaide Hospital Admission Registers, 1841-1952

Jennings, R. (1998). The Medical Profession and the State 1836-1975, Department of Public Health, University of Adelaide.

National Archives of Australia. Record of a Fahy and Schulz travelling on the Pilbarra, arriving 4 August 1900 at Fremantle. National Archives of Australia passenger records.

Register Personal Notices Volume 3 1866-1870, Compiled by Reg Butler & Alan Phillips (1991), Gould Books, Ridgehaven

SAGHS Adelaide Catholic Archives Index, Original Registers, Compactus F, Shelf 6 (at SAGHS, 201 Unley Rd, Unley), Baptisms, Card Indexes to Baptisms, Kapunda 1849-1881, SRCD, Baptisms – Microfiche Copies Kapunda 1849-1901. (information on the baptisms of Michael Patrick (Patrick) Fahy and his brother Edward Fahy)

SAGHS Dis. Adel (Marriage Index book 41, page 194). Certificate 1228 of 1860

SAGHS Royal Adelaide Hospital records (information on Fahy, accessed April 2005)

SAGHS Biographical Index of South Australians 1836-1885, vol 11

SAGHS – Gawler Baptisms, no 952

SAGHS Biographical Index of South Australians 1836-1885, Vol 11 (Edmund Fahy)

SAGHS Shipping Index - information on the arrival of Fahy/Fahey family (Lady Ann 57/11)

SAGHS Death Index (1866) Dis. Adelaide reference b18 p268, Death Index, vol 560, pg. 2919, dist. 1, Adelaide

Sands and McDougall Directories (no 192, pg 1010)

South Australian Births – Index of Registrations 1842-1906, b 593, pg270

White, Rev. P *History of Clare* (SAGHS library)

Newspapers

Border Watch, 5th November 1913

Border Watch, 3rd July 1915

Border Watch, 26th July 1916

Border Watch, 10th June 1919

Border Watch, 20th June 1919

Border Watch, 9th November, 1919

Border Watch, 18th November, 1919

Border Watch, 25th November, 1919

Border Watch, 5th December 1919

Border Watch, 5th July 1920

Border Watch, 5th April 1921

Border Watch, 12th April 1921

Border Watch, 19 July 1934

Kapunda Herald, 27 June 1890

Kapuna Herald, 25 December 1891

Kapunda Herald, 9 May 1893

Kapunda Herald, 28th April 1893, Football Notes

Leader (Angaston), 7th January 1937

South Australian Chronicle 2 July 1892, Kapunda Coursing Meeting

SA Government Gazette, 10 May 1888. Government Gazettes 1841-1889

South Australian Register, 13th November 1899

South Australian Archives, Lady Ann shipping list: https://www.archives.sa.gov.au/__data/assets/pdf_file/0006/831660/GRG35_48_1_57-11_Lady-Ann.pdf

SA Police Gazette, 14th Sept 1921

South Eastern Times, 16th March 1917

Southern Cross, 10th December 1909

Stratton and *The News*, 4th Sept 1933

The Advertiser, 7th February 1906

The Advertiser, 13th January 1910

The Advertiser, 8th November 1927

The Advertiser, Monday 28th Aug 1967, copied from the State Library of South Australia microfiche, accessed 14th January 2005 (Death Notice of Iris McDermott)

The Chronicle, 22nd May 1915

The Chronicle, 20th September 1919

The Irish Harp and Farmers' Herald, 16 Apr 1870

The Observer, 10th January 1925

Photos:

Moorak School Committee photo from Les Hill Photographic Collection, Mount Gambier Public Library.

Photos of Iris Fahy courtesy the late Pat Nash

Personal communication:

Marea O'Brien

Nash, Pat (Mrs) & son Anthony Nash (letters, telephone conversations and photographs) August 2005

Websites:

Clan Stirling online: http://www.cockpitcountry.com/stirling.html

FamilySearch - Probate and Administration Records: Probate Registry 1890-1891

Health Museum SA: https://www.healthmuseumsa.org.au/menu/1991-tuberculosis-control-in-south-australia/

Ireland information:

Clare Heritage and Genealogical Research Centre: www.clareroots.com (see also www.clareroots.com/emigration.htm)

Clare Library Griffith's Valuation 1855: www.clarelibrary.ieolas/coclare/genealogy/griffiths/griffithf1.htm

Views of the Famine: http://adminstaff.vassar.edu/sttaylor/FAMINE/index.html

Irish names: http://scripts.ireland.com/ancesto

Immigrant ships: https://www.immigrantships.net/v12/1800v12/ladyann18591001.html

Clare Library: http://www.clarelibrary.ie/eolas/coclare/history/emigrate.htm

Clan Stirling Online

Shipping List, Octavia

The Gramp Family

Adams, W. The German Americans: An Ethnic Experience. Willi Paul Adams, translated and adapted for an American audience by LaVern J. Rippley and Eberhard Reichmann https://library.indianapolis.iu.edu/static/collections/kade/adams/toc.html

'Angas, George Fife (1789–1879)', Australian Dictionary of Biography, National Centre of Biography, Australian National University, http://adb.anu.edu.au/biography/angas-george-fife-1707/text1855 published first in hardcopy 1966, accessed online 21 May 2020.

Australian Dictionary of Biography, Frederick Hansborough Dutton (1812-1890) by Geoffrey Dutton Biography - Frederick Hansborough Dutton - Australian Dictionary of Biography

Australische Zeitung, 19 February 1908 (accessed via Trove, NLA)

Baker, T. *A heritage of innovation. Orlando Wines 1847-1997*. Anvil Press.

Baker, T. (1987). *The Orlando Way. A Celebration of 150 Years 1837-1987*. G. Gramp and Sons 1987

Bunyip (newspaper), 29th October 1937

Crundwell, Lynette, personal communication by email, 12th February 2024

Crush, P. (2013). *A chronology of Orlando Wines with sources*. Unpublished archival information.

Dimboola Banner and Wimmera and Mallee Advertiser, 3 April 1914, 'Lutheran Conference'

Encyclopaedia Britannia. Germany 1871 to 1918. https://www.britannica.com/place/Germany/Germany-from-1871-to-1918

Find and Connect, Australian Government. https://www.findandconnect.gov.au/entity/koonibba-childrens-home/

German settlers in South Australia: miscellaneous papers 1776-1964. https://www.adelaide.edu.au/library/special/mss/german_settlers/box_f_folder_b.html

Gogler, K. and Philp, B. (2018). Pioneer Vignerons: Johann GRAMP: (1819-1903). https://www.pir.sa.gov.au/__data/assets/pdf_file/0006/347343/Pioneer_Vigneron_-_Johann_Gramp.pdf

'Gramp, Johann (1819–1903)', Australian Dictionary of Biography, National Centre of Biography, Australian National University, published first in hardcopy 1972, accessed online 17 May 2020. http://adb.anu.edu.au/biography/gramp-johann-3651

Iwan, W. (edited by David Schubert). (1995). *Because of Their Beliefs. Emigration from Prussia to South Australia*. David Schubert

Kingdom of Bavaria, https://en.wikipedia.org/wiki/Kingdom_of_Bavaria

Lutheran Sunday School Convention, 24 September 1932

Marsden, S. *Travels in time: the Barossa Valley in the 1850s, around 1900, and in the 1940s*. Available online at: https://studylib.net/doc/8612743/the-barossa-valley-in-the-1850s--around-1900

Munchenberg, R. S., Proeve, H.F.W., Ross, D.A., Hausler, A., Saegenschnitter, G. B. (1992). The Barossa: A vision realised. The nineteenth century story. Lutheran Publishing House.

Oliver, H. (2001). *The Barossa Valley – A Human Tapestry*. State-wide & Global Group.

Probate and Administration Books - Probate Registry, Supreme Court of South Australia, Volume GRS_11585_1_61_61, Family Search

South Australia Company archives. SLSA. BRG 42/36/1. http://guides.slsa.sa.gov.au/c.php?g=410270&p=2794886

SLSA South Australian Company http://www.samemory.sa.gov.au/site/page.cfm?u=1483

Schubert, D. (1997). *'Kavel's People. From Prussia to South Australia*. David Schubert. 2nd edition.

Schulze, J. (n.d.). Timeline of known facts about Johann Gramp. Unpublished timeline.

Schulz, Clive, personal communication with Raelene Linden

Scholz, K, personal communication with S. Battams, 2023

South Australian Migration Museum. (2003). 'German Geographic Origins' pamphlet.

State Records of South Australia, Land Tax Return of 1885

South Australian Register, Croner's Inquest, The Tragedy at Angaston, 30th August 1890

The Advertiser, 14th August 1926 (Advertisements)

The Australian Lutheran, 23rd June, 1965

The Chronicle, 18 May 1939, Obituary

Lola Montez, Dancer and King's Mistress, The Goethe Institut, https://www.goethe.de/ins/ie/en/kul/sup/deutsche-spuren-in-irland/25702166.html

The Leader (Angaston), 28th October 1937

The Observer, Lutheran Mission, 18 March 1911

The Sydney Gazette and New South Wales Advertiser, 31 October 1837

South Australian Chronicle and Weekly Mail, 22nd May 1880

Tolley, J. (2004). *A social and cultural investigation of women in the wine industry of South Australia.* Project Number TOL 01/01.

Tour Kangaroo Island website https://www.tourkangarooisland.com.au/experiences/old-mulberry-tree

United Status, Census, 1840, Ancestry

West Coast Sentinel, Koonibba Mission Station, 28 Aug 1914

Young, G., Harmstorf, I., Langmead, D. *Barossa Survey* (1977), SA Institute of Technology and Adelaide College of Advanced Education for the Australian Heritage Commission https://data.environment.sa.gov.au/Content/heritage-surveys/3-Barossa-Survey-Vol-3-1977.pdf

Ziblatt, D. *Structuring the State: The Formation of Italy and Germany and the Puzzle of Federalism.* Princeton University Press.

Wikitree https://www.wikitree.com/wiki/Gramp-9

Lola Montez, Wikipedia

https://en.wikipedia.org/wiki/Lola_Montez#:~:text=For%20more%20than%20a%20year%2C%20Montez%20exercised,at%20Montez's%20insistence%2C%20to%20close%20the%20university.

Baturina Homewear: https://baturina-homewear.com

Photos:

Johann Gramp and photo of the Gramp family in the vineyard, (from Baker, *The Orlando Way*), used with permission from Vinarchy

Aerial view of Gramps Orlando in 1946, Source: SLSA, BRG 397/2/84/1

The Schulz Family

Ancestry DNA Results

FamilyTree DNA Results

MyHeritage DNA Results

International Union in Global Affairs Conference III, Brussels (The Role of The European Union in Global Health)

Iwan, W, edited by Schubert, D, (1995) *Because of their Beliefs Emigration from Prussia to Australia*, edition first published 1995, published by H Schubert, Highgate, South Australia. First published in German 1931

Marsden, S. *Travels in time: the Barossa Valley in the 1850s, around 1900, and in the 1940s.* Available online at: https://studylib.net/doc/8612743/the-barossa-valley-in-the-1850s--around-1900

Migration Museum Adelaide (2003), German *'Geographic Origins'* pamphlet, accessed April 2005

Munchenberg, R. S., Proeve, H.F.W., Ross, D.A., Hausler, A., Saegenschnitter, G. B. (1992). *The Barossa: A vision realised. The nineteenth century story*. Lutheran Publishing House.

Oliver, H. (2001). *The Barossa Valley – A Human Tapestry*. State-wide & Global Group.

Probate and Administration Books: South Australia. Probate Records 1903, Family Search

SAGHS South Australians 1836-1885 Book Two (information on Schulz family, contributor W168U is EE Wilson, accessed February 1998)

Schubert, D, (1997) *Kavel's People From Prussia to South Australia*, 2nd Edn, published by H Schubert, Highgate, South Australia

South Australians 1836-1885, Book 2, Genealogy SA

Supreme Court of South Australia – Will of F. W. Schulz 1902

The Advertiser, 18th October 1932

The Leader, Angaston, 27th October 1938

Family Histories:

- Moad Family history website http://homepage.mac.com/graememoad/Family/WC_TOC.HTM and emails (Graeme Moad) (Information on the Schulz family)
- Wilson, E. E, 1999, Victor Harbor, mail correspondence dated 20th May 1999 (Information obtained on the Schulz family)
- Schulze, John – various information provided

Images:

Painting: Klemzig, SA, Angas George French, courtesy National Library of Australia 7342551-v

Nixon Drawing; Kelmzing, German Village on the Torrens, South Australia, 1845, State Library of South Australia [PRG280/1/40/72]

Will, Friedrich Wilhelm Schulz (courtesy the late Earle W. Wilson)

Photos;

All photos of the Schulz family courtesy the late Clive Schulz and Mavis, Tanuna, via Raelene Linden, September 2000 (photographs of Schulz family, story of Friedrich Wilhelm Schulz)

The Rumbelow Family

Australian Dictionary of Biography https://adb.anu.edu.au/biography/heading-sir-james-alfred-jim-10467

Deceased Wife's Sister Act 1871 1870-1 -1875

Recorder, 20 May 1942

The Advertiser, 20 June 1945

The Advertiser, 7 July 1909

The Advertiser, 24 August 1954

The Advertiser 14 September 1954

The Advertiser 15 September 1954

The Advertiser, 24 Sept 1954

The Advertiser, 28 September 1954

The Advertiser, 5 October 1954.

The Advertiser, 6 October 1954

The Advertiser, 9 October 1954

The Advertiser, 15 October 1954

The Advertiser, 16 October 1954

The Advertiser, 27 October 1954

The Advertiser, 28 October 1954

The Advertiser, 5 November 1954

The Advertiser, 13 November 1954

The Chronicle, 23rd April, 1921

The Observer, 15 June 1907

The Observer, 24th April 1920

The Register, 21 Jan 1918

The Victor Harbor Times and Encounter Bay and Lower Murray Pilot, 23rd April 1920

Victor Harbour Times, 27 July 1977

Steven Page, HerStory Project, 'Mrs Mahalia Philps', SA History Hub, History Trust of South Australia, https://sahistoryhub.history.sa.gov.au/people/mrs-mahalia-philps accessed 19 August 2023.

SA Genealogy and Heraldry Society – online databases (births, deaths and marriages)

What's in a name? https://names.gukutils.org.uk/Rumbelow.shtml

Family Histories:

- Rumbelow, P, with Lesley Avery, Mary George & Matthew Rumbelow (2005) '*The Rumbelows of Encounter Bay 150 years of the family in Australia*'. Launched April 2005 at a family reunion attended by S.Battams

Photos:

Photos from M. Miller, Rumbelow and Descendants https://www.rumbelow.net/ and personal photos (S.Battams)

The Lomman Family

Ancestry.com.au

A short history of the Register newspaper 1836-1931, SA Memory, SLSA https://www.samemory.sa.gov.au/site/page.cfm?c=2564

Adelaide Observer, 17 September 1859

Adelaide Observer, 26 June 1866

Adelaide Observer, 9 October 1869, Lunatic Asylum Committee

Adelaide Times, 17 May 1851

Athelstone Gorge Methodist Church, *The Register*, 30th Dec 1914, Trove

Australian Christian Commonwealth (SA : 1901 - 1940), Mr Harry Lomman, 11 January 1929, page 5

Booker, D. Making Connections through Oral History, *Word of Mouth*, Autumn 2018

Casenote Translation for Henry Loman, Glenside Hospital Historical Society, translated by David Buob (entry F9)

City of Campbelltown, Indigenous History, https://www.campbelltown.sa.gov.au/__data/assets/pdf_file/0018/234504/Indigenous-History.pdf

Clyne, R. (1987). *Colonial Blue, A history of the South Australian Police Force 1836-1916*, chapter 6, Wakefield Press, Adelaide

Diane Cummings, Bound for South Australia, John from London, 1840, https://bound-for-south-australia.collections.slsa.sa.gov.au/1840John.htm

East Torrens Council Report, December 1859, Trove

Golden Wedding Anniversary, Mr and Mrs John Heading, *The Observer,* 2 March 1918, Trove

Government Land Sale,' *South Australian*, 14th October 1850, and 'Land Sales and Contracts', *South Australian gazette and Mining Journal*, 12th October 1850
'Sale of Crown Lands. Last Thursday's Land Sale', *Adelaide Observer*, 25th February 1854

Government Land Sale, 1849, Trove

James Fort advertisement, December 1856, Trove

John Lowman picture, SLSA, https://collections.slsa.sa.gov.au/find/lomman

MacDonnell Bridge, Campbelltown City Council, https://www.campbelltown.sa.gov.au/library/local-history-room/localhistoryarticles/local-history-articles-places/macdonnell-bridge

Obituary of Hannah Austin nee Lomman, The Advertiser and The Register, 10 Aug 1927, Trove

Obituary of Martha Lomman, *The Advertiser*, 26th August 1897, Trove

Police Court, *The South Australian Advertiser*, 15 December 1860, Trove

South Australian Advertiser (Adelaide, SA : 1858 - 1889), Thursday 31 May 1877, page 6

South Australian Chronicle and Weekly Mail (Adelaide, SA : 1868 - 1881), Saturday 2 June 1877, page 11

South Australian Register, 16 March 1844, page 3

South Australian Register, 20 February 1850, Loman vs Loman

South Australian Register (Adelaide, SA : 1839 - 1900), Thursday 14 February 1861, page 3

South Australian Register, 21 September 1861

South Australian Register, Tolmer Testimonial, 10 May 1852

South Australian Weekly Chronicle, 15 December 1860, page 2

The Advertiser, 7 April 1898, The death of Mr S. Beddome

The Express and Telegraph, 11 October 1869, The Lunatic Asylum Inquiry, https://trove.nla.gov.au/newspaper/article/207683967?searchTerm=parkside%20asylum&searchLimits=l-state=South+Australia|||l-decade=186#

The Express and Telegraph, 8 May 1868, The New Lunatic Asylum, https://trove.nla.gov.au/newspaper/article/207737980?searchTerm=parkside%20asylum&searchLimits=l-state=South+Australia|||l-decade=186

Wikitree, Leandra Ford

Women's Suffrage Petition, South Australia

https://www.ncbi.nlm.nih.gov/pmc/articles/PMC539549/

Heslop Miller and Abbott Families

Abbott, S. (1998) *Womenfolks: Growing Up Down South*. University of Arkansas Press

'A Bethshan Scandal. Pastor Abbott on his Defence. Charges of Immorality Refuted. A Queer Story. A Queer Family. A Queer House. And a Queer Religion.' *The Herald*, 28 November 1892

'A Clairvoyant's Divorce. Turner vs Turner. Husband Charged with Desertion.' *The Age*, 9 November 1909

'A Clerical Scandal. Pastor Abbott in the Stocks. Scene at a Meeting.' *Barrier Miner*, 28 November, 1892

'A Divorce Suit.' *Bairnsdale Chronicle*, 9 November 1909.

'A Religious Scandal. To the Editor of the Age.' *The Age*, 29 November 1892

'A Religious Scandal.' *The Age*, 28 November 1892

'Among the Seers. Police Crusade. Prosecution at Fitzroy. Great Audience of Women. Case of Mrs Turner.' *The Herald*, 27 January 1909

'An Agency Marriage. The Girl Underaged. Police Court Sequel. The Young Couple Charged.' *The Herald*, 19 March 1902

'Assault on Pastor Abbott,' Kerang New Times 20 February 1906'Assaulting a Clergyman' *The Ballarat Star*, 27 February 1906

'Bethshan Miracles. Faith Healing versus Medicine. Pastor Abbott and his Wonderful Cures.' *The Herald*, 1 December 1892

'Bigamy Charged.' *The Herald*. 4 August 1900

'Charged with Bigamy.' *The Herald*. 18 June 1902

'Christchurch Horticultural Society.' *Star*, Issue 5981, 16 July 1887

'Church Service Scene. Assault on Pastor Abbott. Mrs Haldane fined 5s.' *The Argus,* 27 February 1906

'Clairvoyant in Divorce Court. Annie Turner and "Pastor" Abbott. Relationship Reviewed. Jealous Husband Seeks Justice.' *Truth*, 27 November 1909

'Clerical Scandal at Collingwood,' *The Age*, 29 December 1893

'Conan Doyle's Australian Wanderings.' *The Herald*, 19 November 1921

'Crusade against Fortune Tellers. The Case of Mrs Turner. Remarkable Evidence.' *Bendigo Advertiser*, 28 January, 1909.

'Crying "Shame on Angus," Lecturer is Attacked.' *The Daily Telegraph*, 11 May 1934

'Deaths.' *The Age*, 8 June 1894

'Devilish Duper Dowie and Minatory Minister McCullagh.' *Truth*, 18 October 1903

'Dowie and Dynamite.' *The Herald*, 7 September 1885

'Empire Day to Be Remembered.' *The Daily Telegraph*, 23 May 1935

'Exhibition Flowers,' *Lyttelton Times*, Volume LXIX, Issue 8457, 16 April 1888

'Horticultural Society.' *Lyttelton Times*, Volume LXIX, Issue 8490, 24 May 1888

'Horticultural Society.' *Star*, Issue 6034, 16 September 1887

'Husband and Pastor.' *The Australasian*, 13 September 1909.

'Identified. A Yarra Victim. Remarkable Case.' *The Herald*, 22 September 1900

'Intense Culture, Silk and Scent Production,' *Mornington Standard* (Vic), Saturday 13 August 1904, page 4

'Lady Herbalist Seeks a Divorce. Mrs Annie Turner's Petition. Husband Opposes it. Interesting Evidence. The Decree Nisi Granted.' *The Herald*, 8 November 1909.

'Letter from "Pastor" Abbott.' *The Age,* 19 February 1906

'Lovers' Vows.' *The Herald*, 28 August 1901

'Matrimonial Agencies. City Court Disclosures.' *The Argus*, 19 March 1902

'Meetings, Amusements, & c.' *Lyttelton Times*, Volume LXX, Issue 8580, 6 September 1888

'Mercy is Asked For,' *The Herald*, 28 November 1902

'Not Related to Monkey says Savant.' *The Daily Telegraph*, 22 January 1934

'Pastor Abbott. Sunday's Sensation. Origin of the Trouble.' *The Herald*, 20 February 1906

'Pastor Abbott', *Mt Alexander Mail*, 27 February 1906

'Pastor Abbott's Adventures.' *The Bendigo Independent*. 21 February 1906

'Pastor Abbott's Explanation,' *The Ballarat Star*, 20 February 1906

'Pastor Abbott's Troubles,' *Kerang New Times*, 27 February 1906

'Pastor and Clairvoyant. Husband's Objections. Interesting Divorce Case.' *The Argus*, 9 November 1909.

'" Pastor" Abbott's Friend. The P.M. Cuts it Short.' *The Bendigo Independent* 28 February 1906

'"Lines Wanted." Hence a Wedding Ceremony. With a Married Man.' *The Herald*, 17 May 1900

'"Medical" and "General" Pastor Abbott and Mrs Turner in Sydney.' *The Bendigo Independent*, 11 September 1909.

'"Pastor" Abbott. Lady Charged with Assault.' *Weekly Times,* 3 March 1906

'Scene in a Church. Pastor Abbott Interviewed. A remarkable story.' *The Argus,* 20 February 1906

'Scene in a Church. Rebecca Haldane Interviewed. Pastor Abbott's Story denied.' *The Argus,* 21 February 1906

'Secret History.' *Smith's Weekly*, 3 September 1921

'Sheisms.' *Truth*, 21 August 1921

‘Shipping.’ *Lyttelton Times*, Volume LXX, Issue 8663, 12 December 1888

‘Spiritualist Roguery in Excelsis. Stanford-Bailey “Apports” Fraud.’ *Truth*, 13 June 1914

‘Spooks and Spondulux. “Mrs Foster-Turner” and “Pastor Abbott” Resume Business. Amazing Antics of Artful Annie.’ *Truth*, 18 March 1916.

‘Spooks in London. Old Melbourne Friends. A Well Known Trio at Work. Mrs Turner and Charles Bailey. A Cruel Sceptic at Caxton Hall.’ *The Herald*, 28 August 1911.

‘Subtle Craft Cases. Appeals Against Convictions. Case of Mrs Turner. Judgement Reserved.’ *The Age*, 20 March 1909

‘Subtle Craft. The Practices of Sham Spiritualists.’ *The Age*, 25 June 1909.

‘Suppressing Clairvoyants. Police Crusade.’ *Geelong Advertiser*, 28 January 1909.

‘Suspected Murder. A Young Couple Charged. Four Months Old Baby. Found in the Yarra.’ *Weekly Times*, 1 February 1902

‘The Bethshan Faith Healing Scandal.’ *The Bendigo Independent*, 30 November 1892

‘The Bethshan Scandal. What Mr Jonas Says.’ *The Herald*, 29 November 1892

‘The Dental Act.’ *The Herald*, 13 December 1905

‘The Ketch Margaret,’ *Press*, Volume XXIX, Issue 4012, 4 June 1878

‘The Religious Scandal. Vote of Confidence in Pastor Abbott.’ *The Bendigo Independent*, 2 December 1892

‘Thrashing a Preacher. Enraged Woman’s Attack. Sensational Scene at the Temperance Hall.’ *The Age*, 19 February 1906

‘Thrashing Pastor Abbott. Assailant Fined. Lively Scene in Court.’ *The Age*, 27 February 1906

‘Town and Country.’ *Lyttelton Times*, Volume LXIX, Issue 8454, 12 April 1888

‘Weren’t in Least Interested. Invitation from New Guard.’ *The Labour Daily*, 24 June 1932

1888 North Canterbury earthquake, Wikipedia

Abbott, S. (1984). *Womenfolks: Growing up Down South* Houghton Mifflin, US.

Death Notice, *The Age and The Argus*, 28 May 1941

www.Encyclopedia.com – Julia’s Bureau

History of the Kaiapoi Woollen Mills https://libraries.waimakariri.govt.nz/heritage/local-history/places-of-the-waimakariri/kaiapoi/history-of-the-kaiapoi-woollen-mills

Keenan, L (2024). *The Space Between*, Penguin Books Australia

Lyttelton Times, Volume LXXIV, Issue 9289, 18 December 1890

Lyttelton Times, Volume XXVI, Issue 1810, 5 October 1866

Papers Past, New Zealand

Passenger List, Zealanda http://freepages.rootsweb.com/~ourstuff/genealogy/Zealandia1859.htm

Press newspaper, 12 August 1876

Press newspaper, 18 August 1876

Press newspaper, 6 May 1867

Professions and Trades advertisement, *The Daily Telegraph*, 25 April 1928 and 16 October 1928

South Coast Times and Wollongong Argus, 15 August 1941

The Argus, Death Notice, 22 September 1920

The Daily Telegraph, 18 October 1926

The Daily Telegraph, 22 May 1923

The Globe, 11 August 1876

The Herald, 12 March 1953

Family Histories:

- Miller, M *The History of Heslop, Miller, Thompson Families complied by Margaret Miller* (available SAGHS)

Websites:

Canterbury Photography:

https://canterburyphotography.blogspot.com/2008/08/blog-post_29.html?fbclid=IwAR0WprGIpfuQAxY8BUJykLHf5NRYKyHyBpHtBWzekrnRSd09hnahZjmk7Zg

Canterbury Association Passenger Manifests: http://freepages.genealogy.rootsweb.com/~nzbound/canterbury.htm

Passenger Lists, NZ and Australia, 1800s: http://freepages.genealogy.rootsweb.com/~donegal/family/fpasslist.htm

http://freepages.genealogy.rootsweb.com/~shipstonz/ships_uk&i.html

W.T. Stead:

- William T. Stead, Wikipedia
- Government by Journalism, Wikipedia
- Rhodes, M. 'Julia's Bureau: The Temperance Virtuoso, the Father of Journalism and Life after Death in the Spiritualist Anglo-Atlantic https://digpodcast.org/2022/07/10/julias-bureau-the-temperance-virtuoso-the-father-of-journalism-and-life-after-death-in-the-spiritualist-anglo-atlantic%EF%BF%BC/
- Wimbledon Heritage: The journalist who 'sank' the Titanic https://www.wimbledonguardian.co.uk/news/9450699.wimbledon-heritage-the-journalist-who-sank-the-titanic/

- The W.T. Stead Resource Site - Julia's Bureau: An Attempt to Bridge the Grave https://attackingthedevil.co.uk/w-t-stead-the-review-of-reviews/julias-bureau-an-attempt-to-bridge-the-grave/

The Battams Family

Adelaide Observer, 1855

Adelaide Observer, 2nd October 1880

Adelaide Observer, 31st May 1851

Adelaide Observer, 5 June 1847

Battams, Len (deceased 2000), personal communication

Bendigo Advertiser, 22 July 1881

Bishop, C. (2021), *Too Much Cabbage and Jesus Christ. Australia's 'Mission Girl' Annie Lock.* Wakefield Press.

Commonwealth of Australia Gazette, 14th March 1986

Evening Journal, 12th June 1869

Evening Journal, 21st July 1881

Frederick Robe, Lieutenant-Governor. Passed by the Legislative Council 12 March 1847, Government Gazette

National Archives of Australia, WWII , Intelligence report from Loveday internment camp

National Archives of Australia, WWI Record, Joseph Wesley Battams

National Archives of Australia, WWI Records, Daniel Potter

National Archives of Australia, Series B883: Army, 2nd Al F, Record of Leonard George Battams Service Number - SX28857, Item, 6395962

Reg Butler's unpublished computer working files, 2014

Rodda, M. *Miss Mary Jane (Mae) Battams 18 July 1897 – 5 June 1974. A Little Women with a Big Heart-And Gave So Much.* Unpublished.

SA Advertiser, 1859.

SA Advertiser, January 1861

SA Advertiser, January 1861, February 1861 (Mt Remarkable Reports)

SA Register, 10th October 1859

SA Register, The Pioneers of South Australia, 6 November 1877

SAGHS Marriage Registrations, 5/189

Shipping List, The Phoebe, 1847

South Australian Chronicle and Weekly Mail, 19th September 1874

South Australian Government Gazette, 14th January 1864

South Australian Register 19th April 1862

South Australian Register, 11th October 1856

South Australian Register, 14th October, 1876

South Australian Register, 22nd July 1857

South Australian Register, 22nd July 1881

South Australian Register, 3rd August 1855

South Australian Register, 9th April 1862

South Australian Register, 9th February 1881

South Australian Weekly Chronicle, 10 March 1866

South Australian Weekly Chronicle, 13th September 1862

South Australian Weekly Chronicle, 17th November 1860

South Australian Weekly Chronicle, 1st July 1882

South Australian Weekly Chronicle, 26th May 1860

State Records of SA (GRG 45/43 and 5/30) record

The Advertiser, 10th March 1894

The Advertiser, 20th March 1913

The Advertiser, promotion of Captured Lives (2018)

The Age, 22nd July 1881

The Express and Telegraph, 11th November 1874

The Express and Telegraph, 13th April 1874

The Express and Telegraph, 16th June 1881

The Express and Telegraph, 2 November 1867, Visit of H.R.H. The Duke of Edinburgh

The Express and Telegraph, 20th September 1876

The Express and Telegraph, 9th June 1881

The Mail, 6th August 1932

The News, 13th June 1949

The SA Advertiser, 21 June 1866

The SA Advertiser, The Telegraph Demonstration, 16 November 1872

The South Australian Advertiser, 30th December 1879

The South Australian Advertiser, 30th December 1879

The South Australian Advertiser, 8th March 1871

The Sydney Daily Telegraph, 23rd July 1881

The Sydney Morning Herald, Blind Hold Exhibition of Crafts, 30th April 1953

The United Aborigines Messenger, Vol 4, no 10, 1 July 1933

The Wallaroo Times and Mining Journal, 14th October 1876

The Wallaroo Times and Mining Journal, 20th February 1878

The Wallaroo Times and Mining Journal, 20th June 1877

The Wallaroo Times and Mining Journal, 23rd July 1881

The Wallaroo Times and Mining Journal, 28th November 1877

The Wallaroo Times and Mining Journal, 30th December 1874

The Wallaroo Times and Mining Journal, 30th December 1876

The Wallaroo Times and Mining Journal, Inquest at Kadina, 1 May 1875

The Wallaroo Times and Mining Journal, Visit to Barunga Gap, 29th April 1876

UK Census, 1841 (Ancestry)

UK Census, 1851 (Ancestry)

Wachtel, J.A. (1982) *Moorook, Bend in the River*, Investigator Press, Adelaide

Yorke's Peninsula Advertiser, 9 April 1880

South Australian Heritage Council application, 2021, 92 Brougham Place, North Adelaide

Marilyn Ann Rodda, care of Croydon, Dudley, Devon & Renown Parks (South Australia) Local History (Facebook Group)

Photo of grave courtesy South Australian Police Historical Society, Kym Hardwick and Ms Kate Woodcock, Manager of the Society's Photographic Records Section

Websites:

Daniel Battams (misspelt Batham in the original), deposition taken before EB Gleeson, 18 December 1849, GRG 24/6/1849/2331, SRSA, EB Gleeson to Colonial Secretary, 22 December 1849, GRG 24/6/1849/2331, SRSA, all cited on SLSA The South Australian Frontier and its Legacies Interactive Map https://experience.arcgis.com/experience/4755c59ae93447a9b0acf9b2b0b265f6/page/Interactive-Map

Newsbeta website

https://www.lostkatanning.com/hettner-family/

https://www.lbma.org.uk accessed 31st October 2025

https://www.gdaypubs.com.au/SA/kadina/51493/royal-exchange-hotel.html

First Families website 2001 (Battams family) http://pandora.nla.gov.au (accessed 1st April 2006)

Maureen M Leadbeater, Family History South Australia website

Photos:

Families arriving at Pompoota Station, 1917, Wachtel, 1982

Frederick Alfred Roy Battams, Virtual War Memorial Australia https://vwma.org.au/explore/people/555904

Freemasons Tavern, Pirie Street, Adelaide, once owned by Daniel Battams, Grand Lodge of Freemasons SA/NT, Facebook page

Moorook-Kingston Football Club, Wachtel 1982

NAA, Leonard George Battams upon enlistment

Other photos of Len Battams and family (S. Battams)

Picture Postcard WWI, S. Battams

Red Lion Inn, Lost Pubs of Adelaide, Adelaide Economic Development Agency 2025.

Marilyn Rodda, photo of Miss Mary (Mae) Battams

Royal Exchange Hotel, Kadina, https://www.gdaypubs.com.au/SA/kadina/51493/royal-exchange-hotel.html

Conclusion:

Donohue, J. (2023) *Anam Cara: Spiritual Wisdom from the Celtic World*. Penguin Books.

Keenan, L (2024). *The Space Between*, Penguin Books Australia

O'Sullivan, M and Graydon, N. (2013). *The Ancestral Continuum*, Simon and Schuster, UK.

Acknowledgements section:

Bott, Merrie, Genealogical Charts, Personal Communication

Genealogy SA – Online Databases

Miller, M. (2005). *The Miller Family by Margaret Miller, available from SAGHS 2005*

Miller, M. (2000) *This history of Heslop, Miller, Thomson Families is compiled and submitted by Margaret Miller (2010)*

Miller, M. (2000). *The Heading Family History (2000)*

Pearce, Cate (2021). *DNA Analysis Report* prepared for Samantha Battams

Rumbelow, P., Avery, L, George, M., Rumbelow, M. (2005). *The Rumbelows of Encounter Bay: 150 years of the family in South Australia,* Openbook Print, Adelaide

Rumbelow, M. Rumbelow and Descendents website https://www.rumbelow.net/

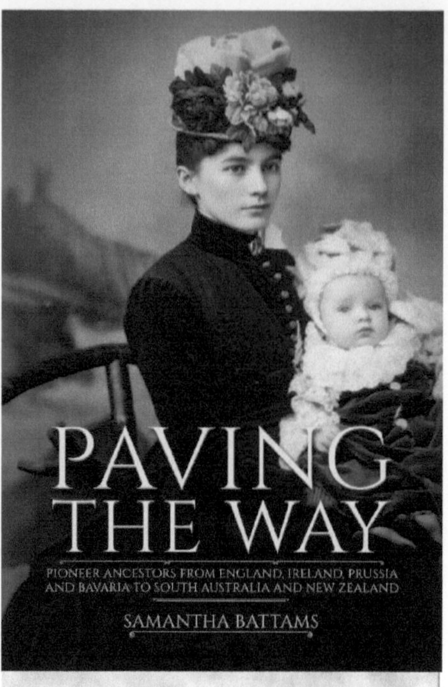
PAVING
THE WAY
PIONEER ANCESTORS FROM ENGLAND, IRELAND, PRUSSIA AND BAVARIA TO SOUTH AUSTRALIA AND NEW ZEALAND
SAMANTHA BATTAMS

THE RED DEVIL
The Story of South Australian Aviation Pioneer,
Captain Harry Butler, AFC
'Luck, Pluck and Ability'
'This book retrieves a wonderful story from the annals of South Australia's history, dusts it off and gives it wings to fly.'
Peter Monteath
Les Parsons and Samantha Battams

SAMANTHA BATTAMS
The Secret Art of Poisoning
THE TRUE CRIMES OF MARTHA NEEDLE
THE RICHMOND POISONER
SAMANTHA BATTAMS
The Rhynie Poisoning Case
THE TRUE CRIMES OF ALEXANDER NEWLAND LEE

www.ingramcontent.com/pod-product-compliance
Ingram Content Group UK Ltd.
Pitfield, Milton Keynes, MK11 3LW, UK
UKHW041900190726
13854UKWH00002B/996